A Paradise Inhabited by Devils

Unknown, *Pianta di Napoli a Volo* (early seventeenth century)

A Paradise Inhabited by Devils

The Jesuits' Civilizing Mission in Early Modern Naples

JENNIFER D. SELWYN

LONDON AND NEW YORK

First published 2004 by Ashgate Publishing

Published 2016 by Routledge
2 Park Square, Milton Park, Abingdon, Oxon OX14 4RN
711 Third Avenue, New York, NY 10017, USA

Routledge is an imprint of the Taylor & Francis Group, an informa business

Copyright © 2004 Jennifer D. Selwyn

Jennifer D. Selwyn has asserted her moral right under the Copyright, Designs and Patents Act, 1988, to be identified as the author of this work.

All rights reserved. No part of this book may be reprinted or reproduced or utilised in any form or by any electronic, mechanical, or other means, now known or hereafter invented, including photocopying and recording, or in any information storage or retrieval system, without permission in writing from the publishers.

Notice:
Product or corporate names may be trademarks or registered trademarks, and are used only for identification and explanation without intent to infringe.

British Library Cataloguing in Publication Data
Selwyn, Jennifer D.
   A Paradise Inhabited by Devils: The Jesuits' Civilizing Mission in Early Modern Naples –
   (Bibliotheca Institutum Historicum Societatis Iesu) (Catholic Christendom, 1300–1700).
   1. Jesuits—Missions—Italy—Naples—History—16th century. 2. Jesuits—Missions—
   Italy—Naples—History—17th century. 3. Missions—Italy—Naples—History—16th
   century. 4. Missions—Italy—Naples—History—17th century. 5. Missionaries—Italy—
   Naples—History—16th century. 6. Missionaries—Italy—Naples—History—17th
   century. 7. Naples (Italy)—Church history. 8. Naples (Italy)—Social conditions. 9.
   Naples (Italy)—Social life and customs. 10. Naples (Italy)—History—1503–1734.
   I. Title. II. Institutum Historicum Societatis Iesu.
   266.2'4573'09031

Library of Congress Cataloging in Publication Data
Selwyn, Jennifer D.
   A Paradise Inhabited by Devils: The Jesuits' Civilizing Mission in Early Modern Naples /
   Jennifer D. Selwyn.
      p.   cm. – (Catholic Christendom, 1300–1700)
   Includes bibliographical references and index.
   1. Jesuits—Italy—Naples (Kingdom). 2. Naples (Kingdom)—Church history. I. Title.
   II. Series.
   BX3738.N3S45 2004
   271'.5304573–dc22   2003064040

ISBN 9788870413571 (hbk)

Typeset by SetSystems Ltd, Saffron Walden, Essex

Contents

Publishers' note		vii
Series Editor's Preface		ix
Acknowledgments		xi
Abbreviations		xiii

Introduction: Situating the Jesuits and Naples in the early modern world		1
	Historical treatments of the Jesuits	12
1	A paradise inhabited by devils	21
	The urban landscape of Naples	36
	Spiritual disorder in Naples	44
2	'Planting many virtues there': Early Jesuit missions in Naples, 1550–1620	55
	The urban missions in Naples	69
	The infidel at home: Converting Muslim slaves	88
3	Reverberations from the New World	95
	The lure of the Indies	98
	The Model Missionary: Francis Xavier	105
	The lucky ones: Neapolitan Jesuits in the New World	110
	José de Acosta and the Jesuits' civilizing mission: From Peru to Naples	117
	Toward a collective missionary identity	136
4	'Use every means that you will judge opportune': Instructions to Jesuit missionaries	139
	Institutional directives and the varieties of instructional documents	142
	Logistical concerns in the instructional manuals	147
	Maintaining good relationships with fellow clergy	161
	Reforming illicit behaviors	166

CONTENTS

5 Taming the beast: Confronting discord in early modern Naples 183

'Blessed are the Peacemakers for they Shall be Called the Sons of God' (Matthew 5:9) 186

The heroic image of Jesuit peacemakers 188

'Exhorting the people to live peacefully': The Jesuits and the Revolt of Naples, 1647–48 194

After the Revolt: The social drama of peacemaking 201

6 Perfecting one's craft: Jesuit missionary theater in Naples 211

Staging the missions 212

Schools of mortification 227

Promise and danger in the penitential missions 237

Conclusion 243

Bibliography 251

Index 275

Publishers' Note

This volume is a co-publication between Ashgate Publishing and the Jesuit Historical Institute.

As well as being part of Ashgate's *Catholic Christendom, 1300–1750* monograph series, it is the 57 volume in the Jesuit Historical Institute's series *Bibliotheca Instituti Historici Societatis Iesu*.

ASHGATE

Ashgate Publishing   *Institutum Historicum Societatis Iesu*

Series Editor's Preface

The still-usual emphasis on medieval (or Catholic) and reformation (or Protestant) religious history has meant neglect of the middle ground, both chronological and ideological. As a result, continuities between the middle ages and early modern Europe have been overlooked in favor of emphasis on radical discontinuities. Further, especially in the later period, the identification of 'reformation' with various kinds of Protestantism means that the vitality and creativity of the established Church, whether in its Roman or local manifestations, have been left out of account. In the last few years, an upsurge of interest in the history of traditional (or Catholic) religion makes these inadequacies in received scholarship even more glaring and in need of systematic correction. The series will attempt this by covering all varieties of religious behavior, broadly interpreted, not just (or even especially) traditional institutional and doctrinal Church history. It will to the maximum degree possible be interdisciplinary, comparative and global, as well as non-confessional. The goal is to understand religion, primarily of the 'Catholic' variety, as a broadly human phenomenon, rather than as a privileged mode of access to superhuman realms, even implicity.

The period covered, 1300–1700, embraces the moment which saw an almost complete transformation of the place of religion in the life of Europeans, whether considered as a system of beliefs, as an institution, or as a set of social and cultural practices. In 1300, vast numbers of Europeans, from the Pope down, fully expected Jesus' return and the beginning of His reign on earth. By 1700, very few Europeans, of whatever level of education, would have subscribed to such chiliastic beliefs. Pierre Bayle's notorious sarcasms about signs and portents are not idiosyncratic. Likewise, in 1300 the vast majority of Europeans probably regarded the Pope as their spiritual head; the institution he headed was probably the most tightly integrated and effective bureaucracy in Europe. Most Europeans were at least nominally Christian, and the Pope had at least nominal knowledge of that fact. The papacy, as an institution, played a central role in high politics, and the clergy in general formed an integral part of most governments, whether central or local. By 1700, Europe was divided into a myriad of different religious allegiances, and even those areas officially subordinate to the Pope were both more nominally Catholic in belief (despite colossal efforts at imposing uniformity) and also in allegiance than they had been four hundred years earlier. The Pope had become only one political factor, and not one of the first rank. The clergy, for its part, had virtually disappeared from secular governments, as well as losing much of its local authority. The stage was set for the Enlightenment.

Thomas F. Mayer,
Augustana College

Acknowledgments

When I began the preliminary work on this book project more than ten years ago, I could have scarcely imagined that I would spend a good part of the next decade immersing myself in the institutional history of the Society of Jesus during its first incarnation in the 'Old Europe,' nor that the story of the Jesuits' civilizing mission, as I have come to call it, would reveal as much about the order itself as about any of the subjects of its missionary endeavors. But conducting the research for this book, from its earliest incarnation as a doctoral thesis, to its current book form, has been a pleasure and an adventure, thanks in large part to the help and encouragement of many people.

Great thanks must begin at the beginning. I thank my family for encouraging my vocation as a teacher and a scholar, as well as for support of various kinds over the years. At UC Davis, I was fortunate to work within an excellent History Department, filled with many generous and helpful people. Many thanks to Debbie Lyons, UCD's History graduate secretary. I was fortunate to have the wonderful inspiration and direction provided by my doctoral thesis committee, Paula Findlen, William Bowsky, and Pauline Watts (gracious enough to work with me, even from a distance of three thousand miles). Paula Findlen, especially, helped to guide and shape the dissertation and then, over the last few years, has been wonderfully helpful in its transition to book form. Throughout the publishing process, she has offered unstinting support, wise counsel, and reminders that a sense of humor and thick skin would be valuable assets along the way. How right she has been! I also thank Susan Mann who has been a real mentor to me since my undergraduate days, who encouraged me to return to graduate study in History at UC Davis, and who has continued to show great interest in this project and in my work, more generally. Other Davis *compadres* who have shared friendship and a passion for history work are: Tara Nummedal, Seth Rockman, Cheri Barkey, Rachel Sturman and Antonio Barrera.

In Italy, I benefitted from the aid and counsel of a number of people. In the Jesuit Archives and Historical Institute, I thank especially Mark Lewis SJ, Tom McCoog SJ, Martín Morales SJ and Nicoletta Basilotta for their graciousness, and for the warm working environment that they foster. For their help during earlier stages of this research, I also thank Father Viktor Grammatowski SJ and the late Father Mario Zanardi SJ for their help with accessing archival materials. Many thanks to the helpful and knowledgeable staff at the *Archivio Segreto Vaticano* and the *Biblioteca Apostolica Vaticana*. In Naples, Father Filippo Iapelli SJ showed me great kindness and generous assistance. Soprintendente Nicola Spinosa, Dottoressa Fernanda Capobianco and their staff at the *Soprintendenza Speciale per il Polo Museale di Napoli*, especially Signora Mena Patruno, provided kind assistance in accessing the images provided in the book and offering permission for their reproduction. Julia Hairston, Elisabetta Constantini and Gregor Kalas made my various stays in Italy a real pleasure.

A number of individuals have offered invaluable suggestions for improving the clarity of my arguments and/or the grace of my prose throughout the development of this project, though I hold none of them responsible for any errors in judgment, or execution. Thanks in particular to Mark Lewis, Tom McCoog, Tom Mayer, David Gentilcore and Paul Murphy, but also to Jodi Bilinkoff, Michelle Fontaine, Tony Grafton, Kathy Lualdi, Ken Mills, John O' Malley, Duane Osheim and Anne Thayer. Many thanks, too, to the most helpful editorial staff at Ashgate Publishing, especially Tom Gray and Kirsten Weissenberg, and to Huw Jones for his copy-editing.

The History Department and the College of Liberal Arts at the University of New Hampshire have been a wonderful home for me since 1998. Among my terrific History colleagues, special thanks to Bill Harris, Janet Polasky, Jan Golinski, David Frankfurter and Julia Rodriguez. Thanks, too, to Dean Marilyn Hoskin for the College's generous support of my research and manuscript preparation, and to Bruce Mallory, Provost (and former Dean of Graduate Studies) at UNH, for additional assistance and a shared love of things Italian. Also, a warm thank you to Burt Feintuch and Jennifer Beard of the UNH Center for the Humanities for awarding me a Gustafson Junior Faculty Fellowship in 2002 to complete the drafting of the book manuscript, and for offering ongoing financial and moral support as the book has drawn closer to publication. I thank Jill Silos for her work on the index.

I am very fortunate to have a wonderful community of friends in far-flung places. At UNH, among friends and colleagues who have offered help of various kinds and friendship are Robin Hackett, Piero Garofalo, Tonda Liggett, Julie Newman and Linda Blum. I also thank Left Coast friends, especially Sherri Patton, Diana Curiel, and Carla Schick.

Finally, I am deeply grateful to my life partner, Judeth McGann. While I'm sure that she never imagined that she would get to know so much about the Jesuits and their fascinating history, she has shown great understanding for my strange obsessions and unwavering encouragement at every stage in this sometimes arduous process. This book is dedicated to her with thanks for all of the laughter and joy that she brings into my life.

Abbreviations

ARSI	Archivio Romano Societatis Iesu
ASV	Archivio Segreto Vaticano
BAV	Biblioteca Apostolica Vaticana
AHSI	*Archivum Historicum Societatis Iesu*
De Procuranda	José de Acosta, *De Procuranda Indorum Salute* (1588)
Della Vita	Antonio Barone, *Della Vita del Padre Pierantonio Spinelli* (Naples, 1707)
F.G.	Fondo Gesuitico
Istoria	Francesco Schinosi, *Istoria della Compagnia de Giesù appartenente al Regno di Napoli*, Vols 1 and 2 (Naples, 1706–11); Saverio Santagata, *Istoria della Compagnia di Giesù Appartenente al Regno di Napoli*, Vols 3 and 4 (Naples, 1756–57)
Missioni	Scipione Paolucci, *Missioni de Padri della Compagnia di Gesù nel Regno di Napoli* (Naples, 1651)
Neap.	*Litterae Annuae Historia Provinciae Neapolitanae*
Opp. Nn.	*Operum Nostrorum*
Pratica delle Missioni	Paolo Segneri and Fulvio Fontana, *Pratica delle Missioni Del P. Paolo Segneri d.C.d. G. Predicatore Pontificio, continuata dal P. Fulvio Fontana delle Medesima Religione, per lo spazio d'anni ventiquattro, per una gran parte d'Italia e di la da monti nella Elvezia, Rezia, Valesia e Tirolo, con l'aggiunta delle prediche, discorsi e metodo distinto tenutosi nelle funzioni sacre* (Venice, 1714)

For Judy

Introduction:
Situating the Jesuits and Naples
in the early modern world

This book explores the Jesuits' global civilizing mission in the early modern period by focusing on an unusual mission field on the geographical and cultural frontiers of Europe: the City and Kingdom of Naples. I consider the significance that internal missionary activity held within the Society of Jesus from *c.* 1550 to 1700, arguing that Spanish Naples offers an important case study in the creation of collective identity. The study also provides a window on the Society of Jesus' contribution to the cultural mapping of the early modern world.

Emerging as a new religious order in the wake of the expansion of European power to the Americas and Asia, the Jesuits were deeply interested in promoting religious and cultural reforms both within Europe and in non-Christian lands across the globe. Scholars have taught us a great deal about the Jesuits' innovative educational endeavors since the Society of Jesus' founding in 1540 and a few of the numerous missions that the Jesuits instituted from Brazil to India during the first century and a half of the order's existence have been captured vividly in feature films on Jesuit endeavors in the Americas, such as *The Mission* and *Black Robes*, or in fascinating narrative studies of Jesuit cultural activity in China, such as Jonathan Spence's *The Memory Palace of Matteo Ricci* (1984). Up to now, though, fewer scholars have paid attention to the nature of the Society of Jesus' global mission as a key feature of the Jesuits' institutional character, nor has sufficient attention been paid to the relationship between Jesuits' efforts to evangelize and civilize nominal Catholics in places like the Kingdom of Naples and their missionary endeavors as far afield as Peru or China.

Referred to since the late Middle Ages as 'a paradise inhabited by devils,'[1] Naples presents a fascinating set of paradoxes: it was an ancient city, noted for its archeological and natural wonders, and considered an

---

[1] For a discussion of the historical development of this conceptualization of Naples, see Benedetto Croce, 'Il "Paradiso Abitato Da Diavoli,"' in *Uomini e Cose della Vecchia Italia* (Bari: Laterza, 1927), 68–86. (N.B. All translations are the author's unless otherwise noted.)

2 A PARADISE INHABITED BY DEVILS

important center of Renaissance high culture, yet populated by a vast population of urban poor who were often seen by contemporaries as uncivilized, violent and immoral. Many of Naples' residents had migrated from the rural outposts of southern Italy during the sixteenth and seventeenth centuries to escape punishing poverty. They sought refuge in Europe's second largest city, with a population in excess of 300 000 by the early seventeenth century.[2] But the paradoxes did not end there. Aside from its notoriety as a major European city in the early modern period, Naples was also the name given to the Spanish viceroyalty that was instituted there in 1503, usually called the *Regno di Napoli* (Kingdom of Naples). The Kingdom of Naples encompassed an area of southern Italy, today known as the *Mezzogiorno*, that stretched from just south and east of Rome to the tip of the Italian peninsula. While special stereotypes developed around urban Naples and certain other regions of the Kingdom, contemporaries often blurred the lines between city and countryside, using the appellation 'Naples' to refer to both the urban sphere and the broader Kingdom.[3] This occurred despite the fact that the twelve provinces that comprised southern Italy were (and remain) both geographically and culturally diverse. Although the Jesuits sometimes mirrored the approach of referring indiscriminately between urban Naples and other parts of the Kingdom, they were ever sensitive to the nuances of their missionary endeavor, recognizing those challenges peculiar to working in the capital Naples, and other southern Italian cities like Lecce v. work in the more remote hinterlands. Still, the Jesuits' civilizing mission embraced the Kingdom of Naples in its totality; they believed that the strategies honed in the urban missions could be adapted to the Kingdom's outlying provinces, just as they drew connections between domestic missionary activities in Italy and those across the globe.

A popular image in the early modern period portrayed Naples as a

---

[2] On the demographic explosion in early modern Naples, especially before the 1656 plague, see Claudia Petraccone, *Napoli Dal '500 al '800: problemi di storia demografica e sociale* (Naples: Guida, 1974).

[3] For the tendency among early modern commentators to stereotype the Italian *Mezzogiorno* as an 'undifferentiated reality,' see Giuseppe Galasso, *L'Altra Europa. Per Un'Antropologia storica del Mezzogiorno d'Italia*, new revised edn (Lecce: Argo, 1997), 184. Throughout this book, I will attempt to distinguish when I am referring to Naples the city, and when I am considering the region as a whole. In some cases, however, the point is to demonstrate the vagueness with which contemporaries identified southern Italians, given the predominant images that colored their perceptions. In using the term *Mezzogiorno* to refer to southern Italy, I am cognizant of the fact that sixteenth-century folk did not use the term in the value-laden manner that later commentators would invoke to describe an ostensibly backward region of Italy.

INTRODUCTION

3

site of spiritual and social disorder. In part for this reason, Naples and its residents became the object of intense interest by the Jesuits, among others. Not only did the Jesuits devote considerable manpower to Naples and its environs, but members also wrote a number of popular histories of their missions in the *Mezzogiorno* and explicitly linked work there to their broader global civilizing mission. Through their writings and their active intervention in the religious and cultural life of Naples from their arrival in early 1552 to their expulsion from the Kingdom in 1767, the Jesuits helped to disseminate the 'myth' of Naples to a broader European public. But Naples also made its mark on the rapidly expanding Society of Jesus, serving as a training ground for members, as an internal frontier that shaped the Jesuits' missionary praxis, and as a place from which to recruit leading members of the Society of Jesus, including those destined for far-off mission fields beyond Europe.

This story is about the Jesuits' efforts to civilize Naples, a task which they undertook with great zeal and a highly articulated, methodical approach and that they regarded as part and parcel of a broader, global missionary project to civilize the early modern world. It is also, in part, the story of the early modern roots of the myth of Naples, a myth that often depicted an ungovernable, backward urban jungle, peopled by a bloodthirsty, incorrigible and superstitious population. This image was not the sole view of Naples or Neapolitans, of course, as I will demonstrate. I should be clear as well that my purpose is not to endorse the Jesuits' early modern world view of a paradise inhabited by devils, in need of spiritual cleansing and moral reform, which I do not share, nor to validate the often triumphal rhetoric that characterizes much Jesuit literature on the civilizing mission, but instead to understand what drove members of the Society of Jesus and like-minded contemporaries to craft and perpetuate a cultural map that continues to resonate down to our own times.

The causes of Christianization and moral reform were inextricably linked within the broader context of the Jesuits' global civilizing mission. As dedicated reformers, the Jesuits saw themselves as embodying an apostolic vocation handed down from the early Church fathers and retooled for a modern age. Whether they found themselves in Lima, Peru or Naples, effecting true conversion among the faithful involved not simply providing basic instruction in orthodox Catholic doctrine, but also promoting broader cultural transformations. The call for moral reform began with the individual sinner, but bespoke a more generalized campaign to rid early modern society of the rampant violence, immorality and irreligiosity that apparently plagued it. As the historian Adriano Prosperi has shown us, the Jesuits and others referred to the Kingdom of Naples as the *Indies Down Here*, a suggestive image that

4 A PARADISE INHABITED BY DEVILS

certainly was meant to entice young novices to consider the pursuit of missionary glory closer to home, but also indicative of the reformers' view that Naples, no less than the Americas, was a pivotal site in the Jesuits' global effort. In *Tribunali della Coscienza. Inquisitori, confessori, missionari* (1996), Prosperi's compelling exploration of the institutional Church and religiosity in early modern Italy, the author devotes attention to analyzing the multiple functions of the Jesuits' internal missions in the *Mezzogiorno* as part of his wider argument about how missionary work complemented other disciplinary forms that the Catholic Church deployed in early modern Italy.[4] While I appreciate Prosperi's broader argument, my study places the Jesuits front and center in order to understand how they viewed their own work within the wider context of early modern Catholic reform campaigns and, especially, how missionary activity came to form a central pillar of Jesuit identity.

A few scholars have considered the internal, or 'popular' missions in early modern Europe in full-length studies, focusing almost exclusively on the rural missions in France and (to a lesser degree) Italy. About three decades ago, in *Catholicism between Luther and Voltaire: A New View of the Counter-Reformation* (1971; 1977), Jean Delumeau posed the still controversial argument that the internal missions of the Jesuits and other religious orders in the French countryside in the early modern period were belated efforts at Christianizing a fundamentally pagan population of peasants. Others, like Louis Châtellier in *The Religion of the Poor: Rural Missions in Europe and the Formation of Modern Catholicism, ca. 1500–ca. 1800* (1997), have detailed the missionary strategies that shaped the rural popular missions in France and Italy. While both of these monographs have generated considerable interest in the European theater for evangelization during this period, neither they, nor the small number of other works that have appeared in English on this broad topic, have sought to examine extensively the role of internal missionary activity in the development of the institutional identity of a specific religious order, nor have they considered such missionary labors in the urban context.[5]

---

[4] Adriano Prosperi has done much formative work on the relationship between the internal missions in places like southern Italy and on the global missionary endeavor and I have drawn inspiration from his analyses. See his '"Otras Indias": Missionari della Controriforma tra Contadini e Selvaggi' in *Scienze, Credenze, Occulte e Livelli di Cultura* (Florence: Olschki, 1982), 205–34 and, more recently, *Tribunali della Coscienza. Inquisitori, confessori, missionari* (Turin: Einaudi, 1996), esp. 551–99.

[5] Jean Delumeau, *Catholicism Between Luther and Voltaire: A New View of the Counter-Reformation*, trans. Jeremy Moiser (Philadelphia: Westminster Press, 1977); Louis Châtellier, *The Religion of the Poor: Rural Missions in Europe and the Formation of Modern Catholicism, ca. 1500–ca. 1800*, trans. Brian Pearce (Cambridge: Cambridge

INTRODUCTION 5

In recent years, scholarship on early modern Catholicism has taken new and exciting turns. In a field once riddled with confessional divisions and characterized by tendencies either to demonize the Catholic Church as an uncompromisingly repressive institution or to celebrate uncritically its victories during the Catholic Reformation, scholars have produced careful, well-researched studies of specific individuals, institutions and locales.[6] Even the term 'Counter Reformation,' long a staple of histories of the Catholic Church in the early modern period, has come under scrutiny. John O'Malley has argued persuasively that there is much value in avoiding highly charged terms like 'Counter Reformation' in order to capture the full richness of early modern Catholic culture and society.[7] Historians have challenged received ideas about periodization and the complex relationship between 'elite' and 'popular' religion, have debated the usefulness of concepts like 'social discipline' that seek to analyze the power dynamics involved in religious reform efforts, and have argued for producing different kinds of institutional histories that avoid either lionizing or demonizing members of the 'official' Church and its personnel.[8]

University Press, 1997). On the Jesuits' internal missions in Brittany, see Alain Croix, *La Bretagne aux 16e et 17e siècles: la vie, la mort, la foi* (Paris: Maloine, 1981); David Gentilcore does provide a nice introduction to missionary strategies in the rural missions of the Italian South in his article ' "Adapt Yourselves to the People's Capabilities": Missionary Strategies, Methods and Impact in the Kingdom of Naples, 1600–1800,' *Journal of Ecclesiastical History* 43, No. 2 (April 1994): 269–96. Likewise, see Dominique Deslandres's suggestive, if all too brief, comparative analysis of Jesuit missions in France and New France, 'Exemplo aeque ut verbo: The French Jesuits' Missionary World,' in *The Jesuits. Cultures, Sciences, and the Arts, 1540–1773*, eds John W. O'Malley SJ, Gauvin Alexander Bailey, Steven J. Harris and T. Frank Kennedy SJ (Toronto: University of Toronto Press, 1999), 258–73.

[6] Among relatively recent English-language monographs that take nuanced approaches to Catholic reform (and reformers) in Italy, see, for example, Thomas F. Mayer, *Reginald Pole. Prince and Prophet* (Cambridge, UK: Cambridge University Press, 2000); Wietse de Boer, *The Conquest of the Soul: Confession, Discipline and Public Order in Counter-Reformation Milan* (Leiden and Boston: Brill, 2001); Elisabeth G. Gleason, *Gasparo Contarini: Venice, Rome, and Reform* (Berkeley and Los Angeles: University of California Press, 1992); Christopher Black, *Italian Confraternities in the Sixteenth Century* (Cambridge, UK: Cambridge University Press, 1989); Nicholas Terpstra, *Lay Confraternities and Civic Religion in Renaissance Bologna* (Cambridge, UK: Cambridge University Press, 1995).

[7] For the most thorough review of the history of naming the period of Catholic reform in its many forms, see John W. O'Malley, *Trent and All That* (Cambridge, MA: Harvard University Press, 1999).

[8] For two excellent analyses of periodization, see Elisabeth G. Gleason, 'On the Nature of Sixteenth-Century Italian Evangelism: Scholarship, 1953–1978,' *Sixteenth Century Journal* 9, No. 3 (1978): 3–26, and Anne Jacobson Schutte, 'Periodization of Sixteenth-Century Religious History: The Post-Cantimori Paradigm Shift,' *The Journal of Modern*

6   A PARADISE INHABITED BY DEVILS

Inspired in great part by this new tradition of scholarship, this study of the Jesuits' civilizing mission in early modern Naples seeks to present the Society of Jesus, and the individuals and communities among whom its members worked, in all the complexity and multi-dimensionality at the heart of any historical subject. I define this civilizing mission as a highly articulated program of moral reform that could accommodate to local conditions and cultural realities. In order to situate the Jesuits and their missions within their early modern world, I have tried to take seriously the historical actors who have left some record of their words and deeds, treating them as neither heroes nor villains, while also providing a critical historical analysis. Sadly, the surviving record is uneven, so the voices that come across to us do not represent the broadest swath of the population that we would wish to know and understand.

Using Naples as the primary (though not exclusive) locus for examining the complex interplay between the Jesuits and the laity during the era of Catholic reform, I attempt to incorporate the best of these historical inquiries, emphasizing the degree to which the Jesuits' (and others') perceptions of Neapolitan backwardness must be read not as fact, but rather as significant contributors to historical images of this beleaguered city and region. While the numerous Jesuit primary sources examined here emphasize the victories won by the order in its apostolic efforts in southern Italy and elsewhere, I illuminate the highly contested nature of efforts to reform society and religion, whether urban or rural. As several recent historical treatments of early modern religious culture have indicated, while social disciplining may indeed have been one goal of reformers, negotiation always lay at the heart of the complex relationships between institutions, communities and individuals. In this regard, I concur with scholars like Wietse De Boer. In his excellent study of efforts to forge a disciplinary regime in Borromean Milan, *Conquest of the Soul. Confession, Discipline, and Public Order in Counter-Reformation Milan* (2001), De Boer reminds us that 'a considerable distance

---

History 61 (1989): 269–84. Craig Harline argues the need for new kinds of institutional histories and a re-assessment of received notions about elite and popular religion in 'Official Religion–Popular Religion in Recent Historiography of the Catholic Reformation,' *Archiv für Reformationsgeschichte* 81 (1990): 239–62. Finally, in William V. Hudon's 'Religion and Society in Early Modern Italy – Old Questions, New Insights,' *American Historical Review* 101, No. 3 (June 1996): 783–804, the author cautions historians to avoid the casual adoption of meta-theories like 'social discipline' to explain complex phenomena such as the relationship between religious reform efforts and the apparent responses of the laity. Hudon urges historians to remain sensitive to the subtleties in historical documents and to be self-conscious in examining the biases scholars themselves bring to their subject matter.

INTRODUCTION   7

separated this ideal [social discipline] and its implementation.'[9] While the notion of social disciplining has been applied more frequently to efforts by religious and secular authorities to impose religious uniformity and to regulate individual and collective behavior, the notion of a civilizing mission characterizes more accurately the Jesuits' own program of religious and cultural reform. The Jesuits, after all, were jealous to protect their own institutional prerogatives and collective identity in all their varied spheres of activity, even when they shared the broader goals of other reformers.

Much of the archival research for this book comes from the Jesuits' main archive in Rome, the *Archivio Romano Societatis Iesu* (ARSI), and from the *Archivio Segreto Vaticano* (ASV) and *Biblioteca Apostolica Vaticana* (BAV). I have consulted a variety of documents in order to understand the Jesuits' missionary labors in Naples and their efforts to forge a strong collective missionary identity within the order. These sources include missionary reports (called 'relations'), correspondence among members, the Jesuits' foundational documents, institutional directives, instructional manuals, letters requesting placement in foreign missions (*Indipetae*) and both unpublished and printed histories of the order's work in the Kingdom of Naples. While the sources that are intended for a Jesuit audience (such as instructional manuals) seem to have a more obvious purpose toward institution-building, printed sources like the popular histories by the Jesuit authors Scipione Paolucci, Francesco Schinosi or Saverio Santagata were meant to extol the order's apparent successes. All three of these works are presented to demonstrate the Jesuits' strategic efforts to represent themselves favorably to a wider audience of the faithful. Wherever possible, I attempt to leaven the Jesuit author's perspective with that of an independent source, but I am also interested in what these institutional histories can reveal to us about the development of a collective Jesuit missionary identity in Naples in the early modern period, and how they build upon and reinforce secular perceptions of Naples and its people. These are rich sources for constructing a history of Jesuit missionary activity in Naples in the early modern period, if they are read with a critical eye.[10]

---

[9] See, for example, Peter Burke, 'A Question of Acculturation?,' in *Scienze, credenze, occulte*, 197–204; Michael Carroll, *Veiled Threats: The Logic of Popular Catholicism in Italy* (Baltimore and London: Johns Hopkins University Press, 1996), esp. 10–15. For his part, Wietse De Boer uses the social disciplinary model judiciously in *Conquest of the Soul*, arguing in his conclusion that 'bishoprics were certainly the best places to take on comprehensive projects of social discipline,' see 324–27.

[10] Three seventeenth- and eighteenth-century popular histories of Jesuit activity in Naples figure prominently in this study: Scipione Paolucci, *Missioni de Padri della Compagnia di Giesù nel Regno di Napoli* (Naples, 1651); Francesco Schinosi, *Istoria della*

8   A PARADISE INHABITED BY DEVILS

In order to provide a fuller picture of non-Jesuit perceptions of Naples, and of the supposed spiritual and social crisis plaguing the *Mezzogiorno*, I have also consulted a range of printed primary sources by contemporaries of the Jesuits, including popular histories of Naples written by secular authors, viceregal statutes, diplomatic correspondence and other commentaries. This primary research has been supplemented by consultation with the very rich secondary literature on southern Italy in the early modern period, much of it unavailable to English-language readers.[11]

Until fairly recently, much of the scholarship on southern Italy in the early modern period was mired in a discourse of 'backwardness.' For many nineteenth- and twentieth-century scholars, particularly those of a nationalist bent, the primitiveness of Naples was an apparent given. Even for one of its most noted native sons, the prolific philosopher, literary theorist and historian Benedetto Croce (1866–1952), Naples had been irremediably tainted by its supposedly sordid and anarchic past, thus failing to progress at the same rate as the rest of the peninsula. In his general survey of the region, *Storia del Regno di Napoli* (1925), Croce argues that Naples failed to produce a lasting legacy of liberal political institutions and values. Departing from previous historical accounts of the *Mezzogiorno* that had either been written to extol local virtues, bemoan the deleterious effects of centuries of Spanish domination, or argue that a combination of insurmountable geographical and cultural 'defects' had forever doomed the South to poverty and under-development, Croce advances a highly idealistic interpretation of Neapolitan history. He tells the story of a small, intellectual elite whom he deems were the engine of whatever positive developments the South might have witnessed over the centuries. Croce maintains that this 'active element' in Neapolitan society, which might have been expected to

---

Compagnia di Giesù Appartenente al Regno di Napoli (Naples, 1706–11), and Saverio Santagata, *Istoria della Compagnia di Giesù appartenente al Regno di Napoli* (Naples, 1756–57).

[11] Among some of the important works focusing on religion and society in the early modern Kingdom of Naples, see Gabriele De Rosa, *Vescovi, popolo e magia nel Sud. Ricerche di storia socio-religiosa dal XVII–XIX secolo* (Naples: Guida, 1971); Mario Rosa, *Religione e Società nel Mezzogiorno tra Cinque e Seicento* (Bari: Donato, 1976); *Per La Storia Sociale e Religiosa del Mezzogiorno d'Italia*, eds Giuseppe Galasso and Carla Russo (Naples: Guida, 1982), two vols; Romeo De Maio, *Religiosità a Napoli, 1656–1799* (Naples, Edizioni Scientifiche Italiane, 1997), and, most recently, Elisa Novi Chavarria, *Il Governo delle Anime. Azione pastorale, predicazioni e missioni nel Mezzogiorno d'Italia. Secoli XVI–XVIII* (Naples: Editoriale Scientifica, 2001). For a rare English-language study focusing on the southern Italian province of Terra d'Otranto (Apulia), see David Gentilcore, *From Bishop to Witch. The System of the Scared in Early Modern Terra d'Otranto* (Manchester, UK: Manchester University Press, 1992).

INTRODUCTION 9

advance progressive institutions and values – namely, the intelligentsia – had been held back by the 'negative element,' or, as Croce labels them, 'the inert and heavy and reluctant mass (which exists in every people, and in southern Italy was perhaps more inert and heavy and reluctant than elsewhere).'[12] Thus, in Croce's view, the modern history of Naples is indeed a negative history.

By contrast, in the Italian Marxist tradition, largely influenced by Antonio Gramsci, southern Italy is represented as an autonomous region where a 'peasant civilization' seemed frozen in time. Never mind that a large portion of the *Mezzogiorno*'s population lived and worked in and around urban Naples in this view; the popular classes in the South had been separated from what should have been their natural allies, the more 'developed' working class of the rest of Italy, thus leading to their historic 'backwardness' and apparent inability to effectively resist a ruling class's efforts to impose cultural and economic hegemony upon them.[13]

Writing in the 1960s, the influential Neapolitan anthropologist Ernesto De Martino challenged what he deemed Gramsci's historically static view of southern Italian popular culture to argue instead that the continued vitality and existence of 'subaltern cultures' in the Italian South demonstrated the limits of efforts at cultural hegemony on the part of secular and religious institutions. Curiously, some of those most sympathetic to the historic plight of Neapolitans and other southern Italians have endorsed the view that the persistence of magic and superstitious beliefs and practices contributed to the failures of economic, social and political development in this region. As Annalisa Di Nola has compellingly demonstrated in a recent essay on De Martino's magisterial study of southern Italian popular religion, *La terra del rimorso* (1961), even a critic of the results of modernization (and 'civilization') for his neglected and misunderstood *Mezzogiorno* could accept many of the terms of the debate itself. De Martino, for example, cited the deleterious effects of the failure of Catholic reforms to eliminate supposedly 'backward' popular religious practices, like highly emotional mourning rituals, even as he championed the dignity of persistent local

---

12 Benedetto Croce, *Storia del Regno di Napoli* (Bari: Laterza, 1925); also available as Benedetto Croce, *History of the Kingdom of Naples*, ed. H. Stuart Hughes, trans. Frances Frenaye (Chicago and London: University of Chicago Press, 1970), esp. 195. For an argument for the modern development of the discourse of southern Italian backwardness, see Nelson Moe, *The View from Vesuvius. Italian Culture and the Southern Question* (Berkeley and Los Angeles: University of California Press, 2002).

13 For a thoughtful, if brief, discussion of the Gramscian view of southern Italian cultural politics, see Galasso, 'Introduzione,' *Per la Storia sociale e religiosa del Mezzogiorno d'Italia*, x–xi.

rituals often deemed pagan by other scholars.[14] While De Martino ultimately rejects the simplistic notion of an all-powerful Catholic Church trying to impose its vision of religiosity on a passive and backward populace, many subsequent scholars of southern Italian religious history have focused upon the more 'magical' and 'superstitious' aspects of local religious practice, linking the 'failure' of Church reformers to enforce orthodox Catholicism in this region to the persistence of such practices and attitudes.

In the last thirty years, several important studies have delved into the nature of the supposed 'weakness' of southern Italian religious culture in the early modern period. For example, Gabriele De Rosa has argued that an analysis of religious life in the *Mezzogiorno* confirms the ultimate failure of Tridentine reformers in the late sixteenth and seventeenth centuries.[15] As one of his fellow southern Italian historians, Mario Rosa, has argued, De Rosa presents a fundamentally negative history of the South, endorsing the idea of a division between a localized Neapolitan Church which was steeped in a 'magico-religious syncretism' and a centralized Tridentine Church which sought in vain to set things to right. But although Rosa may argue with De Rosa over the primary features of religious 'backwardness' in the Kingdom of Naples, noting the dearth of adequately trained clergy and a general sense of economic and social disorder in the region that led to the slow implementation of religious reforms, he, too, seems preoccupied with documenting a history of failure.[16]

More recently we have seen a more nuanced, less negative approach to the study of the *Mezzogiorno*. Southern Italian historians like Giuseppe Galasso and the late Carla Russo, working independently and as co-editors of an invaluable collection of essays, *Per la storia sociale e*

---

[14] Ernesto De Martino, *La Terra del Rimorso: Contributo a una storia religiosa del Sud* (Milan: Il Saggiatore, 1961). To this point, De Martino's fascinating work has not been translated into English. For a critical assessment of his work, however, see Annalisa Di Nola, 'De Martino's "Critical Ethnocentrism" in South Italy,' in *Italy's 'Southern Question': Orientalism in One Country*, ed. Jane Schneider (New York: Berg, 1998), 157–75. Two other important English-language works consider especially De Martino's contributions on the Apulian ritual of Tarantism: see Michael P. Carroll, *Madonnas that Maim: Popular Catholicism in Italy Since the Fifteenth Century* (Baltimore: Johns Hopkins University Press, 1992), esp. 77–81, and David Gentilcore, *From Bishop to Witch. The System of the Sacred in Early Modern Terra d'Otranto* (Manchester, UK: Manchester University Press, 1992).

[15] Gabriele De Rosa, *Vescovi, Popolo e Magia nel Sud. Ricerche di Storia Socio-Religiosa dal XVIIaXIX Secolo* (Naples: Guida, 1971), esp. 305–306.

[16] Mario Rosa, *Religione e Società nel Mezzogiorno tra Cinque e Seicento* (Bari: Donato, 1976). For his critique of De Rosa, see 145–56, esp. 148–9; Rosa's own negative view of Neapolitan religious history is evident, esp. 27–35.

INTRODUCTION   11

religiosa del Mezzogiorno d'Italia (1982), have helped to shift discussions away from a preoccupation with the deficits in southern Italian religiosity and culture to provide a richer and more variegated view of this complex region. The recent publication of collected essays by Elisa Novi Chavarria, *Il Governo delle Anime. Azione Pastorale, Predicazione e Missioni nel Mezzogiorno d'Italia* (2001) offers another invaluable resource for scholars.[17]

One important area of work on early modern religiosity in southern Italy that I do not consider here in great depth is art and architectural production and patronage. Naples was, of course, a major center for Baroque art and architecture, as were other important southern Italian cities like Lecce. Scholars such as Romeo De Maio have provided critical analyses of the relationship between Catholic Reformation piety, institution-building and artistic development in early modern Naples. A substantial scholarship also exists on the Jesuits' patronage of the arts and architecture, including the complex story of the construction of Jesuit churches in Naples and other centers of activity in the South. While much of this scholarship has been done by Italian art and architectural historians, both Maria Ann Conelli and Helen Hills have explored the religious landscape of early modern Naples and the visual arts and architecture in more recent, English-language studies. Unfortunately, this fascinating story is beyond the purview (or expertise) of this book.[18]

Although historical studies of early modern southern Italy that focus

---

[17] The list of publications by Giuseppe Galasso is too long to include. In addition to *Per La storia sociale e religiosa*, for Galasso also see esp. *L'Altra Europa*; for Russo, see esp. *Società, Chiesa e vita religiosa nell'Ancien Regime* (Naples: Guida, 1976), and *Chiesa e Comunità nella Diocesi di Napoli tra Cinque e Settecento* (Naples: Guida, 1984). For a stimulating and comprehensive survey of post-war work on popular religion which goes beyond the Italian context, see Russo's 'La religiosità popolare nell'età moderna. Problemi di prospettive,' *Prospettive Settanta* 1 (1979): 345–79.

[18] See, for example, Romeo De Maio, *Pittura e Controriforma a Napoli* (Rome-Bari: Laterza 1983), and *Seicento Napoletano. Arte, costume e ambiente*, ed. Roberto Pane (Milan: Edizioni di comunità, 1984). There is also, of course, a vast literature on Jesuit patronage of the arts and the building and adornment of Jesuit churches in Naples and other parts of the Kingdom of Naples. Useful sources include Filippo Iapelli SJ, 'Gesuiti e Barocco fra Napoli, Sardegna, e Roma,' *Societas* 38 (1989): 112–24 and Michele Errichetti, 'La Chiesa del Gesù nuovo in Napoli. Note storiche,' *Campania Sacra* 5 (1974): 34–75. On the important topic of the patronage of religious buildings, especially convents, and the appropriation of urban space within the social landscape of Naples, see Helen Hills, 'Cities and Virgins: Female aristocratic convents in early modern Naples and Palermo,' *Oxford Art Journal* 22, No. 1 (1999): 29–54; Maria Ann Conelli, 'The *Guglie* of Naples: Religious and Political Machinations of the Festival *Macchine*,' *American Academy in Rome Publications* 45 (2000), 153–83. I thank both authors for providing me with offprints of these articles.

12   A PARADISE INHABITED BY DEVILS

on religion and culture have been quite limited in English language scholarship, one of the primary voices in this field, David Gentilcore, has offered a number of valuable cautionary arguments in the spirit of Galasso and Russo's work. Challenging historical studies that seek to document 'failure' and do not adequately interrogate their sources, Gentilcore raises the important point that Gabriele De Rosa's perspective, for example, allows for too much uncritical adoption of 'the opinions of the reformers,' and the possibility of accepting their definition of what constitutes 'superstition.' Ironically, however, Gentilcore falls victim to this tendency to keep score in his own work. While he rightly challenges scholars to be aware of their own biases and hidden (or not so hidden) agendas while conducting research, the author also ends up reifying the historians' common preoccupation with seeking to gauge success or failure in post-Tridentine religious reform.[19]

Historical treatments of the Jesuits

If historical studies of Naples have often been characterized by an obsession with documenting failure, until fairly recently institutional studies of the Jesuits have been alternately uncritical and apologetic tributes to the Society of Jesus, often written by members of the order, or ideologically driven hatchet jobs, penned by a range of hostile critics. As John W. O'Malley argued several years ago in his pivotal study, *The First Jesuits* (1993), until quite recently much of the research on the Society of Jesus has been produced internally, working within a well-defined tradition, and too often posing familiar questions.[20]

The tradition of internally produced historical studies of the Society of Jesus began early. By the mid-seventeenth century, just about one hundred years after the order's official founding, the Jesuits had produced a number of institutional studies and hagiographies in Latin and in several vernacular languages. Although the purpose of such

---

[19] For useful cautionary notes, see David Gentilcore, 'Methods and Approaches in the Social History of the Counter-Reformation in Italy,' *Social History* 17, No. 1 (January 1992): 73–98. In a more recent historical investigation, however, Gentilcore appears to be searching for evidence to determine the 'success' or 'failure' of Tridentine reforms in early modern Southern Italy: see '"Adapt Yourselves to the People's Capabilities": Missionary Strategies, Methods and Impact in the Kingdom of Naples, 1600–1800,' *Journal of Ecclesiastical History* 45, No. 2 (April 1994): 269–96.

[20] John W. O'Malley, *The First Jesuits* (Cambridge, MA: Harvard University Press, 1993), 2; cf. O'Malley, 'The Society of Jesus,' in *Religious Orders of the Catholic Reformation: Essays in Honor of John C. Olin on His Seventy-Fifth Birthday*, ed. Richard L. De Molen (New York: Fordham University Press, 1994), 139–63, esp. 158–9.

INTRODUCTION   13

publications was to extol the successes of the order in its varied activities, these histories are rich resources for a student of the Society of Jesus, if they are read with a critical eye. Naples, too, became a popular site for studies of the Jesuits, particularly with regard to their mission history in Europe. Four of these early Jesuit histories in the Kingdom of Naples figure prominently in this study.

Although his *Cronica* was not published until just a few years ago, Giovan Francesco Araldo (1528–99) wrote the first detailed history of Jesuit activities in Naples, tracing the order's work in the southern Italian capital from the events leading up to the Society of Jesus' arrival early in 1552 until illness prevented him from continuing his account in 1596.[21] While the work emphasizes the Jesuits' self-conscious articulation of their own importance in sixteenth-century Naples, the *Cronica* provides a valuable window onto the order's increasingly reform-oriented activities in Naples during the latter half of the century. It also considers the wider context of Neapolitan social and political life.

The first comprehensive, published history of the missions in Naples came a little more than fifty years after Araldo's internal chronicle. Scipione Paolucci's *Missioni de Padri della Compagnia di Giesù nel Regno di Napoli* (Naples, 1651) was written on the heels of the Revolt of Naples (1647–48), a troubled time for the Kingdom of Naples, and a challenging atmosphere for the Society of Jesus. Paolucci's compendium of missionary relations strives both to edify and entertain its presumably secular readership. Although the author selects and dramatizes tales of miraculous conversions for his audience, he also reveals the evolution of what we might call Jesuit missionary science. Some of the stories Paolucci tells are humorous, and the author does not fail to remark upon the challenges that Jesuits faced in their missionary endeavors, yet Paolucci's primary goal remains quite singular: to celebrate the Society of Jesus' activities in the Kingdom of Naples and argue for their invaluable service to the Catholic world in general.

Some half a century later, Francesco Schinosi, another Jesuit, composed *Istoria della Compagnia de Giesù Appartenente al Regno di Napoli* (Naples, 1706–11). In this two-volume work, Schinosi presents a highly detailed account of the Society of Jesus' first fifty years in the

---

[21] For a vast bibliography of works written by Jesuits, from the origins of the Society of Jesus, see Carlos Sommervogel, *Bibliothèque de la Compagnie de Jésus*, 11 vols (Brussels: O. Schepens; Paris: A. Picard, 1890–1932). Araldo's *Cronica della Compagnia di Gesù di Napoli del P. Giovan Francesco Araldo* (hereafter, *Cronica*), which I originally consulted in manuscript form, is now available in print for the first time in a modern, edited volume, *Napoli, L'Europa e la Compagnia di Gesù nella 'Cronica' di Giovan Francesco Araldo*, ed. Francesco Divenuto (Naples: Edizioni Scientifiche Italiane, 1999).

14   A PARADISE INHABITED BY DEVILS

Mezzogiorno of Italy, examining notable members of the order, missionary activity and the vital development of Jesuit colleges in urban Naples and the southern Italian hinterlands. Like Giovan Francesco Araldo, Schinosi traces the Jesuits' involvement in important historical events of the period, but the degree of historical analysis that he offers is limited and the rendering of certain events inaccurate. Schinosi seems mainly concerned with arguing for the heroic value of Jesuit activities in Naples and thus interesting a broader reading public in news of the order's successes, rather than presenting any critical evaluation of their progress, which might aid novices and veterans alike. Despite its limitations, however, I do not agree with Ulderico Parente's ultimate dismissal of the value of Schinosi's work. If viewed with a critical eye, Schinosi's account can tell us a great deal about how the Jesuits chose to represent themselves to potential supporters.[22]

The historical weaknesses of Schinosi's work are self-consciously addressed by his successor in chronicling the Jesuits' history in Naples, Saverio Santagata. Completing Schinosi's history by taking events from 1600 to 1630, in the *Istoria della Compagnia di Gesù appartenente al Regno di Napoli*, Volumes 3 and 4 (Naples, 1756–57), Santagata attempts to distance himself from his predecessor by arguing that he will show more faithfulness to the chronological order of historical events and offer a more precise account of the truth. Santagata's invocation of the truthfulness of his account (which includes identifying the primary sources which form the basis of his history) may represent a defensive gesture at a time when the Jesuits were facing increasing criticisms, but it might also signal the Jesuits' shifting historical consciousness by the mid-eighteenth century, a period fraught with troubles for the order as it faced expulsion from nearly every European and American outpost where the order placed its men. Although the work was composed over a century after the events that it describes, it, too, can provide an important insight into how the Jesuits constructed the story of their own labors in the Kingdom of Naples, and offer an intriguing, if only partial, view of the early seventeenth-century landscape.

Taken together, these works demonstrate the Jesuits' strategic efforts to represent themselves favorably to a wider audience of the faithful. Wherever possible, I attempt to leaven the Jesuit author's perspective with that of an independent source, but I am also interested in what these chronicles can reveal to us about the development of a collective

---

[22] For Parente's critique of Schinosi, whom he rightly judges 'apologetic' and thus largely 'unreliable,' see his valuable consideration of Alfonso Salmerón's contributions to Catholic reform in sixteenth-century Naples, Ulderico Parente, 'Alfonso Salmerón a Napoli (1551–1585),' *Campania Sacra* 20 (1989): 14–51, esp. 14.

INTRODUCTION

Jesuit missionary identity in Naples in the early modern period, and how these authors build upon and reinforce secular perceptions of Naples and its people.

In the modern period, the earlier tradition of advancing a positive representation of Jesuit activity in Italy (including the Kingdom of Naples) is continued in Pietro Tacchi Venturi's multi-volume *Storia della Compagnia di Gesù in Italia* (1930–50). Tacchi Venturi's encyclopedic series provides a wealth of information on important people, events, and institutional shifts within the first nearly half century of Jesuit activity. In the tradition of other noted Catholic scholars who attempted to shift the historical understanding of early modern Catholicism away from a defensive posture, the Jesuit scholar Tacchi Venturi and his successor, Mario Scaduto, emphasize the creative and proactive evolution of the Jesuits' apostolic and educational endeavors, but they provide little in the way of critical analysis of the Society of Jesus within its historical context.[23]

Until recently, most English-language treatments of the Society of Jesus have tended toward outright confessional hostility or apologetics. In the last couple of decades, however, several historians of the order have composed useful historical studies of individual Jesuits and Jesuit corporate culture, as well as broad surveys of the Society of Jesus' work in a variety of mission fields. Many of these studies are characterized by the new questions that they pose, attention to primary sources, critical perspectives and careful historical methodology.[24]

---

[23] The entire early history of the Jesuits in Italy through *c.* 1570 comprises six volumes, beginning with Pietro Tacchi Venturi SJ, *Storia della Compagnia di Gesù in Italia*, 3 vols (Rome: La Civiltà Cattolica, 1930–50); Mario Scaduto SJ, *L'Epoca di Giacomo Laínez, 1556–1565*, 2 vols (Rome: La Civiltà Cattolica, 1964–74), and Scaduto, *L'Opera di Francesco Borgia, 1565–1572* (Rome: La Civiltà Cattolica, 1992). An edited volume covering the Mercurian generalate (1573–80) is currently in press.

[24] See, for example, William V. Bangert's very useful study, *Claude Jay and Alfonso Salmerón. Two Early Jesuits* (Chicago: Loyola University Press, 1985), and the posthumous work by the same author, *Jerome Nadal, S.J. (1507–1580): Tracking the First Generation of Jesuits*, ed. and completed by Thomas M. McCoog SJ (Chicago: Loyola University Press, 1992). One excellent study of the formation of Jesuit consciousness and decorum is A. Lynn Martin, *The Jesuit Mind: the Mentality of an Elite in Early Modern France* (Ithaca: Cornell University Press, 1988). In terms of regional studies, on the Jesuits in Portugal see Dauril Alden, *The Making of an Enterprise: The Society of Jesus in Portugal, its Empire, and Beyond, 1540–1750* (Stanford: Stanford University Press, 1996); on missions to Japan and China, see Andrew C. Ross, *A Vision Betrayed: The Jesuits in Japan and China, 1542–1742* (Edinburgh: Edinburgh University Press, 1994). And for a wide-ranging look at the breadth of scholarship on many aspects of the Society of Jesus by an international array of scholars, see *The Jesuits. Cultures, Sciences, and the Arts, 1540–1773*, eds John W. O'Malley SJ, Gauvin Alexander Bailey, Steven J. Harris and T. Frank Kennedy SJ (Toronto: University of Toronto Press, 1999).

16   A PARADISE INHABITED BY DEVILS

In this book, I hope to build upon such work as O'Malley's *The First Jesuits*, a critical introduction to understanding the complex maturation of this early modern religious organization within the broader sweep of sixteenth-century society and culture. O'Malley's investigation, which covers the first twenty-five years of Jesuit history, offers an excellent model for writing a rich, layered institutional history. I follow his example by exploring the development of the Jesuits' missionary project in Naples through the end of the seventeenth century, focusing upon the evolution of a collective missionary identity within the order, and understanding better how the Jesuits were influenced by and contributed to an early modern mythologizing of Naples.

There was a complex relationship between the myth of Neapolitan backwardness that took root in the sixteenth century and the Jesuits' pursuit of an active apostolate in the southern Italian capital and the hinterlands of the Kingdom of Naples. Chapter One, 'A Paradise Inhabited by Devils,' considers the early modern perceptions of supposed Neapolitan backwardness within the context of the shifting political, social and religious features of southern Italian and European society more generally. What was the relationship between stereotype and reality in early modern Naples? As numerous historians have noted, this period witnessed a dramatic shift in the fortunes of the Mediterranean world as economic power moved northward and centered increasingly on the Atlantic. This process accelerated in the seventeenth and early eighteenth centuries; and, while Naples continued to be an important trade outpost, the marginalization of the Italian South took hold from this period forward.

From the sixteenth century on, negative images of the Neapolitan populace grew in number and ferocity. Although the bulk of such invective was directed at the urban and rural poor, the Neapolitan nobles did not escape unscathed. If secular observers found much to criticize in the Neapolitan landscape, so too did their religious contemporaries. From papal visitors like Tommaso Orfini, who did a reconnaissance throughout the southern Italian peninsula in 1568, to a string of Neapolitan bishops, religious reformers sought to identify critical problems like inadequately trained clergy and the apparently rampant immorality among clergy and laity alike.

While the Jesuits were drawn to Naples by powerful benefactors who urged them to establish a college there, the development of urban missions in Naples, and later the rural missions in the southern Italian countryside, became increasingly important as a response to growing social and economic tensions in the southern Italian capital and this perceived spiritual crisis. At the same time, the missions came to be a model for the Society's work throughout other parts of Europe. Provid-

INTRODUCTION   17

ing a close analysis of missionary innovators like Pierantonio Spinelli, the Neapolian Provincial early in the seventeenth century and the man usually credited with designing the first urban missions, Chapter Two, ' "Planting many virtues there": Early Jesuit missions in Naples, 1550–1620,' argues that in response to the broader contemporary perceptions of Naples, and in keeping with the Jesuits' own global missionary project, the Society devoted considerable efforts to establishing itself in early modern Naples and hoped to publicize its efforts there.

Jesuit writings also reveal a fascinating relationship between the *Indies* of Asia and the Americas, and the so-called *Other Indies* of southern Italy as real and imaginary sites of missionary activity. As Jesuit missionary theorists and early practitioners like Francis Xavier and José de Acosta traveled to India and America, respectively, they provided two very different models for a civilizing mission that would eventually have major implications for work in southern Italy. Especially Francis Xavier, the first Jesuit to venture beyond the borders of Europe in 1543, provided a model for a heroic missionary vocation which would be emulated by literally thousands of young Jesuit novices for centuries to follow. In southern Italy, a religious cult grew around the Spanish Jesuit which the Society used both to recruit members to the order and for religious propaganda purposes. Using a collection of letters requesting placement in the Indies, including marginal notations by Provincial leaders, I discuss the kinds of missionaries that the order sought to conduct its extra-European missions and the sophisticated means by which young Jesuits hoped to make their case to superiors.

As much as the personal model of Xavier contributed to the development of a missionary ideal in the young Society of Jesus, the Jesuits' conceptualization of a global civilizing mission and the methods that would be required to work among various populations required more detailed theorizing about evangelization. The work of José de Acosta (1540–1600), a Spanish Jesuit who spent fourteen years laboring in Peru and then Mexico was particularly important in this regard. In his book *De Procuranda Indorum Salute*, Acosta developed a thoroughgoing framework for assessing any given culture's 'level of civilization' and the specific missionary strategies appropriate for its conversion. While he did not speak specifically of conducting missionary work among the urban or rural poor of Europe, Acosta, like Xavier, provided another model for the Jesuits to follow in conducting missionary work at home and abroad, demonstrating the extent to which the Jesuits contributed to changing definitions of superstition and savagery and the remedies needed to eradicate them.

Chapter Four, ' "Use every means that you will judge opportune": Instructions to Jesuit missionaries,' continues the comparative analysis of the Jesuits' developing institutional identity by focusing on the instructional manuals written by and for missionaries in Naples, in other parts of Italy, and beyond Europe. As much as the heroic models offered by missionaries deployed to the Indies contributed to the development of a collective identity within the Society of Jesus, the composition of instructional documents that could guide novice Jesuits also facilitated the creation of the Society of Jesus' distinctive approach to its civilizing mission and helped shape the profile of the 'ideal' Jesuit. The Jesuits forged their institutional identity as much through the creation and dissemination of instructions to missionaries as they did through human models like Xavier or Acosta, among others. Across the seventeenth century, the Jesuits composed increasingly detailed and comprehensive instructions to guide the actions of the order's rapidly expanding membership. Far more than their medieval forebears like the Franciscans and Dominicans, the Jesuits sought to systematize the missionary vocation, anticipate potential obstacles to success and draw the necessary lessons from past mistakes.

One of the other cornerstones of Jesuit practice in Naples, and elsewhere, was their accommodation to local religious rituals and emphasis on spectacle to effect their ambitious civilizing mission in Naples. While certainly not the only order to adapt theatrical techniques in their missionary arsenal, the Jesuits are intriguing for the degree to which they adapted local, often 'unorthodox', practices, even as they decried the supposedly damaging effects of overly ecstatic or artificial spectacle. Chapter Five, 'Taming the beast: Confronting discord in early modern Naples,' examines peacemaking and reconciliation rituals as central activities in the Jesuits' mission. Just as the turmoil unleashed by an earlier revolt in 1585 led the Jesuits to increase their reform activities among the poor, inspiring the urban missions, so the more cataclysmic Revolt of 1647–48 inspired greater attention to the reconciliation role that missionaries believed they must play to maintain social peace. In moments of violent unrest and crisis, the Jesuits self-consciously employed ritualized religious spectacle to try to convince the population to submit to traditional religious and secular authorities.

Chapter Six, 'Perfecting one's craft: Jesuit missionary theater in Naples,' continues the investigation of the complex relationship between religious spectacle and Jesuit missionary methods by exploring the Jesuits' deft use of missionary theater to accomplish their civilizing mission in early modern Naples, just as they employed theater in their colleges as both a pedagogical tool and to dazzle wealthy patrons. There are two central ironies in the phenomenon of missionary theater: first, although the Jesuits were among the most vocal critics of secular theater, such as the *commedia dell'arte*, from the early seventeenth century on,

INTRODUCTION

they employed many of the same techniques as these theater artists, despite their polemics. Prominent Jesuit missionary theorists from Naples and other parts of Italy contributed to a broader vision of the efficacy of theatricality in evangelization. Second, although the Jesuits employed a highly dramatic rhetorical style in order to achieve their civilizing mission, they were ultimately accused of fostering the very superstitious, gimmicky religiosity that they presumed to eradicate. This was especially true for the Jesuits' encouragement of that most southern Italian of religious rituals, the penitential exercises, which formed the dramatic centerpiece of Jesuit missions in both urban Naples and the countryside.

As a civilizing project, the Jesuits' missions in the Kingdom of Naples began from the premise that the urban poor and their rural neighbors were backward, and sought specific remedies to reform their behaviors, cultural practices and religious values. In this regard, they echoed their secular counterparts, who forged a discourse of southern Italian backwardness which continues to be disseminated through modern literary images such as *Cristo si è fermato a Eboli* (1963), as well as cinematic representations and contemporary journalism. Early Jesuit commentators saw an explicit connection between the efficacy of Jesuit missionary intervention in the Italian *Mezzogiorno* and the newer mission fields of the Indies. They noted the importance of Naples and its hinterlands as a proving ground for the order's apostolic activity, making it a critical locus for experimentation, the pursuit of patronage and publicizing the Society's work. By detailing the myriad challenges which missionaries faced from what the Jesuits viewed as a predominantly uncivilized and sometimes unruly population, the order celebrated its own efficacy, providing further justification for the global civilizing mission which it sought to realize.

This book provides a critical window onto a group of reformers who devoted a prominent place to Neapolitans in its missionary program. The Jesuits' moral universe was informed by a bifurcated view of the world as a paradise in which good and evil battled for supremacy. Naples was no different, but served as a microcosm of the larger struggle in which the Jesuits were engaged. As such, it provides object lessons in the institutional history of one of the most important new religious orders of the early modern period. One unexpected consequence of this book has been its timeliness. When I began the project, I felt comforted in the belief that such an absolutist moral universe as that of the early Jesuits lay well in the past. Recently, however, I have had my doubts. Apparently, good and evil are afoot in the world and are easily identifiable.

CHAPTER ONE

A paradise inhabited by devils

While the mythology of a beautiful but culturally backward southern Italy holds less power today than it did in earlier times, the intensity of stereotypes that represent southern Italians as overly emotional, violence-prone and lazy is still evident to a visitor in contemporary Italy. From at least the late Middle Ages forward, as Naples' economic and political fortunes became increasingly bound up with the policies of the powerful monarchies that claimed sovereignty over it, and as the machinations of its own evidently anarchic and self-interested nobility took their toll, prominent images of the city likewise became more alarmist. The sixteenth and seventeenth centuries brought a dramatic influx of immigrants into the city. Individuals and families migrated from the southern Italian countryside, bringing with them a host of social problems not unfamiliar to other burgeoning early modern cities and towns, but apparently magnified in the minds of observers because the social problems that they observed in Naples took place in such an apparently idyllic climate.

When the first twelve Jesuits arrived in Naples in 1552 to establish a college and begin their program of moral reform in the southern Italian capital, they were no doubt aware of the stereotypes of the *Mezzogiorno* that prevailed by the mid-sixteenth century. In time, the Jesuits would join the chorus of those who duly noted the troubles in Naples, reifying many of those stereotypes even as they celebrated the challenges that the City and Kingdom offered to the Society of Jesus in its ambitious apostolic program. The period from the mid-sixteenth century through to the end of the seventeenth century saw an explosion in the publication of local and regional histories, 'descriptions' and travel guides for Naples. During this roughly 150-year period, some 36 works were published in vernacular Italian, 15 in Latin and an additional 7 in other vernacular languages.[1]

---

[1] Cf. Elisa Novi Chavarria, ' "Las Indias de Por Açà" Nelle Relazioni dei Gesuiti Napoletani,' now available in her *Il Governo delle Anime* (2001), 141–56. Novi Chavarria follows Adriano Prosperi in considering how the Jesuits contributed to the 'literary topos' of the 'other Indies,' while she argues that the image ceased to have much relevance to Jesuit missionaries by the latter half of the seventeenth century. On the burgeoning genre of 'descriptions' of Naples of various kinds, see Rosario Manfredi, 'Le "Descrittioni" di Napoli (1450–1692). Appunti per una Ricerca Bibliografica,' *Rendiconti della Accademia di Archeologia Lettere e Belle Arti*, Vol. 63 (1992): 63–108; Maria Rosaria Pelizzari,

22 A PARADISE INHABITED BY DEVILS

Dominant views of early modern Naples and its citizenry were shaped by a curious paradox: the city and its surroundings were viewed as an earthly paradise, while many Neapolitans, especially the poor, were seen in a different light. Benedetto Croce (1866–1952), the highly prolific and influential Neapolitan philosopher, historian and literary critic, noted that by the sixteenth and seventeenth centuries it was almost a cliché to refer to Naples as a 'paradise inhabited by devils.'[2] For the Jesuits, however, this characterization of the city reflected in microcosm the world that they hoped to reform through their educational and apostolic ministries.

To understand fully the paradoxical view of the southern Italian capital, we must begin by examining early modern perceptions of Naples within the context of the shifting political, social, economic and religious features of southern Italy in the late medieval and early modern periods. The sixteenth century is a critical period of transition in this respect, both because of the city's rapid demographic growth and the larger political and economic changes that moved southern Italy further from the gravitational center of international commerce and trade.[3]

What were the key features of the emerging profile of Naples? Out of the anecdotal impressions of the city, penned by a vast array of commentators both foreign and native to the *Mezzogiorno*, we can trace several unifying themes. For many, Naples came to be defined as a city and region plagued by criminality and moral decay, including rampant prostitution and violent social unrest. Observing its complex urban landscape, many commentators produced vivid discourses of a barbarous *popolo minuto* (common folk) and, in a usually less derisive manner, spoke of the decadence of the southern Italian nobility that flocked to the city in the late sixteenth and seventeenth centuries. A few, like the sixteenth-century Neapolitan author Camillo Porzio, found common attributes across the social spectrum to highlight. Writing in a late sixteenth-century account of the Kingdom of Naples for the new viceroy, Porzio argues that both noble and lower-caste Neapolitans share 'common qualities.' Despite apparent differences, they are equally 'desirous of new things, little fearful of the judicial system, make much

---

'Dalle Descrizioni per I Forestieri Alle Guide Turistiche: Cinque Secoli di Napoli in Vetrina,' *Campania Sacra* 32 (2001): 429–57. A few English translations of such documents are now available in Jeanne Chenault Porter, ed., *Baroque Naples. A Documentary History* (New York: Italica Press, 2000), esp. 23–41.

[2] Croce, 'Il "Paradiso Abitato Da Diavoli,"' 68.

[3] Some historians, like Rosario Villari, argue for identifying the latter half of the seventeenth century as the crucial moment in the 'eclipsing' of southern Italy and the onset of its 'permanent backwardness.' See Villari, *The Revolt of Naples*, trans. James Newell, (Cambridge, UK: Polity Press, 1993), 1–2.

esteem of honor, love appearances more than substance, [and are] courageous, [and] homicidal.'[4] Porzio's comments reveal a rather ambiguous rendering of Neapolitans that seems derisive and yet betrays a grudging admiration. In common with other commentators, he appears to scorn Neapolitans' supposed love of novelty and superficiality, combined with a notorious violent streak. But he also seems to approve of their 'courage' and love of honor, suggesting the complexity of such representations.

Beyond broader stereotypes of Neapolitan character, early modern secular and religious critics alike were often troubled by the seemingly contradictory presence of ecstatic (and sometimes unorthodox) religious rituals and practices with evidence of irreligiosity, or laxity. Much of this irregularity was blamed on an ignorant and/or corrupt clergy that either could not or would not lead its flock, and on the supposed lack of civility among average Neapolitans. The prevailing view, as we shall see, suggested that radical reform of Neapolitan religious practices was both necessary and desirable, even if it apparently failed in the minds of many modern commentators. This argument has been echoed by several prominent scholars, who have often uncritically accepted the idea that southern Italians could not or would not practice orthodox Roman Catholicism and have focused their research on exploring the failures of Tridentine Catholicism to take hold in the Kingdom of Naples. My question is not whether or not religious and moral reform was a success or a failure in the Kingdom of Naples, but how contemporaries like the Jesuits understood the social, cultural and spiritual landscape of early modern Naples and the tasks set before them.

If Naples and its environs came to be viewed as a troubled urban center in the early modern period, such negative perceptions were not so prominent in the medieval period, or even into the fifteenth century. While the city had long been a battle ground among competing powers, from the Normans in the twelfth century to the Angevin and then Aragon monarchs in the thirteenth, fourteenth and fifteenth centuries respectively, Naples had also enjoyed a strong reputation as one of the premier cultural centers of medieval Italy. During the fourteenth century, both Francesco Petrarch and Giovanni Boccaccio, two central figures in early Renaissance humanist culture, sought out the patronage of the Angevin King, Robert 'the Wise' (r. 1310–43). While Petrarch spent little time in the southern Italian capital, Boccaccio arrived there as a

---

[4] Camillo Porzio, *Relazione del Regno di Napoli al Marchese Di Mondesciar, Vicere di Napoli* (1579), in *La Congiura dei Baroni del Regno di Napoli Contra il Re Ferdinando Primo e Gli Altri Scritti*, ed. Ernesto Pontieri (Naples, 1964), 339. Cf. Galasso, *L'Altra Europa*, 174.

24 A PARADISE INHABITED BY DEVILS

youth and spent fifteen years in Naples, writing a number of his early works in and around the Angevin court.

Perhaps more than their Angevin predecessors, however, the reigns of Aragonese rulers (1442–1504) like Alfonso V (r. 1442–58) and Ferrante (r. 1458–94) were associated with artistic and cultural patronage and urban renewal. Alfonso began his effort to conquer the city from the Angevin Kingdom that had ruled it for nearly two centuries (1268–1435) in 1432, while the Spanish took formal control of Naples as part of its viceroyalty in 1503, after several years of struggles with the French for hegemony over peninsular Italy. Unlike the Angevin rulers who came before him, Alfonso V was credited with minimizing the power of the barons in the Kingdom of Naples, an important development since historians have long maintained that a selfish and anarchic nobility contributed in great part to Naples' economic and political misfortunes.[5]

For his part, Ferrante is often credited with facilitating urban renewal in Naples, patronizing the arts and providing for at least a modicum of political stability until the Aragon kings' overthrow by the French at the turn of the sixteenth century, and then the rapid return of the Spanish to southern Italy through their creation of the long-standing Viceroyalty of Naples. It was precisely during Ferrante's long reign that a Florentine commentator, Francesco Bandini, could praise Naples' apparently calm and cultured environment, noting that Naples was the kind of city where one 'does not feel the blows of the citizens, [. . .] seditions, the shrieks of oppressed people.' Bandini also commended Neapolitans 'as most eloquent and very erudite and excellent.'[6] Such praise should not be surprising from the Florentine commentator, given the incessant warfare and political chaos which city-states like his own were experiencing during the same period.

At the same time, the Kingdom of Naples was a prominent player in the fractious politics of late medieval Italy. As the single secular mon-

---

[5] Jerry Bentley, *Politics and Culture in Renaissance Naples* (Princeton: Princeton University Press, 1987), 9. For an idiosyncratic but interesting assessment of the relative merits of the Aragon kings, see Benedetto Croce, *History of the Kingdom of Naples*, ed. H. Stuart Hughes, trans. Frances Frenaye (Chicago: University of Chicago Press, 1970), originally published as *Storia del Regno di Napoli* (Bari: Laterza, 1925). 53–4; 89–94. A more traditional narrative history of Alfonso's reign is Alan Ryder, *The Kingdom of Naples Under Alfonso the Magnanimous. The Making of a Modern State* (Oxford: Clarendon Press, 1976).

[6] Francesco Bandini, as cited in Atanasio Mozzillo, *Passaggio a Mezzogiorno*, 85. But for a much less complimentary view of the Aragonese rulers, especially Ferrante and Alfonso II, see Jacob Burckhardt, *The Civilization of the Renaissance in Italy* (New York: Harper Torchbooks, 1958), 51–3.

archy among the five major powers in fifteenth-century Italy (Naples, the Papal States, the Republics of Venice and Florence and the Duchy of Milan), the Aragonese Kingdom of Naples wielded considerable influence by lending its support to the various players that formed the constantly shifting alliances in Italian politics during this period. For example, in 1443 Alfonso shrewdly forged alliances with the papacy and the Milanese ruler Filippo Maria Visconti against the upstart *condottiere* Francesco Sforza's threat to expand his power base in central Italy while they served his interests. Later, the Aragonese king shifted allegiances in the mid-1550s to work alongside his former rival and now ruler of Milan, Sforza, in their common interests in the Italian League.

Internally, too, the Kingdom of Naples achieved a brief period of relative consolidation of central power, allowing the monarchy to minimize threats posed to it by a restive nobility, moving away from feudal modes of warfare toward the use of *condottieri* who served the state, and reforming the state bureaucracy, largely through the efforts of non-noble state managers. In this respect, Naples was well within the mainstream of late medieval European states, in spite of the consensus picture of its later backwardness.[7]

Yet while Naples' image in late medieval Europe may have been more favorable on the whole than it was to become in the following centuries, troubling signs were already on the horizon. As Benedetto Croce argued nearly a century ago, the idea of Naples as 'a paradise inhabited by devils' had been widely applied to Naples since at least the fourteenth century, even if the specific appellation, credited to Bernardino Daniello, was coined in a letter sent by the Florentine Dante scholar in 1539. In that letter, dispatched from Naples, Daniello remarks on the gifts of the city 'whose location seems to me marvelous and the most beautiful that I have ever seen,' surrounded as it is 'by the mountains on one side and the sea on the other.' Such beauty, however, was tainted for Daniello because he saw Naples as full of unsavory sorts of people.[8]

Even before Daniello, Italian commentators had called attention to the apparently dramatic juxtaposition between the attractive environment of Naples and its 'evil' populace. One early critic of Neapolitans, writing in the fifteenth century, was the Florentine satirist Arlotto Mainardi (1396–1483). In one of his little stories, Arlotto responds to a stock question about why Naples, if it is rightly called an 'earthly paradise' and produces 'an enormous quantity and abundance of

---

[7] For background on the Aragonese king's foreign policy moves, see Bentley, *Politics and Culture in Renaissance Naples*, 13–18; on his 'modernization' of the central state in Naples, see Ryder, *The Kingdom of Naples*, esp. 367–71.

[8] Bernardino Daniello, as cited in Croce, 'Il "Paradiso Abitato Da Diavoli," ' 70.

26 A PARADISE INHABITED BY DEVILS

innumerable goods and many exquisite types of fruits for the nourish-
ment . . . and the sustenance of men,' is a city full of people 'of little
ingenuity,' who are 'malignant, bad and full of treasons.' Arlotto
answers that if 'Naples had perfect men of goodness and ingenuity, it
would not be called a terrestrial paradise, but instead the sphere of the
Sun. And so, that air [of Naples] produces bad and treasonous men.[9]
Such early commentators herald the emergence of what would soon
become a common perception of the Neapolitans (and especially of the
poor). In this view, all of the wonders that Naples had to offer seem
ephemeral, or vulnerable to destruction at the hands of its anarchic
population.

Certainly, some authors chose to play down this human threat to
emphasize the glories of the city. Indeed, it seemed to many to be a
truism that cities had a civilizing influence on their populations. Such
attitudes could be traced back to Plato and Aristotle and had strong
currency in the sixteenth and seventeenth centuries. For Giulio Cesare
Capaccio, the Neapolitan author of *Il Forastiero* (1634), a history of
Naples and guide for foreign visitors, the relationship between city and
countryside was more complex still. As much as the city might ennoble
at least some of those who made it their own, so too these newcomers
could bring their own energies to the urban sphere. Speaking of these
immigrants from the far-flung towns and villages of the *Mezzogiorno*,
Capaccio comments admiringly:

> Now many other inhabitants have been added here [. . .] Calabrese,
> Abruzzese and from closer by, coastal dwellers [. . . and] they have
> filled up the entire city with such a frequency that they make up
> almost a third of it [. . .] and from what I have heard, [just] as the
> inhabitants are frequenting and developing the city, they are enno-
> bling it.

Beyond his recognition that provincials might add flavor to the growing metropolis, however, Capaccio does not entirely depart from the
dominant view that city life civilizes people, reminding his imaginary
visitor that 'the City of Naples also ennobles all those who come to
live in it. Because speaking of those of the Kingdom, when some arrive
here, they are reborn and change customs and that roughness of the
countryside becomes civility, and a freedom proper to Naples makes
itself felt.'[10]

Capaccio's remarks are intriguing for two important reasons. First,
because they differ markedly from those contemporaries who felt that

---

[9] Piovano Arlotto Mainardi, *Facezie Motti e Burle del Piovano Arlotto*, ed. Chiara
Amerighi (Florence: Libreria Editrice Fiorentina, 1980), 232-3.

[10] Giulio Cesare Capaccio, *Il Forastiero* (Naples, 1634), 690.

A PARADISE INHABITED BY DEVILS

the rural outposts of the Kingdom of Naples were true backwaters, paling even in comparison with the troubled capital city and all of its urban woes.[11] Authors such as Camillo Porzio began a long-standing trend of highlighting the virtues and vices of the City of Naples, and its province, the Terra di Lavoro, while offering less developed images of the Kingdom's other eleven provinces and their diverse populations. While Capaccio does not offer much evidence of the 'nobility' of the Calabrese or Abruzzese that he mentions, their inclusion in and of itself is remarkable. But another fascinating feature of Capaccio's passage is that it seems to imply that the city itself could offer a civilizing influence, despite the presence of the very sort of people whom the author will castigate in the very same text, as we shall see. In Capaccio's *Il Forastiero*, we see a fascinating blend of a kind of idealized depiction of Naples that occasionally butts up against the harsh realities against which the author wishes to warn his foreign visitor. Ironically, then, like so many other of his contemporaries, Capaccio appears fixated on emphasizing the tension between people and place, despite the apparent contradictions in his representation of city and region.

What happened to Naples that could transform these few, anecdotal disparagements of the local population into a chorus of urban stereotyping, creating a discourse of backwardness that has largely persisted over time, if changing according to the dynamics of the particular historical moment and the viewpoint and agenda of the critic in question? Historians have generally agreed that the sixteenth and seventeenth centuries witnessed several crucial developments that affected Naples' fortunes in the early modern world, including a shifting economic order, the vagaries of Spanish imperial policy, and the demographic transformation of southern Italy as a whole.[12]

Several decades ago, Fernand Braudel traced the shift away from a

---

[11] Compare the comments of Camillo Porzio, whose characterizations of rural southern Italians are less complimentary. See Porzio, *Relazione*, 312–31. For a fascinating discussion on the tradition among southern Italian commentators of valorizing the capital city and its immediate hinterlands to the exclusion of other areas of the Kingdom, when they do not simply collapse the entire Kingdom into a discussion primarily of the urban center, see Galasso, *L'Altra Europa*, esp. 184–200.

[12] Among those historians who have traced the economic eclipsing of the *Mezzogiorno* as part of a broader marginalization of the Mediterranean in the early modern period, see esp. Fernand Braudel, *The Mediterranean and the Mediterranean World in the Age of Philip II*, 2 vols (Berkeley and Los Angeles: University of California Press, 1995). For a fascinating consideration of the changing dynamics of noble life and economic activity during this period, also see Tommaso Astarita, *The Continuity of Feudal Power. The Caracciolo di Brienza in Spanish Naples* (Cambridge, UK: Cambridge University Press, 1992).

28   A PARADISE INHABITED BY DEVILS

Mediterranean-based economy toward the Atlantic by the late sixteenth century, including a consideration of its deeper impact on the Italian economies during the early modern period.[13] While Naples had never seen the degree of urban proto-industrial production found in northern and central Italian city-states like Florence and Venice, by the late Middle Ages Naples had a significant role in the production of silk and wool.[14]

Indeed, Camillo Porzio, in a late sixteenth-century description of the Kingdom of Naples and its people, evokes the still-bustling economic activity that characterized the city and Kingdom in this period. He notes that the local landscape contained minerals such as salt, alum and sulphur, along with agricultural products like fruits, and hemp for manufacturing ropes and sails. In the urban sphere, Porzio stresses the production of cloth, especially silks, but also outlines other forms of artisanal production: 'In the city of Naples they spin every sort of silk cloths with great skill; and fruits and flowers are seasoned most exquisitely with sugar, and there are carpenters who fashion tables, primarily out of walnut [. . .].' In brief, Porzio declares, the province containing Naples, the Terra di Lavoro, could provide all one would need for human pleasure.[15]

Despite such glowing reports, however, by the late sixteenth century the City and Kingdom of Naples became less active contributors to the early modern economic order, precisely during an important period of transformation in the global economy. Scholars of early modern southern Italian history have offered a number of hypotheses to explain this development that suggest both internal and external factors.[16] This was a signal moment of transition.

Some historians have noted that the role of the entrepreneur had never been valued in southern Italy and that the Spanish had done little to encourage local business endeavors. As the Neapolitan scholar Giu-

---

[13] Braudel is careful to note, however, that the overall decline of the Mediterranean as a center of trade was not uniform, and that a group of Italian merchants continued to benefit from this commerce into the seventeenth century. See *The Mediterranean*, 228–30.

[14] Claudia Petraccone, *Napoli Moderna e contemporanea* (Naples: Guida, 1981), 12. Petraccone cites the significance of the monopoly that Naples held on the production of these two important commodities, although she also notes the decline of wool production in the sixteenth century. Also see Petraccone, *Napoli dal '500 al '800*, 5. For a thorough discussion of the significance of silk production, and especially its decline, in the Kingdom of Naples in the seventeenth century, see Antonio Calabria, *The Cost of Empire*, 22–5.

[15] Camillo Porzio, *Relazione*, 313.

[16] For a brief but useful overview of the broader trends in Neapolitan historiography, particularly related to the explanatory schools of thought epitomized by scholars like Benedetto Croce and more recent treatments of the South that are anthropologically inspired, see Astarita, *The Continuity of Feudal Power*, esp. 10–12.

seppe Galasso aptly suggests, 'the general opinion has prevailed that entrepreneurship was paralyzed due to various elements related to its socio-political and socio-cultural context, or, [because it] did not correspond to the anthropological characteristics of the southern populations.' According to this 'stereotyped' view of Neapolitans, which Galasso does not necessarily accept, 'southerners lack a spirit of initiative and permit foreigners to enrich themselves at their expense; that their needs are limited, a little due to their laziness and a little because of the ease of satisfying themselves with little efforts thanks to the generosity of nature in their country.'[17] Once again, the link between people and place is invoked to explain Neapolitans' economic behaviors.

Writing from Naples in the late sixteenth century, Francesco Marcaldo, an agent of the Grand Duke of Tuscany, remarked upon the nobles' lavish lifestyle and apparent disinterest in commercial activity: 'The nobles live very grandly, considering it a disgrace to look after merchandise, nor even to domestic affairs, in person.'[18] Indeed, well into the latter part of the early modern period, several key Neapolitan reformers seemed swayed by the notion that certain characteristics inherent in southern Italians might contribute to the region's backwardness, permitting others to control their destinies. In the second half of the eighteenth century, as a growing chorus of reformers bemoaned the lack of economic development in the *Mezzogiorno*, Giuseppe Maria Galanti, one of the most noted of these critics, complained that Neapolitan elites tended too often to turn toward the professions, rather than busying themselves with commerce: 'All those among us who have talent and a small fortune apply themselves to law, to medicine, to being a notary, [or] a priest, and thus procure for themselves subsistence from the people.' Galanti worried that too many Neapolitans (both residents of the City and of the Kingdom as a whole) pursued a 'lazy, good for nothing' existence, or labored not in their own interests, but for the benefit of outsiders, lamenting: 'The foreigners profit from our stupidity.'[19] In this view, Neapolitan elites were, in a

---

[17] Galasso, *L'Altra Europa*, 227–8.

[18] Francesco Marcaldo, 'Cose principali di una Relazione sul Regno di Napoli, fatta al Granduca di Toscana da Francesco Marcaldo, nell'anno 1594,' in 'Documenti Sulla Storia Economica e Civile del Regno Cavati dal Carteggio degli Agenti Del Granduca di Toscana in Napoli, Dall'Anno 1582–1648,' *Archivio Storico Italiano* 9 (1846): 245–353, esp. 247.

[19] Giuseppi Maria Galanti, *Della descrizione geografica e politica delle Sicilie* (1769), cited in ibid., 228. For an interesting consideration of the eighteenth-century debate on economic development in southern Italy, see Biagio Salvemini, 'The Arrogance of the Market: The Economy of the Kingdom Between the Mediterranean and Europe,' in *Naples in the Eighteenth Century. The Birth and Death of a Nation State*, ed. Girolamo Imbruglia (Cambridge, UK: Cambridge University Press, 2000), 44–69

30   A PARADISE INHABITED BY DEVILS

sense, responsible for their own ill fortunes because they had remained
mired in old ways of doing things, while allowing outsiders to determine their collective fate.

Others have shared Galanti's emphasis on the impact of foreign
investors, especially the Genoese and Dutch, on the local economy, and
the newly urbanized nobility's disdain for commerce, while also stressing
the poor infrastructure in the South that hampered trade with the rest of
Italy and the further reaches of Europe.[20] Nor can one ignore the impact
of Turkish incursions on the Adriatic coast of southern Italy on the
decline of the *Mezzogiorno* as a trading entrepôt.

While the diminution of Naples' role in the burgeoning commerce
and trade of the early modern period probably resulted from a combination of these problems, Spanish imperial policy must also be considered an essential factor. From almost the beginning of the Viceroyalty
(1503), the Spanish Crown faced a number of challenges in centralizing
its authority and reducing the threat of the resistant nobility. While
Ferdinand I strove to be conciliatory toward the nobility, and chose
viceroys who did not govern with a heavy hand, matters shifted under
the rule of his grandson, Charles V.[21] A letter sent to Charles V by his
Secretary, Gattinara, early in his reign (1521) reveals a number of
problems that the Crown faced in Naples that would remain nagging
concerns in decades to follow. First, Gattinara notes that Naples 'evaded'
the Crown's requests for money. He also bemoans the fact that the
Neapolitan nobility had a monopoly on the administration of justice.
And finally, he warned his sovereign that the aristocracy expressed its
independent streak through support for the French.[22] This last charge
was especially troubling for the Spanish because throughout much of
the sixteenth century, war raged between the Spanish and French
Crowns over the spoils of European hegemony.

Subduing Naples became critical for the Spanish in order to secure
supply lines to troops in northern Italy and, increasingly, as a fiscal
source for ongoing war efforts. But as important as Naples became for
Spanish imperial prerogatives, the City and Viceroyalty also caused
innumerable headaches for the Crown. By at least 1530, a sense of crisis
pervades perceptions of Naples as the Spanish government worried over

---

[20] For the broader problems of transportation across Mediterranean Europe in this
period, see, for example, Braudel, *The Mediterranean*, 282–90.

[21] Giuseppe Galasso, 'Trends and Problems in Neapolitan History in the Age of
Charles V,' in *Good Government in Spanish Naples*, 13–78, esp. 19–20.

[22] Galasso, 'Trends and Problems,' 30. Compare with Croce's argument that the
Neapolitan barons never had any independent political agenda, nor aspirations to succeed
reigning monarchs in his *History of the Kingdom of Naples*, 66–7.

the destabilizing presence of unpaid Spanish troops in the City, and problems of brigandage, banditry and piracy.[23]

The long regime of the Viceroy Pedro de Toledo (r. 1532–53) marked an important turning point in Spain's relationship to its southern Italian imperial possession, setting in motion a number of policies that would particularly affect Naples' long-term economic health and the fiscal pressures it faced from its Spanish overlords. Historians have noted Toledo's important part in the urban renewal of sixteenth-century Naples. In 1533, Toledo proceeded with his plans to build new city walls and streets and to renovate older structures, though not without widespread and ongoing dissent from many quarters. Scholars have stressed the limited investment that the Spanish made in the local economy as a whole, while fiscal demands increased upon the rapidly growing population of the city. During this period, the tax burden upon commoners across the viceroyalty increased significantly. Nobles paid only one-third of tax levies, while commoners paid three-quarters. To finance the paving of roads and other parts of his urban renewal project, Toledo had levied a number of other taxes, starting with a tax on the sale of wine and bread. This inevitably led to violent resistance from the population, and not for the last time.[24] In 1542, a hearth tax was introduced, alongside new *gabelles* (indirect taxes) on important trade items, such as silk. Indirect taxes were also added to export items. Over the course of the seventeenth century, such fiscal burdens had an increasingly deleterious effect on the local economy and, some historians would argue, contributed over the long term to the region's social unrest, culminating in the so-called Revolt of Masaniello of 1647.[25]

---

[23] Galasso, 'Trends and Problems,' 33; 40. Rosario Villari also traces growing Spanish concerns over the Viceroyalty and an atmosphere of lawlessness in *The Revolt of Naples*, esp. 19–55.

[24] Ibid., 43; for more on the pivotal nature of Toledo's Viceroyalty, see *Il 'Liber Visitationis' di Francesco Carafa Nella Diocesi di Napoli (1542–1543)*, ed. Antonio Illibato (Rome: Edizioni di Storia e Letteratura, 1983), esp. xiv–xvii. The best, detailed, early modern account of Toledo's reign, including his many government pragmatics, is Domenico Antonio Parrino, *Teatro Eroico e Politico dei Governi de' Vicere del Regno di Napoli*, 2 vols (1692; 1875), esp. I, 193–224. Although Parrino is an often uncritical chronicler of his subjects, the viceroys of Naples through the end of the seventeenth century, his account is informative if one ignores the often florid and hyperbolic prose. On Toledo's efforts at urban renewal, see also Antonio Ghirelli, *Storia di Napoli* (Milan: Einaudi, 1973), esp. 28–30; Franco Strazzullo, *Edilizia e Urbanistica a Napoli dal '500 al '700* (Naples: Arte Tipografica, 1995).

[25] For a compelling discussion of the impact of fiscal pressures on urban Naples, and the Viceroyalty more broadly in the sixteenth and seventeenth centuries, see Calabria, *Cost of Empire*. For a useful discussion of the varieties of taxes and other fiscal burdens placed

32 A PARADISE INHABITED BY DEVILS

The combination of fiscal pressures from the new Spanish state, the rapacity of local feudal lords and widespread famine in the countryside drove many of the rural poor into the City of Naples in the early sixteenth century. Even during the first half of the century, Naples witnessed significant population increases. During the roughly twenty-year period from 1528 to 1547, coinciding with much of Toledo's term as Viceroy, the city's population reportedly grew from about 168 000 to 245 000,[26] while no corresponding efforts toward economic development promised an easing of poverty in any real sense. Like the pre-modern forebears of many twenty-first-century immigrants who flock to contemporary metropolises, there were several 'push/pull' forces that drew masses of folk to urban Naples in search of something better, regardless of how chimeric such hopes for improved livelihood might have been. Hunger was, as it always has been, a significant factor in these migrations to the capital, but there was also the tyranny of landlords with which to contend, feudal and royal imposts, and the hope of finding a better livelihood in the city.

If we trace the dramatic population growth of Naples in the sixteenth century alongside a series of severe famines and attendant epidemics, we can see the connection between hunger and urban population growth. Throughout the second half of the sixteenth century, southern Italy as a whole suffered through several famine cycles, while the population of urban Naples continued to grow dramatically.[27]

For his part, Toledo seemed acutely aware of the dangers presented by a bloated population and took steps to minimize the dangers, even if these proved ultimately ineffectual. Providing bread for the poor was one essential reform that Toledo and subsequent viceroys took quite seriously. Toledo, in fact, created a special office, the *Grassiero*, to assure the adequate provisioning of the city's population.[28] But as

---

upon Neapolitans by the Spanish government, see ibid., esp. 39–53. Also see Rosario Villari, *The Revolt of Naples*, trans. James Newell (Cambridge, UK: Polity Press, 1993), esp. 74–97, and Astarita, *The Continuity of Feudal Power*, 164.

[26] Illibato, *Il 'Liber Visitationis,'* xiv; cf. Petraccone, *Napoli dal '500 al '800*, 3–10. Petraccone notes the difficulties in gaining precise population figures for Naples, given the inconsistencies of available census data and their incorrect reporting in early modern chronicles, 12–17.

[27] Petraccone, *Napoli dal '500 al '800*, 15. As Petraccone is careful to relate, such growth is merely an estimate, based on problematic census figures. Further, she notes that this average annual growth was not consistent throughout the years 1547–1606, but averaged about 13 per cent from 1547 to 1595, increasing further between 1595 and 1606.

[28] For an excellent discussion of the provisioning of grain for Naples' expanding and hungry population, within the larger context of the complexities of grain and wool production in the Kingdom of Naples, see John Marino, *Pastoral Economics in the*

A PARADISE INHABITED BY DEVILS

Naples' rulers would learn to their displeasure, bread was not simply a staple in the meager diet of Naples' poor. Rather, as in so many other struggles among pre-modern social groups beyond southern Italy, it could become either a symbolic bargaining chip to ease tense social relations, or, when lacking, a trigger to violence and revolt.[29] In fact, the viceregal government's concern to determine how much bread would be required to feed the urban poor who were facing starvation in Naples motivated one of the early urban census projects to be undertaken by Toledo in 1547.[30]

Yet despite the best efforts of the civic and viceregal governments, famine was a constant threat in sixteenth- and seventeenth-century Naples, as several contemporary accounts reveal. In a fascinating series of dispatches from Naples over the course of the late sixteenth to mid-seventeenth centuries, several agents of the Grand Duke of Tuscany comment on a wide range of economic and political stresses upon the City of Naples, and the Kingdom of Naples more generally. Apparently written to advise the Tuscan rulers of land investment opportunities in the *Mezzogiorno*, these reports provide a generally unromanticized view of life in the southern Italian capital, eschewing much of the hyperbole and vitriol found in other contemporary chronicles.[31] They also provide great insight into the economic privation chronically faced by the mass of Neapolitans, and the magnet that the city provided to the rural poor, especially during times of great want. For example, in one early seventeenth-century report, the Tuscan agent, Fabrizio Barnaba, notes the influx of newcomers to the city:

> The famine is so great throughout the Kingdom that the communities come together in Naples, and they go throughout the city, crying: 'Bread, Bread.' And there is such a concentration of the poor

---

Kingdom of Naples (Baltimore: Johns Hopkins University Press, 1988), esp. 176–80. Marino's study examines the significant and complex economic, social and cultural roles played by the sheepherders of Puglia in the economic life of the Kingdom of Naples, and of the sometimes intractable contradictions between the grain and wool trades in the Italian South. On the creation of the office of *Grassiero*, and its implications, also see Claudia Petraccone, *Napoli moderna e contemporanea* (Naples: Guida, 1981), 17.

[29] By way of comparison, for a classic analysis of the complexities of pre-modern bread riots in England, see E.P. Thompson, 'The Moral Economy of the English Crowd in the Eighteenth Century,' in *Customs in Common: Studies in Traditional Popular Culture* (New York: New Press, 1991), 185–258.

[30] Petraccone, *Napoli dal '500 al '800*, 4.

[31] On the principal purpose for which these dispatches were written, to advise the Grand Dukes of Tuscany on the sale of feudal or Spanish royal lands and make recommendations on potential purposes, see 'Documenti Sulla Storia Economica e Civile,' 262n.

34   A PARADISE INHABITED BY DEVILS

> that God forbid there is an infestation of plague; because the people
> are dying on the streets and no one is taking any chances.[32]

The specter of famine struck early modern commentators like Barnaba,
not simply because of the obvious and widespread misery that it caused,
and the fears that a high concentration of newcomers could increase the
risks of disease, but also because contemporaries felt that hunger made
people more susceptible to sinful behaviors and vice. Secular historians,
such as Giovanni Antonio Summonte, noted the grave threats to public
morality that were posed by the vicious cycle of famine, epidemic and
flood that plagued Naples periodically during the second half of the
sixteenth century. Referring to a severe famine that hit the southern
Italian capital in 1565, Summonte laments:

> In the month of February 1565 there was a very great shortage of
> bread in Naples . . . there was also a shortage of greens, so much so
> that they were selling old leaves of cabbage as good stalks, and this
> famine lasted inside and outside of Naples until the month of May,
> which was the cause of great calamity, and many of the poor died
> of hunger, and others in order not to die, sold away the virginity of
> their own daughters with great disservice to Our Lord, [and] not
> without great penalty from the Royal Ministers.[33]

Indeed, as Summonte suggests, famine led people to take dramatic
actions, with grave consequences for their bodies and souls, and those
of their families. In the most serious of cases, as we will see in the next
chapter, hunger and desperation could lead to outright rebellion, as in
the case of the Revolt of 1585. Clearly, poverty and desperation were
troubling phenomena of urban life in the *Mezzogiorno*, but moral
reform, as we shall see, was the primary solution promoted by early
modern reformers, not just for the urban commoners, but for the
apparently decadent and violence-prone urban nobility as well.

If population growth in Naples was marked by the huge influx of
rural poor, the nobility also flocked to the city throughout the sixteenth
and seventeenth centuries, bringing with them large retinues of family
members, servants and retainers, as well as importing their lavish
lifestyles to the rapidly growing southern Italian metropolis. For the
Spanish Crown, bringing the rural nobility to the capital from the

---

[32] Fabrizio Barnaba, agent of the Grand Duke of Tuscany, 23 April 1607, 'Documenti
Sulla Storia Economica e Civile del Regno,' 266. For a sample of other accounts of the
omnipresent hunger and desperation in Naples, see ibid., 250; 256; 264–6; 290.

[33] G.A. Summonte, *Historia della Città e Regno di Napoli*, 4 vols (Naples, 1602–43),
Vol. 4, 339. Compare A. Bulifon, *Giornali di Napoli dal 1547 al 1706*, ed. Nino Cortese
(Naples: Società Napoletana di Storia Patria, 1932), I, 36. As cited in Petraccone, *Napoli
dal '500 al '800*, 7–8. For a later seventeenth-century perspective, see Innocenzo Fuidoro,
Successi del Governo del Conte D'Oñatte, ed. Alfredo Parente (Naples, 1932), 69.

provinces represented an effort to dilute its potentially disruptive power by incorporating elites within the viceregal court.[34]

Whether hungry or prosperous, ragged plebes, respectable artisans or well-heeled urban nobles, the sheer bulk and density of the Neapolitan population struck both natives and visitors. Although estimates vary widely, figures for the population of the city prior to the devastating plague of 1656 range between 250 000 and 400 000 people.[35] It was no wonder, then, that Giulio Cesare Capaccio's fictional visitor to Naples in *Il Forastiero* could remark upon this great mass of humanity, comparing the omnipresent crowds to swarms of bees:

> I go throughout the city and beyond the artisans [. . .] that are innumerable, beyond those who remain in their homes, I see on every street, in every alley, [around] every corner such a frequency of people who bump into me, [and] trample me [. . . that] I have difficulty going out among them. I go into the churches where there is preaching [. . .] and I discover that they are full of people, and throughout the city it seems as if no one is missing. I go to the court houses and it is a miracle to see such an assembly, and not just one, or ten of the streets, but all of them are so full of people on foot, on horseback, and in carriages, with such a murmur everywhere as if they were a swarm of bees.[36]

The sheer volume of people who called Naples home struck Capaccio's fictional visitor at a visceral level, causing him to wonder aloud, with all the people whom he encountered, who could be missing? But beyond the broad social groupings that the foreigner mentions, the artisans, those assembled in the law courts, the parishioners, and passersby on the streets, who were these individuals? We need to know more specific information about the distinct social groups that populated the early modern metropolis, their means of livelihood, contributions to the urban environment and how contemporaries viewed them in order to understand how reformers like the Jesuits viewed their missionary agenda in the City of Naples.

---

[34] Nino Leone, *Napoli ai Tempi di Masaniello* (Milan: Biblioteca Universale Rizzoli, 1994), 20.

[35] Petraccone's best estimate for the pre-plague population of Naples in the mid-seventeenth century is about 300 000. See *Napoli dal '500 al '800*, 51.

[36] Giulio Cesare Capaccio, *Il Forastiero*, 847. Also notable was the extreme overcrowding in the city, due in part to a ban on building outside city walls that was instituted in 1566 and remained in effect well into the eighteenth century. On this prohibition, see Ghirelli, *Storia di Napoli*, 27.

The urban landscape of Naples

> I want you to understand some things about the inhabitants of Naples [. . .] All of these, I differentiate as nobles, people [*popolo*], and Plebeians [*Plebe*]. The first ones, [include those] from the noble jurisdictions and those untitled. The second [. . . are] of middle condition. The third, from the lower orders.[37] – Giulio Cesare Capaccio, *Il Forastiero* (1634)

While the demographic evidence remains problematic for developing a clear picture of Naples' early modern social fabric, it is possible to identify the main social groupings in the city, their relative weight within the population as a whole and the professional or artisanal makeup of at least their male constituents. In the absence of comprehensive population records like those available elsewhere, such as, for example, the Florentine *catasti* (tax records) or other reliable census data, demographic historians of Naples have had to use sources such as the so-called *processetti matrimoniali* (marriage contracts), surveys drawn up by post-Tridentine parish priests on the occasion of a couple's marriage, to draw a picture of urban Naples in the seventeenth century. Such sources are limited by the fact that they provide data primarily on those of marriageable age and largely neglect women's social identities, but in combination with chronicles of the period, they can provide rich documentation of the different layers of Neapolitan society upon whom reformers like the Jesuits pinned their hopes for effecting reform.[38]

The social group that would become most central to the Jesuits' missionary efforts in both the City and Kingdom of Naples – as patrons and benefactors, but also as missionary subjects – was the nobility.

---

[37] Ibid., 692. Capaccio goes on to describe the titled nobility, or those 'in Piazza,' as the privileged nobility, those holding military title as 'Cavaliero,' or knight, belonging to an elite Equestrian Order. More specifically, the term 'di Piazza' refers to those noble families recognized as among the five noble *Seggi*, or administrative units that, together with the single *Seggio popolare*, elected representatives to Naples' civic government, the Tribunale di San Lorenzo. For a useful overview of this administrative structure that also notes the efforts of non-*Seggio* noble families to attempt to gain access to the governing process in the sixteenth century, see Astarita, *Continuity of Feudal Power*, 24–5. I thank the author for personal correspondence that helped clarify part of Capaccio's passage for me.

[38] Petraccone, *Napoli dal '500 al '800*, 56–7. Petraccone defines the *processetti matrimoniali* as 'la documentazione richiesta ai futuri sposi dall'autorità ecclesiastica, prima di dare il consenso alla celebrazione del matrimonio.' Such contracts, which were published as banns by the local parish clergy, were mandated by the Council of Trent, although they did not come into frequent usage in Naples until the early seventeenth century. Much of the following demographic information and the interpretation of data relies upon Petraccone's careful analysis.

Nobles were represented by a group of feudal landholders from throughout southern Italy, many of whom made their way to the viceregal capital during the sixteenth century. But a slightly large group of urban elites with aspirations to nobility might well include the independently wealthy (*viventi del proprio*) patriciate, comprising perhaps 5 per cent of the population of Naples during this period.[39] Add in other powerful groups of leading citizens, especially professionals like attorneys, notaries and doctors, and the total percentage of urban elites grows to about 7 per cent, according to available figures.

Nobles were drawn to Naples by the attractions of the viceregal court and its attendant institutions, as well as the cultural offerings of the urban capital. They shaped its identity and destiny to a significant degree. Generally residing in the northern districts of the city, an area also heavily populated by clergy, their growing presence in the city, along with retinues of employees, servants and hangers-on whom they brought with them, transformed the urban landscape in several ways.[40] First, the heavy concentration of nobles in Naples, especially by the early seventeenth century, only increased their overall socio-economic power in the Viceroyalty, *vis-à-vis* other social castes. From the city, the nobility continued to collect feudal revenue from their fiefs back in the provinces. In Naples, they alone held the juridical right to control local militias, to access the keys to the city's gates and to use certain kinds of weaponry as well.[41] Yet the Spanish authorities knew well that they needed to maintain good relationships with a potentially restive and violence-prone nobility in order to keep order in the capital and prevent incursions by their two greatest nemeses in the South: the French and the Ottoman Turks.

While Catholic reformers like the Jesuits also looked to the nobility to help finance and provide human capital for ambitious projects like their colleges and reform congregations, over time they, like the Spanish viceregal government, also might cast a wary eye on at least some among the nobility, given their notorious propensity toward factional disputes and blood-letting. As we will see, Jesuit missionaries had to tread carefully with Neapolitan elites who were both among their most significant patrons and potential subjects of their wide-ranging civilizing mission.

We get a sense of the problems that the viceregal government might

---

[39] Whether of noble birth or not, Tommaso Astarita notes that 'by the mid-sixteenth century [. . .] the old urban patriciate and the provincial baronage had become much more integrated,' *Continuity of Feudal Power*, 36.

[40] Petraccone, ibid., 70–71.

[41] Leone, *Napoli ai Tempi di Masaniello*, 34–5.

38   A PARADISE INHABITED BY DEVILS

face from the nobles in an intriguing narrative of the sixteenth- and seventeenth-century viceroys, Domenico Parrino's *Teatro Eroico e Politico dei Governi de'Vicere* (1692; 1875). This work provides a distinctive look at early modern Naples and its government. While Parrino's chronicle is intended as a paean to two centuries of viceroys, the Neapolitan author does provide interesting insights into contemporary perceptions of the Neapolitan social orders, as well as listing the pragmatics, or legislative initiatives, of the various viceregal administrations.

In his discussion of Neapolitan resistance to Pedro de Toledo's viceregal regime, Parrino notes that the nobility was bound to take umbrage at the strict measures that Toledo employed, given their own tendencies toward ruling the roost in the City and Kingdom more broadly. From Parrino's perspective, Toledo lost the nobles' support by forcing them to conform to the rule of law and the authority of the central government, noting that because they were: 'accustomed to living with excessive license, and with imperious customs, [so] they could not stand that he took from them the absolute sovereignty that they exercised over their vassals, and that insolent authority that they used with the artisans and the commoners [. . .]'.[42]

Indeed, beyond the sheer power and influence that the nobility came to wield in Naples, they made their presence felt in the city, according to contemporaries, through their lavish spending, displays of wealth and pomp and frequent duels. Like other members of the European nobility during the Baroque period, Neapolitan noblemen and women sought to demonstrate rank and influence through outward signs of magnificence. As one recent author has demonstrated evocatively, the sheer expenditures of Naples' elites were staggering. Describing one marriage contract drawn up in the seventeenth century between a noblewoman and a wealthy commoner, we learn that one of the betrothed, Anna Acquaviva, member of an illustrious noble family, received a dowry worth 40 000 ducats. To put this figure in perspective, we need to know that: 'with a single ducat, one could buy 35 liters of first class wine and 55 of grain [. . .], a live lamb, piglet, or kid goat, assure fifteen days of pay to a workman or to a bricklayer, [or] have a chaplain celebrate twelve masses.'[43] Thus, the income disparities that separated a small, noble elite from the mass of the Neapolitan populace are truly staggering.

---

[42] Parrino, *Teatro Eroico*, 194.

[43] Leone, ibid., 10. Cf. Braudel, *The Mediterranean*, 733. Braudel uses this story to illustrate the hostility that might accompany a marriage between social unequals, noting that although the groom-to-be, Bartolomeo D'Aquino, was a 'wealthy financier,' he represented the sort of *nouveau riche* upstarts that certain members of the Neapolitan

A PARADISE INHABITED BY DEVILS

As a result of their tremendous power and influence in Naples and across the Kingdom, the nobles also inspired a great deal of enmity from other members of the social body. Early on in the period of Spanish viceregal rule, members of the *popolo* might express their resentment toward these noble elites by challenging their faithfulness to the Crown, in contrast with the *popolo*'s own apparently faithful service to the Spanish. In the wake of Toledo's suppression of the first uprising against efforts to impose the Spanish Inquisition in Naples in 1547, for example, citizens decried the Viceroy's apparent blindness to the crimes of the nobility and the nobles' own hostility to the citizenry:

> All the citizens cried because they remembered the many good and faithful services rendered by the common citizens, who had shed their own blood to recover this Kingdom of Naples from the French; [and this] the nobles had not done, but instead, had always plotted and ordained treaties of rebellion among the greater part of them. And on this unfavorable occasion, they stayed by themselves, and rejoiced, like iniquitous men, saying without any mercy or charity, let the vile rabble hang.[44]

Although many of the Jesuits themselves came from non-noble backgrounds, they would have been quite reluctant to level such criticisms at the nobility.

Often less socially prominent, but still quite wealthy, were the merchants and businessmen who involved themselves in trade in textiles, wine and foodstuffs. Such commoners, who would generally be considered respectable members of the *popolo*, also represented roughly 5 per cent of the population, though their precise social standing might differ from one commentator to the next. Among small-time business owners and shopkeepers, most numerically prominent were those involved in the sale and distribution of foodstuffs, an essential economic niche amidst a large and hungry populace like Naples. Such individuals represented perhaps 9 per cent of the workforce for which the *processetti matrimoniali* offer evidence.[45]

Contemporary observers seemed to disagree over the finer distinctions between the *popolo* and the plebeians, suggesting that urban social

---

nobility resented. Braudel notes that this cross-caste marriage was to be ill-fated, as Acquaviva's male relatives intervened to prevent the young woman from marrying beneath her station, kidnaping her and taking her to a convent in Benevento for safe keeping.

[44] Anonymous, 'Racconti di storia napoletana,' as cited in Galasso, 'Trends and Problems in Neapolitan History,' 73. Cf. Parrino's vivid description of events surrounding Toledo's efforts to impose the Spanish Inquisition in Naples, in *Teatro Eroico*, esp. 205–13.

[45] Petraccone, ibid., 60–62.

40   A PARADISE INHABITED BY DEVILS

castes beneath the nobility were both more fluid and more subjectively drawn than traditional elites. For one seventeenth-century observer, the *popolo* were differentiated from those beneath them more by their greater respectability and degree of virtue than by membership in specific trades, or strict economic conditions. For Camillo Tutini, Naples was divided among nobles, the plebeians and 'another sort of person, who, by reason of birth, doesn't belong to the nobility, and for virtue and riches is very distant from the Plebeians [. . .].' This intermediate group 'constitutes a third species, that with the name of People, come by this to be specially called [. . .].' Tutini goes on to compare the Neapolitan *popolo* to their ancient Roman counterparts, implying that they were due a certain degree of political power and influence that was forbidden to the lower orders that constituted the Plebe.[46]

Other early modern commentators, however, provided a somewhat different read on the social landscape, linking one's trade much more tightly to socio-economic status. For C.F. Riaco, by contrast, admission to the middle tier in Neapolitan society was largely limited to those belonging to the liberal professions, merchants and 'respectable' artisans, such as printers, barbers, architects, jewelers, chemists/druggists and silk weavers. What separated these artisans from the many others who were consigned to a lower status was apparently their professional credentials and perhaps, as one historian has argued, the degree to which their work brought them into direct contact with the nobility.[47]

Finally, the third group of Neapolitans that populated the urban landscape were the plebeians. A large, amorphous group that could encompass a whole range of artisans, laborers, servants and the infamous *lazzari* – the poorest of commoners with no legitimate livelihood according to contemporary observers – the plebeians escape easy definition or differentiation from the more respected and respectable *popolo*.

Nevertheless, even if commentators could not always agree on who precisely belonged within the lowest social caste, they concurred on one thing: a generalized disdain for Naples' lower orders and an anxiety over the anarchic potential of this group for creating social mischief and undermining good order. Early modern chroniclers like Giulio Cesare Capaccio capture vividly the hostile representation of Neapolitan 'backwardness' associated with the plebeians which forms the basis for such historiography:

---

[46] Camillo Tutini, *Dell'origine e fondazione de' Seggi di Napoli* (Naples, 1644), cited in Petraccone, *Napoli dal '500 al '800*, 57–8.

[47] C.F. Riaco, *Il giudicio di Napoli. Discorso del passato contaggio rassomigliato al giudicio Universale* (Perugia, 1658), as cited in ibid., 58–9. The argument is Petraccone's.

A PARADISE INHABITED BY DEVILS

> Nowhere in the world is there anything so obtrusive and undisciplined, the result of the mixture and confusion of so many races [as the Neapolitan *popolo minuto*] . . . miserable, beggarly, and mercenary folk of a kind such as to undermine the wisest constitution of the best of republics, the dregs of humanity, who have been at the bottom of all the tumult and uprisings in this city and cannot be restrained otherwise than by the gallows.[48]

In this encapsulation of a common view of the Neapolitan lower classes, Capaccio captures the sense that Naples was overrun by a riotous and criminal mob who might only be controlled through the most rigorous measures of social control.

These sorts of perceptions of the apparent criminality of Naples' poor also seem to have occurred to lawmakers, for we find among the pragmatics of a number of sixteenth- and seventeenth-century Neapolitan viceroys efforts to control lawlessness in its many forms in urban Naples and the kingdom itself. For example, Pedro de Toledo ordered that anyone prosecuted of 'night-time thefts' in Naples be subject to capital punishment, certainly not an unusual penalty for thievery in early modern Europe.[49] In the second half of the sixteenth century, Viceroy Don Parafan Di Ribera ordered all vagabonds to leave the Kingdom or face similar penalties.[50] But such directives were apparently ineffectual, because by the early seventeenth century, we still have reports of 'vagabonds' being rounded up by local authorities and sent to the gallows. Writing to the Grand Duke of Tuscany in 1606, an unnamed agent based in Naples reports that a criminal judge has taken to 'going at night to the hotels, and taverns, and jailing all those who seem to him to be vagabonds and useless ones [. . .].' Within a few days, the agent remarks, up to 400 men had been rounded up and sent to the gallows, much to his relief: 'And so it is, and one can walk a little bit more securely at night throughout the city,' rather than fearing thieves in his midst.[51]

Beyond urban Naples, other areas of the Kingdom were also noted for their apparent lawlessness and criminality and religious danger. Calabria was commonly viewed as among those provinces of the King-

---

[48] Giulio Cesare Capaccio, 'Descrizione di Napoli' (*c.* 1607), *Archivio Storico per le province napoletane* VII (1882), 535.

[49] For a list of pragmatics issued by Pedro de Toledo and subsequent viceroys through the mid-seventeenth century, see Pedro de Toledo, 'Pragmatic V,' in Parrino, *Teatro Eroico*, 1, 222. On the broader rise in lawlessness and violence by the turn of the seventeenth century, both in real terms and in popular perception, see Villari, *Revolt of Naples*, 33–55; Leone, *Napoli ai Tempi di Masaniello*, 25–7.

[50] Pragmatics of Parafan Di Ribera (1559–1571), as cited in Parrino, *Teatro Eroico*, 279.

[51] See Bibliography, p. 253.

42   A PARADISE INHABITED BY DEVILS

dom most infamous for criminality and violence. The southernmost provinces of the Kingdom, Calabria Ultra and Calabria Principata, closer to Sicily than to the capital in Naples, were also among the poorest provinces throughout this period, subject to dire social conditions, especially during periods of more generalized economic downturn. Along with the Abruzzi provinces northeast of Naples, Calabria was marked in the late sixteenth century by a high incidence of banditry. It was in this province, too, where landowners, including the Church, worried over peasant resistance to paying tithes. Finally, the link between lawlessness and unorthodox religiosity was noted in midsixteenth-century Calabria. There, even before the Jesuits established a permanent presence in the Kingdom of Naples, both Nicolás Bobadilla and Cristóbal Rodríguez were dispatched by the Holy See to seek the conversion of some cells of Protestant heretics in a number of small communities.[52]

While various commentators decried the violence and crime-ridden nature of Neapolitan life, some also linked the apparent instability and volatility of the Neapolitan *popolo minuto* to its supposed proclivity to superstitiousness and love of the ephemeral. One anonymous sixteenth-century author declared the lower orders to be 'unstable, reckless and angry,' noting their tendency to be 'easy to piety and to evil.' Such people, the author argued, partly echoing Camillo Porzio's remarks cited above, were 'lovers of festivals and novelties,' but could also be fickle in their passions, even toward their political rulers: '[The common folk] receive the new viceroys with much applause, but soon they become satiated and [then] bored.'[53]

Yet still others implied that the majority of Neapolitans, not just the lower orders, were dissatisfied with their lot and dangerous as a result of this. In an idiosyncratic reference to conditions in Naples contained in a 1559 report to the Venetian Senate, the Venetian ambassador to the

---

[52] For perceptions of criminality and violence in Calabria, see Galasso, *L'Altra Europa*, 186; 196; compare Mozzillo, *Passaggio a Mezzogiorno*, 345, and Rosario Villari, *The Revolt of Naples*, trans. James Newell (Cambridge, UK: Polity Press, 1993), esp. 36–7 and 40; Villari also points to the perceptions of prevalent banditry in the Abruzzi in the late sixteenth century, especially under the leadership of the colorful figure Marco Sciarra. See ibid., 48–55. On the religious concerns related to sixteenth-century Calabria, see Novi Chavarria, 'Le Missioni dei Gesuiti in Calabria,' in *Il governo delle anime*, 113–39; cf. Ulderico Parente, 'Nicolò Bobadilla e gli esordi della Compagnia di Gesù in Calabria,' in *I Gesuiti e la Calabria*, ed. V. Sibilio (Reggio Calabria: Laruffa, 1992), 19–56.

[53] Anonymous, 'Discorso politico intorno al governo di Napoli (undated),' as cited in Galasso, *L'Altra Europa*, 184. The *popolo minuto*, of course, did not have a monopoly on violence, as we have pointed out. For a discussion of the broader atmosphere of violence, especially in the early seventeenth century, see Leone, *Napoli ai Tempi di Masaniello*, 14–15.

A PARADISE INHABITED BY DEVILS   43

Spanish Crown, Michele Suriano, warned that the local population might prove disloyal to its Spanish overlords, given a general atmosphere of discontent and demoralization in the city. First, he noted, Neapolitans felt burdened by the weight of taxation and its detrimental effects on their livelihoods:

> The Kingdom of Naples yields revenues of a million in gold and has expenses of a million and a half. They make up the difference with grants, assessments, subsidies, new taxes, and increases in the old ones [. . .] As a result a majority of Neapolitans are bankrupt and desperate, and many of them take to the streets because they have no other way to make a living.[54]

The danger, of course, was that desperate people might resort to crime, leading Suriano to repeat the common view that the economy in Naples 'breeds more thieves and outlaws than there are in all the rest of Italy.'[55] Leaving aside the question of whether or not Suriano's specific argument is valid, his account reinforces a general consensus that early modern contemporaries shared: hardship and social tensions in Naples bred violence and desperation. To that he added his own caution to the Spanish viceregal government, warning of the potential disloyalty of the Neapolitan populace: 'As for the morale of the Neapolitans, I can only repeat what they themselves always say: every government sickens them and every state displeases them.'[56]

In the worst instances, economic desperation and dissatisfaction could and did lead to urban rebellion. The intense fiscal demands upon the viceregal government placed a strain upon its ability to satisfy a potentially restive population. In subsequent chapters, we will consider two of the most explosive Revolts to rock early modern Naples (those of 1585 and 1647–48) in greater depth, considering both the causes of these uprisings and their implications, particularly for Jesuit missionaries' reform efforts in and around Naples. Yet aside from these better-known revolts, early modern chroniclers paint a picture of constant instability in Naples. Such incidents were often due to some combination of three factors: popular resentment over the issuance of new taxes, changes in the price of bread, or reductions in the weight of bread, the principle staple in the meager diet of most Neapolitans. In one case, from 1606,

---

[54] Michele Suriano, 'Diplomatic Report to the Venetian Senate,' (1559), as cited in *Pursuit of Power. Venetian Ambassadors' Reports on Turkey, France, and Spain in the Age of Philip II*, ed. and trans. James C. Davis (New York: Harper Torchbooks, 1970), 46–8, esp. 46.

[55] Ibid.

[56] Ibid. Suriano goes on to present a rather odd discussion of the respective sources of noble and popular discontent which implies a kind of topsy-turvy world of social hierarchy under the Spanish which cannot be borne out by source evidence.

44 A PARADISE INHABITED BY DEVILS

one of the Tuscan agents residing in Naples captures the visceral fear of imminent popular rebellion, due, as usual, to the levying of new taxes, while also revealing a certain air of resignation when he observes: 'Here, we are without bread and without wine, [due to] the imposition of new gabelles [. . .] I hope to God that this rabble [*popolaccio*] does not make some revolt.'[57]

Spiritual disorder in Naples

By the late sixteenth century, the image of an unruly, violent and immoral Naples had become as well entrenched as the picture of the southern Italian city as an earthly paradise. With its soaring population of newly emigrated rural poor, its supposedly decadent nobility and rampant criminality, Naples seemed a city in dire need of reform. Into this mix of urban ills we must add concerns over the very spiritual fiber of Italy's largest city. For another layer of the paradoxical nature of representations of Naples and its populace that struck commentators was the apparent propensity toward immorality and clerical corruption in the city, combined with an overly ecstatic piety that often took on highly materialistic ritual forms. From sixteenth-century episcopal reports, to papal visitors, to Jesuit reformers' own accounts, we see a picture of Naples as troubling to observers in the realm of the sacred as it is in the secular.

Even before the Council of Trent (1545–63), Church reformers in Naples railed against clerical absenteeism, ignorance and the all-too-frequent practice of clergymen living openly with concubines.[58] By the mid-fifteenth century, it was a common practice for Neapolitan archbishops to reside in Rome and to leave many of their pastoral duties to underlings. This, of course, was a practice common to many dioceses throughout Catholic Europe. So, too, clerical cohabitation with concubines was deemed a serious problem well before it was taken up by Tridentine reformers. As early as the fourteenth century, a Neapolitan bishop Giovanni Orsini (r. 1328–57) threatened local clergy that they would lose their offices and benefices if they did not send away their mistresses within two months' time.[59] Two centuries later, Francesco

---

[57] Fabrizio Barnaba, Agent of the Grand Duke of Tuscany, 27 July 1606, 'Documenti Sulla Storia Economica e Civile del Regno,' 264.

[58] On the lack of religious instruction among clerics and laity in the *casali* which ringed the City of Naples, see Carla Russo, *Chiesa e comunità*, 34–5. On the impetus for pre-Tridentine reforms by local Church officials, see *Il 'Liber Visitationis,'* esp. xiii–xx.

[59] *Il 'Liber Visitationis,'* xviii–xix.

Carafa, Archbishop of Naples from 1541 to 1544, sought to reverse the same practices by threatening excommunication to any cleric caught in an illicit relationship.[60] But in the wake of the marathon Council, reforming bishops like Alfonso Carafa (1557–65) hoped to formalize ecclesiastical reforms by publicizing the results of a diocesan synod (1565) which called for major improvements in the religious life of Naples.[61]

Other sixteenth-century observers, such as the papal visitor Tommaso Orfini, noted a range of disturbing features of southern Italian religious life that they believed required urgent reform.[62] Orfini, soon to become the Archbishop of Foligno, was delegated by Pope Pius V to conduct an official apostolic visitation in the Kingdom of Naples in 1566. His visit to the region, which included a whirlwind tour of some twenty-five locales over several months, represents one of the first glimpses at local efforts to effect Tridentine reforms and reinforces other contemporary perceptions of disorder throughout the region.[63] Originally dispatched to Naples during the winter of 1566 after having proven himself an able visitor in the Roman dioceses, Orfini was held up in his duties for over a year as a jurisdictional dispute between the papacy and the Spanish Crown developed.[64] He finally began his visitation in February 1568, working his way from the southeastern coastal port city of Brindisi northward toward Naples. Many of Orfini's reports deal with towns and cities in the provinces of Terra di Otranto and Terra di Bari, on the southeastern flank of the Kingdom. Even given the Naples-centered view of many contemporaries, these two provinces had two important provincial cities, Lecce and Bari, and were thus viewed by at least some as more 'civilized' than remote and less

---

[60] Carafa issued the following order in his *Constitutioni*, published in 1542: 'Commandammo sotto pena di escommunicatione, e di privatione de beneficii, et mille libre di cera, che nissuno clerico ne Preite debba tenere concubine publice, ne in casa sua, ne di altri.' As cited in *Il 'Liber Visitationis*,' xix.

[61] On Alfonso Carafa's reform efforts and the results of the 1565 Synod, see L. Parascandolo, *Memorie storiche critiche diplomatiche della chiesa di Napoli* 4 (Naples, 1851), 76–84; 252–62.

[62] Pasquale Villani, 'La Visita Apostolica di Tommaso Orfini nel Regno di Napoli (1566–1568): Documenti per la Storia dell'Applicazione del Concilio di Trento,' *Annuario dell'Istituto Storico Italiano per l'età moderna e contemporanea* 8 (1956): 5–79. Orfini's original documents are from ASV, *Arm*, XXXV, t. 93.

[63] On the significance of Orfini's apostolic visitation and the novelty of Pius V's order – the first papal visitation in over 200 years – see Villani, 'La Visita Apostolica,' 5–23.

[64] This jurisdictional dispute, which hinged on a fifteenth-century Spanish precedent requiring all important decisions emanate from the central government, led to a papal interdict. For the specifics of this conflict, which was resolved by Philip II in the early part of 1568, see Villani, 'La Visita Apostolica,' 10–18.

46 A PARADISE INHABITED BY DEVILS

populated agricultural and pastoral regions of the *Mezzogiorno*, such as Basilicata or Calabria.[65]

Orfini's documentation of religious life in the Kingdom of Naples is valuable for a number of reasons. First, by covering a large number of locales, both large and small, his commentary reveals recurrent themes and problems. Although much of the evidence upon which Orfini bases his observations is anecdotal or simply hearsay, Orfini presents a vivid account of official Church perceptions of disorder in the *Mezzogiorno*. In addition, Orfini's field notes reinforce the Jesuits' own subsequent reports of clerical incompetence, and the woeful lack of Christian education in both the urban center of Naples and in other regions of the Kingdom. Finally, Orfini's account reflects the predominant concerns of Tridentine reformers, and his general recommendations for reforming the Neapolitan landscape provide a useful context in which to place Jesuit efforts. Although the report covers towns and cities outside the urban center in Naples, it is worth citing here because of the integral relationship that urban Naples played in the broader life of southern Italy.

Among the key themes which reappear throughout Orfini's visitation reports are comments on local episcopal leadership, clerical conduct and the often miserable state of church buildings and finances. The issue of episcopal residence was stressed during the Council of Trent and Orfini takes pains to note whether archbishops live in their dioceses or not. Often, the failure of bishops to reside in their dioceses seems linked to other problems. In Polignano, a town in the present-day province of Brindisi, for example, Orfini notes the absence of the bishop alongside other concerns such as the number of clergy living with concubines, sexual misconduct in monasteries and the presence of heretics. Orfini cites a local man, Gerolamo Parrino, as the source for much of his information on the poor state of affairs in the town. On the immorality of a group of monks, Parrino tells him: 'I hold the brothers of Saint Vitus to be living very bad lives, and so does everyone else in Polignano [. . .] Most of them are concubinaries, and Brother Giovan Pietro and the others have syphilis (*mal francese*), and it is said that Giovan Pietro has a son, whom I have seen living in his house in Polignano.'[66]

But even in towns where there was a resident bishop, Orfini notes numerous indiscretions. In Conversano, in the province of Terra di Bari, he reports one Franciscan who had 'made a bordello in [his] monastery.'

---

[65] Orfini, 'Visit to Polignano,' as cited in Villani, 'La Visita Apostolica,' 44. Orfini does not title each of his visitation reports, but I have chosen to label them as such for the reader's convenience.

[66] Compare the comments of Porzio, *Relazione*, 312.

A PARADISE INHABITED BY DEVILS

Elsewhere, he cites clergy accused of dancing publicly with prostitutes, being drunkards, playing cards and dice and committing homicides.[67] Sometimes, however, the most illicit member of the local clergy was the bishop himself. In the town of Ruvo, Orfini remarks upon a 'dishonest' bishop who is reported to have a concubine, is suspected of committing numerous homicides, and is known to have 'scandalized' women of the community in church.[68]

In less sensational cases, Orfini focuses not so much upon the immorality of local clergy and episcopal officials as on the lack of education or proper training which clerics receive and the dire consequences of clerical ignorance on the laity. In his first stop, the Adriatic port city of Brindisi, Orfini notes that despite the presence of a resident bishop, the clergy seem ineffectual. There is no specific person delegated to administer the sacraments and, because the priests are not attending adequately to the care of souls, local women are taking on such care: 'The priests were found greatly wanting in going to see to the sick and dying; in their place, the women went with words that they call orations, which have something of the superstitious [about them].'[69]

In Ostuni, as in Brindisi, no one has been charged with administering sacraments, and Orfini reports that communion and confession are conducted 'indifferently by those who are called [upon], as is the marriage ceremony.' Far from following the Tridentine recommendation to establish diocesan seminaries, Orfini complains that many local priests seem to have no notion of what a seminary is: 'Not only wasn't there a seminary, but there wasn't even close to any understanding of this name seminary by some of these priests; there was no equivalent, nor any lessons for the clergy, who are very ignorant.'[70] Elsewhere, Orfini complains that the vast majority of clergy are not even adequately trained in grammar.[71]

The problem of working with ill-trained or immoral clergy posed one of the central challenges to Jesuit missionaries. Orfini's representation of ongoing conflicts between episcopal leaders and local clergy also jibes with the Jesuits' missionary relations, which are full of anecdotes regarding the need to reconcile warring members of the religious community. Orfini identifies the need for outsiders, such as the Jesuits, to come in and aid in the reforming process. In Brindisi, for example, where Orfini has already lamented the lack of clerical training, the clergy

---

[67] Orfini, 44–6.
[68] Orfini, 'Visit to Ruvo,' 53.
[69] Orfini, 'Visit to Brindisi,' 38.
[70] Orfini, 'Visit to Ostuni,' 41 [author's emphasis].
[71] Orfini, 'Visit to Rutigliano,' 45–6.

48 A PARADISE INHABITED BY DEVILS

charge their archbishop with being overly harsh and accusing them of
sedition. An additional controversy involves a dispute between the same
archbishop, the abbess of a Benedictine convent and several nuns. In
response to this deteriorating situation, Orfini suggests the need for
outside help, 'a father sufficiently jesuitical or similar for vicar.' Such a
person 'will greatly aid in the governing of that clergy and could easily
relieve the poor relationship between the archbishop and the clergy, and
also encourage a good turn by the nuns of that monastery with their
continued supervision.'[72]

As this selective overview of Orfini's visitation records suggests,
anecdotal though it is, Church officials perceived southern Italy as ripe
for serious and sustained reforms. It is important to stress that the kinds
of spiritual disorder that commentators pinpointed were seen as evidence
of the Church's own failings – quite a sensitive subject given the spread
of a Protestant threat across large swaths of Europe.

If many ecclesiastical officials blamed inept or immoral clergy for the
problems of impiety among the laity, the ecstatic and supposedly unorthodox piety of the lay folk could trouble other commentators. Scholars
of southern Italian religiosity have generally agreed upon its key characteristics, even if they have debated how to interpret the distinctive
practices of piety that mark the region. Without wishing to engage the
question of whether or not southerners were 'superstitious' or 'pagan,' a
highly problematic and polemical debate that relies upon a subjective
interpretation of popular religious beliefs and practices, it is important
to sketch the broad outlines of Neapolitan piety and ritual practice in
order to understand the spiritual landscape that Jesuit missionaries
encountered in their reconnaissance in urban Naples and the Kingdom's
rural hinterlands, and how they tried to negotiate among communities
of the faithful.[73]

Popular religious piety in the *Mezzogiorno* shared many characteristics with other parts of early modern Europe in that it was marked by
a highly localized, concretized and personalistic form of Catholicism. As
a number of scholars have suggested, *local religion* connotes community
or region-specific variations on Roman Catholic piety that cut across
traditional boundaries of social caste, or even education level.[74] Thus

---

[72] Orfini, 'Visit to Brindisi,' 37–9.

[73] Among the many important studies of southern Italian religiosity in the early
modern period, this overview draws heavily from the work of Giuseppe Galasso, *L'Altra
Europa*, esp. Ch. 2, 'Santi e Santità,' 79–144; Romeo De Maio, *Religiosità a Napoli,
1656–1799* (Naples: Edizioni Scientifiche Italiane, 1997).

[74] The literature on what William Christian has referred to as 'local religion' in early
modern Europe is large. For comparable works on Iberia, see Christian's own *Local
Religion in Early Modern Spain* (Princeton, NJ: Princeton University Press, 1981); Allyson

A PARADISE INHABITED BY DEVILS 49

'popular' should not be construed to include only the urban poor or peasantry. In the case of Naples and the disparate communities of southern Italy, as elsewhere, a panoply of local saints and other protective figures were worshiped by the laity and seen as valuable potential intercessors in their often difficult lives.

In his remarkable study of southern Italian historical anthropology, *L'Altra Europa* (1997), Giuseppe Galasso provides an invaluable overview of the distinctive features of *Mezzogiorno* religious culture past and present, while challenging the historiographical tendency common among too many scholars of the Italian South who borrow early modern reformers' assumptions about the 'pre-christian' or 'achristian' nature of such piety.[75] Galasso justly highlights the eclectic nature of this piety, given the multiple ethnic and religious influences on the region historically. There is also the decidedly personalized nature of southern Italian cult worship, which includes its supposedly 'feminized' and 'positive and consolatory' features, as well as the emphasis placed on individuals' and communities' sense of ownership over local cult figures, and concern for the efficacy and sacred power of given figures, manifested through the success of ex-voto prayers invoked in moments of crisis, or need.[76]

Using evidence from a modern survey of the prevalence and distribution of local patron saints in over 1700 southern Italian communities, Galasso has interpreted the significance of these data for understanding the contours of religious piety in an earlier age.[77] Among the 300 or so patron figures that appear, Galasso cites the unsurprising prevalence of different localized versions of Mary as characteristic of *Mezzogiorno* piety. It seems to state the obvious that the Virgin Mary should be a central figure in popular Catholic piety in the early modern period, appearing in about 17 per cent of the communities surveyed as a patron figure. But, as Galasso suggests, Marian devotion was quite widespread across Italy (not to mention beyond); in the Kingdom of Naples, local Marian cults took on much more localized forms, becoming associated with specific natural–geographical sites, such as Mary of the Mountain;

Poska's fine study of religiosity and reform efforts in Galicia, *Regulating the People. The Catholic Reformation in Seventeenth-Century Spain* (Leiden: Brill, 1998); Sara Nalle, *God in La Mancha: Religious Reform and the People of Cuenca, 1500–1650* (Baltimore: Johns Hopkins University Press, 1992).

[75] Galasso, *L'Altra Europa*, 80.

[76] Ibid., 115 and 83–5.

[77] Ibid., 95–100. While noting the difficulties of using recently gathered data to project back to an earlier age, Galasso argues effectively that if such anthropological evidence is used carefully, alongside other historical evidence, it 'possesses [. . .] a strong retrospective value.' Ibid., 95.

50 A PARADISE INHABITED BY DEVILS

or the Sea; or the Forest; of miraculous place-names; or denoting specific functions that emphasized the miraculous nature of the cult figure.

What made these expressions of Marian devotion and cult practice so characteristically southern Italian was not necessarily that the worship was deeper, or more central to Catholic piety than elsewhere. Instead, its distinctiveness lay in the fact that despite 'this terminological richness, this superabundance of figurations and of variations of the figure of Mary' across local communities, Marian piety retained a surprising degree of consistency across the Kingdom of Naples.[78]

Similarly, other saints' cults emerged out of specific local conditions and needs, even if these sacred figures were prominent in late medieval and early modern Catholic worship beyond the region, such as St Anthony of Padua. In the southern Italian context, not surprisingly, local cults often emerged within the context of the all-too-frequent outbreaks of the plague, beginning especially in the fourteenth century, thus taking on special functions.[79] For urban Naples, of course, the figure and cult of San Gennaro became a central symbol of local, urbanized piety. The annual summer ritual of noting and celebrating the liquification of the saint's blood became a marker of Neapolitan devotion, and the occasions on which this did not occur were greeted with great consternation and could be read as evidence of disunity and/or divine disfavor.

In the face of this highly localized religious practice, the Council of Trent (1545–63) was meant to usher in important changes in the practices of the laity and reform the Church in significant ways. In the post-Tridentine period, and especially by the early seventeenth century, there is certainly an increase in the number of saints' cults that are associated with religious orders, like the Society of Jesus.[80] Here, although the Tridentine Church might have preferred to emphasize the more edifying aspects of these saints' lives in order to improve the religious education of the laity, they continued to find that communities responded to cult figures because of their abilities to produce results and mitigate the more challenging aspects of daily life: the deaths of children, bad harvests, illness, plague, natural disasters. Religious processions, pilgrimages and participation in popular local rituals had to be adapted to excite communities of the faithful. Thus, in the Kingdom of Naples, as in so many other sites of missionary endeavor, a strong dose of accommodation to local practices and prerogatives underscored efforts to civilize the laity.

---

[78] Ibid., 99.
[79] Ibid., 103.
[80] Ibid., 109.

A PARADISE INHABITED BY DEVILS

By the end of the sixteenth century, it appears by all accounts that the perception of social disorder among local ecclesiastical leaders had not declined, but had perhaps increased. A 1595 report on the need for parish reforms to the Vatican's *Congregatione di Concilio* (the organ created to follow up on the implementation of Tridentine decrees in local jurisdictions), written on behalf of then Neapolitan Archbishop Annibale di Capua, complained that the inability of parishes to deal with a rapidly expanding, complex population could lead to dire results. The inadequacy of parishes led to a lack of accurate information on how many souls were being administered care, difficulties in providing for the administration of sacraments during times of illness or plague, the excessive travel time required by priests to attend to their numerous parishioners and, perhaps most worrisome, the difficulty in 'keeping tabs' on foreigners, especially those suspected of spreading heretical ideas.[81]

A few years later, in 1599, a pastoral visit by the new Archbishop Alfonso Gesualdo voiced wider concerns. Gesualdo bemoaned the difficulties in maintaining a necessary level of discipline among clergy in the city of Naples. This was particularly a problem, he noted, because of the vast number of clergy living in Naples without proper benefices. Gesualdo also commented upon the undue power that the laity supposedly held over the churches, the problem of merchants not observing religious holidays, unruly convents of female religious and, echoing his predecessor, an overabundance of clergy and religious houses in Naples. Such clerics, Cardinal Gesualdo remarked, 'the unobservant ones, and those that live in certain little places over which there cannot be regular observance, cause many disturbances [and] . . . many scandals.'[82]

Even well into the seventeenth century, in the wake of the dual crises represented by the Revolt of Masaniello and the cataclysmic plague of 1656, visitation reports from a number of Neapolitan archbishops suggest an ongoing concern with the shortcomings of the Neapolitan clergy, and the continuing need for episcopal reform. Among the most vigorous of reforming bishops, Innico Caracciolo (1667–85) focused his efforts on two areas of reform: educating the clergy and efforts to eradicate concubinage. Referring derisively to the mass of ill-informed, corrupt and/or unworthy clergy who populated late seventeenth-century Naples, Caracciolo compared Naples to 'a forest,' providing a 'con-

---

[81] ASV, *Congregatione di Concilio/Relationes ad Limina, Neapolitana I & II*, ff. 27–36v/113–22v, Alfonso Gesualdo, *Visita Limina Apostolorum*, 'Relationi del[lo] stato della Chiesa di Napoli per il 4' et 5' triennio,' 1599, f. 28.

[82] Gesualdo, 'Relazioni,' ff. 28–31v.

52 A PARADISE INHABITED BY DEVILS

venient hiding place for crimes and criminals.'[83] With regard to the problem of poorly trained clergy, one historian uses a wonderful metaphor to evoke the paucity of seminary-trained clergy in Naples at least at the turn of the eighteenth century. The seminary, Romeo de Maio notes, was like 'an aquarium for privileged fish compared with an ocean that contained every species.'[84]

As a group, the Jesuits arrived in the City of Naples in early 1552, largely at the behest of their many noble benefactors and supporters, guided initially by the primary objective of establishing a college that would provide a humanist education to local elites and recruit new men into the Society of Jesus.[85] Once formally established there, however, the Jesuits could not help but seize upon the opportunities that Naples presented for refining the civilizing mission that the Society of Jesus began to undertake in earnest in the second half of the sixteenth century. Over time, Naples became a laboratory for reform and institutional innovation, and a training ground for missions (and missionaries) far beyond the borders of southern Italy.

The environment of spiritual disorder that contemporaries saw as plaguing Naples was precisely the kind that Ignatius Loyola had envisioned when he advised his brethren to labor in 'that part of the vineyard ... which has the greater need, because of the lack of other workers or because of the misery and weakness of one's fellow men in it and the danger of their eternal condemnation.'[86] For the Jesuits, the challenges were tremendous, but the rewards potentially great. They set for themselves an ambitious agenda, striving not just to improve the religious climate in Naples by encouraging more frequent attention to the sacraments or instructing the laity in Christian doctrine, but to combat other social ills, like prostitution, criminality and the polluting impact of having so many non-believers (predominantly Muslim slaves) in the growing city. But determining which areas of religious and social reform were most pressing and those strategies best suited to building an active

---

[83] Innico Caracciolo, *Relationes ad Limina*, 19 January 1683, cited in Romeo de Maio, *Religiosità a Napoli, 1656–1799* (Naples: Edizioni Scientifiche Italiane, 1997), 48.

[84] De Maio, ibid., 47. Beyond urban Naples, Elisa Novi Chavarria remarks that despite the emergence of several new diocesan seminaries in the late sixteenth century, mostly in the Neapolitan hinterlands of Campania and in the two Calabrias (38 in the years between the close of Trent and 1594), the majority of secular clergy continued to receive limited instruction. See Novi Chavarria, 'Pastorale e Devozioni,' in *Il Governo delle Anime*, 27.

[85] Araldo, *Cronica*, 3v–8v.

[86] Ignatius Loyola, *The Constitutions of the Society of Jesus*, trans. and with an introduction by George E. Ganss (St Louis: The Institute for Jesuit Sources, 1970), 274. *The Constitutions* was originally published *c.* 1558–59.

ministry required a high degree of institutional innovation and an effort to forge a strong sense of collective purpose. What was the distinctive institutional identity that the still-young Society of Jesus brought to Naples in the second half of the sixteenth century, and how did the Jesuits forge their broad campaigns for reform?

CHAPTER TWO

'Planting many virtues there': Early Jesuit missions in Naples, 1550–1620

In 1553, soon after the Society of Jesus had established itself in Naples, the Jesuit chronicler Giovan Francesco Araldo (1522–99) argued confidently that the Jesuits were gaining a growing influence in the troubled but bustling hub of commercial, imperial and religious activity. In a report written for Ignatius Loyola, Araldo celebrates the arrival of the Jesuits in the southern Italian capital. After recounting the initial activities of the small group of twelve Jesuits who had ventured to Naples in early 1552, Araldo suggests that their presence was not only welcomed by the populace, but that they had already made an important contribution to re-establishing piety and a moral order in the city:

> From this humble and low beginning, and with the singular example of patience, and with simple, devoted, and useful conduct, the Society in Naples began to be held in great esteem and to have many in Church, as in the largest schools [. . .] And publicly, one heard thanks for the Grace that had sent [the Society of Jesus] at so opportune a time, eradicating many vices and planting many virtues there; training the youth in the fear of God and introducing them to the attendance of the sacred sacraments, along with teaching them good sciences and Christian doctrine.'[1]

While it might be tempting to dismiss Araldo's words as mere hyperbole, or the aggrandizement of local successes in a bid to win approval from institutional superiors, his comments none the less tell us a great deal

---

[1] ARSI, *Litterae Annuae Historia Provinciae Napoletanae* (hereafter *Neap.*) 72, Document II, ff. 5–10v; Giovanni Araldo, 'Historia . . . provinciae Neapolitanae ab anno 1551 ad 1567,' esp. f. 6. A slightly different version of these comments found their way into Araldo's longer *Cronica della Compagnia di Gesù di Napoli* (hereafter *Cronica*), f. 11v (21). This chronicle provides an invaluable account of Jesuit activity in the southern Italian capital from their arrival in 1552 through 1596. For a helpful, if brief, biographical sketch of Araldo, see Mark A. Lewis SJ, 'The Development of Jesuit Confraternities in the Kingdom of Naples in the Sixteenth and Seventeenth Centuries,' in *The Politics of Ritual Kinship. Confraternities and Social Order in Early Modern Italy*, ed. Nicholas Terpstra (Cambridge, UK: Cambridge University Press, 2000), 210–27, esp. 215.

about how the Jesuits viewed themselves and their mission in Naples from the outset.

But aside from providing insight into the order's evolving collective identity, Araldo's account is important for an additional reason. As the earliest historian of the Jesuits' educational and reforming mission in Naples, he attempts to provide a detailed and thoroughgoing account of the Society of Jesus' wide-ranging initiatives in Naples, providing a bird's eye view of the order's close ties to key elite benefactors and reform allies, and its complex relationship to the dynamic, often conflict-ridden, social climate of late sixteenth-century Naples.

If the Jesuits first came to Naples with the primary goal of instituting a college, lending its citizens the excellent preaching skills of its most noted orators like Alfonso Salmerón[2] and participating in charitable activities that sought to respond to increasingly dire conditions in the southern Italian capital, over the course of the sixteenth century, they became increasingly involved in a civilizing mission that might respond to such wide-ranging social ills as prostitution, an expanding prison population and the disturbing presence of a large population of Muslim slaves. From the Jesuits' own perspective, their apostolic labors required something more than the teaching of Christian doctrine or reinvigorating the laity in the frequent practice of the sacraments, important though these were. Rather, their vocation demanded that they try to convince missionary subjects to adopt a new set of values and behaviors that conformed to the mood of post-Tridentine European society.

Naples became an important training ground for leading members of the Society of Jesus in the second half of the sixteenth century, as well as an important site for experimentation with new forms of religious and cultural reform activity. The Jesuits' chronicles of their urban missions both publicized the Society's reform efforts by highlighting their self-described successes, but, ironically, these accounts also contributed to the images of incivility and barbarism that were already abroad in the city.

Individual Jesuits had been working throughout the Kingdom of Naples since Ignatius Loyola first went to the ancient monastery at Monte Cassino in 1538 to teach his *Spiritual Exercises* to Pedro Ortiz, the Holy Roman Emperor Charles V's Neapolitan agent. By mid-century, however, influential members of the Neapolitan political and economic elite were making determined efforts to install the Society of Jesus in the southern Italian capital, seeing value in having a Jesuit

---

[2] On the central role played by Salmerón in Naples, where he was not only viewed as an outstanding preacher and theologian, but also led the Jesuit province as its first provincial from 1558–76, see Parente, 'Alfonso Salmerón.'

EARLY JESUIT MISSIONS IN NAPLES, 1550–1620

college in their own city. As Giovan Francesco Araldo tells it, the initial driving force behind the eventual establishment of a Jesuit base in Naples was Hieronimo Vignes, the Neapolitan son of a Spanish merchant. While studying in the highly respected university in Padua, Vignes became acquainted with local Jesuits and was apparently impressed by their work in the noted town in the Veneto. After returning to Naples, Vignes used his personal connections to convince a powerful noble, Ettore Pignatelli, the Duke of Monte Leone, to put his considerable influence behind establishing the Jesuits in Naples and to win the approval of the Viceroy, Pedro de Toledo. Crucially, by the spring of 1551, the Jesuits had secured financial commitments from a number of the wealthiest and most powerful members of the Neapolitan elite to establish their college and preparations began in earnest. In keeping with the Jesuits' apostolic aspirations, Ignatius Loyola sent twelve Jesuits to Naples on 16 January 1552. Within this initial group, just two were fully professed priests, Nicolás Bobadilla and Andrea Oviedo, while the rest were scholastics like Araldo himself.[3]

The establishment of the Jesuit college at Naples in 1552 (and later in other parts of the Kingdom) had important implications for early missionary activity there.[4] Part of the Jesuits' 'way of proceeding' was to combine missionary activity with the establishment of educational institutions. The colleges would ideally provide the manpower needed to fulfill the order's ambitious apostolic agenda and, by participating in such activities, novices would gain much needed training in missionary work. In practice, however, things were a bit more complicated. As a corollary to developing a range of ministries throughout the communities in which they worked in Europe and the Indies, the Jesuits founded colleges at a brisk pace. In Italy, there were 30 colleges by 1565, while in the Kingdom of Naples alone, 16 had been founded by the end of the

---

[3] For the 'prehistory' of Jesuit activity in Naples, see Araldo, *Cronica*, esp. 3v–8v/ 13–17; cf. Schinosi, *Istoria*, 1: 2–32. The significance that the Jesuits placed upon their noble benefactors is immediately evident in Araldo's chronicle by his listing of the original patrons of the college. This list appears again at the end of the account, including the amounts given to the Society of Jesus by each donor. See *Cronica*, 332r–v/377–8.

[4] On the foundation of the College of Naples (1552) and its attendant problems, see Tacchi Venturi, *Storia della Compagnia*, 2/2: 433–47. A more recent historical study of the Neapolitan college during the sixteenth century is Mark A. Lewis SJ's ' "Preachers of Sound Doctrine:" The Social Impact of the Jesuit College of Naples, 1552–1600' (PhD diss., University of Toronto, 1995). Lewis and I have arrived independently at similar conclusions about the importance of Naples as a 'training ground' for the Society of Jesus in the sixteenth and seventeenth centuries, although his focus remains primarily on Jesuit education in Naples, while mine traces the Society's other apostolic activities.

58   A PARADISE INHABITED BY DEVILS

sixteenth century.[5] The college in Naples was both an important recruiting ground for the order and the source for the earliest experiments with missionary reform activity across the city.

The Jesuits' dual orientation made sense, given the emphasis which Loyola and other founding members of the order had placed on the importance of the colleges to the overall work of the Society. This emphasis is highlighted in a letter which the first Secretary of the Society of Jesus, Juan Alfonso de Polanco, wrote to fellow members on behalf of Loyola's successor as general, Diego Laínez, in 1560. In this letter, Polanco placed the importance of the colleges squarely beside the ministries, arguing that the Jesuits had two primary means of serving others:

> one in the colleges through the education of youth in letters, learning and Christian life, and second in every place to help every kind of person through sermons, confessions, and the other means which accord with our customary way of proceeding.[6]

The growth of the colleges encouraged an expansion of missionary activity for the very simple reason that they provided the physical infrastructure for the new community of Jesuits in Naples. From the outset, efforts were made to combine the work of the colleges with broader attempts at religious and social reform.

Early on, Neapolitan Jesuits found the colleges to be ideal bases from which to launch missionary activities. As early as 1554, Araldo helped to found a lay confraternity, the *Congregation of the Veneration of the Most Holy Sacrament*, also known as the *Zitti*, which met in the Neapolitan College's chapel. This confraternity was composed largely of men from leading Neapolitan families who sought to combine charitable work such as 'assistance to the infirmed and to the incarcerated' with encouraging more frequent practice of the sacraments. Its charge extended beyond this, however, to include surveying neighbors and community members for evidence of heretical activities.[7]

---

[5] On the growth of the Jesuit colleges throughout the order in the early years, along with attendant problems, cf. O'Malley, *First Jesuits*, 208. Several of the colleges founded in the Kingdom of Naples in the sixteenth century did not survive long, due to the perennial problems of inadequate funds and/or personnel. Some of these colleges, like the ill-fated Civitá Sant'Angelo, lasted only seven years (1566–73), while others, like the college in Salerno, barely made it through a year (1589–90). For a handy list of Jesuit Colleges in the Province of Naples (1552–1609), see Lewis, 'Preachers of Sound Doctrine,' 249. On additional problems that the order faced with its early colleges, see Parente, 'Alfonso Salmerón,' esp. 36–40.

[6] Polanco, Letter of 10 August 1560, cited in O'Malley, *First Jesuits*, 200.

[7] Araldo, *Cronica*, 13v/23. Cf. Armando Guidetti, *Le Missioni Popolari: I Grandi Gesuiti Italiani. Disegno Storico Biografico delle Missioni Popolare dei Gesuiti d'Italia*

EARLY JESUIT MISSIONS IN NAPLES, 1550–1620

In a letter to Polanco, Araldo highlights the significance of the *Zitti* for increasing the esteem in which the order was held, but he also stresses the positive benefits that the confraternity might contribute to the general atmosphere of the college. Araldo cites the range of important men who took part in the Congregation (among these, doctors, 'learned and zealous priests,' and 'many unmarried students, merchants and nobles'). He stresses the value that the organization had to the work of the college and the Society as a whole. For Araldo, as for Alfonso Salmerón, the colleges were ideal sources from which to develop lay spiritual and charitable institutions.[8]

One gets a similar impression of the vitalizing influence of early Jesuit activity in Naples from the observations of a young Antonio Possevino, later to become an important Jesuit participant in anti-Protestant missions in the Piedmont region of northern Italy. Writing to Margherita Gonzaga, Duchess of Mantua in 1558, one year before he joined the Society of Jesus, Possevino begins his narrative by providing a brief history of the order from its origins in Paris, where Ignatius joined together the original members, to its first years in Naples. Not surprisingly for a young student and courtier writing to a renowned Italian noblewoman, Possevino exaggerates the noble composition of the Society's membership, arguing that in Naples, as elsewhere, 'some knights left the vanities and the frivolities of the world' to become Jesuits.[9]

Commenting enthusiastically upon Jesuit piety and simplicity of livelihood, Possevino seems especially impressed by the breadth of Jesuit endeavors. In his description of the Neapolitan College, he offers a vivid, if idealized, portrait of the order's attempts to combine humanist educational principles with efforts to Christianize its charges:

---

dalle Origini al Concilio Vaticano II (Milan: Rusconi, 1988), 38; Lewis, 'The Development of Jesuit Confraternities,' 215–17, and Parente, 'Alfonso Salmerón,' 23.

[8] Araldo's letter to Polanco, dated 20 November 1557, cited in Pasquale Lopez, 'Una Famosa Congregazione Laica Napoletana nel '600 e L'Opera Missionaria di Padre Corcione,' in *Clero, Eresia e Magia nella Napoli del Viceregno* (Naples: Adriano Gallina, 1984), 115–50, esp. 119. On Salmerón's efforts to keep the 'Communicants' meeting at the college, against the recommendations of Cristoforo Madrid, Jesuit Visitor to the Province of Naples in 1560, see 120.

[9] Possevino's letter to Margherita Gonzaga, as cited in Tacchi Venturi, *Storia della Compagnia* 1/2, 65–72, esp. 66–8. As for the social profile of early members of the Society, based on a survey conducted by Jerónimo Nadal, the majority of early Jesuit priests and students in the colleges came from merchant or professional families, mostly urban. For a brief discussion of the social makeup of the order through 1568, see O'Malley, *First Jesuits*, 59. For a fuller discussion, see Thomas V. Cohen, 'The Social Origins of the Jesuits, 1540–1600' (PhD diss., Harvard University, 1973), 1: 214–74.

60 A PARADISE INHABITED BY DEVILS

> [F]irstly, they [the Jesuits] live not only by themselves and in the service of their [own] salvation, but for their neighbors and generally for everyone. They teach Greek, Latin and vulgar letters to more than three hundred schoolboys without [financial] reward. Friday and Sunday, they demonstrate to them [the schoolboys] Christian doctrine, teaching them that which they should believe, which are the mortal sins, the precepts of the Holy Roman Church.[10]

Possevino explicitly contrasts the Jesuit schools with the public schools that, according to the author, were examples of 'scandal,' partly responsible for the desolate state of spiritual affairs in the southern Italian capital. Invoking the commonly accepted idea that where spiritual disorder flourishes, social disorder cannot be far behind, Possevino cautions those elites who are complacent with the current state of affairs: 'And whoever [. . .] wants to begin to see ruin and the blows of the multitudes, will find that where religion has been lost, there it has followed.'[11] To this pious young observer, then, sixteenth-century Naples was ripe for the kind of religious and social reforming zeal that the Society of Jesus appeared to embody.

Despite such glowing descriptions of Jesuit activity in mid-sixteenth-century Naples, the Society of Jesus was plagued by certain problems that limited its effectiveness. One of the most serious concerns was the shortage of experienced personnel. This could create unforeseen difficulties when the demands for Jesuit services overwhelmed the capabilities of the order's many young, inexperienced members.[12] Because of the rapid growth of the Society of Jesus, the demand for its services increased at an ever greater rate. This demand placed additional pressures on available personnel and meant that Jesuit superiors were often unwilling to remove even those individuals whom they considered liabilities to the work in Naples. For example, when Alfonso Salmerón (1515–85) complained to his colleagues in Rome about the inadequacies of the Neapolitan College's rector, Cristobal Mendoza (whom even Juan Polanco had recognized as early as 1556 to be 'terrible' and desirous of being 'more feared than loved' by his colleague), nothing was done to remove the school official. Despite

---

10 Possevino, as cited in Tacchi Venturi, *Storia della Compagnia* 2/2: 68. For a brief discussion of 'free' Latin schooling in sixteenth-century Naples, of the non-Jesuit variety, see Paul Grendler, *Schooling in Renaissance Italy. Literacy and Learning 1300–1600* (Baltimore and London: Johns Hopkins University Press, 1989), 106.

11 Possevino, as cited in Tacchi Venturi, *Storia Della Compagnia*, 1/2: 68–9.

12 Cited in Bangert, *Claude Jay and Alfonso Salmerón*, 301.

EARLY JESUIT MISSIONS IN NAPLES, 1550–1620   61

numerous complaints, Mendoza could still be found in his post six years later.[13]

On still other occasions, however, it was Rome that sought to relieve its own personnel shortages by removing desperately needed workers from Naples. In such cases, Salmerón, in his capacity as Provincial of the Society of Jesus in the Kingdom of Naples (1558–76),[14] struggled to keep individuals from leaving. One case in point is the story of Luigi Massella, who sought removal from his duties in Naples, ostensibly because of depression and ill-health. Salmerón's impassioned plea to the Society's third general, Francisco Borja, underscores the frustrations of operating with limited manpower and under ever-expanding demands upon the order's energies:

> My Father, it is simply not right that anyone can take off from the Province merely by saying, 'I am depressed,' or 'I am not happy in this particular work.' [...] If one priest quits the Province, then another, and then still another, and if we are not empowered to go ahead and ordain others, what is going to become of the Province?[15]

Salmerón's comments reveal two ongoing difficulties that Jesuit provincial superiors faced throughout the early modern period in Naples: a fairly high number of members with health problems and/or emotional difficulties, and restrictions on their ability to ordain an adequate number of priests in order to fulfill the Society of Jesus' ambitious goals for its schools and apostolic missions.

This complex web of promise and challenges made Naples an important training ground for the Society of Jesus and a locus for the emergence of Jesuit leadership with close ties to the region. Three key figures played crucial roles in both the development of Jesuit apostolic activity in the Kingdom of Naples and in the broader life of the Society. Alfonso Salmerón was among the most respected early leaders of the Jesuits, not simply in Naples, where his preaching skills were renowned, but throughout the order, and beyond. Salmerón's great knowledge of theology made him a key figure at the Council of Trent, taking him from Naples from 1551 to 1554. Yet he was a figure not immune to

---

[13] For a broad treatment of the personnel problems associated with the Jesuits' Neapolitan College during its early years, see Scaduto, L'Epoca di Giacomo Laínez, 4: 361–8; for the specific debacle with Mendoza, cf. Lewis, ' "Preachers of Sound Doctrine," ' 67–71.

[14] In fact, Salmerón's provincial leadership was interrupted between 1561 and 1564 by his duties at the Council of Trent, where he played a key role as a theologian.

[15] Salmerón's letter to Borja, dated 12 September 1568, in MHSI, Epistolae P. Alphonsi Salmeronis (Madrid, 1906–07), 2: 176–7; cf. Bangert, Claude Jay and Alfonso Salmerón, 317.

62   A PARADISE INHABITED BY DEVILS

controversy. His apparently sudden disappearance from Naples in 1561 led to wild rumors that he had followed in the path of earlier popular preachers, like Bernardino Ochino, accused of heresy and escaped to Geneva.[16] But upon his return a few years later, such rumors were finally put to rest.

Another notable leader of the Jesuits who received important training in Naples was the fifth General of the Society of Jesus, Claudio Acquaviva (1543–1615). The son of one of the leading Neapolitan noble families, Acquaviva was born in the Abruzzi, the northeastern-most region of the Kingdom of Naples. Before becoming General at the age of 37, Acquaviva received much of his training in Naples, including a stint as Provincial after Salmerón's resignation from the position in 1576. During his long tenure as superior of the order, Acquaviva helped to shape the emerging identity within the Society of Jesus and was instrumental in making internal missionary activity central to the Jesuits' broader civilizing mission.

Finally, Pierantonio Spinelli (1555–1615) was also among the central figures in the early civilizing mission in Naples. Like Acquaviva, his rough contemporary, Spinelli came from one of the most powerful Neapolitan families, and belonged to the second generation of Jesuits who crafted the still-new organization's ambitious (and increasingly global) agenda. In Naples, Spinelli expanded areas of reform to include work with prostitutes and prisoners, and for the conversion of Muslim slaves, providing a model for urban missionary endeavors across Italy.[17]

The provincial leadership in southern Italy during the second half of the sixteenth- and the early seventeenth century included some of the most noted members of the order and there seem to have been close and important ties between Rome and Naples in this period. In addition to Salmerón's long-term role as the Jesuits' Neapolitan Provincial, Claudio Acquaviva, Pierantonio Spinelli, Muzio Vitelleschi and Vincenzo Carafa all held this same office during a crucial period in Neapol-

---

[16] Ulderico Parente has rightly noted that Salmerón's broader contributions to Catholic reform in sixteenth-century Naples have been strikingly under-analyzed in the range of works that consider other aspects of the Spanish Jesuit's contributions to Jesuit history, or to Tridentine reforms.

[17] Unfortunately, the most expansive source for the life and work of Spinelli is Antonio Barone's hagiographic account, *Della Vita del Padre Pierantonio Spinelli della Compagnia di Giesù* (Naples, 1707). Published nearly one hundred years after its subject's death, Barone's book has a poor organizational style and suffers the lack of balance characteristic of such sources. Nevertheless, when read against other sources, it offers valuable information on this significant, but far less known, contributor to Jesuit activity in the urban realm of the late sixteenth to early seventeenth centuries. Spinelli served as Provincial of Naples twice: from 1606 to 1609, and again in 1612.

EARLY JESUIT MISSIONS IN NAPLES, 1550–1620

itan history and a formative moment in the growth and maturation of the Society of Jesus. Interestingly, three of these men (all southern Italians by birth), Acquaviva, Vitelleschi and Carafa, also ultimately rose to the position of Superior General in the order. Increasingly, over the course of the late sixteenth and seventeenth centuries, this Jesuit leadership forged a missionary praxis for the Society's growing membership in the Kingdom of Naples. For while the original members of the order, like Ignatius Loyola, had early outlined the broad contours of a missionary philosophy for the Society of Jesus, it was in locales like Naples where theory and practice came together through trial and error, and innovation.

If the Jesuits derived their broadly defined, flexible concept of mission from a long historical legacy among religious orders and individuals, they also sought to strike a balance between a core theory of missionizing and adapting to the particularities of any mission field. In a fine study of the development of European missions, Adriano Prosperi argues that the missionary form derived from a growing consciousness among medieval Europeans of 'having a message and a truth to carry to others.'[18] In contrast to scholars who have posited a historic opposition between the concept of 'crusade' and 'mission,' Prosperi instead suggests that forms were modified to suit the specific needs of the historical moment. Thus, for example, the thirteenth-century Franciscan missions to the Mongol emperors appear to be somewhat hybrid forms of religious and cultural intervention.[19] Acknowledging the awesome military might of these non-Western rulers and lacking the firepower which European armies might provide, the Franciscans had to adapt a traditional 'crusading' strategy. Instead, mistakenly believing that the Mongols might prove open to Christianization and the adoption of certain Western practices through persuasion, individual missionaries sought to influence those at the top.

During the early sixteenth century, at the outset of the European evangelizing experience in the Americas, the notion of mission as a kind of pilgrimage held sway among the first mendicant missionaries. For these early Franciscans and Dominicans, the results of the mission were not as important as the model itself; the missionaries saw themselves as 'instruments of Divine Providence,' newly arrived in the Americas to prepare the Amerindians for the 'last days.'

The Jesuits, by contrast, largely rejected the mendicants' prophetic view of history, and, with it, an apocalyptically driven missionary

---

[18] Adriano Prosperi, 'L'Europa Cristiana e il Mondo: Alle Origine dell'Idea di Missione,' *Dimensioni e Problemi della ricerca storica* 2 (1992): 189–220, esp. 210–17.

[19] Prosperi, 'L'Europa Cristiana,' 191–2.

methodology. Innovators like José de Acosta argued that history itself was not prophetic, but 'natural and moral,' and recommended missionary strategies based upon observation and the careful gathering of data about specific societies and their practices.[20]

The Jesuit concept of mission both built upon the experiences of other orders and models and was widely interpreted to fit local conditions and objectives. The purpose of apostolic activity was outlined early in the order's 'Formula of the Institute of the Society of Jesus (1540).'[21] In this document, Ignatius Loyola defined as the primary purpose of the order: 'to strive especially for the defense and propagation of the faith and for the progress of souls in Christian life and doctrine, by means of public preaching, lectures, and any other ministrations whatsoever of the word of God.' He also elaborated upon some specific areas of emphasis, including instruction in the *Spiritual Exercises*, a program of searching self-reflection and purification which formed an essential part of the Jesuit ministry,[22] the education of 'children and unlettered persons' in Christian doctrine, and more traditional pastoral duties such as hearing confessions and administering sacraments. Although Loyola does not use the word mission in this context, he invokes a number of activities which will come to be considered staples of the missionary regime, notably calling upon his brethren to serve as peace-makers and to 'assist those who are found in prisons or hospitals.'[23] Although these apostolic activities were by no means unique to the Jesuits, they became important areas of focus within the emergent internal missions.

What is clear from the 'Formula of the Institute' is that missionary activity itself lay at the heart of the Society's endeavors. This focus is revealed in Part VII of the Jesuits' *Constitutions*, 'The distribution of the incorporated members in Christ's vineyard and their relations there with their fellow men,' where the Jesuits pledged a special vow to the Pope to be ready to 'go to any place whatsoever where he judges it expedient to send them for the greater glory of God and the good of souls, whether

---

[20] Cf. Prosperi, 'L'Europa Cristiana,' 198–204.

[21] The 'Institute,' which outlines the purposes for which the new religious order was established, was first approved by Pope Paul III in his bull, *Regimini militantis Ecclesiae*, 27 September 1540. It was re-approved, with some clarifications added, in the bull *Exposcit Debitum*, 21 July 1550, by Pope Julius III. Reprinted in Loyola, *Constitutions*, 63–73.

[22] For an overview of the purposes of the *Spiritual Exercises* and the uses to which they were put, see 'Introduction,' *The Spiritual Exercises of Saint Ignatius*, trans. and commentary by George E. Ganss (St Louis: The Institute of Jesuit Sources, 1992), 1–14, esp. 1–4. *Spiritual Exercises* was first published in 1548.

[23] Loyola, 'Formula of the Institute,' as cited in *Constitutions*, 66–7.

EARLY JESUIT MISSIONS IN NAPLES, 1550-1620   65

among the faithful or the infidels.'[24] Such a vow implied a readiness to respond unquestioningly to the requests of the pontiff, but the language of the document also reveals the Jesuits' desire to maintain as much autonomy as possible within this vow and to minimize potential disruptions to the Society of Jesus.

The importance of maintaining a certain degree of autonomy can best be understood by examining the Jesuit principle of accommodation. This principle was embedded in foundational documents like the *Spiritual Exercises*, which could be practiced in a variety of ways, depending upon the needs and particular constraints of the individuals involved. The order placed a premium upon its members' ability to interact effectively with a wide range of people and to maximize their impact upon the communities within which they worked. Such an approach necessitated the utmost flexibility and the superiors of the Society jealously protected this autonomy, even in the case of pontifical missions. Jesuit leaders sought to exert their discretionary power whenever it seemed appropriate. For example, the *Constitutions* suggests that where the Pope has not named a specific individual to undertake a mission, the superior of the order should 'judge who would be most fit for such a mission . . . while pondering the greater universal good and also the minimum damage possible to the other employments which are undertaken.'[25]

Similarly, the Jesuits sought to clarify the precise purpose of the missions by encouraging the pontiff to make his intentions explicit, while reserving some discretionary power for the order's superior where this was lacking:

> It is highly expedient that the mission should be entirely explained to the one who is thus sent, as well as the intention of His Holiness and the result in hope of which he [the missionary] is sent. This should be given in writing, if possible, that he may be better able to accomplish what is entrusted to him by the order [. . .] The superior can also be helpful by some instruction, not only in his own missions but also in those of His Holiness, in order to attain better the end which is sought.[26]

While some historians have interpreted the Jesuits' Fourth Vow as evidence of the order's slavish obedience to the whims of individual popes, this argument fails to consider the order's pragmatic approach to its work. While it is certainly true that the Fourth Vow demonstrates the

---

[24] Loyola, *Constitutions*, 267–71, esp. 268. For a detailed consideration of the Jesuits' Fourth Vow, see John W. O'Malley, 'To Travel to Any Part of the World: Jerónimo Nadal and the Jesuit Vocation,' *Studies in the Spirituality of Jesuits*, 16, No. 2 (1984).

[25] O'Malley, *First Jesuits*, 38–9; 81–2; 111–12, esp. 81.

[26] Ibid.

66 A PARADISE INHABITED BY DEVILS

Society's close links with the papacy, the Jesuits clearly sought to pursue their own complex agenda through the pontifical missions.[27] Ever careful to express such desires for autonomy in guarded language, the *Constitutions* nevertheless establishes this precedent. Loyola argued that when a pontifical mission lasted longer than the customary three months' duration, and when such activity would not harm the overall goals of the 'principal mission,' a Jesuit might 'make some excursions to aid the souls in neighboring regions' and 'consider, but without prejudice to his mission, as has been said, in what other things he can employ himself for the glory of God and the good of souls.'[28] In this modest way, then, Ignatius placed some parameters around the conduct of the pontifical missions, safeguarding the interests of the Society while still ensuring that the order would maintain a special relationship with the Pope.

Like other areas of Jesuit endeavor, the Jesuits' Fourth Vow needs to be interpreted beyond its obvious spiritual content. The Fourth Vow represents both a practical and an ideological position: the order looked to the papacy for protection from its enemies within the Church as well as without. But the Fourth Vow also grew out of the Jesuits' conviction that the pope, as head of a universal church, was the best vehicle to 'distribute them for the greater glory of God.'[29]

In recommending to Jesuit superiors how they might determine the most fruitful missions to undertake, Ignatius was ever mindful of potential patrons. For example, in determining the location for missions, he recommended choosing those places 'where the greater fruit will probably be reaped,' where a Jesuit college or house was already established, where 'important and public persons' had sought out spiritual aid from the Jesuits, or where 'the enemy of Christ our Lord has sown cockle, and especially where he has spread bad opinion about the Society.'[30] In other words, the Jesuits had to make strategic use of limited human resources with an eye toward achieving the greatest success.

One of the hallmarks of Jesuit missionary activity in Naples, as elsewhere, was the Society of Jesus' reliance upon elite patrons for financial and administrative assistance. Like the special vow to the pope, this early orientation toward the wealthy and powerful was both prag-

---

[27] Loyola, *Constitutions*, 269–70.

[28] On the complex relationship between the Society and the papacy, especially regarding the Fourth Vow, see O'Malley, *First Jesuits*, 296–310.

[29] Loyola, *Constitutions*, 270.

[30] On the Jesuits' practical reliance upon the papacy for legitimation and protection, cf. O'Malley, *First Jesuits*, 296–7. O'Malley argues that early Jesuits believed that the Holy See had the 'broad vision required for the most effective deployment in the vineyard of the Lord,' 299.

EARLY JESUIT MISSIONS IN NAPLES, 1550–1620

matic and philosophical: the Jesuits relied upon the financial good graces of lay and clerical elites to support their apostolic and educational projects; but it also reflected the commonly held belief of the time that a 'universal good' would be generated from above. Or, as Loyola argued:

> The more universal the good is, the more it is divine. Therefore, preference ought to be given to those persons and places, which, through their own improvement, become a cause which can spread the good accomplished to many others who are under their influence or take guidance from them.[31]

In Naples, too, local elites formed the backbone of Jesuit apostolic activities. Whether through their association with pre-existing lay confraternities, like the Confraternity of the Bianchi of Justice, or through those established by Jesuit innovators like Araldo, the Jesuits sought to forge close ties with an enthusiastic layer of reform-minded elites.[32] Whatever the benefits of such an orientation, however, it might also prove troublesome when social strife among the popular classes erupted, as it so often did in the tumultuous Naples of the sixteenth and seventeenth centuries.

Aside from this strong bias toward courting the powerful, the *Constitutions* offered few recommendations of specific missionary strategies beyond considerations of the urgency of certain undertakings over others, the availability and talents of personnel and the length of time that might be devoted to such tasks. But Ignatius did empower the order's provincial superiors to provide explicit instructions to those being sent into the field, encouraging missionaries to communicate frequently with superiors and to gather information relevant to their work.[33] He hinted at the usefulness of a 'division of labor' among missionaries, advising that at least two Jesuits be sent among the people to 'be more profitable to those to whom they are sent.' Such an arrangement was useful for a number of reasons. On a purely practical level, it meant that one missionary could preach and lecture in Christian doctrine while one or more heard confessions and conducted the *Spiritual Exercises*. Loyola also imagined that sending out pairs of Jesuits would allow people with complementary levels of experience or temperaments to serve most effectively. In this way, novices would be paired with seasoned veterans, or 'one very ardent and daring ... could well go [with] another more circumspect and cautious.'[34] While the Jesuits were not the first religious order to send pairs of missionaries out into

---

[31] Loyola, *Constitutions*, 274–5.
[32] Lewis, 'Jesuit Confraternity Activity,' 213–14.
[33] Loyola, *Constitutions*, 275–80.
[34] Loyola, *Constitutions*, 277–8.

68   A PARADISE INHABITED BY DEVILS

the field, this approach proved to be a hallmark of Jesuit missionary strategy in Naples, as elsewhere.

The idea of promoting a 'division of labor' among members while on missions seems to have developed through practical experience. In Schinosi's history of the Jesuits' early years in the Kingdom of Naples, he describes the practice of sending pairs of Jesuit novices from the Neapolitan College on small-scale missions throughout the popular quarters of the city. The novices would set out each afternoon to preach in the *piazze*, ideally attracting crowds of people who would then follow them to an *osteria* (tavern) where the novices would continue to preach through supper (and perhaps a few drinks). If they could win over some new converts, the rector of the college, Andrea de Oviedo, would 'spend a good part of the night listening to confessions.'[35] This activity represented both a response to suggestions found in the *Constitutions* and an accommodation to the particular conditions of sixteenth-century Naples. The active street life that characterized the southern Italian capital meant that missionaries needed to go outside, where their labors would bear the most fruit.

Such early forays into the popular quarters of the city represented an initial experiment with the urban mission that Pierantonio Spinelli would formalize in Naples in 1601.[36] They also reflected the deep concern over the social disorder that observers believed plagued Naples and its surroundings. Although the Jesuits would have been much more cautious about making public criticisms of their fellow clergy, their establishment of an urban missionary strategy speaks volumes about the order's conviction that it could play a central role in reestablishing social peace and Catholic orthodoxy in early modern Naples.

---

[35] Schinosi, *Istoria*, 1: 38–9 On the early popular missions in Naples, also see Guidetti, *Le Missioni Popolari*, 36–40.

[36] On Spinelli's crucial role in developing the urban mission in Naples and the wider impact of this innovation on the order as a whole, cf. Barone, *Della Vita del Padre Pierantonio Spinelli*, 116–21; Santagata, *Istoria*, 3: 32–4; Guidetti, *Le Missioni Popolari*, 40. Lance Lazar is quite right to argue that the earliest initiatives associated with the urban mission began at the heart of Jesuit activity in Rome, by the 1540s, yet this does not diminish the significance of the innovative work in Naples. For a wonderful discussion of early Jesuit confraternities in Rome and their work with urban ministries, see Lance Lazar, 'The First Jesuit Confraternities and Marginalized Groups in Sixteenth-Century Rome,' in *The Politics of Ritual Kinship. Confraternities and Social Order in Early Modern Italy*, ed. Nicholas Terpstra (Cambridge, UK: Cambridge University Press, 2000), 132–49, esp. 136.

The urban missions in Naples

For the Jesuits, the urban missions represented one of the most significant developments to emerge out of southern Italy in the second half of the sixteenth century. Not only did they foster efforts at religious and cultural reform in Naples, but the design and the objectives of the urban missions were, to a large extent, transferred to work in the rural areas of the Kingdom of Naples which flourished during the seventeenth and early eighteenth centuries.[37]

Several other religious orders, individuals and lay groups had begun to promote moral reform in early sixteenth-century Naples and charitable activities had grown more focused and urgent some decades before the Jesuits arrived. The spirit of fostering Christian renewal through charitable acts and preaching was already alive and well in small circles of reform-oriented clergy and laity who met around notable early sixteenth-century figures like the Dominican preacher Girolamo da Monopoli and the Augustinian Callisto da Piacenza. This work was furthered with the arrival in Naples of Ettore Vernazza in 1518. Vernazza, a notary from Genoa, was a key figure in the establishment of several chapters of the Oratory of Divine Love across Italy, including Naples. The Oratory movement, whose roots lay in Genoa and Vicenza from the late fifteenth century, expressed the Christian Humanist's dual orientation toward the development of individual spiritual reformation and moral reform of the communities through charitable activity. Both Gaetano Thiene and Gian Pietro Carafa (future Pope Paul IV), co-founders of the Theatine Order, were early members of the Oratory and helped establish the group's presence in Naples. With the considerable help and patronage of the wealthy Spanish widow Maria Longo, a fascinating figure in her own right, Vernazza sought to open a new hospital in the southern Italian capital, aimed primarily at syphilitics, who were banned from other hospitals. As an outgrowth of the work of this *Ospedale degl'Incurabali*, the *Compagnia dei Bianchi*, a lay confraternity, took up the work of seeking the gallows conversion of condemned prisoners. Furthermore, Longo, anticipating another of the Jesuits' important missions to prostitutes, sought the conversion of these 'fallen women' and their vulnerable daughters by venturing out on the streets of Naples and beseeching her charges to return with her to the *Ospedale*.[38]

---

[37] Novi Chavarria, 'Le Misssioni dei Gesuiti in Calabria in età moderna,' 107.

[38] For a brief narrative of the establishment of the *Ospedale*, and especially of the important contributions of Maria Longo to this reform work, see Araldo, *Cronica*, 91v–93v; cf. Giuliana Boccadamo, 'Maria Longo, L'Ospedale degli Incurabili e la sua Insula,'

70 A PARADISE INHABITED BY DEVILS

Building upon these earlier initiatives, the Jesuits created urban missions in a variety of forms. Narrowly speaking, the 'urban missions' were those systematic preaching missions which proceeded, district by district through urban centers, beginning in Naples in 1601. But in a broader sense, the urban missions encompassed a wide range of urban ministries that aimed at the social and cultural reform of Neapolitans, most notably the popular classes. While such initiatives were often welcomed by secular and religious officials alike, they also expressed the prerogatives of the Society of Jesus for both institution-building and placing a distinctive imprint on the city's cultural map. In this way, they were the local expression of the Jesuits' more global civilizing mission.

The Jesuit most closely associated with the emergence of the urban missions in Naples was Pierantonio Spinelli (1555–1615). Although Spinelli probably borrowed generously from contemporaries in terms of missionary methodology, in his role as Neapolitan Provincial and as an orator and reformer, he worked to make the urban missions a staple of Jesuit apostolic activity.[39] Spinelli was born into a noble family in Seminara, Calabria. As a youth, he was drawn to a spiritual life, and after a brief stay at the Jesuit College in Messina (Sicily), Spinelli moved to Naples to begin the long process of becoming a Jesuit at the young age of 17.

Like many young novices in the Society of Jesus, Spinelli sought a missionary vocation in the Indies. Instead, he was fated to spend the bulk of his life shuttling between the Jesuit colleges in Naples and Rome, and developing the formal structures of urban missions as Provincial of Naples during the early seventeenth century. He served as Provincial in two separate stints: first from 1606 to 1609 and then again in 1612. From his early days in Naples, Spinelli was instrumental in expanding Jesuit activity. Following in the path of the medieval mendicants, the Franciscans and Dominicans, Spinelli and a companion wandered through the poorer quarters of Naples, preaching and teaching Christian doctrine. Such forays, sometimes referred to as 'missions of the street,' resemble those taken by many Jesuit theology students.[40] Spinelli's

---

Campania Sacra 30 (1999): 37–170; Francesco Saverio Toppi, *Maria Lorenza Longo. Donna della Napoli del '500* (Pompeii: Pontificio Santuario, 1997), 108.

[39] Armando Guidetti notes Spinelli's signal role in advocating the urban missions while serving as Provincial (1601), but also mentions the importance of individuals like Giulio Mancinelli (1537–1618) in developing a missionary method suitable to the urban missions. See Guidetti, *Le Missioni Popolari*, 39–40.

[40] Guidetti, *Le Missioni Popolari*, 36–7. These 'Missioni della strada' seem to have become formally organized sometime around 1580.

hagiographer, Antonio Barone, offers a vivid, if highly romanticized, description of Spinelli's improvised processions:

> He extended himself also to the suburbs, singularly to those areas inhabited by gypsies, or such people [as were] extremely ignorant of spiritual matters and had been totally abandoned by those who should have ministered to them. There, with pious processions, he [Spinelli] traveled everywhere through those distressing alleys, and in front of their hovels, he instructed the wretched creatures in the Sacred mysteries and the Divine Precepts; extracting from them the vices and errors of which they were full.[41]

This description reveals not only Spinelli's missionary style, but also the extent to which the Jesuits saw themselves as both religious and cultural reformers. Beyond filling the gap left by absent or unsuitable clergy in attending to poorer parishioners, Spinelli's preaching missions also sought to transform people's behavior, 'extracting from them the vices and errors of which they were full.'

According to the image of Spinelli that Barone and other chroniclers offer us, Spinelli fit very much within the mainstream of the Society of Jesus in his missionary orientation. For although the Jesuits shared much with their medieval predecessors in terms of prescribing a simple, pious way of life for members, their primary emphasis on an active ministry set the order apart. The Jesuits were distinct from other religious orders in several key ways: the requirement that novices attain experience in active ministry before taking solemn vows; their residence in 'houses' instead of monasteries; an emphasis on pilgrimage, or mission; and their outward orientation toward cultural reform.

The first distinctive feature of the Jesuit vocation, the requirement that novices gain experience in active ministry before taking solemn vows, speaks to the Jesuits' emerging institutional identity as early as the second half of the sixteenth century. The Society of Jesus prided itself on being highly selective in choosing members and sought to insure that those who finally took vows would represent the order in the best possible light. Since apostolic activity was at the center of the Jesuit vocation, it is unsurprising that superiors would want to evaluate novices' commitment to this kind of work before admitting them fully into the fold.

The Jesuits' residence in 'houses' rather than monasteries appears fairly trivial on first glance, but reveals a far more important distinction between the Society of Jesus and members of monastic orders. While the monastic life was highly regulated by daily schedules, requirements such as the singing of vespers, vows of silence and frequently geographic

---

[41] Barone, *Della Vita*, 39.

72   A PARADISE INHABITED BY DEVILS

isolation from laity, the Jesuit vocation required that members be free of rigid schedules. The 'houses' were both residences and sites for a range of activities in the world, including the meetings of lay congregations that might meet under the supervision of members of the order to organize charitable ventures, or simply to receive the sacraments. The Society's avowed willingness to send members wherever their labors were most required meant that individuals could not be tied down to restrictive schedules or burdensome duties. In the interest of maintaining such flexibility, the Jesuits sought exemptions from typical duties such as the office of choir.[42]

Finally, the Jesuits' outward orientation toward religious and cultural reform set them apart from many contemporaries. We can see this distinction between the Jesuits and their peers by examining the Capuchins' 'General Chapter' (1536), and comparing it with Ignatius Loyola's views on the significance of missionary work. Like the Jesuits, the Capuchins were one of the emerging religious orders formed in the heat of the Reformation era. As Louis Châtellier has characterized the Capuchin vocation: 'The true missionary, according to the Capuchin rule, should thus dedicate the greater part of his time to meditation, in silence, in seclusion, in dispossession, in order to be able to then descend from the 'mountain,' when he has been awakened by the impetuous Spirit, to speak to the people.'[43]

The Jesuits, instead, were called upon to make apostolic activity central to their purposes. In the middle section of the *Spiritual Exercises* (1548), Loyola admonishes those who would follow his guide to choose the 'Standard of Christ' and prioritize missionary work:

> Consider how the Lord of all the world chooses so many persons, apostles, disciples, and the like. He sends them throughout the whole world, to spread his doctrine among people of every state and condition. Consider the address which Christ our Lord makes to all his servants and friends whom he is sending on this expedition. He recommends that they endeavor to aid all persons [. . .][44]

Thus, at the heart of Jesuits' spirituality and organizational practice lay a commitment to reforming the outside world, in this way demonstrating their commitment to fulfilling their apostolic vocation.

This emphasis on active ministry with an eye toward social reform characterized much of Spinelli's work in developing new areas of religious and cultural intervention in late sixteenth- and early seventeenth-century Naples. In addition to ministering to the poor, Spinelli

---

[42] Cf. John O'Malley, *First Jesuits*, 67–8.
[43] Châtellier, *The Religion of the Poor*, 18–21, esp. 19.
[44] Ignatius Loyola, *Spiritual Exercises*, 65–7.

EARLY JESUIT MISSIONS IN NAPLES, 1550–1620

and others placed special emphasis on working with so-called 'fallen women' and prisoners. They also sought to Christianize Muslim slaves, mostly North Africans, though referred to generically as 'Turks.' This group was said to represent over 20 000 people in early modern Naples, according to one recent estimate.[45] In this sense, then, the civilizing mission was adapted to what the Jesuits saw as the most urgent social concerns of urban Naples. By attempting to acculturate these groups, whose very existence posed a threat to a unified Christian community as well as post-Tridentine values, the Jesuits believed that they could make a vital contribution to bringing order to the troubled city.

Although an active ministry characterized the Jesuits' work from their first years in Naples, the impetus to respond creatively to dire social conditions was certainly fueled by the Revolt of 1585. The May Revolt, described as one through which Naples became a 'theater of the most inhuman barbarities,' was certainly not the first time that ordinary Neapolitan citizens took up arms to protest economic conditions in the city. It began, like so many others, as a simple protest against the increase in the price of bread. City fathers had decided to export a large portion of the communal store of wheat to Spain at a time when much of the Neapolitan population was struggling with falling wages and inflationary trends. Within days, Giovan Vincenzo Starace, the Elector of the People and a wealthy silk merchant, had been publicly lynched and the popular quarters were in uproar.[46]

Jesuit sources present the revolt as largely driven by starvation among the lower classes and there is no doubt that hunger played a significant role.[47] But Rosario Villari makes a convincing case that the insurrection was in fact much more highly organized than many early modern bread riots. He highlights, for example, the extent to which the rhetoric of the revolt was directed at both the power of the unpopular Viceroy, Pedro

---

[45] Salvatore Bono, 'Schiavi Musulmani in Italia nell'età moderna,' *Erdem* 3, No. 9 (July 1987): 829–38, esp. 830–32. Frustratingly, Bono does not cite the source for his figures.

[46] For a good overview of the causes and consequences of the Revolt of 1585, see Rosario Villari, *The Revolt of Naples*, Chapter One. For Barone's assessment, see *Della Vita*, 122–5. Also see Michelangelo Mendella, *Il Moto Napoletane del 1585 e il Delicto Storace* (Naples: Giannini, 1967). Mendella refers to the public official as 'Storace,' but most sources, including Villari, call him 'Starace.' For an interesting, anonymous eyewitness account of the revolt, see N. Faraglia, ed., 'Il Tumulto Napolitano dell'anno 1585,' *Archivio storico per le province napoletane* 11, nos 1–4 (1886), 433–41; cf. Araldo, *Cronica*, ff. 199v/239; ff201v–r/244. Curiously, Araldo does not make mention of specific Jesuit interventions to calm the situation.

[47] Schinosi, for example, argues: 'Meanwhile [it was] hunger, impatient by its nature and a poor counselor, [which] incited the lower orders against the unlucky Storace.' Schinosi, *Istoria*, 2: 2.

74 A PARADISE INHABITED BY DEVILS

Téllez-Girón, the Duke of Ossuna, and toward that portion of the rising commercial and professional elite that was benefitting in a largely depressed economy. Villari sees the revolt as an important turning point in the legacy of pre-modern social protests, precisely because of the widespread support for the insurrection and evidence of autonomous organizing among reform-minded merchants and some of the intelligentsia.[48]

Despite the brutal repression of the revolt, concerns over increasing social tensions in Naples grew throughout the remainder of the sixteenth century and beyond. A number of synodal decrees under the auspices of both Neapolitan and other local bishops explicitly forbade the operation of any confraternities without express permission from the episcopal authorities.[49]

For their part, the Jesuits made much of their apparent role in helping to restore order in the face of the revolt. While Giovan Francesco Araldo is strangely silent on the Jesuits' supposed role in quelling the violence, Antonio Barone paints a picture of Jesuits boldly responding to the requests of the military and local officials to calm the masses by venturing into the streets, crucifixes in hand, 'summoning the people to follow Christ and with that leading them away from uniting themselves with the seditious ones.'[50] Francesco Schinosi also offers an image of the Jesuits prevailing over the chaos. Citing Carlo Mastrilli's argument to his brethren that the Jesuits should get involved in attempting to quell the revolt, Schinosi suggests the confidence that the order felt regarding its abilities to intervene effectively:

> *One has a duty*, with such a temperament governing the affair . . . I only want to open the streets to everyone. If they kill me, the loss (which won't even be a loss) will stop with me only. But if they will acknowledge me and my counsels, to their benefit, (which wouldn't be hard to [have] happen, because among them, many love me) then

---

[48] Villari, 'Naples: The Insurrection of 1585,' 311–16. On the question of motives, however, and challenging Villari's advocacy of a 'ritual magical' reading of the vicious dismemberment of Storace and the parading of his remains through the streets of Naples, see Mendella, *Il Moto Napoletano*, 50–51. Mendella disagrees with Villari's rendering of events, charging his fellow historian with an 'illegitimate application to the urban population of sixteenth-century Naples of methods and attitudes that only today ethnology and social science have put into circulation in the culture . . .' ('. . . ci sembra una illegittima applicazione alla popolazione urbana della Napoli cinquecentesca . . . di metodi ed atteggiamenti che solo oggi l'etnologia e le scienze sociali hanno messo in circolazione nella cultura . . .').

[49] Villari, 'Naples: The Insurrection of 1585,' 324–6.

[50] Barone, *Della Vita*, 125

EARLY JESUIT MISSIONS IN NAPLES, 1550–1620   75

all of you, *for that space which your fervor will create*, will want to aid [me] in my operations.[51]

The 'space' to which Mastrilli referred was precisely the opportunity for the Jesuits to place their imprint upon the religious and cultural life of the city. Mastrilli believed that his personal powers of persuasion, and (by extension) those of his fellow Jesuits, could overcome any popular sentiments in favor of the revolt. This was part and parcel of an emerging 'ideal' of the Jesuit missionary. Partly influenced by the example of early Jesuits like Francis Xavier who had set out to Christianize the East Indies, this image of the heroic missionary became both a means to bind members of the order to a common purpose and a wonderful public relations tool.

In the immediate circumstances, however, the Jesuits also became targets of popular anger. Schinosi admits as much when he refers to the popular perception that the Jesuits were 'favored by the Viceroy, the Duke of Ossuna.'[52] In fact, both Schinosi and Santagata's histories of the Society of Jesus in the Viceroyalty of Naples are replete with examples of the Jesuits' close ties to local and regional notables. The Jesuits' orientation toward elites was both a matter of principle and pragmatism. Although the majority of individual Jesuits came from 'middle-class' backgrounds, their close relationships with Neapolitan nobility, historical ties to at least some of the viceroys and the noble background of leading members such as Acquaviva and Carafa certainly would have fueled popular suspicions.

The Society of Jesus emerged from the insurrection of 1585 with a greater sense of urgency about the need to expand its ministries, and a new commitment to winning over the popular classes to its projects of religious and cultural reform. The intensification of the order's reforming activities following 1585 attests to the impact of the event on the Society as a whole.[53] By 1590, the fifth General of the Society, Claudio Acquaviva, issued his first directive on the conduct of internal missions. He urged his brethren to conduct missions in order to inspire penitence, increase popular understanding of Christianity and extirpate vices. Beyond outlining the motivations for conducting these missions, however, Acquaviva also offered strategies for the appropriate means of evangelization, made suggestions for dealing with other clergy and identified those personal qualities that missionaries should ideally pos-

---

[51] Schinosi, *Istoria*, 2: 4. (The emphasis on 'One has a duty' is in the original text; the emphasis on 'for that space' is mine).

[52] Schinosi, *Istoria*, 2: 3. Compare also Mendella, *Il Moto Napoletane*, 34.

[53] Schinosi discusses the new congregations which the Society instituted in Naples as attempts to 'procure in the lower orders these better behaviors,' see *Istoria*, 2, 9–11.

76   A PARADISE INHABITED BY DEVILS

sess. These general recommendations would be expanded upon in subsequent letters to members of the Society of Jesus over the next ten
years.[54]

Whatever the degree of their actual involvement in calming the streets
in the aftermath of the revolt, it is certain that the Society of Jesus
established a number of new congregations in Naples in an attempt to
'procure in the common people these better behaviors.' If the urge
toward social rebellion was demonically inspired, as the Jesuits and
many of their contemporaries believed, then the poor would need to
learn to accept God's supremacy and their own responsibility to obey
those whom He had placed above them in the social order. Linking
dissolute behavior with a propensity to question the divinely ordained
social arrangement, the Jesuits thus promoted submission to ecclesiastical and secular authority as a prerequisite to leading a holy life.

Where they had once emphasized the elite character of the confraternities with which they were associated, the Jesuits now strove to
encourage greater piety and reforming activity among the poor. As they
would go on to demonstrate in their rural missions across southern Italy,
conversions would not be accomplished through merely encouraging
more frequent confessions, or Eucharistic devotion, but required reforming the poor habits of the people. And while the poor did not corner the
market on dissolute practices, Jesuit rhetoric served to reify the commonly held belief that popular ignorance bred immorality. The Jesuits
stressed the internal transformation of its subjects and urged the newly
converted to win others over. In service of this goal, the Jesuits made
frequent use of lay instructors in reform efforts. This approach, which
envisioned the poor leading one another into a more domesticated
existence, challenges any simplistic reading of Jesuit missionary strategy
as merely an effort to bully the lower orders into submission. But just as
we should be cautious not to deny some degree of agency to those who
were attracted to the Jesuits' reforms, nor should we accept the Society's
often triumphal rhetoric as evidence of the unquestioning consumption
of their civilizing mission by the Neapolitan popular classes.

For the Jesuits in Naples, it was not enough to preach against social
disruptions like the 1585 Revolt, though they had certainly done that

---

[54] For General Acquaviva's 1590 letter to the Jesuits' Neapolitan Provincial, Antonio
Lisio, see ARSI, *Neap.* 202, ff. 31–3v, 'Lettera di N.P. Generale Claudio Acquaviva
quando mando il 2ᶜ Giubileo impresato da Nostra Compagnia. Sisto V' et ordina che si
mandino alcuni padri in missione, Dei 2ᶜ maggio, 1590. Al Padre Antonio Lisio, Provinciale di Napoli.' Although the letter was directed to Lisio, it was reflective of wider changes
which Acquaviva sought to encourage throughout the Society's broad geographic sweep.

EARLY JESUIT MISSIONS IN NAPLES, 1550–1620

when Carlo Mastrilli lashed out against the 'demonic' inspiration behind the insurrection.[55] Rather, in much of their apostolic activity, the Jesuits favored an approach that encouraged congregants to internalize their religious values and practices and spread them to others.[56] Participants were encouraged not to be passive observers, but rather active participants in evangelizing efforts. That was precisely the purpose of a new Neapolitan congregation initiated in 1588, where:

> in the manner of domestic birds that obtain other birds [for] the hunter, these congregants emerged from our Residence during the festive days and, [by] combining friendship and using opportune means with others, drew them [along] with them to confessors, and to a more settled life.[57]

This practice of training the laity to perform both apostolic and charitable functions also made sense, given the shortage of parish clergy to which I have referred. The problem of inadequate clergy did not just plague the City of Naples. In other parts of the Kingdom, the Jesuits often found themselves turning to the laity to perform (or assist in performing) essential spiritual tasks.[58] The strategy took root in other cities such as Lecce, the largest city in the region of Apulia and a major center of Jesuit activity. A missionary report from 1590 discusses the work of Father Bernardo Ottaviano, who began to labor among the paupers and beggars of the Apulian city. Characteristically, Ottaviano's missionary work was aided by the presence of a Jesuit college in Lecce.[59] The many demands upon the energies of the small Jesuit community

---

[55] Schinosi, *Istoria*, 2: 4–5.

[56] Sherrill Cohen argues that this approach to conversion, 'the spiritual rebirth and transformation of the individual soul,' coupled with calling on the converted to convert their peers, is common to all religious movements during periods of intense reform, such as the Catholic Reformation or, later, the Great Awakening. While there is certainly truth in this comment, it does not negate the fact that the Jesuits linked their missionary strategies and apostolic orientation to this broader view of conversion to a greater extent than most other religious orders. See Cohen, *The Evolution of Women's Asylums Since 1500. From Refuges for Ex-Prostitutes to Shelters for Battered Women* (New York and Oxford: Oxford University Press, 1992), 7.

[57] Schinosi, *Istoria*, 2: 93

[58] The Jesuits founded a number of congregations in Naples during the late 1580s. Five of these, each representing a distinct social group (nobles, clergy, merchants, artisans and servants, respectively) operated out of the Jesuits' Professed House. For a summary of their composition and dates of origin, see Gennaro Nardi, 'Nuovo Ricerche Sulle istituzioni napoletane a favore degli schiavi. La Congregazione degli Schiavi dei PP. Gesuiti,' *Asprenas* 14 (1967): 294–313, esp. 304.

[59] On the use of laity for ministering to the poor in Lecce, see ARSI *Neap.* 72, Document 10 (1590), ff. 42–42v; the college, founded in 1579, had been constituted five years earlier as a Jesuit residence. For its history, see Tacchi Venturi, *Storia della Compagnia*, III, 507.

78 A PARADISE INHABITED BY DEVILS

precluded members of the order from devoting much time to such activity, thus necessitating the involvement of lay folk:

> And because our Fathers, due to the many other occupations of that College, could not totally involve themselves in said work, the said father [Ottaviano], founder of this work, chose some people [from] among those in the oratory of artisans . . . Those people took care of assembling the poor, of requesting alms throughout the city on Saturday, in order to distribute them to said poor on Sunday, when the poor congregated in our above mentioned church.[60]

This approach, like so much of the Jesuits' work, reflected the principle of accommodation in action.

In assessing the work of the Oratory, the author of this report, Alessandro Ferrari, praised the use of the laity in ministering to the poor, noting that not only had this created more social stability in Lecce through the systematic distribution of alms, but had also provided a vehicle for more people to hear Mass and make confessions on a regular basis. Finally, echoing the work of the new congregations in Naples, the activity in Lecce had the welcome result of encouraging peer education, as 'some of those well-instructed poor have the function of teaching Christian doctrine to the others.'[61] If one of the primary goals of a civilizing mission was to encourage individuals to internalize new values, then Lecce appeared, at least to Jesuit sources, to be a success.

In general, in the aftermath of the Neapolitan Revolt of 1585, the Jesuits stepped up their apostolic activity. They placed renewed emphasis on open-air preaching in the piazzas, founded new congregations and promoted works of Christian charity. In all of these spheres, Naples became a vital center for experimentation with missionary strategies and areas of intervention, providing a model for the order at large. Three areas of focus deserve special attention, however, because they illuminate the Jesuits' efforts to implement a civilizing mission in urban Naples, while also demonstrating the difficulties that such work entailed: reform of prostitutes or 'fallen women,' prisoners and attempts to convert Muslim slaves to Christianity.

Early modern European elites were deeply concerned to preserve female honor and prevent poor but 'decent' women from falling into prostitution. By the sixteenth century, with the spread of syphilis,

---

[60] ARSI, *Neap.* 72, Doc. 10, ff. 42–42v., Alessandro Ferrari, Rector of College of Lecce, 'Report on the work of P. Bernardo Ottaviano from Lecce' (1590) (sent to Giovanni Maremorti, Rome, 1608); cf. Lewis, 'Jesuit Confraternity Activity in Naples,' 217.

[61] ARSI, *Neap.* 72, Doc. 10, f. 42v.

prostitutes were increasingly viewed as a threat to public health.[62] Religious officials viewed the dangers posed to poor women's honor as reflective of wider social decay. Some blamed the supposedly lax morals and decadence of Renaissance culture for the severity of the crisis, pointing to the social and cultural status attained by a small number of courtesans, such as the Venetian *letterata* Veronica Franco, as indicative of a wider tolerance for such behavior.

The perception that prostitutes comprised a vast, amorphous population pervades much of the literature of the time. One contemporary, when asked to venture a guess as to the number of prostitutes in Venice (a city renowned for the visible presence of prostitution), argued with some exaggeration that such a task would be 'an intolerable labor [...] like wanting to count the stars in the sky.'[63] Although accurate numbers are hard to come by for Naples, contemporaries certainly noted an expansion in prostitution and growing concern over its effects from the late fifteenth century.[64] Naples followed Venice and Rome among those European cities best known for the sex trade and, as the often scandalous poet Pietro Aretino mused, 'of those many Neapolitan women [who are courtesans] it would be too much to count the entire genealogy.' Aretino waggishly claimed that the foremothers of the Neapolitan prostitutes of his day dated back to the times of Alexander the Great. Of course Aretino spoke of the courtesan, a semi-respectable figure of late medieval urban culture, especially in Italy, who was often renowned for her intelligence, artistic skill and social connections.

By the end of the fifteenth century, however, both the Catholic Church and secular authorities began to make a proper distinction between the work of courtesans and that of common street prostitutes. For example, the notoriously unchaste Pope Alexander VI distinguished between 'whores by candlelight' and 'honest Courtesans.'[65] In Naples,

---

[62] Two views of changing perceptions of prostitution in early modern Italy are Cohen, *Evolution of Women's Asylums*, and Lucia Ferrante, 'Honor Regained: Women in the Casa del Soccorso di San Paolo in Sixteenth-Century Bologna,' in *Sex and Gender in Historical Perspective*, ed. Edward Muir and Guido Ruggiero (Baltimore and London: Johns Hopkins University Press, 1990), 46–72. For a fascinating comparative perspective, see Lyndal Roper, *The Holy Household. Women and Morals in Reformation Augsburg* (Oxford: Clarendon, 1989), esp. 89–131.

[63] As cited in Mario Scaduto SJ, *L'Epoca di Giacomo Laínez* IV, 639–41, esp. 640.

[64] Salvatore di Giacomo, *La Prostituzione in Napoli Nei Secoli XV, XVI, e XVII. Documenti Inediti* (Naples, 1899), 71.

[65] Pietro Aretino, *Capricciosi e piacevoli ragionamenti*, cited in Di Giacomo, *La Prostituzione in Napoli*, 71–2. According to available figures, Florence's pre-Plague population of 1630 was *c.* 72 000, compared to Naples' *c.* 250 000. For population figures, see Eric Cochrane, *Italy 1530–1630*, ed. Julius Kirshner (London and New York:

80 A PARADISE INHABITED BY DEVILS

city fathers demonstrated increased concern over an apparently burgeoning sex trade by arguing for stiffening penalties for pimps (*ruffiani*). Such a request is evident in the following letter sent to the Spanish King Ferdinand of Aragon in 1505:

> [D]ue to the prostitutes and dishonest women there are many pimps in this city, both citizens and foreigners, we beg your Catholic Majesty to order and command the regent of the grand court of the royal prison (*vicaria*) that he must hunt down, prosecute and punish them, and not permit any ruffian in said city for any reason [. . .] and for greater efficacy, that Your Majesty concede power to the Electors of this City . . . to act against these said pimps . . . [66]

Just two years later, in 1507, Naples' first viceroy, Consalvo Ferdinando di Cordova e di Aguilar, ordered that all pimps be banished from the City and Viceroyalty of Naples and forbidden re-entry without the 'express license of His Majesty,' on pain of 'being placed in galley labor.' As for the prostitutes themselves, while they were warned against harboring pimps, the viceroy took no action to curtail the sex trade altogether.[67]

From the early sixteenth century at least, contemporaries in Naples and members of the Viceregal court noted the presence of street prostitution and were especially concerned to enforce local taxes on the sex trade. Known in Neapolitan dialect as the *ngabellate*, these taxes were collected on a regular basis, anywhere from once per week to once per month, depending upon the scrupulousness of the local authorities.[68] A quick look at the court records from the Tribunale di San Lorenzo from the second half of the sixteenth century reveals the scale of the problem. Neighbours brought numerous cases against local women accused as prostitutes, their pimps and their clients. Interestingly, students are often among the targets of these legal proceedings. In July 1567, for example, the governors of the convent The Virgins of the Holy Spirit pleaded with the courts to evict (*sfrattare*) the inhabitants of an adjacent building, a group of 'students, prostitutes, and dishonest women,' in order to protect the honor and sanctity of their female charges. Apparently, this effort was successful.[69]

But beyond the moralizing of humanist reformers and local com-

---

Longman, 1988), 280; see also Carlo Cipolla, *Before the Industrial Revolution. European Society and Economy, 1000–1700* (New York: Norton, 1976), 281.

[66] *Privilegi et Capitoli con altre gratie concesse alla fidelissima città di Napoli* (1505), as cited in Di Giacomo, *La Prosituzione in Napoli*, 74.

[67] Viceroy Ferdinando di Cordova e d'Aguilar, as cited in ibid., 74–5.

[68] Ibid., 96–7.

[69] Acts of the Tribunal of San Lorenzo, Archivio Municipale di Napoli 1566–1575, as cited in ibid., 99–100.

EARLY JESUIT MISSIONS IN NAPLES, 1550–1620   81

munity members, and some seemingly ineffectual efforts at legislation, the problem of prostitution in Italy had complex causes and social implications. Because civic and viceregal government in Naples played such a relatively small role in social reform in this period, religious orders and lay congregation took up much of the work of housing women who, for various reasons, required shelter.[70] The Protestant Reformation certainly had an impact upon the development of these institutions, as Catholic reformers sought to deflect criticism of the supposedly debauched state of morality in Italian towns and cities, while also endorsing the notion that the conversion of the most despised members of society would facilitate an overall cleansing of the social body.

Part of the intensification of Catholic reform fervor in the sixteenth century lay in efforts to regulate social behavior more effectively through partnerships between religious reformers and the laity.[71] The Jesuits were just one among many religious orders that aimed to redress a range of social ills through the development of new institutions or the reorganization of old ones. The confraternities, for example, were a popular vehicle for such reform efforts. The revival in the demand to reform prostitutes, using coercive means if necessary, was only part of this larger movement. Where during the fifteenth century, public officials in many Italian cities sought to regulate prostitution, viewing it as a 'necessary evil,' by the sixteenth century, one can perceive a 'hardening of attitudes,' resulting in the greater stigmatization of prostitutes.[72]

The institutions specifically designed to house so-called 'deviant' women fell into two broad categories: refuges for so-called *convertite*, reformed prostitutes, and conservatories to prevent those in danger of falling into prostitution. Institutions of the former variety could be found in Naples from the early sixteenth century, often under the joint sponsorship of religious and lay reformers; the conservatories, however, developed somewhat later.[73] While it is hard to gauge the numbers of

---

[70] Cohen, *Evolution of Women's Asylums*, 63–7.

[71] See Brian Pullan, *Rich and Poor in Renaissance Venice: The Social Institutions of a Catholic State to 1620* (Cambridge, MA: Harvard University Press, 1971). For a comparative perspective across urban Italy, see his more recent study, 'Support and Redeem: Charity and Poor Relief in Italian Cities from the Fourteenth to the Seventeenth Century,' *Continuity and Change* 3 (1988): 177–208. The growth of custodial institutions, especially for prostitutes and/or vulnerable young girls, was part of a broader movement toward institutional responses to growing impoverishment in the sixteenth century.

[72] Cohen, *Evolution of Women's Asylums*, 32–3.

[73] Such was the case for the Neapolitan reform efforts sponsored by the religious reformer and founder of the Theatines Gaetano Thiene and the lay women Maria Lorenza

82 A PARADISE INHABITED BY DEVILS

women who availed themselves of such institutions, some figures do serve to illustrate the growing demand for female refuges over the latter part of the sixteenth century. Within the Neapolitan conservatories, largely run by the vast confraternity, the Compagnia dei Bianchi dello Spirito Santo, with whom the Jesuits and other orders worked, the population grew from 400 residents in 1587 to 1890 residents in 1608.[74]

For their part, the Jesuits became involved in reforming prostitutes almost from the outset, and this work retained an important place in their apostolic mission throughout the early modern period and beyond. The image of the unrepentant female sinner, often a prostitute, or a woman of supposedly questionable morals, was a standard feature of Jesuit missionary rhetoric, as it was of much medieval and early modern moral discourse. Because women were characteristically viewed as more prone to the seductions of the devil, providing 'stable, ordered culture' (*stabil cultura*) to poor women, so that they might become pious Christians, was considered all the more urgent.[75]

In 1543, Ignatius Loyola was instrumental in organizing the refuge of Santa Marta in Rome. During the next decade, similar institutions were established in such cities as Florence, Milan, Messina and Palermo. We get a sense of the purposes of such institutions in a 1551 memorandum by the Jesuits' Secretary, Juan Polanco. According to Polanco, the refuge had been instituted to cope with the growing number of women who sought a monastic vocation, but could not be accommodated by existing convents. Thus, the Casa Santa Marta functioned as both a permanent home for up to twenty nuns and a refuge for unmarried prostitutes and married women who had turned to prostitution. As founders of the refuge, the Jesuits assisted the confraternity that ran the facility in collecting alms and gaining papal approval for its operation; they selected the Casa's female director, and provided preachers and confessors for residents.[76]

Like other religious and lay reformers, the Jesuits saw three possible 'solutions' to reforming prostitutes, or preventing those in danger of falling into prostitution from doing so: matrimony, domestic service or entrance into a convent. To facilitate the former, they sought to

---

Longo and Maria Ayerbe. See Scaduto, *L'Epoca di Giacomo Laínez*, II: 641. The first refuge for *convertite* in Naples was established in 1538. Meanwhile, the first conservatory opened in Naples in 1564.

[74] Black, *Italian Confraternities*, 208. The Compagnia dello Spirito Santo, Naples' largest confraternity, boasted some 7000 members in 1563. On their wide-ranging reform activities, see 51.

[75] Santagata, *Istoria*, 3: 470.

[76] For a general discussion of the Jesuits' early ministry to prostitutes, cf. O'Malley, *First Jesuits*, 178–85, esp. 183.

EARLY JESUIT MISSIONS IN NAPLES, 1550–1620

collect dowries for refuge and conservatory residents alike. Confraternity members assisted in this work. The confraternities not only collected funds from members, but were apparently not shy about commenting on individual women's prospects for securing marriage proposals.[77]

As we have seen, the concern over reforming prostitutes had taken institutional shape in Naples prior to the mid-sixteenth century, but the Jesuits took an active role in promoting the reform of prostitutes from their first years there. As in other areas of Jesuit activity, Jesuit work among prostitutes was characterized by the order's particular strain of early modern Catholic Reformation piety and cultural values. When female confraternities were established under the guidance of Giovan Francesco Araldo in 1554, members were urged to take prostitutes into their homes, if necessary, until appropriate placements could be found.[78] Somewhat later, the Jesuits were instrumental in establishing residences for young women, such as the Conservatory of the Holy Spirit. This institution, established in the late sixteenth century, more closely resembled a prison than anything else, but its purpose was very much in keeping with Spinelli's wider goals for the urban missions:

> a Conservatory newly planted for worldly women, those enlightened by Heaven to see themselves before the entrance of Hell, where in order to burn [away] the foulness of their shameless lives, they resolved to close themselves as in a prison of Holy Penitence, to cleanse [their lives] again with tears, and to extinguish with these [tears] the flames they had earned.[79]

These new Jesuit-inspired institutions sought nothing less than the internal transformation of their subjects. But occasionally, if we glimpse beneath the triumphal rhetoric of Jesuit documents, there are traces of resistance to this kind of cloistering. Francesco Schinosi describes one such incident in which a group of about twenty residents escaped the confines of the Conservatory. These girls, who had been living in the Conservatory and had taken up the vestments of nuns, returned

---

[77] Christopher Black notes that the confraternity of SS Crocefisso in Naples offered higher dowry payments, on the whole, than those available in other Italian cities, though he gives no reason for this discrepancy. But despite the higher dowry price, the confraternity was known to delay disbursement for up to twenty years! For the seventeenth century, dowries averaged between 50 and 60 ducats. Black notes that in investigating claims to collect dowry payments: 'The officials investigating the cases made personal comments: "has the requisites and is, moreover, beautiful;" "of mediocre appearance, aged seventeen . . ."' Black, *Italian Confraternities*, 183–4.

[78] Araldo, *Cronica*, f. 15v/25; cf. Lewis, 'The Development of Jesuit Confraternities,' 215.

[79] Barone, *Della Vita*, 105.

84   A PARADISE INHABITED BY DEVILS

to the popular quarters of the city from which they had come. What is perhaps more revealing in the account is the Jesuits' incredulity that anyone might wish to escape their confinement to, as they characterized it, 'live as slaves of their relatives, miserable artisans, in miserable hovels.'[80]

This episode bears a striking resemblance to missionary incredulity when faced with Amerindian children's solidarity with their own parents during rebellions in New Spain. In both cases, the Fathers believed that their missionary subjects (whether MesoAmericans or young Neapolitan women from the popular classes) did not know what was best for themselves, because their 'level of civilization' (to use Acosta's character-ization) did not equip them for such efforts at self-reflection.[81] After all, the Jesuits imagined their project as one of cultural uplift. So central was the notion of the civilizing mission as an ethic of cultural betterment at the heart of the Jesuit ministry that they seemed baffled at such examples of popular non-compliance. This attitude can be understood best by referring to the analogy of a parent seeking to discipline an errant child. In a discussion of the work of the Jesuit reformer Benedetto Palmio with a Venetian conservatory, one historian argues: 'Palmio and his disciples were not attempting mere hand-to-mouth charity, by the temporary relief of physical needs: instead, they aimed at a takeover bid, at establishing an institution which would, in the interests of the soul, assume all the functions of a zealous and exacting parent.'[82] Cleansing Naples of the scourge of prostitution was just one of the ways in which the Jesuits imagined themselves purifying Naples and combating demonic influences on its apparently vulnerable population.

Another important area of reform work for the Jesuits' civilizing mission in Naples was in the prisons, where Jesuit missionaries aimed to alleviate some of the most dire conditions that prisoners faced, but expected certain behaviors from inmates in exchange for their assistance. The Neapolitan royal prison (which, along with the royal court, was known as the *Vicaria*) was notorious among early modern Italian penal institutions for the levels of violence within its walls, as well as the apparent extortion of prisoners by fellow inmates, jailers and custodians. The bulk of the prison population, apart from those awaiting trial, or execution, consisted of debtors and beggars. Imprisonment was not

---

[80] Schinosi, *Istoria*, 1: 377–8.

[81] See Richard Trexler, 'We Think, They Act: Clerical Readings of Missionary Theater,' in *Understanding Popular Culture. Europe from the Middle Ages to the Nineteenth Century*, ed. Steven L. Kaplan (Berlin and New York: Mouton, 1984), 189–227, esp. 227n.

[82] Pullan, *Rich and Poor in Renaissance Venice*, 390; cf. O'Malley, *First Jesuits*, 188.

EARLY JESUIT MISSIONS IN NAPLES, 1550–1620

envisioned as punitive, by and large, but as custodial. And though it was supposedly a short-term proposition, many individuals (and whole families) could spend a long period incarcerated.

If we examine a few of the relevant pragmatics issued by the viceregal administration during the late sixteenth and early seventeenth centuries, we can get some idea of the scope of the problem. One ongoing problem in the Neapolitan prisons was the assaults that took place inside the cells. As early as 1579, a pragmatic was drawn up to punish those who attacked fellow inmates.[83] But just ten years later, another pragmatic was needed to address the problem of weapons being smuggled into the *Vicaria* in the guise of apparel. According to this statute: 'all those who are incarcerated, as much for civil causes as for criminal, of whatever state, grade and condition, as much noble as commoner, present and future, are ordered and commanded not to dare, nor presume to carry, nor keep inside said cells said leather belts.'[84] Yet by 1593, authorities were still troubled by violence, apparently, because another pragmatic was issued banning all types of weapons that might lead to violent incidents.

Violence among prisoners was not the only concern within Neapolitan jails, however. In 1592, the problem of extortion was addressed by a statute that sought to combat the practice of powerful inmates extorting their fellows by 'making them pay for oil [for lamps] and making them give other illicit payments [. . .].'[85] In this way, powerful prisoners would set themselves up as 'bosses' and profit from their prison experiences.

But if the pragmatics demonstrate examples of prisoners taking advantage of one another, they also suggest that jailers and prison custodians also exploited vulnerable prisoners. One of the most egregious of these abuses, and one that directly affected religious reformers who sought to provide some basic necessities within the *Vicaria*, such as bedding and medical care, was the 'renting' of beds to prisoners for exorbitant prices. In theory, jailers were expected to provide some

---

[83] L. Giustiniani, *Nuova Collezione delle Prammatiche del Regno di Napoli* (Naples, 1804), Tomo 3, 141, cited in Romano Canosa and Isabella Colonello, *Storia del Carcere in Italia. Dalla Fine del Cinquecento all'Unità* (Bari: Sapere2000, 1984), esp. 77–86; 77. On the controversial practices of religious reformers in exacting confessions from condemned prisoners, see Giovanni Romeo's excellent study, *Aspettando il Boia. Condannati a morte, confortatori e inquisitori nella Napoli della Controriforma* (Florence: Sansoni, 1993). For a general discussion of the emergence of prisons in sixteenth-century Italy, see Dario Melossi and Massimo Pavarini, *The Prison and the Factory. Origins of the Penitentiary System*, trans. Glynis Cousins (London: The Macmillan Press, 1981), 63–80.

[84] Pragmatic of 5 May 1589, cited in *Storia del Carcere*, 78.

[85] *Storia del Carcere*, 79.

86   A PARADISE INHABITED BY DEVILS

finances to the confraternity that provided assistance to prisoners, but often, according to one source, jailers neither provided beds, among other necessities, nor reimbursed the reformers.[86]

The Jesuits became involved with reforming prisoners and prison conditions largely through pre-existing lay congregations like the *Compagnia dei Bianchi della Giustizia*, founded in Naples *c.* 1519, and through Jesuit-led initiatives like the 'Congregation of the Veneration of the Most Holy Sacrament,' spearheaded by Giovan Francesco Araldo in 1554, which devoted at least part of their charitable activities to working in the prisons, alongside work in hospitals and other service to the laity.[87] From at least 1579, according to Santagata's *Istoria*, the Jesuits established a nominal presence in the jails of the *Vicaria*. The Jesuits wrote about their experiences, for example, in a text that Pierantonio Spinelli produced based on his experiences working with the prison population, entitled 'Manual of Spiritual Reminders' (1601), which he presented to Cardinal Alfonso Gesualdo. The Jesuit historian presents an unproblematic portrait of the Jesuits selflessly working for the better conditions of prisoners and seeking ways to improve their spiritual health.[88]

But some scholars have raised important questions about the apparent benignity of the Jesuits' (and others') labors within the prisons in the sixteenth and seventeenth centuries, casting a jaundiced eye in particular on the efforts of reformers to secure a 'good death' for condemned prisoners by any means necessary. In a powerful recent study, Giovanni Romeo has argued that far from serving prisoners altruistically to provide spiritual and material aid, missionaries and the lay reformers whom they increasingly guided as 'comforters' required condemned

---

[86] Ibid.

[87] The Jesuit-led confraternity the Congregation of the Most Holy Sacrament was created in 1554, under the guidance of Giovan Francesco Araldo. On the early history of the confraternity and its place within the wider picture of Jesuit missionary activity in sixteenth- and seventeenth-century Naples, see Pasquale Lopez, 'Una Famosa Congregazione Laica,' in his *Clero, Eresia e magia*, 116–17; in his *Cronica*, Araldo himself makes only an oblique reference to the congregation, but notes that it will take up the work 'already instituted in Naples (after that most illustrious Compagnia de Bianchi, that was annihilated and destroyed through the work of the devil and the malignity of men [. . .]),' an apparent reference to the expulsion of several members of the confraternity in the mid-sixteenth century because of suspicions of heresy. See *Cronica*, f.13v/23. The exact origins of the *Bianchi* are somewhat murky, but it seems clear that the organization had strong ecclesiastical leadership by at least the 1530s, initially under strong guidance by the newly formed Theatine order; cf. Romeo, *Aspettando il Boia*, 105–108.

[88] Santagata, *Istoria*, 3: 344–5. I have been unsuccessful in tracking down this document, which may well have been destroyed; cf. Araldo, *Cronica*, f.184r/224. Cf. Lewis, 'The Development of Jesuit Confraternities,' 218.

EARLY JESUIT MISSIONS IN NAPLES, 1550–1620

prisoners to confess and repent for their sins before their execution, or face harangues, physical deprivations and even torture. Without mincing words, Romeo contends that the 'comfort' offered by reformers was less about 'rescuing souls' than work in the service of upholding an evolving disciplinary regime: 'more than a service of charity given to the forsaken in the name of the sacrifice of Christ, between 1500 and 1700, comfort represents the principal instrument for the legitimation of worldly justice, the stamp [of approval] affixed by the authorities that control souls to the decisions of the authorities that control bodies.'[89] In further support of his argument that reformers used unsavory tactics to coerce contrition that was meant to be given freely, Romeo cites a particularly striking example of a small group of Neapolitan Jesuits haranguing a condemned prisoner in a vain effort to exact his confession and assure his 'good death' at the scaffold. It is the case of Agostino D'Argenzio, a young Neapolitan condemned to death in 1610, and the account is reproduced from a document in the archives of the *Compagnia dei Bianchi della Giustizia* in Naples. The account describes D'Argenzio as afflicted by the devil, dying 'impenitent and obstinate,' and refusing confession, despite being:

> exhorted, implored, and compelled to do it for seven continuous days, night and day, by the entire Company, with great effort, ardor and anxiousness on the part of the brothers, who attended to this [matter] with exquisite diligence [. . .]And beyond the brothers with the vests, in order perhaps to inspire in him [D'Argenzio] greater fear and shame, Father Carlo Mastrillo, Father Pietro Antonio Spinelli, and Father Stefano Citarelli of the Society of Jesus, were also sent there [. . .]

In the end, rather than carry out his execution in a swift and merciful manner, the grim public execution was continuously interrupted, even as D'Argenzio was up on the gallows, by the priests' vain and dramatic efforts to force his confession. Finally, the report reveals that the condemned man, 'never wanting to receive the confession, was hanged miserably, mourned by everyone present there in the great concourse of the Mercato.'[90]

One can empathize with Romeo's distress at the misery that Jesuit 'comforters' inflicted upon a condemned man in their attempts to 'save his soul,' but it is also crucial to understand that it was precisely within the logic of the Jesuits' civilizing project that combating criminal or

---

[89] Romeo, *Aspettando il Boia*, IX.

[90] 'Il Martirio di Antonio D'Argenzio, alias il sergente Pacione' (15 February 1610), from an account preserved in the *Archivio della Compagnia dei Bianchi della Giustizia*, cited in Romeo, ibid., Appendice 3/3: 257–8; 147–8.

88   A PARADISE INHABITED BY DEVILS

immoral behavior, however defined, required such dramatic (and, by our standards, extreme) efforts on the part of missionaries. Just as Carlo Mastrilli had hoped to demonstrate to the laity in the aftermath of the 1585 Revolt, the Jesuits were ready and willing to stand in the breach in order to combat the 'evil' that they perceived was plaguing the city and infecting its population with dangerous ideas.

As in their work among prostitutes, the Jesuits hoped that missionary activity among prisoners might produce internal as well as external transformations. In a report written in the early seventeenth century, an unnamed Jesuit missionary remarks upon the founding of a congregation within the walls of the *Vicaria*, apparently instituted to both encourage greater piety and to train prisoners to 'learn Christian doctrine in order to teach others.' This idea of emphasizing internal education rested on the conviction that once prisoners got out of jail, they would be thankful for the opportunity to become better Christians and thus more likely to help convert the 'ignorant ones.' Since many came from rural backgrounds which were notoriously under served by parish clergy, Christianized former prisoners could serve in the latter's stead. This, in turn, would result in an overall increase in religious piety: 'Such people, when they get out of jail, praise and thank God, who has sent them to prison . . . [M]any confess to having known God as a result of being in jail and after they get out, they go back to their lands, teaching Christian doctrine to the ignorant and performing many other works of charity.'[91] The Jesuits looked to the newly converted former prisoners to further the aims of their civilizing mission and to publicize their good works in the villages and hamlets to which these subjects would presumably return. Inevitably, the Jesuits no doubt hoped that their efforts would encourage new followers, both within their urban ministries and in the rural missions which flourished in the seventeenth century.

The infidel at home: Converting Muslim slaves

Although the lure of foreign missions was always strong in the Society of Jesus, providing the most direct inspiration for the civilizing mission at home, efforts to convert Muslim slaves permitted novices to work with 'real' infidels while supporting the personnel needs of the Neapoli-

---

[91] ARSI, *Neap.* 73 [1613–39], Anonymous, 'Breve Relatione dell'opera instituta dentro le carceri della vicaria di Napoli,' no date given, ff. 100–101, esp. 100. Cf. Christopher Black's observations on Jesuit prison reform work in Italy generally, *Italian Confraternities*, 222.

tan Province.[92] Such work was important not only as a strategy to win more souls to Catholicism, but also because it constituted a kind of consolation prize for young Jesuits who failed to win placement in the more highly coveted missions to the Indies.[93] A number of Neapolitan Jesuits, notably Pierantonio Spinelli, made such work a priority, ostensibly because they saw the unchristian treatment of Muslim slaves as antithetical to Catholic reform values. Their criticism was not of slavery per se, but of the failure of slave owners to work for their slaves' conversion.

In this respect, the Jesuits were following in a long tradition of Church ambiguity on the question of slavery. According to the concept of 'just war,' articulated by Thomas Aquinas in the thirteenth century and later used by many to justify the enslavement of Turks, Africans, Amerindians and Slavs, any captive taken in battle could legitimately be enslaved.[94] Although individual popes might speak out against the immorality of slavery, the papacy clearly accepted the enslavement of Muslims and the economic viability of the slave trade and even availed itself of domestic slaves.[95]

Given the size of the slave population in early seventeenth-century Naples, there is surprisingly little information available on the early modern slave population in Italy, let alone Naples. Nevertheless, the Italian scholar Salvatore Bono estimates the early seventeenth-century figure for domestic slaves in Naples at 20 000, or roughly 10 per cent of the population of the city! Although this number may seem extraordinary, given Spain's extensive reconnaissance of North Africa during the sixteenth and early seventeenth centuries, as well as ongoing skirmishes with the Turks, many captives would have been taken to

---

[92] As with broader discussions of the prison population and prostitution, there is little empirical research on the Muslim slave population of Naples. For two brief considerations of the early modern slave experience which include references to southern Italy, see Salvatore Bono, 'Schiavi Musulmani in Italia nell'età moderna,' *Erdem* 3, No. 9 (July 1987): 829–38, and Corrado Marciani, 'Il Commercio degli Schiavi alle fiere di Lanciano nel sec. XVI,' *Archivio Storico per le province napoletane* 41 (1961): 269–82. (I thank Bob Davis for these citations). For an assessment of the congregations to convert Muslim slaves, especially the reform work sponsored by Naples' reforming bishop, Burali d'Arezzo, see Pasquale Lopez, 'La Riforma Tridentina a Napoli nell'Opera Pastorale del Burali d'Arezzo (1576–1578),' in his *Clero, Eresia e magia*, 57–111, esp. 102–109, and Gennaro Nardi, 'Nuove Ricerche,' 294–313.

[93] See Prosperi, 'Il Missionario,' 179.

[94] For a discussion of the application of the 'just war' argument to the sixteenth-century debate over the enslavement of Amerindians, see Anthony Pagden, *The Fall of Natural Man. The American Indian and the Origins of Comparative Ethnology* (Cambridge, UK: Cambridge University Press, 1982), esp. 27–33.

[95] Marciani, 'Il Commercio degli schiavi,' 270–72.

90 A PARADISE INHABITED BY DEVILS

Naples.[96] In general, the majority of male captives in early modern Italy would have worked as galley slaves on merchant or battle ships. The Mediterranean, in particular, was the scene of brutal warfare during this period. Just as Christians were captured and returned to the Ottoman Empire or North Africa to work as slaves, so the 'Turks' (a generic term which referred to all Muslims whether or not they were Turkish) were viewed as a legitimate source of forced labor. Captives were part of the 'booty' acquired in the corsair battles of the period. While many male captives worked the galleys, women and children were sent into domestic service. Not surprisingly, women were frequently subject to sexual exploitation, and young children were often seen as a source of amusement, a curiosity in Baroque court society.[97]

Partly in the interest of insuring decent treatment for Christian slaves in Muslim lands, but also inspired by the broader Catholic reform spirit of the time, missionaries and religious reformers worked to improve the treatment of Muslim slaves.[98] In 1601, the Congregation of the Epiphany was founded to direct conversion efforts. The new congregation was begun by the Jesuit Girolamo di Alesandro, an instructor in the Jesuit college who was inspired by a conversion story passed along to him by one of his students. When he heard of the youth's success, di Alesandro 'was greatly inflamed in his desire to make some similar conquest: so much so that he obtained license from his Rector [along with another Jesuit, Giacomo Antonio Giannoni] ... and both of them, during vacation days, took to intervening in the stables of the noble palaces, well furnished with slaves destined to work as stable hands.'[99] Di Alesandro boasted of converting twelve slaves within the course of a month, and took on the task of coordinating future efforts. But his work was not without nay-sayers. Some slave owners were suspicious of these activities. Just as some young girls had resisted their confinement in conservatories designed to protect them from the dangers of living in the popular quarters of the city, so some Muslim captives rejected the Jesuits' conversion efforts in favor of escaping their own confinement. Because of these escapes, slave owners may have looked upon these works of religious reform as potentially injurious to their financial well-being. Despite this kind of opposition, however, the Jesuits continued to

---

[96] Bono, 'Schiavi Musulmani in Italia,' 830–32. Frustratingly, Bono does not cite the source for his figures.

[97] Bono, 'Schiavi Musulmani in Italia,' 830–31.

[98] For a recent study of the enslavement of European Christians during the period of Barbary corsair battles, see Robert Davis, 'Counting European Slaves on the Barbary Coast,' *Past and Present* 172 (2001): 87–124.

[99] Santagata, *Istoria*, 3: 28–30.

EARLY JESUIT MISSIONS IN NAPLES, 1550–1620   91

build upon early missions to Muslim slaves, because they viewed their ill treatment as part of the wider environment of Neapolitan disorder and violence. No doubt, too, the reformers saw the potentially successful conversion of Muslims as an especially sweet victory, and one that they would be only too happy to publicize.

For Pierantonio Spinelli, there were two interrelated abuses associated with Neapolitans' treatment of Muslim slaves. The first abuse was that of Neapolitans' 'purchasing for themselves the most vile services of infidel house slaves,' without 'giving thought to winning them [over] to Christ.' The 'purchase of vile services' was a probable reference to the sexual exploitation of female (and perhaps male) domestic slaves, cited above. Equally objectionable for Spinelli was the fact that certain slave owners refused to provide any spiritual instruction to those slaves who might have shown some interest in 'the holy and new laws that they had taken to profess.' For Spinelli, both of these 'disorders' were 'so disagreeable to Christ and so prejudicial to souls that [they required] the most zealous fervor to repair [them].'[100] In this regard, Spinelli echoed the concerns expressed half a century earlier by Bartolomé de Las Casas over the *encomienda* system that predominated in Spanish America. For Las Casas, the *encomenderos* endangered the souls of Amerindians, as well as their own salvation, by exploiting their labors and failing to provide them with an education in Catholic doctrine.[101] As an enticement, Spinelli promised that those slaves who proved amenable to Jesuit conversion would enjoy better treatment and, in some cases, could use this avenue to win their freedom.[102]

In order to facilitate conversions and respond more effectively to abuses, Spinelli recommended that missionaries learn the mother tongue(s) of slaves, to better serve such potential subjects. In keeping with the broader Jesuit strategy of accommodation, he argued that the Jesuit college should offer novices instruction in languages like Turkish and then send them out to convert the 'infidels.' His biographer, Antonio Barone, describes Spinelli's approach: 'Father's idea was to send them touring through Naples, looking everywhere for these slaves. [And] these

---

[100] Barone, *Della Vita*, 100.

[101] For a synthesis of Las Casas' opposition to the *Encomienda* system as an obstacle to the evangelization of Amerindians, see *Witness. Writings of Bartolomé de Las Casas*, ed. George Sanderlin (Maryknoll, NY: Orbis Books, 1971), esp. 151–8.

[102] The reforming Archbishop Burali d'Arezzo, for example, advocated just such a 'deal' for converted slaves. See Lopez, 'La Riforma Tridentina a Napoli,' in his *Clero, eresia e magia*, 107–109. Although freedom may have been held out as an enticement toward conversion, neither Burali nor Pasquale Lopez makes clear how many individuals actually benefitted from this practice. Similarly, though Jesuit sources cite the 'benefits' which might accrue to Christianized slaves, they are not explicit on this score.

92   A PARADISE INHABITED BY DEVILS

[slaves], hearing for themselves those impassioned Religious announcing the Word of God [to them] in their mother tongue, little by little became tame with [the missionaries], and more easily gave them a hearing.'[103]

Beyond advocating for language instruction for Jesuit novices, Barone's account of Spinelli's intervention demonstrates the kind of confidence that the Jesuits apparently had in their civilizing mission among slaves. In this view, linguistic accommodation could be combined with Jesuit mastery and charisma to produce effective conversion and civilizing of the most alien members of Neapolitan society: infidel slaves. This kind of linguistic accommodation was noted in other parts of the Kingdom as well, where Jesuit missionary reports cite the distinct advantage of having missionaries conversant in local languages. This was particularly true among islanders who, due to their geographic isolation, might not have had previous exposure to Tuscan Italian, the common language of Jesuit missionaries in southern Italy. Southern Italian dialects remain geographically distinct even today, blending remnants of Arabic, Spanish and Greek with regional vernacular.

Another benefit to be gained from this work with Neapolitan slaves was that it fit well with the order's need to accommodate the desires of its members. In a 1603 visit to Naples, the Society's Superior General, Claudio Acquaviva, approved of the work of the Congregation of the Epiphany, a more formal institution designed to direct conversion efforts. In responding to those Jesuit novices who had not been selected to take up the much sought-after missions in the Indies, Acquaviva offered conversion efforts among Neapolitan infidels as a potentially attractive alternative. He was described as asking these novices 'to prepare themselves for the conversion of the Infidels, [and] . . . to win the existing slaves [residing] in Naples to the Holy Faith [. . .]. He also advised them that their linguistic inexperience was an insurmountable impediment to converting those who didn't yet know how to speak Italian.'[104]

Acquaviva encouraged the novices to pursue their language studies as an essential tool to win over new converts. To facilitate this process, he announced the foundation of an academy of languages, to be organized by Spinelli. Thus the work among Muslim slaves, like much of the order's apostolic activity in Naples, combined the development of educational institutions with social reform efforts. The Jesuits hoped that the newly converted Muslim slaves would in turn encourage the conversion of their compatriots. There is no solid evidence to indicate that significant numbers of Muslim captives actually converted. But like their

---

[103] Barone, *Della Vita*, 101–102.
[104] Santagata, *Istoria*, 3: 28.

EARLY JESUIT MISSIONS IN NAPLES, 1550–1620

work among prostitutes and Neapolitan prisoners, Jesuit attempts to effect cultural and religious reform among 'infidels' led to the development of local initiatives and institutions. All of these projects were aimed at a broader civilizing mission to address the apparent inadequacies of the Neapolitan popular classes and to try to prevent upheavals like the 1585 Revolt.

By the early seventeenth century, the Jesuits' urban missions had begun to take root in Naples. Preaching to the poor, working with prostitutes, ministering to prisoners and converting Muslim slaves became vital activities for the growing missionary order, allowing members both to respond to the specific challenges of the southern Italian city and to define for itself a wider reforming agenda. Pierantonio Spinelli played a key role in the evolution of the urban missions, which soon spread to other parts of Italy. Beyond the urban missions, however, Spinelli's innovations led to a number of other changes in the development of popular missionary practice. Popular preaching spread beyond churches to hospitals, prisons and the rural hinterlands. The Jesuits stressed the issuing of religious medals, sacred images, crowns and little spiritual books as 'gifts' to offer to those who responded to their endeavors. Women and children were brought into the popular practice of sacred processionals, though always according to the rules of propriety, and penitential disciplining grew more widespread. Finally, the Jesuits attempted to popularize the ritual of the *Quarant'Ore*; or forty continuous hours of religious observance as an alternative to the revelries of Carnival. Such practices were intended to sacralize popular practices, but even so, troubles might sometimes ensue. Flavio Rurale has shown, for example, how one Jesuit preacher in Milan, Giulio Mazzarino, was drawn into a dispute with Archbishop Carlo Borromeo and the Inquisition in 1579 over a controversial sermon delivered on the last day of Carnival. In this case, the issue was not so much one of Mazzarino's indulging superstitious practices, but of breaking one of the cardinal rules set out for Jesuit preachers: avoiding controversy in popular sermons. None the less, Mazzarino's case suggests the potential pitfalls inherent in encouraging a certain degree of autonomy among individual Jesuit personnel.[105]

By the end of the sixteenth century, all Jesuits were required to

---

[105] Barone, *Della Vita*, 118–21. On the institution of the 'Quarant'Ore', see Schinosi, *Istoria*, II, 89–91. For the discussion of Mazzarino's difficulties, see Flavio Rurale, 'Carlo Borromeo and the Society of Jesus in the 1570's,' in *The Mercurian Project: Forming a Jesuit Culture, 1572–1580*, ed. Thomas M. McCoog SJ (St Louis and Rome: Jesuit Historical Institute, in press). Many thanks to Tom McCoog for making this as yet unpublished essay available to me.

94 A PARADISE INHABITED BY DEVILS

participate in popular missions. Yet despite this directive, it was the actual experience of developing flexible missionary strategies and institutions appropriate to meeting the challenges of the day which gave life to the Jesuits' missions. Within this context, Naples represented a laboratory out of which much of the raw material for the popular missions emerged between 1550 and 1620. Following upon Spinelli's example, the Society of Jesus would initiate systematic preaching missions in both urban and, increasingly, rural parts of Italy. Within the complex agenda of such missions, strategies arrived at through practice would be balanced with the broad pastoral goals outlined by Loyola and his early companions. Although the principle of accommodation dictated the utmost flexibility in assessing each mission field, those areas of reform that had provided the Neapolitan Jesuits with a proving ground – popular preaching, teaching Christian doctrine, reforming prostitutes – would continue to engage their energies.

CHAPTER THREE

Reverberations from the New World

O, my dearest father, if you could see the extreme ruin of many souls and how they are lost on account of the dreadful ignorance that reigns in these mountains, as much in the ecclesiastic [realm] as in the secular, you would have compassion for them. And just as some of ours [Jesuits] go to the Indies, here, it seems to me, they could accomplish as much in the service of God [. . .] because there is a great necessity to extirpate many errors, superstitions and abuses of which there are an abundance.[1]

Miguel Navarro's 1575 letter to the Society of Jesus' fourth Superior General, Everard Mercurian, presents a striking example of how one Jesuit missionary viewed southern Italy as an ideal locus for the Jesuits' Christianizing efforts. By invoking the Indies, Navarro repeats what had by then become a common analogy between a missionary project in the New World (or, just as often, the recently colonized parts of East Asia) and an equally urgent call for civilizing the 'Indies down here.' Just as the urban missions in Naples sought to promote moral reform among the citizenry, rural missions might confront a parallel 'savagery' that supposedly dominated the more remote reaches of the Kingdom.

For Jesuits like Navarro, much could be gained by working to combat the supposed ignorance and barbarity of southern Italian communities. Navarro's letter raises a number of interesting questions about the nature of the Jesuits' civilizing mission and the relationship between work in the Indies and the more 'backward' regions of Europe such as the Kingdom of Naples. For example, by citing the 'dreadful ignorance that

---

[1] For Navarro's letter to Mercurian, dated 24 January 1575, see Pietro Tacchi Venturi, *Storia della Compagnia*, 1/2: 92–5, esp. 92–3. Navarro set out with a companion from the Jesuit college at Messina (Sicily) in the winter of 1575 to conduct preaching missions in the mountains of southern Calabria, then still considered a part of the Sicilian Province. Well before Navarro, however, other Jesuits had made the linkage between work in the Indies and in more remote parts of southern Europe. According to Adriano Prosperi, Silvestro Landini was the first to make an explicit connection between the task of evangelizing among Amerindian pagans and their European counterparts, in this case Corsicans, in 1552. Prosperi also notes that Ignatius Loyola was aware of the need to provide consolation to those Jesuits rejected from missionary service in the Indies by reminding them that they could provide much service in 'our Indies.' See Prosperi, *Tribunali della Coscienza*, esp. 551–8.

96   A PARADISE INHABITED BY DEVILS

reigns in these mountains, as much in the ecclesiastical [realm] as in the secular,' Navarro anticipates the observations of José de Acosta, a notable proponent of the Jesuits' missionary efforts in the Americas. Like Acosta, Navarro links a lack of civility with religious ignorance, implying that true Christianization would require a concerted program of cultural reform, in addition to religious training.

Navarro's mention of the need to 'extirpate many errors, superstitions, and abuses' suggests a curious parallel in the missionary impulse at home and abroad. According to this view, southern Italian peasants and herdsmen, like urban commoners, were nominally Christians, unlike their Amerindian or Asian counterparts. And yet, their 'ecclesiastical and secular ignorance' rendered them equally fruitful targets for the Jesuits' labors. Even so, the Society's administrators recognized the need to convince novices that such less than glamorous work was as vitally important as the apparently more glorious missions to the Indies. After all, not all Jesuits were suited to the rigors of life in far-flung mission fields. Hundreds of Neapolitan Jesuits hoped to follow heroic models like Francis Xavier, or his successor in leading the East Asian missions, the southern Italian Alessandro Valignano, to distant locations around the globe.[2] Yet this was not practical for the order. Jesuit leadership in Naples (and elsewhere) had to consider how to meet increasing demands for its services at home with a finite number of laborers.

Navarro highlights such practical considerations as the most effective use of limited personnel and resources in his recommendation to General Mercurian that Jesuit novices should be sent to the rural hinterlands of southern Italy as a proving ground before being shipped off to the Indies:

> I believe that just as the Society has houses of probation for the novitiates, these mountains of Sicily [and Calabria] could be a place where those who desire to go to the Indies can prove their worth. I am certain, in fact, that whomever will prove himself well in these, *our Indies*, will be successful in those more remote ones; and, on

---

[2] Valignano (1529–1606), born in Chieti (Abruzzo Citra), Italy, was sent to Goa, India in 1574 to serve as Visitor, in charge of all Jesuit missionary activity and personnel across the continent. Valignano was particularly known for his principles of cultural adaptation, which he articulated in missionary instructions and treatises from his work in Japan, in particular, and which became a source of controversy in the order (and beyond) later in the seventeenth century. On Valignano, see especially Josef Franz Schütte SJ, *Valignano's Mission Principles for Japan*, trans. John J. Coyne SJ (St Louis: The Institute of Jesuit Sources, 1980); cf. Andrew C. Ross, *A Vision Betrayed: The Jesuits in Japan and China, 1542–1742* (Edinburgh: Edinburgh University Press, 1994).

REVERBERATIONS FROM THE NEW WORLD   97

the contrary, those who have trouble here will not be of much use elsewhere.[3]

These comments represent a relatively early recognition that the missions in southern Italy and the Indies were parallel efforts, part of a larger project for religious, cultural and social reform. But they also show the pervasive concern with pragmatism in the order.

This chapter explores the complexities of the Jesuits' civilizing mission in the Kingdom of Naples and abroad. In the first part of the chapter, I consider the lure of the Indies for Neapolitan Jesuits and how their superiors evaluated whom to send to distant mission fields, while balancing the needs of the order closer to home. Adriano Prosperi has argued persuasively that the powerful lure of the Indies was not only pervasive within the Society of Jesus in the sixteenth and seventeenth centuries, appealing to a variety of needs among individual members of the order, but that news of Jesuits' labors in 'exotic' locales could bolster the sprits of those working in more mundane conditions, even when the Jesuits faced their most troubling times.[4]

Francis Xavier became an important early model for young novices seeking a missionary vocation in distant lands and, after his death in 1552, became the source for a popular religious cult that had special resonance in the Italian *Mezzogiorno*. But the Jesuits obviously could not send all the young novices who requested missions in the Indies and still meet the demands for their labors closer to home. The order responded to growing concerns over the supposed backwardness and incivility of Naples and its hinterlands by making direct comparisons between work among 'gentiles' in the Indies and among their very own

---

[3] Letter of Navarro, in Tacchi Venturi, *Storia della Compagnia*, 1/2: 93 (emphasis mine). Although there is no evidence that Mercurian ever considered formally implementing Navarro's plan, the suggestion alone speaks volumes about the perceptions of rural southern Italy as an appropriate 'staging ground' for broader missionary activity. On wider problems with personnel in southern Italy during the formative generalate of Everard Mercurian, see Mark A. Lewis SJ and Jennifer D. Selwyn, 'Jesuit Activity in Southern Italy during the Generalate of Everard Mercurian,' in *The Mercurian Project: Forming a Jesuit Culture, 1573–1580*, ed. Thomas M. McCoog SJ (St Louis and Rome: Jesuit Historical Institute, in press).

[4] For examples of several earlier letters that invoke the 'other Indies,' and the uses of rhetorical value of this term, cf. Prosperi, *Tribunali della Coscienza*, esp. 551–61 and 561. While Prosperi notes the degree to which the deployment of the notion of 'our Indies' represented a practical 'substitution' for the order's superiors, his gaze is much broader than exploring the Society of Jesus's internal missions in the *Mezzogiorno*; cf. Elisa Novi Chavarria, '"Las Indias De Por Acà" Nelle Relazioni dei Gesuiti Napoletani,' now available in *Il Governo delle Anime*, 141–56, esp. 143. Novi Chavarria's most interesting (if debatable) suggestion is that the use of this discourse of the familiar 'other,' who is one's neighbor, declines after the mid-seventeenth century.

98   A PARADISE INHABITED BY DEVILS

neighbors. In so doing, the Jesuits elaborated a missionary program for cultural and religious reform that was truly global in nature, yet ever vigilant to balance the order's broader vision with adaptation to local realities and challenges.

José de Acosta, a fellow Spanish Jesuit, was also a crucial figure in the elaboration of the cultural map upon which the Jesuits' civilizing mission in the Americas was based. Like Xavier, Acosta's writings help us to appreciate the emergence of a 'heroic' missionary identity that was being forged in the Society of Jesus by the end of the sixteenth century.

The lure of the Indies

Young Jesuits coming of age in the second half of the sixteenth century were certainly raised on the discovery literature which held wide appeal among literate Europeans across the continent. From the early publication of Columbus's letters to Ferdinand and Isabella to published accounts by chroniclers ranging from Bernal Díaz to Francisco Lopez de Gómara, these novices would have been imbued with a strong sense of both the apparent valor of the European conquerors in the New World and the daunting but 'glorious' challenges which faced would-be evangelizers in the Americas.[5] We have a rich source for understanding the profound draw that the Indies held on the imaginations of young Jesuit novices in a collection of formal letters requesting missionary vocations beyond Europe's borders. The *Indipetae* illuminate both the widespread appeal of the Indies for Jesuit novices and the means by which members of the Society of Jesus attempted to convince superiors of their suitability for such vocations. The occasional annotations by provincial leaders on a prospective missionary's qualifications also provide a fascinating glimpse at the Jesuits' emerging notion of the 'ideal' missionary. They show the evolution of key criteria for judging prospective missionaries, which included an emphasis on such personal qualities as: good health, piety, sound judgement and obedience, as well as novices's ability to exploit patronage networks. Because the *Indipetae* for Italy include

---

[5] A recent exploration of the 'desire for the Indies' among Italian Jesuits is Gian Carlo Roscioni, *Il Desiderio delle Indie. Storie, sogni e fughe di giovani gesuiti italiani* (Milan: Einaudi, 2001). Bernal Díaz and Francisco Lopez de Gómara are two of the most important early chroniclers of the New World conquests. There have been countless studies of the nature and impact of discovery literature on early modern European consciousness, but just to name two excellent overviews: John H. Elliott, *The Old World and the New, 1492–1650* (Cambridge, UK: Cambridge University Press, 1970) and, on the Italian reception to discovery literature, Rosario Romeo, *Le Scoperte Americane nella Coscienza Italiana del Cinquecento* (Milan-Naples: R. Ricciardi, 1971).

REVERBERATIONS FROM THE NEW WORLD 99

hundreds of letters, dating from 1589 to 1649, it is possible to suggest both the numerical predominance of requests from the Neapolitan Province and trace periods of more intense interest in such missions in southern Italy.[6]

Although many letter writers clung to formulaic recitations of their qualifications and motives for seeking placement in missions to the Indies, the *Indipetae* also contain several poignant letters, most notably from individuals who desperately sought placement in foreign missions over a period of years, only to be rejected again and again. Young Jesuits in the Neapolitan Province actively pursued missions in the Indies. Besides the obvious motivation of obtaining glory through the possibility of martyrdom in far-off, 'exotic' locales, novices also apparently looked to promote the greater glory of the Neapolitan Province through such labors. The Society encouraged its leaders to distribute letters from the Indies among the novices to inspire their continued fervor and to build a sense of solidarity and commitment to forging a universal evangelizing strategy. Finally, some Neapolitan Jesuits made direct linkages between their own work in the Indies and the tasks facing communities in southern Italy, suggesting an awareness among at least some members of the order of the ties that bound places like Naples and the wider world to be conquered for the Catholic Church and civilization.

During one of his early visits to Naples as the fifth General of the Society of Jesus in 1586, Claudio Acquaviva brought just such letters to motivate the eager novices with the promise that if they continued to pursue their studies, they might have reasonable hopes of being sent to the Indies. According to one Jesuit chronicler, these letters apparently had an immediate impact on the novices: '[W]hether from India or from Poland,' the letters inspired 'great enthusiasm, announcing the arrival in those countries of some Fathers of our Kingdom.' Novices were especially inspired by the news of Neapolitan missionaries like Michele Ruggieri, one of the first Jesuits in China, and Pietro Paolo Navarra, an early Jesuit martyr in Japan. By invoking Navarra, Acquaviva stirred the instinct toward martyrdom that drove many religious enthusiasts during

---

[6] According to my consultation of the *Indipetae Italia* for the years 1589–1648, ARSI, F.G. 733–745, there were well over three hundred requests for placement in missions to the Indies in the Provinces of Naples and Sicily alone. For the year 1620, for example, southern Italy accounted for 55 out of 113 requests among all the Society's Italian provinces. That same year, according to available figures, there were approximately 579 members of the Society of Jesus in its Neapolitan Province. Population figures for the Jesuits are scattered throughout the provincial documents, see esp. ARSI, *Neap.* 72 and 73. For a useful table with reliable membership figures, cf. Mario Rosa, 'Appendix 1,' *Religione e Società*, 271.

100 A PARADISE INHABITED BY DEVILS

the early modern period, noting that the missionary had 'made illustrious the Japanese flames by dying in these.' Even beyond death, through the dissemination of his letters, Navarra 'set fire to the Youth here, studying to go there to work in those missions, [and] at the end to perpetuate the glory of the Law of Christ *and of our Province* with their sweat and blood.'[7]

Why did Jesuit novices seek placement in missions in the Indies? As the description above suggests, novices were often 'set afire' by the letters from their brethren in the field and the promise of serving the greater glory of God and the Society in the Indies of the East, or the Americas. But some, too, may have hoped to escape the drudgery of less glorious activities closer to home. We get this impression, for example, in an early letter by Nicolò Mastrilli, written to Claudio Acquaviva in 1590:

> It has been close to seven years since I wrote to Your Paternity when I was a first-year novice who desired to go to the Indies or to China . . . now that same desire has grown in great measure through all this time, [and] judging that it is a most evident sign of a Divine Vocation, it seems [worthwhile] to represent myself [to you] with much more affection than before.

Although Mastrilli tries to assure Acquaviva that he receives great consolation from his work teaching Christian doctrine to young boys, he suggests that his skills, and the divine will of God, might be better served by sending him to the Indies. Thinking about being sent abroad fills him 'with fervor and incredible happiness.' And while he claims that he is also gratified by his work teaching Catholic doctrine to school boys, 'an occupation *which with great contentment I would spend my life*,' the tone of the letter bespeaks a certain weariness with such mundane tasks. Nevertheless, Mastrilli knows better than to make his possibly baser motives explicit to the Father General. Instead, he relies upon a tried and true method of invoking God's will and the persistence of his dream of a missionary vocation: 'However, seeing other signs through which the Divine Vocation is more manifestly demonstrated, which conquests . . . makes my hope [of being sent to the Indies] grow marvelously. This vocation [to the Indies] seems to me to naturally have the ability to resist whichever impediment stands in its

---

[7] Schinosi, *Istoria*, 2: 54–5 (emphasis mine). Although Schinosi mentions the reporting of the active participation of Jesuits in the battle against heresy in places like Poland, my reading of the *Indipetae* does not reveal a groundswell of interest in placement in missions in Central or Eastern Europe.

way . . .'.[8] No doubt Mastrilli did feel that he was following God's plan for him, yet his letter reveals an awareness of rhetorical strategies that might help his dream along.

Others explicitly invoked the Society's vocation to 'help one's neighbors' as a primary motivating factor in their desire to serve in far-flung missions. Such is the case with Francesco Pavone in a 1590 letter to his superiors in Rome. Like Mastrilli, Pavone wrote his letter shortly after receiving news of his fellow member of the Neapolitan Province Michele Ruggieri's arrival in China. Pavone makes specific reference to Ruggieri within his more customary recitation of an apparently uncontrollable desire to be sent to the Indies: 'Truly, this desire has always been resolute in my soul, and everyday, it has been growing [so that] now, it seems to me that I should manifest it in every way . . . that it is my particular obligation, that I am a member of the Society of Jesus where one makes this profession to help one's neighbors, especially those who have the greatest need of it.[9] By invoking the 'greater need' of his services in the Indies, Pavone seeks to move beyond expressing the seemingly more personal motivation of fulfilling a 'desire' to realize this vocation, even if it is couched in the language of serving the divine will. With his subtle reference to Loyola's admonition to his brethren to serve in that part of 'Christ's Vineyard' where they might be most effective, Pavone demonstrates an understanding of his institutional duties and purpose. By mentioning to Acquaviva that he has been counseled by his provincial superior, Pierantonio Spinelli, to demonstrate 'something in the service of God' and to consider learning the requisite languages, Pavone also shows a sensitivity to the patronage networks within the order that might enable a novice to achieve his desired vocation.[10]

---

[8] ARSI, *F.G.* 733, *Indipetae 2 Italia*, Doc. 11/1, Nicolò Mastrilli, 'Letter to Claudio Acquaviva' (Naples, 28 June 1590) (emphasis mine). Interestingly, although he discusses the activities of his two brothers, Gregorio and Carlo, Araldo does not mention Nicolò Mastrilli.

[9] ARSI, *F.G.* 733, *Indipetae 2 Italia*, Doc. 12, 'Letter of Francesco Pavone' (Naples, 24 June 1590). Other Neapolitan Jesuits who make specific reference to Ruggieri's inspiration during the same year are Matteo d'Aruano and Giulano Pesce (ibid., Docs 10 and 11). I have found a total of ten requests for placement in missions in the Indies for the year 1590 in the Neapolitan Province alone.

[10] Although he never achieved his goal of being sent to China, Pavone (1569–1637) did go on to play an important role in the Neapolitan Jesuit community. In addition to teaching Humanities, Philosophy, Theology and Hebrew at the Jesuit College in Naples, Pavone helped to revive an important Neapolitan congregation in the early seventeenth century. Although falsely credited to Pierantonio Spinelli (see Ch. 2, fn 100), Pavone wrote the *Manuale di Alcuni ricordi spirituali, con diverse meditazioni ed istruzioni per introdurre esercizi di pietà* (Naples, 1601). On his numerous publications (over 24), see Sommervogel, *Bibliothèque de la Compagnie de Jésus* 6: 390–95.

102 A PARADISE INHABITED BY DEVILS

If some neophyte Jesuits like Pavone acknowledged both the foundational goals of the Society of Jesus to be of service to others and the more pragmatic concerns of the order's leadership in their letters, these practical matters are even more evident in the comments of provincial superiors that sometimes annotate the *Indipetae*. Superiors looked for a balance of strong personality traits, experience and sound judgment in choosing potential missionaries for sought-after assignments in new lands. Even those who appeared to have strong abilities or talents might fall short of the mark. We see this, for example, in one Neapolitan Provincial superior's evaluation of the novice Carlo di Gennaro. While di Gennaro is credited with possessing 'mediocre ability, good judgment and prudence' and is deemed 'very mature and pleasant,' his apparently limited 'experience of things' concerns his superior. Meanwhile, although di Gennaro strikes his evaluator as singularly virtuous, he is less certain of the youth's potential leadership qualities: 'He is very virtuous, humble, obedient, and very submissive, and of singular devotion and he has the desire to suffer, and is very zealous of soul. But he is very cautious, which impedes him to a great degree from governing well, from confessing, in dealing with his neighbors, and all the other duties of the Society.'[11] Thus, it seems that would-be missionaries to the Indies were expected to be go-getters, self-starters and men who might inspire the confidence of neophyte converts and fellow evangelizers alike.

But while the Society of Jesus certainly shied away from accepting as missionaries those who exhibited excessive timidity, superiors were equally concerned about those who displayed an overly independent demeanor. Of one unfortunate Neapolitan novice, Vito Vignapiano, a Neapolitan Provincial complains: 'He is not very devoted, humble, [nor] obedient, he has his own mind, and is very quick to anger.'[12] Apparently, Father Vignapiano's prospects did not look bright.

While the Neapolitan Provincials evaluated candidates' internal qualities, the late sixteenth-century Sicilian Provincial, Bartolomeo Ricci, seems far more concerned about the physical health of potential missionaries. For example, of one request for a missionary vocation, Ricci cautions: 'Father Antonio Cicala doesn't have the health for such a voyage, [for such] hardships and labors; even if he had the spiritual stability for a similar business, I would not send him.' By contrast, Ricci's consideration of another novice reveals: 'Niccolò Longobardo seems to me to have very good health, fervor and zeal.'[13]

---

[11] ARSI, *F.G.* 733, *Indipetae 2 Italia*, Doc. 30 (Naples, 1592).

[12] ARSI, *F.G.* 733, *Indipetae 2 Italia*, Doc. 36 (Naples, 1592). I would like to thank Julia Hairston and William Bowsky for helping me to translate this tricky passage.

[13] ARSI, *F.G.* 733, *Indipetae 2 Italia*, Doc. 25/1 (Palermo, April 1592). While this

These comments by Jesuit Provincial superiors, with all of their variations in emphasis and tone, reveal the gradual development of notions of the 'ideal' missionary, which find echoes in the writings of Francis Xavier and José de Acosta. They also suggest that, quite apart from the rhetorical flourishes and displays of passionate engagement with which novices tried to imbue their letters, superiors had much more pragmatic concerns. They wanted strong, healthy, stable and judicious missionaries who could combine evidence of leadership abilities with a willingness to comply with directives from above. In seeking out these qualities, southern Italian Provincials were simply responding to a developing notion of collective identity within the growing Jesuit order.

Already by 1550, just ten years after the order's founding, Juan de Polanco (hereafter, Polanco), the Society of Jesus' first Secretary, had drawn up a list of the 16 qualities which an ideal Jesuit should possess. This list highlighted the need for flexibility and a serene disposition. Would-be missionaries, whether they were destined for the Indies or commissioned to European locales like Naples, had to have sufficient training in theology to fulfill the ecclesiastical duties of their office, but character traits seemed to take prominence in Provincials' assessments.[14]

While novices were quick to dispel any potential concerns that superiors might have had over their suitability for a missionary vocation to the Indies, they also became increasingly conscious of the need to demonstrate a commitment to the broader goals of the order. We have already seen the novice Francesco Pavone's reference to the Jesuits' 'profession to help one's neighbors' in his request to be sent to the Indies, but he was not alone in this awareness. For example, the Sicilian novice Niccolò Longobardo, cognizant of the importance of theological training, assured his Provincial Ricci that he would be adequately prepared. While Longobardo hails from the neighboring Jesuit Province of Sicily, his case is also instructive. Longobardo was engaged in the first year of his theological training, Ricci notes, 'with the hope that a second [year] should be enough for him.' Indeed, Longobardo got his wish to be dispatched to the Indies within a few years, embarking for Goa in 1596, and spending a long life as a Jesuit missionary in Asia, before his death in Beijing in1655 at the age of 90.[15] In the case of southern Italy,

---

reference takes us out of the immediate discussion of the Kingdom of Naples, the conceptualization of Sicily as part of the 'Indies down here' makes the comments of both Sicilian Provincials and prospective missionaries valid for this discussion.

[14] For an overview of those qualities considered ideal for Jesuits (whether primarily aimed at a missionary vocation, or otherwise), cf. O'Malley, *First Jesuits*, 81–4.

[15] ARSI, *F.G. 733, Indipetae 2 Italia*, Doc. 25/1 (Palermo, April 1592). On the fortunes of Longobardo and of other Italian Jesuits who were sent to the East in the

104 A PARADISE INHABITED BY DEVILS

novices manifested their awareness of the order's collective aims by citing the urgency of conducting missionary activity in 'the Indies down here,' if only as a training ground for more glorious endeavors further afield. Novices like Giuseppe Cocollo reflect this understanding in their requests to be considered for missions in the Indies after having first proven themselves at home. In a 1602 letter which might have pleased Miguel Navarro, Cocollo writes:

> These past few days the Father Provincial was visiting this college and I expressed to him the desire [that I share] with so many of the others to go to the Indies. Father Provincial said these words to me: 'Giuseppe, Our Father salutes you and tells you to apply [yourself] well to going toward perfection in these Indies down here and later [he will] send you to the other Indies.' [T]hese words have left me with such consolation and happiness.[16]

Similarly, Pierantonio Castelli's 1603 letter casts his explicit interest in serving in Peru within the context of broad experience and education at home. While Castelli does not invoke the promises of his Provincial in efforts to persuade the General, Acquaviva, he provides a detailed list of his responsibilities and areas of training before putting on the rhetorical gloss:

> It has been [for] about fifteen years that, thanks to the singular grace of God, I have served in our Society. I have studied philosophy and three years of theology. I have taught school in [the] humanities and grammar. I have been a minister for three years, and preached for as long ... Currently, I read lessons in church, I lead a congregation of noblemen and [hear] confessions ... I am robust ... I do not have any illnesses nor suffer from any bad habits.[17]

I would like to suggest that both Cocollo's and Castelli's letters reflect the emerging missionary identity which began to take shape in the Society by the early seventeenth century. Just at the period when key figures in the order like Pierantonio Spinelli were forging more systematic approaches to missionizing among urban populations like Naples, novices were also responding to the call by Acquaviva for serious candidates for missionary vocation.

Acquaviva's formal requirement for Jesuits to conduct internal missions in Europe was disseminated throughout the Society of Jesus in a series of letters written between 1590 and 1602. These letters included

---

sixteenth century, see Maria Iris Gramazio, 'Gesuiti Italiani Missionari in Oriente nel XVI Secolo,' *AHSI* 66 (July–December 1997): 286.

[16] ARSI, *F.G.* 733, *Indipetae 2 Italia*, Doc. 144, 'Letter of Giuseppe Cocollo' (Naples, 13 July 1602).

[17] ARSI, *F.G.* 733, *Indipetae 2 Italia*, Doc. 235, 'Letter of Pier'Antonio Castelli' (Palermo, 1 April 1603).

general instructions for carrying out these missions, as well as suggestions for the ideal qualities that potential missionaries should possess. In an early version of his instructions, Acquaviva clarifies the fundamental requirements for the missionary vocation. He echoes the judgment of Provincial superiors by stressing that ideal candidates 'are people of great confidence and maturity.' Moreover, Acquaviva seconds Polanco's concern that would-be missionaries combine academic training with a talent for evangelizing: 'It is well if they have an ample gift for the use of our faculties, and grace in the aid of souls.' Finally, mirroring José de Acosta's emphasis on accommodating to the particularities of local communities and contexts, Acquaviva suggests that regional Jesuit leaders be given some discretion in instructing the missionaries under their charge: 'The other instructions [will be given] according to the qualities of the countries and the [choice of] people, according to the prudence of the Fathers Provincials.'[18] Again, we see an emphasis on the possession of basic talents and experience alongside a demonstration of solid character traits. But at this stage, Acquaviva is not very specific in his instructions.

As much as these kinds of formal suggestions might inform the self-presentation of prospective missionaries in their efforts to secure coveted assignments, real-life models like the early Jesuit missionary Francis Xavier offered concrete examples of the missionary vocation in action. Francis Xavier's life and missionary legacy, like those of some of his important successors, provided direct inspiration to young Jesuits, including those in the Neapolitan Province, where a strong cult grew up around his memory. From the outset of the Society of Jesus, Francis Xavier contributed greatly to an emerging Jesuit missionary identity.

The Model Missionary: Francis Xavier

Francis Xavier (1506–52), who became known as the 'Apostle of the Indies,' played a signal role in establishing a personal model for missionary leadership, aspirations and decorum for generations of young novices in the Society of Jesus. As one of the original members of the

---

18 ARSI, *Neap.* 202, 'Lettera di N.P. Claudio Acquaviva,' f. 33. This cautious approach to determining which members of the order might be well suited to missions in the Indies is echoed by Alessandro Valignano in an earlier letter, written to Everard Mercurian on 4 December 1575, in which Valignano urges his general to be careful not to send men to the East Indies who have misconceptions about missionary work there. See Roscioni, *Il Desiderio delle Indie*, 98.

106 A PARADISE INHABITED BY DEVILS

order and the first to venture beyond the borders of Europe, Xavier became an important symbol not just for the Society of Jesus, but indeed for the embattled Catholic Church in its efforts to defend Roman Catholicism and facilitate its spread among unbelievers.[19] His letters were eagerly distributed among members of the Society, and also published in numerous languages. Within fifty years after Xavier's death, a biography of the missionary was published along with a collection of his letters. By 1622, Xavier, along with Ignatius Loyola, Teresa of Avila and other important Catholic Reformation figures, had been canonized by Pope Gregory XV.[20]

The son of a local government official, Xavier was born near San-güesa, Navarre (in northern Spain) on 7 April 1506. Educated in the Castle of Xavier, he left for theological studies at the University of Paris in 1525, meeting Ignatius Loyola and his early companions-to-be within the next few years. Ordained as a priest in 1537, Xavier was not initially earmarked to make the journey to India for the fledgling Society of Jesus in 1540. Instead, the mercurial Nicolás Bobadilla had been selected to carry out the mission on behalf of the Portuguese sovereign King John III, but at the last moment Bobadilla was too ill to make the journey and Xavier was sent in his stead.

Since the Society of Jesus had not yet been formally approved by Pope Paul III, and because papal interest was so strong in gaining a foothold in Portugal's newly conquered territories in the East, Xavier was officially deployed as a papal *nuncio* (representative) to the Indies. He arrived on the island of Goa in September of 1541 and made subsequent travels along the Fishery Coast of India during his second

---

[19] A good introduction to Xavier's stay in the Indies, if overly heroic in its depiction of the 'Apostle of the Indies,' is William V. Bangert, *A History of the Society of Jesus*, 2nd edn (St Louis: Institute of Jesuit Sources, 1986), 29–37. For a far more critical look at Xavier's legacy, see K.A. Lakshminarasimha, *Debunking a Myth, or the re-discovery of St. Francis Xavier: The true story of his life and deeds* (Bombay: Dikshitji Maharaj, 1964). For the importance of diverse models of 'life writing' in this period, see Thomas F. Mayer and D.R. Woolf, eds, *The Rhetorics of Life-Writing in Early Modern Europe. Forms of Biography from Cassandra Fedele to Louis XIV* (Ann Arbor: University of Michigan Press, 1995). The editors' introduction is especially helpful in thinking about typologies of life-writing in this period and how such works have been theorized. For a briefer but thoughtful work on one of the Jesuits' most prolific early biographers, see Jodi Bilinkoff, 'The Many "Lives" of Pedro de Ribadeneyra,' *Renaissance Quarterly* 52 (1999): 180–95.

[20] The following section, which considers Xavier's life and legacy, relies heavily upon the 'Introduction' to *The Letters and Instructions of Francis Xavier*, trans. and introduced by M. Joseph Costelloe (St Louis: The Institute of Jesuit Sources, 1992), xiii–xxx. For a consideration of the dissemination of Xavier's letters and other writings, as well as the publication history of works on or by the Jesuit saint, see esp. xxiv–xxx.

REVERBERATIONS FROM THE NEW WORLD 107

year in the East. Xavier was to spend ten years in Asia, traveling as far afield as present-day Indonesia, Japan and to the outskirts of China, where he died en route in late 1552.

Even in his earliest letters to his brethren in Rome, Xavier gave detailed accounts of the methods he was developing in efforts to evangelize the vast and diverse populations of South Asian coastal communities. In one of the first of these letters, dated 15 January 1544, Xavier gives us a vivid description of his work along the Malabar coast of India. Like Valignano, who followed him in guiding missionary activity in Asia, as well as those Neapolitan Jesuits who worked among Muslim slaves, Xavier quickly recognizes the necessity of evangelizing in the native tongue of his subjects. Thus, in addition to hurriedly translating prayers from Latin into Malabar (with the help of locals), he apparently memorized the Malabar prayers himself. While Xavier emphasized teaching Christian doctrine, seeking to convince his village parishioners that their salvation depended upon their ability to master the fundamental catechism, as well as knowing and following the Ten Commandments,[21] he also offers dramatic testaments of his struggles with 'pagan' peoples, cites apparently victorious conversions and trumpets the supposed triumph of Catholicism in far-off lands. These accounts, widely distributed within the order through the circulation of Xavier's letters and instructions, no doubt inspired his Neapolitan emulators in their labors closer to home. His letters reveal several qualities that will render him an ideal role model for Jesuit novices seeking placement in missions to the Indies and, on a broader level, for those pursuing a missionary vocation within Europe as well.

First, Xavier paints a vibrant portrait of a missionary who moves easily and effectively among his neophyte charges. In one relatively early letter, dated to 1544, he confidently relates the enthusiastic reception that his ministrations are receiving among the Malabar villagers, leaving him exhausted but clearly satisfied:

> During this time there were so many who came and asked me to come to their homes to recite some prayers over their sick, and others who came in search of me because of their infirmities, that the mere reading of the Gospels, the teaching of the boys, baptizing, translating the prayers, answering their questions, which were never failing, and then the burial of the dead left me no time for other occupations.[22]

---

[21] Francis Xavier, 'To His Companions Living in Rome,' Cochin, India, 15 January 1544, in *Letters and Instructions*, 63–74, esp. 65–6.

[22] Ibid., 67

108   A PARADISE INHABITED BY DEVILS

Xavier proffers an image of himself as fully integrated into the life of this foreign community and trusted by the local population with even the most intimate life cycle rituals, such as care for the sick and dying.

In a letter written the following year, in 1545, Xavier claims phenomenal successes in converting large numbers of Indians to Catholicism, evoking the heroic missionary image that became associated with his legacy: 'I have news to tell you about these regions of India, how in a kingdom where I now am [Travancore] God our Lord has moved so many people to become Christians that within a single month I baptized more than ten thousand persons.'[23]

Beyond these glowing reports that lay claim to adulation and mass baptisms, Xavier also evokes an appealing missionary model by linking the value of theological education in service to one's neighbors. He urges novices to put their theological education to good use in apostolic work. Anticipating José de Acosta's recognition that the conversion of the Indies would fail in the absence of dedicated and well-trained missionaries, Xavier calls upon Jesuit novices to channel their energies toward useful goals like the salvation of pagan people, rather than thinking solely of their studies, or advancement to positions of respect and authority. Addressing his fellow Jesuits back in Europe, Xavier laments the waste of perfectly good young talent in the pursuit of academic fame, or notoriety. Such scholars, he contends, might more profitably use their talents in the global evangelization effort:

> Many times I am seized with the thought of going to the schools in your lands and of crying out there, like a man who has lost his mind, and especially at the University of Paris, telling those in the Sorbonne who have a greater regard for learning than desire to prepare themselves to produce fruit with it: 'How many souls fail to go to glory and go instead to hell through their neglect!' [. . .] I fear that many who study in the universities study more to obtain honors, benefices, or bishoprics with their learning than with the desire of adapting themselves to the demands of these honors and ecclesiastical states . . . I was almost moved to write to the University of Paris . . . how many millions of pagans would become Christians if there were laborers.[24]

Xavier's urgent requests for the Society to send ardent members to the Indies were repeated both in personal letters addressed to Ignatius Loyola and in the circular letters 'to his companions in Europe.' Curiously, although he had initially stressed the need for missionaries with

---

[23] Xavier, 'To His Companions Living in Rome,' Cochin, India, 27 January 1545, in *Letters and Instructions*, 117.

[24] Xavier, 'To His Companions Living in Rome,' Cochin, India, 15 January 1544, in *Letters and Instructions*, 67–8.

REVERBERATIONS FROM THE NEW WORLD 109

theological training, Xavier increasingly emphasizes his need for anyone with 'the desire to come to live and die with these people.'[25] In some of his later missives to Loyola, Xavier is even more blunt, perhaps reflecting a certain desperation for missionary personnel. In one letter, dated 1549, Xavier pleads with the General to send him '[s]ome persons of the Society who have no talent for letters or preaching and would not be missed either in Rome or in other areas,' arguing that such second string talent would 'serve God here more than in Europe if they were truly mortified and much more experienced and had the other qualities needed for being of assistance to these pagans.'[26]

I have already suggested the impact of Xavier's example by the examination of southern Italian Jesuits' enthusiastic letters requesting a missionary vocation to the Indies, but the cult around the Spanish Jesuit was broader than the confines of the Society of Jesus. Like other religious orders of the sixteenth century, such as the Theatines, the Jesuits consciously publicized the purportedly miraculous deeds associated with exemplars like Xavier to increase their influence on the shape and direction of popular religious devotion in regions like the *Mezzogiorno*. Particularly during the seventeenth century, in the wake of the combined effects of years of economic hardship and epidemiological disasters like the Plague of 1656, Neapolitan Jesuits encouraged popular devotion of their sanctified brethren, most notably Xavier. Jesuit missionaries would administer holy water within which the relics of the Saint had been immersed in order to cure illnesses such as malaria and a variety of fevers; and, less frequently, such water was applied to the cure of more permanent physical disabilities. This approach culminated in the publication of an anonymous work detailing Xavier's powers as a protector of the residents of urban Naples, and beyond, in the wake of the Plague, *Ragguaglio della miracolosa protezione di San Francesco Saverio Apostolo delle Indie, verso la città e il Regno di Napoli nel contagio del 1656* (Naples, 1660).[27]

---

[25] Xavier, 'Letter to his companions in Europe,' Amboina (Indonesia), 10 May 1546, in *Letters and Instructions*, 139.

[26] Xavier, 'To Father Ignatius of Loyola in Rome,' Cochin, 12 January 1549, in ibid., 221.

[27] On the Jesuits' efforts to publicize Xavier's efficacious powers, especially the therapeutic effects of 'holy water' which had come into contact with the Saint's relics, see Giulio Sodano, 'Miracoli e ordini religiosi nel Mezzogiorno d'Italia (XVI–XVIII secolo),' *Archivio Storico per le Province Napoletane* 105 (1987): 293–414, esp. 294–313 and 373–5; see also Roberto Rusconi, 'Gli ordini maschili dalla Controriforma alle soppressioni settecentesche. Cultura, predicazione, missioni,' in *Clero e società nell'Italia moderna*, ed. Mario Rosa (Rome-Bari: Laterza, 1992), 207–74, esp. 220. Finally, on the wider influence of Xavier's cult, see the recent special issue of *AHSI* 71 (July–December 2002),

110   A PARADISE INHABITED BY DEVILS

In the eighteenth century, another Neapolitan Jesuit, Francesco Palma, published an account of the many miracles attributed to contact with Xavier's relics throughout the Viceroyalty of Naples. In this document, Palma confidently asserted that 'the water of Saint Francis Xavier is for us the Panacea for all ills.'[28] Thus, Xavier himself represents a fusion of the romantic lure of the foreign missions for neophyte members of the Society of Jesus and the direct and personal influence that members of the order might have on popular devotion in local communities throughout southern Italy. While his legendary status within the order helped to recruit new members into the order who were drawn to a missionary vocation, the miracles apparently associated with him also helped to bind local communities to the Jesuit fathers in their midst. Within the cult around St Francis Xavier, we can also see one of the apparent ironies of the Jesuits' civilizing mission: its accommodation to what Jesuit critics might deem superstitious forms of worship, all in the name of Christianization.

The lucky ones: Neapolitan Jesuits in the New World

The Indies held tremendous appeal for southern Italian Jesuits and missionary innovators like Francis Xavier might inspire neophyte members of the order to pursue such a vocation, but how exactly did the Neapolitans fare in their efforts to obtain those coveted missions in Indies? And, for those who obtained the coveted prize, what impact did their experiences in the New World have on their perceptions of missionary challenges back in Naples? By the time of General Claudio Acquaviva's death in 1615, the Society of Jesus had increased the geographical breadth of its involvement in both the East Indies and the Americas and had also established a popular missionary strategy throughout southern Italy. Saverio Santagata argues that by 1605, the Jesuits' missions in the Kingdom of Naples had advanced in numbers and fervor. This global expansion of missionary activity was deemed one of the great achievements of Acquaviva's generalate.[29]

The end of the first quarter of the seventeenth century also marked

---

on the occasion of the 450th anniversary of the death of Xavier. See, in particular, Maria Cristina Osswald, 'The Iconography and Cult of St. Francis Xavier, 1552–1640,' 259–77. Although Osswald does not mention Xavier's cult in Naples specifically, her article demonstrates the great demand for both relics and images of the 'Apostle of the Indies' throughout the far-flung reaches of the Society of Jesus.

[28] Francesco Palma, cited in Sodano, 'Miracoli e ordini religiosi,' 296n.

[29] Santagata, *Istoria*, 3: 177 and 549.

REVERBERATIONS FROM THE NEW WORLD 111

an increase in the deployment of Neapolitan Jesuits to missions in the Americas. In 1616 alone, six men from the Neapolitan College were chosen to be sent to America.[30] This is a fairly significant number, given that there were approximately three hundred members of the Jesuit community in Naples during these years. In the next year, the election of Muzio Vitelleschi as the sixth General of the Society augured well for the expansion of the Society's universal missionary orientation and the greater inclusion of southern Italian Jesuits in that enterprise. Santagata tells us that a number of Neapolitan Jesuits were successful in obtaining placements in the new missions established in the Viceroyalty of New Granada (centered around modern-day Cartagena, Colombia) in 1605, 'which needed a great number of workers in order to cultivate the vast camp opened to the expansion of the Faith.' He describes how Vitelleschi received a request from Alonso de Sandoval, one of the first Jesuit missionaries in Cartagena, 'for the increase in missionaries in those parts.' Vitelleschi responded favorably to Sandoval, and 'understanding well the desire noted by many [there] to travel to the Indies, gave license to six of them to do it.'[31]

Such news must have emboldened fresh recruits to hope for a similar fate, yet few of those who painstakingly recorded their dreams of a missionary assignment in the Indies succeeded in attaining their desired goals, and even fewer left records of their achievements in the New World. Some, like the unfortunate Francesco Mastrilli, found their numerous requests repeatedly ignored. Born in Nola in 1581, Mastrilli's is one of the more poignant examples of a frustrated missionary vocation. The nephew of three well-respected members of the Society in southern Italy, Mastrilli wrote numerous letters to both Acquaviva and Vitelleschi during his years in the order, but apparently poor health and a vague reference to his insufficient demonstrations of penitence were the primary deterrents to his being assigned to a mission field in the Indies.[32] In the last of five impassioned letters from Mastrilli which are

---

[30] Santagata, *Istoria*, 4: 4. Among those sent in 1616 from the Neapolitan College were: Alfonso di Aragona, Giovanni Battista Sansone, Cesare Graziano, Ortenzio Sabelloni, Claudio Rovilier and Pietro Comentale. For the figures on the Jesuit population of the City of Naples, see ARSI, *Neap.* 73; cf. Rosa, Appendix 1, 'Strategia Missionaria gesuitica in Puglia,' in *Religione e Società*, 271.

[31] Santagata, *Istoria*, 4: 49–50. The six sent in 1617 included: Francesco Ruggi, Francesco Susanna, Diego di Errici, Luigi Marincola and Carlo D'Orta.

[32] We have already encountered two of Francesco Mastrilli's better-known relatives: Carlo Mastrilli, who urged his brethren to restore peace in strife-torn Naples on the eve of the 1585 Revolt, and Nicoló Mastrilli, who obtained his desired goal of gaining a mission to the Indies (Peru). A third uncle, Gregorio Mastrilli, was recognized as a respected orator in the Neapolitan Province. See Santagata, *Istoria*, 4: 225–6.

112   A PARADISE INHABITED BY DEVILS

still extant, the Jesuit writes a four-page plea to Vitelleschi to consider him one more time, arguing that a vocation to the Indies is a 'sure means to my salvation; without this, I will not be eternally saved.' His desperation carries Mastrilli far beyond the standard testaments of obedience and submissiveness to the authority of his superiors, as is evident in his closing remarks: 'For the love of God, give me any other penitence outside of this – not sending me [to the Indies]. God desires that I go; he commands it.'[33]

As much as Mastrilli's story symbolizes the frustration that many Neapolitan Jesuits felt over their failure to secure a mission to the Indies, the example of one who succeeded in reaching the Americas and left a record of his experiences there further enriches our understanding of the relationship between the missions to the Indies and those in southern Italy. In direct contrast to Mastrilli's frustrated pleas, Carlo D'Orta represents a success story. D'Orta emerges from the often faceless mass of would-be missionaries drawn to work in the Indies through his subsequent letters back home and the brief, biographical references to him provided by Saverio Santagata. Through Carlo D'Orta, we can see the impact of Xavier's heroic model on the missionary correspondence of Jesuits in the field. Perhaps more importantly, though, D'Orta's letters demonstrate how missionaries might draw a connection between their labors abroad and the daunting tasks facing colleagues back in southern Italy. His own experiences in Colombia suggest that at least some Neapolitan missionaries viewed themselves as agents of a global civilizing mission that connected work in exotic, far-off lands with the painstaking efforts to reform life back home.

D'Orta was one of the lucky few among the hundreds of Neapolitan Jesuits who enthusiastically requested placement in the Society's ever-expanding range of mission fields during the latter part of the sixteenth and the first half of the seventeenth century. On the surface, D'Orta's request for a missionary vocation in the Indies seems mundane and unremarkable. In fact, the following letter shares a great deal with the formulaic series of *Indipetae* that we have already examined, implying a desire to seek martyrdom in a far-off land, a certain quest for adventure

---

[33] ARSI, F.G. 736, *Indipetae 4 Italia*, Doc. 167, 'Letter of Francesco Mastrilli' (Catanzaro, 12 July 1620). Mastrilli's earlier letters were written between 1612 and 1620 (F.G. 734–6). His name is recorded variously as *Mastrillo* and *Mastrilli*. And, curiously, he refers to himself in his final letter as Giovanni, not Francesco. To add to the confusion, a later Mastrilli, named Marcello Francesco (born in Nola in 1603), was sent to Asia where he died near Nagasaki, Japan in 1637. See *Diccionario Histórico de la Compañía de Jesús. Biografico-Temático* (Rome: Jesuit Historical Institute, 2001), 4: 2566.

– in other words, reminiscent of many such letters of would-be missionary novices:

> Pax Christi:
> As of today, it has been fifteen days since I reminded Your Paternity [General Muzio Vitelleschi] of the desire that I have expressed many times in the past to be employed as an Apostle . . . inside myself, I feel drawn to far-off places, where one could truly consume one's time and one's life . . . I have not yet had a response [from you] . . . For this reason, once again, I beg you to console me [by] sending me on one of the next missions to the East . . . [knowing] that once there, I will remain a most obedient son. From Capua, April 29, 1617.
>
> Most Humble Servant and most obedient son in Christ,
> Carlo D'Orta[34]

Apparently, however, D'Orta's letter held sway with his superiors, though he did not get his wish to be sent to Asia. Just six months after this request, Carlo D'Orta was commissioned to depart for the Americas, where he spent a little more than one year before his untimely death in 1619.

In his portrait of Carlo D'Orta, Santagata provides the barest sketch of a man whose relatively late entrance into the Society (he was 33 when he joined in 1614) was at least in part inspired by his desire for martyrdom. D'Orta hoped to emulate those 'Heroes murdered for Christ' about whom he heard while residing in Naples. According to Santagata, D'Orta spent his novitiate 'accustoming himself to the hardships of India,' by performing acts of extraordinary penitence.'[35]

Unlike other Neapolitan Jesuits, such as Pierantonio Spinelli, D'Orta is not described as destined to a holy life from his childhood. Born in Giuliano, in the diocese of Aversa (just north of Naples) in 1581, Santagata tells us that D'Orta was considered a bright but also 'disobedient' youth. His conversion was brought about by a chance encounter with a Jesuit priest, which led him to Naples to take vows with the order. But significantly, D'Orta's initial work in the Society was in his home territory of Aversa. There, just prior to his placement in New Granada, he returned to work among his *paesani*, founding a congregation called the Nativity of Our Lady, which offered instruction in Christian doctrine and attempted to promote greater attention to the

---

[34] ARSI, *F.G. 735, Indipetae 4 Italia* (1616–18), No. 133, 'Letter of Carlo D'Orta to Muzio Vitelleschi' (Capua, 29 April 1617). I have identified two other letters by D'Orta requesting placement in a mission in the Indies: the first dated 2 January 1616 and the second, to which he refers in the above-cited letter, dated 15 April 1617.

[35] Santagata, *Istoria*, 4: 141. Cf. Sommervogel, *Bibliothèque de la Compagnie*, 5: 1951.

114 A PARADISE INHABITED BY DEVILS

sacraments.[36] This routine Jesuit activity would apparently inspire in D'Orta a strong sense of loyalty to his home community and a source for future reflection.

In his letters from Cartagena, Colombia, D'Orta combines aspects of a travel narrative with social commentary. He provides an inventory of the spiritual tasks facing him and his fellow Jesuits. After reporting on the arduous nature of his eight month voyage from Naples to Cartagena, D'Orta comments upon the unfamiliar weather, quality of food, bad air and the large number of insects with which the missionaries must contend.[37] But he is quick to assure his co-religious that he is grateful for the opportunity to serve the Society of Jesus in the New World: 'I write you these things not out of unhappiness ... but only to inform you of the qualities of this part of the New World.'

While the details of the ship voyage and the Jesuit's initial impressions of Colombia are fascinating, one of the most intriguing features of Carlo D'Orta's letter is his observation of the social leveling present in America. In contrast to the highly stratified society of early modern southern Italy, in Colombia, D'Orta tells us in an implicitly critical tone, any European rustic might advance. Tellingly, D'Orta renders this judgment in the middle of a larger critique of the market in African slaves, 'the trade here that is all the more in use':

> The merchants go to buy them [the Africans] on the coasts of Guinea and of Angola at such a vile price; from there, they transport them on ships well acquainted with this port and once here, they make of them the first sale[s] with incredible earnings [. . .] Those who remain here are put on ships again and carried to other ports until they are all sold. [The slaves] work as miners, on the land, and serve in households, since in all of America, every European, even those of lowly birth and poor condition, refuses to serve in similar positions.[38]

While D'Orta's belief that all Europeans might advance in the New World seems exaggerated, his remarking upon these conditions is a telling reminder that the Jesuits were largely social conservatives. After all, they had argued against the 1585 Revolt of Naples on the grounds

---

36 Santagata, *Istoria*, 4: 134–5.

37 Carlo D'Orta, Circular Letter to Muzio Vitelleschi (1 July 1618), as cited in Santagata, *Istoria*, 4: 51–3.

38 D'Orta, ibid. For a fascinating study of the Jesuits' broader ministries to African slaves in colonial Cartagena, see Ronald J. Morgan, 'Jesuit confessors, African slaves and the practice of confession in seventeenth-century Cartagena,' in *Penitence in the Age of Reformations*, eds Katharine Jackson Lualdi and Anne T. Thayer (Aldershot, UK and Burlington, VT: Ashgate, 2000), 222–39.

REVERBERATIONS FROM THE NEW WORLD   115

that such protest was demonically inspired, so the image of uncivilized, 'rude' Europeans living beyond their station was notable.

It was precisely among African slaves that D'Orta consumed much of his missionary labor during his brief time in the Indies. There, he joined his more famous fellow Jesuit, Pedro Claver (1585–1654), who had arrived in Cartagena in 1610 and later came to be regarded as a 'patron saint of slaves.' Like his mentor Francis Xavier, D'Orta unselfconsciously revels in his many apparent victories over unbelief and savagery. He provides a far more detailed description of this work in an extensive letter written to his congregation in Aversa. In a tone familiar to readers of missionary reports from the Indies, D'Orta compares his charges ('this most miserable people') to children in both their 'simplicity' and in their eagerness to be introduced to the fundamental precepts of Christianity:

> In introducing myself to speak to them of the things of the Holy Faith, I found them [possessed of] a simplicity which is exactly that of a child. When, for the first time [they] begin to discern good from evil, everyone asks to be [a] Christian, some even telling me that for this end [alone] they gladly would have come to America, notwithstanding the duty to be perpetual slaves. Up to now I have not encountered anyone who has failed to embrace the law of Jesus Christ. They entreat [me] to be baptized quickly, hold Christians in great esteem, raise their hands to the Heavens, and cry out *mantegne*, which in their language means God.[39]

This account fits within the Jesuits' customary manner of highlighting their subjects' great reverence toward them in missionary reports. D'Orta's African subjects cannot merely be open to Christianity, but must make the seemingly absurd claim that they would willingly subject themselves again to enslavement for the privilege of becoming Christians. Apparently, D'Orta does not meet any obstinate sinners, a far cry from the situation reported in southern Italy, where we often encounter such individuals (even if they are eventually won over to the true faith). Perhaps this was precisely the point that he wished to impart to his brethren back home: if African slaves could so heartily embrace the Christian faith, then they must not allow for the laxity which was then apparently plaguing so many Christian communities in and around Naples.

By contrast, the missionary relations for the Kingdom of Naples are rife with accounts of people who initially reject the Jesuit missionaries'

---

[39] D'Orta, 'Letter to his colleagues in Aversa' (Cartagena, 15 August 1618), as cited in Santagata, *Istoria*, 4: 136–40, esp. 137. For information on Pedro Claver, see Mariano Picón-Salas, *Pedro Claver, el Santo de los Esclavos* (Madrid: Ediciones de la Revista de Occidente, 1969).

116 A PARADISE INHABITED BY DEVILS

efforts to challenge their sinful ways. Ultimately, such sinners are generally won over through a combination of peer pressure, miraculous signs, or an individual missionary's charismatic appeal, though the truly recalcitrant (as we will see) sometimes meet an untimely death. In D'Orta's America, however, as in Xavier's India, baptisms are heartily requested, and the missionary works with interpreters to teach the basic tenets of the faith to the neophyte Christians.

What is most intriguing about D'Orta's account is both the audience to which it is addressed and the later inclusion of the missionary's recommendations for the work which must be continued in Aversa. Unlike the previously cited letter, which was intended for the widest possible audience within the order and perhaps beyond, this communiqué is directed to a local audience. Although D'Orta never explicitly mentions any discord in Aversa, Santagata reports widespread social tension in the town just a few years after this letter was written.[40] Without speculating as to whether D'Orta was aware of such discord, his representation of the great successes being achieved in the New World must have resonated within his congregation, offering inspiration and reminding his *paesani* of the universal dimensions of the Jesuit mission.

In his letter to his comrades in Aversa, D'Orta spares no opportunity to remind his audience of the enormity of the tasks facing ardent Christians in the Indies (once again remarking upon the challenges posed by the intense heat, the 'formidable winds' and the 'most troublesome insects'), but his most impassioned criticisms seem directed to the spiritual crisis closer to home. Citing the valiant example of early Christian ascetics who renounced the love of friends and family for the greater glory of God, D'Orta bemoans the lack of such rigorous discipline in his own time:

> But alas, how few Christians one finds today who take this way of being to heart. Who is there who has only the aim to honor and [promote] the glory of God! Many don't even avoid bad practices, nor separate themselves from poor companions. The Churches and the congregations find themselves depopulated. The word of God isn't heard, people don't attend to the sacraments. Who is there who has a hatred for pleasures and the acquisitions of this world? [. . .] I have written this [letter] for that person who thinks little or nothing about their Soul, who is not devoted to the Most Holy Madonna, and doesn't come, or unwillingly comes to this congregation: My Dears, greatly beloved of the Virgin Mary, attend your

---

[40] The discord and violence in Aversa prompted the Society's mission to the area in 1621 in order to promote social reconciliation and end the 'cruel factions' between the common folk and the nobility, Santagata, *Istoria*, 4: 202–203.

Congregation, be friends of penitence, of the orations of the word of God. Attend to the sacraments, love all, but don't converse with everyone[.] [E]scape the dangers of sinning, embrace positive occasions, easily pardon those who offend you and don't pay too much attention to that which will soon pass and be over.[41]

In this exhortation to the members of the 'Congregation of the Nativity of Our Lady,' D'Orta seems to be juxtaposing his wildly enthusiastic report of the victories for Christians in the New World with the lack of religious seriousness at home in southern Italy. Although he does not make an explicit comparison between the ardent African slaves who greet the Jesuit fathers by a name given to their indigenous 'God,' D'Orta's overall message could not have escaped his fellow congregants.

Here, then, is an example of how one Jesuit missionary could assume an implicit connection between the popular missions at home and the Christianizing efforts in the Indies. The successes of the conversion efforts abroad were meant to inspire European Catholics. They might also be used to shame those who failed to attend to their Christian duties. After all, if the 'uncivilized' Africans and Amerindians might embrace Christianity as willingly as the Jesuit missionary reports indicated, how could their supposedly more 'civilized' southern Italian counterparts fail to follow suit? Or perhaps that was precisely the problem: civility, as we have noted, was never a certainty in the contemporary perceptions of the *Mezzogiorno*.

With D'Orta's letter to Aversa, a self-conscious, collective Jesuit missionary identity seems to be emerging. Not only does the missionary display those signal qualities which superiors from Juan Polanco to Claudio Acquaviva had enumerated: flexibility, prudence and faithfulness, but he attempts to bridge the gap between the distant mission fields of South America and southern Italy through his own example and advice. The native son of Aversa may have traversed the ocean to Christianize infidels, but he was still passionately committed to the missionary efforts of his brethren back home, recognizing activities like reforming sinful behavior and inspiring greater understanding of Christian doctrine as central to a broader Jesuit vocation.

José de Acosta and the Jesuits' civilizing mission: From Peru to Naples

While the Jesuits' emerging notion of a civilizing mission is evident in the personal model of Francis Xavier and in the letters of Neapolitan novices, the institutionalization of a collective, global missionary agenda

---

[41] D'Orta, as cited in Santagata, *Istoria*, 4: 139–40.

118   A PARADISE INHABITED BY DEVILS

within the Society of Jesus also owes a great deal to the work of the controversial Spanish Jesuit José de Acosta (1540–1600). Acosta's model of a flexible yet comprehensive missionary program in the Indies that accommodated a range of 'levels of civilization' had enormous implications for the development of a popular missionary strategy in southern Italy. Acosta's signal work on the evangelization of Amerindians, *De Procuranda Indorum Salute* (1588), argues that the Jesuits can and should play a vital role in training clergy, teaching Christian doctrine, extirpating idolatries and reforming unseemly behaviors. At the same time, Neapolitan Jesuits were identifying parallel problems closer to home. Whether in Naples, or in far-flung mission fields across the globe, the Jesuits approached their civilizing mission with a combination of deliberateness and flexibility. Neapolitan Jesuits learned to follow Acosta's advice, showing that his admonition to accommodate to local conditions and the specific character of a community had made the long journey across the wide Atlantic to the Italian South, where it would be reshaped to fit the contemporary conditions of a city and a region in crisis.

If Francis Xavier contributed to the development of a Jesuit missionary identity by serving as a personal and institutional model of missionary decorum and heroism, José de Acosta offered a comprehensive program for assessing the 'level of civilization' that any society had reached and those techniques most appropriate to its successful evangelization. Like Xavier, Acosta helped identify important areas of activity for Jesuit missionaries. And like Xavier, too, Acosta's work was adapted to the challenges and dynamic nature of missionary reform work in Naples and beyond. While a charged figure within the Society of Jesus because of his murky role in tensions between the Spanish Crown, certain restive Spanish Jesuits and the Society's central leadership in Rome, Acosta made a significant contribution to a Jesuit missionary science in the New World and in local European communities like Naples.[42]

Neapolitan Jesuits adapted Acosta's missionary philosophy and methods for their own evangelizing work closer to home, developing detailed instructional manuals based upon the principles of accommodation and informed by Acosta's cultural map of civilizations. While missionaries in the Italian South were certainly aware that they were working among

---

[42] The best source of information in English on Acosta's life, controversial position within the late sixteenth-century Society of Jesus and innovative institutional and theological innovations is Claudio Burgaleta, *José de Acosta, S.J. (1540–1600): His Life and Thought* (Chicago: Loyola Press, 1999). For Acosta's role in the so-called 'Memorialista' crisis within the Society of Jesus, and in particular the Spanish Assistancy, see Chapter 4.

REVERBERATIONS FROM THE NEW WORLD 119

nominal Christians, rather than the 'barbaric' neophytes of the Americas, they freely adapted Acosta's notions of superstition and savagery and the remedies necessary to eradicate them to their own work. In order to understand better how this linkage was accomplished, we need to step back to re-examine the earliest missionary endeavors of the Jesuits and other orders in the New World and the challenges that they faced in uncharted territories.

Catholic Missionaries became active in the Americas from the earliest period of European contact with Amerindians, hoping to effect widespread and permanent conversions within culturally disparate societies that they scarcely understood. Shortly after the Spanish conquest of the Valley of Mexico in 1521, a contingent of twelve Franciscan friars was brought from Spain to begin the formal work of converting the indigenous peoples of MesoAmerica. These Franciscans were imbued with a sense of millenarian fervor which inspired them to emphasize mass baptisms over the slower, painstaking work of effecting deeper, perhaps more lasting conversions. Initially, less focus was placed upon attention to missionary methods, because the friars were driven by a sense of apocalyptic urgency. By 1540, however, a series of visible inquisitorial trials of indigenous leaders (*Caciques*) accused of practicing traditional rites called into question the completeness of the conversions.[43] Thus, by the mid-sixteenth century, in addition to the growing attraction of Protestantism among large sections of the populations of Central Europe, France and even pockets in Italy, the Catholic Church had to recognize that its efforts to Christianize the New World were incomplete. Within this troubled context, the Jesuits offered their own missionary alternative. The Society's evangelizing strategies owed much to the inspiration of the mendicants, the Franciscans most notably, but in a number of important respects, the Jesuits' model was novel.

Like the Franciscans and Dominicans before them, the Jesuits envi-

---

[43] Twelve Franciscans arrived in Mexico City in 1524 at Cortés's behest. For a brief but insightful discussion of the Franciscan (and later, Dominican) approaches to the 'spiritual conquest' of Mexico and the problem of incomplete conversions, see Prosperi, 'L'Europa Cristiana,' 197–209. For an exploration of the mendicants' Christianization efforts, with a special emphasis on the distinctive missionary strategies of the Franciscans, in particular, see Robert Ricard's *The Spiritual Conquest of Mexico. An Essay on the Apostolate and the Evangelizing Method of the Mendicant Orders in New Spain, 1523–1572*, trans. Lesley Byrd Simpson (Berkeley and Los Angeles: University of California Press, 1966). Ricard closes his study in 1572, the year in which the Jesuits became established in New Spain, because he considers the work of the Jesuits a distinct departure from that of the earlier orders. For a brief discussion of the Jesuits' distinctive contribution to the evangelization of Mexico, see Ricard, 3. For more on the Franciscan missions, also see John Leddy Phelan, *The Millenial Kingdom of the Franciscans in New Spain*, 2nd edn (Berkeley and Los Angeles: University of California Press, 1970).

120 A PARADISE INHABITED BY DEVILS

sioned their missions as tools for social transformation. In addition to adhering to a principle of accommodation, they stressed the importance of seeing the missionary project as a long-term proposition, emphasizing the value of missionaries as a stabilizing presence in newly converted communities and the necessity of promoting an idea of cultural exchange with their missionary subjects. Jesuit missionaries paid especially close attention to the efficacy of certain strategies over others and increasingly formalized their elaboration of rules, or instructions for missionaries in the field. Perhaps most distinctively from their predecessors, the Jesuits argued that the missionaries' first task was to enforce 'civility' before encouraging baptisms and formal conversion to Christianity. In this way, as Adriano Prosperi has noted, the missions became a project to advance both 'the work of religious propaganda *and* the transmission of political and social models.'[44]

While the Jesuits' global civilizing mission had become a hallmark of their international focus as early as 1540, when Xavier was deployed to the East to Christianize the Portuguese colonies, the Jesuits did not establish missions in Africa or the Americas for at least a decade.[45] Establishing their first residence in the Western Hemisphere in Brazil in 1550, within just three years, this Portuguese colony was one of the six provinces that made up the Jesuits' governing infrastructure. Although the Brazil province held many fewer men than the missions in India (25 in Brazil in 1555, compared with about 55 based in Goa on the west coast of India), this early expansion was notable, especially given the vast distances that separated these provinces from the Society's governing body in Rome and the bulk of its membership.[46] Between 1567 and 1572, the Jesuits had broadened their regional scope to include such parts of Spanish America as Peru and Mexico.

Arriving on the heels of the mendicant orders, the Jesuits worked to establish colleges which, like their European models, might serve as cultural centers for the émigré and creole communities in the New World and bases from which to train future missionaries. Among the indige-

---

[44] Prosperi, 'L'Europa Cristiana,' 210–19, esp. 219 (emphasis mine).

[45] The ill-fated African missions, largely driven by misinformation about the possibility of implanting Roman Catholicism in regions such as Ethiopia and Egypt where other Christian churches had long existed, were initiated after 1555. For a brief survey of the Jesuits' early work in four regions of Africa, Ethiopia, Egypt, Southeastern Africa (near present-day Mozambique) and Angola, see Bangert, *A History of the Society of Jesus*, 89–91. The Jesuits also made an early intervention in the newly conquered Spanish territories of Florida in 1566, but failed miserably in this effort, see ibid., 93–5.

[46] O'Malley notes the unevenness in the distribution of members of the Society in the early years of the order: for example, around 1549, although there were already thirty Jesuits in India, there were just thirteen in Paris. O'Malley, *First Jesuits*, 53–4; 76–9.

REVERBERATIONS FROM THE NEW WORLD 121

nous populations, the Jesuits employed one of the first principles of the civilizing mission, to gather nomadic peoples together into settled communities, under the watchful eye of priests and other 'civilized' individuals. In Mexico, this appeared to be a far more successful enterprise, perhaps because the nature of the Spanish conquest there had been more complete. But the Jesuits also had to contend with the far greater presence of other orders in Mexico, delaying their arrival and limiting their spheres of activity. In Peru, by contrast, the political climate seemed far less stable, but the opportunities for the Jesuits more obvious. By the time José de Acosta arrived there in 1572, he entered a profoundly crisis-ridden colonial situation.

In Peru, there were deep political divisions that grew out of the messy military campaigns of conquest which had been led by Francisco Pizarro and his companion Diego de Almagro. Although Pizarro and his men had fought a brutal war of conquest against the Incas between 1531 and 1536, nearly forty years later they continued to face stiff indigenous resistance. Beyond these obstacles, the Spanish conquerors had themselves engaged in a near civil war over the spoils of their victory. The Spanish sent Viceroy Francisco de Toledo into this troubled climate in 1569 to help complete the pacification of Peru, and Acosta was soon to follow.[47] During his fourteen years in the Americas, Acosta would use his wide-ranging experiences to produce an influential series of publications on the nature of the Americas and the methods best suited to convert its native populations to Roman Catholicism. While he may have never stepped foot in Naples, Acosta's insights into the challenges that evangelization posed to the missionary in the field must have resonated with his southern Italian brethren.

José de Acosta (1540–1600) was born into a merchant family in Medina del Campo, Castile in the year in which the Society of Jesus was formally recognized.[48] He entered the order in Salamanca at the age of twelve, along with four of his brothers. After taking vows as a Jesuit, Acosta spent five years teaching grammar in his hometown of Medina before being sent on a tour of various Jesuit colleges in Spain and Portugal. Finally, in 1559, he settled in Alcalá to study at the university there. Acosta pursued a broad and varied education in Alcalá, studying

---

[47] The area known as 'Peru' actually encompassed its present-day namesake, as well as Colombia, Argentina, Ecuador and Bolivia. An excellent consideration of Acosta's role in the pacification and Christianization of Peru, including an insightful overview and analysis of his formulation of the 'civilizing mission', is Armido Rizzi, 'De Procuranda indorum salute. L'evangelizzazione degli Indios: Problemi e metodi,' *Futuro dell'Uomo* (Special Issue: America Latina: 1492–1992. Quattro Voci del 1500) 29, No. 2 (1992): 69–88.

[48] On Acosta's early life and milieu, see Burgaleta, *José de Acosta*, 3–11.

122   A PARADISE INHABITED BY DEVILS

theology and philosophy, and gaining a solid humanist education. The Spanish Jesuit apparently showed an early interest in the debates still raging among Dominican scholars at Salamanca over the problematic conquest of the Americas and the enslavement of Amerindians. After completing his studies in Alcalá and being ordained as a priest in 1566, Acosta spent about four years working in a variety of ministries in small towns throughout Spain before obtaining his goal of being sent to the Indies as a missionary in 1571. His experience in internal missions in his homeland may well have offered some formative training for the missionary methodology that he developed later, although he does not refer to this explicitly.[49]

Like many young Jesuits, Acosta had enthusiastically sought placement in the missions to the Indies. As early as 1561, when still a student at Alcalá, Acosta had expressed his intentions to Jerónimo Nadal, during one of the superior's periodic visits to Castile. At that time, however, Spanish America remained the exclusive province of the mendicant orders. But between 1566 and 1567, the Spanish monarch Philip II commissioned the Jesuits to evangelize Florida and Peru. In light of these new developments, in 1568 and 1569 Acosta renewed his appeal to set off for the Americas in letters to the recently elected General, Francisco Borja.[50]

Acosta begins his second letter to Borja, dated 23 April 1569, with a gentle reminder that he has written before, but feels compelled to remind his superior of his continuing interest in a missionary vocation in the Indies. His reasons for seeking placement in the Indies are standard enough, resonating with the *Indipetae* that we have discussed above. Acosta cites his desire to serve God and increase his worthiness by being sent to a mission field that will provide greater challenges than he was currently facing in Spain. He notes the greater potential for reaping spiritual fruit where there is a more acute necessity for his labors and refers to his great desire to imitate Christ, preparing to suffer, if need be, to spread the Gospel. Finally, and probably most crucially, Acosta exhorts Borgja to send him to the Spanish Indies because of his specific talents as a preacher and instructor of theology, politely reminding his superior that he (Acosta) can think of nothing else but his desired vocation to the Indies.[51]

---

[49] On Acosta's formative training in Spain and his appointment to a mission in the Indies, see ibid., 25–30.

[50] 'Introducción,' *Obras del Padre José de Acosta*, ed. Francisco Mateos (Madrid: Atlas, 1954), x. Cf. Burgaleta, *José de Acosta*, 30–31.

[51] For Acosta's letter to Borgia, see 'Carta a San Francisco de Borja, General de La

REVERBERATIONS FROM THE NEW WORLD   123

Acosta arrived in the Indies in the spring of 1571, although he would not take up his formal duties in Lima for another year. Once there, Acosta taught theology at the Jesuit college, and apparently became a much admired and respected preacher as well. Within a year, however, the Jesuits' current Provincial in Peru, Padre Jerónimo Ruiz de Portillo, sent Acosta on an extended mission into the interior of Peru. There, Acosta's duties included a visit to the new Jesuit college in Cuzco, but the broader goals were to preach in the colonial cities, 'at the same time, studying the religious situation and the most urgent spiritual necessities of the land.'[52]

Over the course of his fourteen years in Peru, Acosta played a key role in establishing a strong Jesuit presence and in developing influential theories of both the nature of the New World (its human societies, as well as flora and fauna) and the tasks before those who would evangelize this vast territory. After becoming Provincial of Peru in 1576, Acosta was pivotal in developing concrete strategies for the evangelization of its indigenous communities. On the second of his tours of the territory in his capacity as Provincial, in 1578, Acosta participated in the founding of the first Jesuit *doctrina* at Julí. As one recent commentator has noted, the *doctrina* 'represented the attempt at the construction of a Christian Indian community; that is, [one] which realized Christian fraternity inside the frame of indigenous culture and institutions,' but it remained a controversial institution for the Society of Jesus, and not all members were convinced of its efficacy.[53] In 1582, Acosta participated in the Third Lima Council, a gathering of ecclesiastical officials who met to consider the state of the Church in the colony. As a result of his labors at the Council, Acosta ultimately issued three important guides to

---

Compañia de Jesús, En Que Pide Las Misiones de Indias (Ocaña, 23 de Abril, 1569)', *Obras*, 251–2.

[52] 'Introducción,' *Obras*, x–xi. The political climate into which Acosta stepped in 1571 was fraught with great tensions between Jesuit Provincial Ruiz de Portillo, a number of leading members of the Peruvian Jesuit community and the Spanish Viceroy Toledo, largely over the question of the Jesuits leading the *doctrinas* (parishes for Indians). According to Claudio Burgaleta, 'Such curacies were strictly forbidden by the Jesuit Constitutions, which saw them as an obstacle to the desired poverty and mobility that St Ignatius desired for his sons.' On this tension, see Burgaleta, *José de Acosta*, 35–6.

[53] Ibid. Also see Rizzi, '*De Procuranda Indorum Salute*,' 86. Rizzi describes the *doctrinas* as indigenous parishes, but notes that the *doctrina* at Julí represented an early form of the more famous Jesuit evangelizing/civilizing institution, the *reduction*. For a more in-depth view of the experiment at Julí, see Norman Meikeljohn, 'Los Jesuitas de Julí: doctrineros modelo,' Chapter VI in *La Iglesia y los Lupaqas de Chucuito durante la Colonia* (Cuzco: Instituto de Estudios Aymaras, 1988). On the Jesuit *reductions* in Paraguay, see especially Girolamo Imbruglia, *L'invenzione del Paraguay. Studio sull'idea di comunità tra Seicento e Settecento* (Naples: Bibliopolis, 1983).

124   A PARADISE INHABITED BY DEVILS

teaching the catechism, hearing confessions and providing stock sermons.[54]

But Acosta is best known for two major works through which he crystallized his theories of evangelization, the evolutionary development of human societies and the nature of the Americas. It was this work that, in many ways, left the deepest mark upon missionary innovators within the popular missions in southern Italy and elsewhere. *De Procuranda Indorum Salute*, Acosta's first major work, was written in Lima in 1577. Although it is far less known than Acosta's subsequent study, *Historia Natural y Moral de las Indias* (1590), the original work deals more directly with the tasks facing missionaries in the evangelization of the Americas.[55]

As one scholar of early modern empire has noted, the debates around the conquest and evangelization of the Americas reflect broader shifts in the intellectual climate of sixteenth-century Europe. Evaluating Acosta's role in these developments, Anthony Pagden argues that the Spanish Jesuit's inquiries were novel in two primary respects. First, Acosta recognized the cultural uniqueness among discrete Amerindian societies and the importance of this diversity for his classificatory schema. In the *Historia*, Acosta sought to present the 'total history' of the New World, both materially and in terms of human societies. Beyond the ambitious scope of his work, Acosta stressed the value of empirical data; his advocacy of a 'new system of knowledge of the new world' was an important contribution to early modern learned Europeans' world view. Acosta took pride in his empirical approach, while none the less continuing to rely upon biblical sources, patristic writings and the work of the Ancients to authorize his findings.[56]

---

[54] José de Acosta, *Tercero Catechismo y exposición de la Doctrina Christiana, por Sermones. Para que los curas y otros ministros prediquen y enseñen a los Yndios y a las demas personas* (1585), reprinted with a critical commentary in *Monumenta Catechetica Hispano-Americana* (Siglos XVI–XVIII), Vol. 2, ed. Juan Guillermo Durán (Buenos Aires: Facultad de Teologia de la Universidad Catolica Argentina, 1990), esp. 597–631. Acosta's instructional guide reiterates the general philosophy found in *De Procuranda*, while offering more succinct and specific recommendations to would-be missionaries and parish priests.

[55] In the original editions of *De Procuranda Indorum Salute* (1588), a Latin edition of the first two books of the *Historia Natural y Moral de las Indias* (1590) (hereafter cited as *Historia*) was included. For the publication history of both works, including a discussion of the censoring of certain passages deemed anti-Spanish in *De Procuranda*, see 'Introducción,' *Obras*, xxxvii–xl. I have chosen to use the more recent bilingual Spanish–Latin edition of the *De Procuranda* for subsequent citations from the text. *De Procuranda Indorum Salute*, 2 vols, ed. Luciano Pereña Vicente (Madrid: CSIC, 1984; 1987).

[56] Anthony Pagden, *The Fall of Natural Man*, 151–7. Pagden goes to great lengths to demonstrate the eclecticism of Acosta's sources and methods of inquiry. But he is careful

Aside from differences in style and focus, Acosta's two major publications, *De Procuranda* and the *Historia*, were driven by three common objectives. First, Acosta explicitly set out to produce a scientific investigation of remote cultures. He believed that in so doing, he might mitigate some of the misinformation and distorted views of Amerindians which were rampant among sixteenth-century New World travel narratives.[57] Acosta's second goal for his work was to provide instruction for missionaries. Although this implies a purely religious motivation, for Acosta it was inextricably bound up with his desire to unravel the cultural complexities of Amerindian historical development. After all, missionaries needed to understand the cultures that they were attempting to evangelize if they hoped to succeed. Finally, Acosta joined his mendicant predecessor, the Dominican friar and polemicist Bartolomé de las Casas in efforts to challenge the notion that Amerindian cultures were purely irrational. Although Acosta differed with las Casas on a number of important points regarding the nature and appropriate status of Amerindians in colonial America, he remained unquestioningly opposed to viewing indigenous peoples as 'natural slaves.'[58]

Throughout his writings, Acosta presents a set of complex and often contradictory views of Amerindian cultures, capabilities and values. These divergent attitudes are indicative of the broader difficulties inherent in the civilizing mission and have echoes in the popular missions in southern Italy.[59] A closer investigation of Acosta's *De Procuranda* will bring this ambivalence into sharp relief and help to clarify the nuanced

---

to show the limits of Acosta's empiricism, and the extent to which the Jesuit scholar cannot be regarded as a true 'modern.' For Acosta's reliance on ethnographic data about the Inca provided by Don Polo de Ondegardo, one of Viceroy Toledo's advisors, see Burgaleta, *José de Acosta*, 37.

[57] On the representation of *novelty* in New World narratives, see Michael T. Ryan, 'Assimilating New Worlds in the Sixteenth and Seventeenth Centuries,' *Comparative Studies in Society and History* 23 (1981): 519–38, and John H. Elliott, 'The Discovery of America and the Discovery of Man,' in his *Spain and its World, 1500–1700. Selected Essays* (New Haven and London: Yale University Press, 1989), 42–64.

[58] For an insightful discussion of Acosta's 'purposes' in composing these works, stressing the notion that his writings should be seen as an expression of his 'theological humanism,' see Burgaleta, *José de Acosta*, esp. 73–80. Compare Pagden, *The Fall of Natural Man*, 156–7. Pagden considers the historical development of the idea of natural slaves from Aristotle to Aquinas to the Salamanca School debates of the mid-sixteenth century over the New World conquest in ibid., Chapters Three and Four. For a comparative perspective on Acosta's and las Casas's views, see ibid., 146–7.

[59] That the study of the New World should reveal anxieties with home-grown implications should come as no surprise. As Pagden, Adriano Prosperi and numerous others have argued, the study of the New World provided a 'laboratory' for studying non-Christian (or, one might add, semi-Christian) people. For this argument, cf. Pagden, *The Fall of Natural Man*, 150; Prosperi, 'Il Missionario,' 183.

126   A PARADISE INHABITED BY DEVILS

ways in which missionary models and methods developed for use in the New World reverberated back home in Europe. In particular, there is a curious tension between Acosta's discussion of missionary accommodation and his advocacy of the use of coercion or force, where necessary.

Acosta composed his guide to evangelizing Amerindians just one year after being appointed Provincial of Peru for the Society of Jesus and thus the work certainly reflects upon some of the challenges which he was then facing in his new, more responsible role within the order. This examination of *De Procuranda* highlights the implications of Acosta's evangelizing model for Jesuit work in Naples, stressing common themes, the use of similar, edifying anecdotes and the broader relationship between parallel efforts to produce Christianization and religious and social reform in the late sixteenth century.

De Procuranda Indorum Salute is written as both a polemic in favor of evangelizing Amerindians and a missionary manual for the success of such an endeavor. The work begins with a Preface that outlines Acosta's philosophy of the distinct 'levels of civilization' which different societies have reached, advocates the Christianization of Amerindians and establishes Acosta's goal of presenting an 'objective' rendering of the nature of the New World, using empirical methods of inquiry. In his dedication to Everard Mercurian, the fourth General of the Society of Jesus (1573–80), Acosta promises that his work will be based solely upon scrupulously researched information and direct experience, avoiding any hint of 'partiality' toward any party.[60]

Although certain aspects of Acosta's discussion bear little direct relevance for work within European popular missions, much of *De Procuranda* could be applied to the broader pastoral goals of the Society of Jesus in Naples and elsewhere. Particularly in its attention to the centrality of accommodation in the practice of evangelizing, its use of exemplary stories and advocacy of a highly methodical approach, the work can be seen as an important model for future missionary manuals, though by no means the only one. The body of the work is divided into six books, each of which takes up a specific aspect of New World evangelization – exploring the obstacles which missionaries faced, the nature of the initial conquest and evangelization of the Americas, the importance of civil administration, the qualities of an ideal missionary and the most efficacious means for teaching the sacraments and Christian doctrine to indigenous communities:

---

[60] Acosta, 'Dedicatoria' to Everard Mercurian, Lima, Peru, 24 February 1577, *De Procuranda*, 49–53, esp. 49. Acosta was especially eager to make a case for the possibility of evangelizing among Amerindians, given the debate then raging about the viability of such campaigns.

REVERBERATIONS FROM THE NEW WORLD   127

> It is quite difficult to discuss successfully *the* way of achieving the salvation of the Indians. Because, in the first place, various are the nations into which they are divided and [they are] very different among them, as much in terms of climate, habitation and clothing as in ingenuity and customs [. . .] and to establish a common norm for subjecting such diverse peoples to the gospel and at the same time educating and ruling [them], requires an art so elevated and profound that we frankly confess to not have been able to reach it.[61]

In the Preface to his first important publication, Acosta presents an evolutionary argument about the comparative development of distinct civilizations and the implications of these 'levels' for the Christianization of 'barbarian' peoples. As the above comment reveals, Acosta recognized the diversity of Amerindian societies and implicitly endorsed the Jesuit principle of accommodation in missionizing efforts. His insistence that it is foolhardy to seek a single means to evangelize among such a disparate set of communities illustrates this point.

In his social evolutionary schema, Acosta considered all 'barbarian' societies against the normative standard of contemporary Christian Europe. For the Spanish Jesuit (and in this he was not alone), non-Christians might achieve a relatively high degree of civility due to the development of a written language, sophisticated governmental structures, extensive commerce and trading networks and elaborate religious cults and ritual behavior, but 'true' civility could only be synonymous with Roman Catholicism.[62]

According to Acosta's cultural map, barbarians were those who 'hid from right reason and the common way of life of men.' Clearly, the influence of Aristotelian thought is evident here. He divided such people into three categories. The highest category of barbarians was those nearest to learned European in the possession of 'right reason.' According to Acosta, civilizations such as the Chinese, Japanese and East Indian 'have stable republic[s], public laws, fortified cities, judges who are obeyed, and, what is more important, the use and knowledge of letters, because wherever there are books and written monuments, people are more humane and politic.'[63]

Acosta viewed these Asian societies as comparable to the Ancients, the Greeks and Romans, and recommended evangelizing them in a similar manner. He argued: 'Because they are powerful and they possess

---

[61] Acosta, 'Proemio,' *De Procuranda*, 55 (emphasis mine).

[62] By this standard, of course, Protestant 'heretics' and Jews might be considered barbarians, but while such language was occasionally applied to these groups, their 'civility' in other respects, notably literacy, made such appellations absurd, at best.

[63] Acosta, *De Procuranda*, 61–9, esp. 63.

128   A PARADISE INHABITED BY DEVILS

human knowledge, they must be made subject to the Gospel through the use of their own Reason.' Thus, Acosta felt that missionary orders like the Jesuits could effectively evangelize such 'barbarians' in the manner of the Apostles, without the need to rely upon the force of arms or armies to protect them from harm.[64]

Next down on the evolutionary pyramid were the Incas and Mexicas of the New World, those civilizations whose empire-building legacy the Spaniards admired, even as they destroyed the institutions which had perpetuated it. These civilizations were largely urbanized (a sure sign for Acosta of greater civility), economically active and followed complex religious cults, although they had no literary tradition which the Europeans recognized as valid. Acosta reasoned that the experience of the strong, centralized authority which rulers like the Inca had exercised would equip this group of barbarians to submit to the authority of 'Christian rulers and magistrates,' and facilitate their conversion to the true faith. He justified the need to exercise colonial dominion over even such relatively 'civil' indigenous societies by referring to the 'monstrosity of rites, customs and laws' reputedly practiced by such barbarians. This seems a clear reference to the practices of human sacrifice and cannibalism, in particular.[65]

Finally, the third category of barbarians to whom Acosta assigned a place in his cultural scheme were the 'savages,' represented for Acosta by groups like the Caribs, or the Tupinamba of Brazil. These societies, according to Acosta, were composed of peoples who 'scarcely have human feeling' and who existed 'without law, without king, without pacts, with neither judges nor republic.' For Acosta, one sure sign of such societies' savagery was their nomad status. For sixteenth-century Europeans, nomadism was synonymous with a whole panoply of unsavory behaviors and attributes, which Acosta catalogues in this discussion: cannibalism, bestiality, nudity, sodomy, sexual licentiousness and low intelligence.[66]

It was not just the nomadic way of life *per se* that proved troubling for Acosta and others. The very idea that people lived so far from the civilizing influences of cities and towns posed a threat to the construction

---

[64] Acosta, *De Procuranda*, 63. Despite such idealism, the Jesuits had a far harder time effecting successful, long-term conversions in these three East Asian societies. Among the most compelling studies of Jesuit missions to East Asia, see Jonathan D. Spence, *The Memory Palace of Matteo Ricci* (New York: Penguin Books, 1984).

[65] Acosta, *De Procuranda*, 63–5; Pagden notes that in the *Historia*, Acosta credits the Inca and Mexica for having at least a pictographic language, but he likens the function of their indigenous 'books' to the role played by religious icons among illiterate Europeans. Cf. Pagden, *The Fall of Natural Man*, 187–90.

[66] Acosta, *De Procuranda*, 67–9, esp. 67.

REVERBERATIONS FROM THE NEW WORLD 129

of a universal Christian community. Whether in Brazil, Florida, or the mountains of Calabria, the isolation of small, 'disordered' communities represented the victory of primitivism over rationality and civil behavior.[67] This perspective is ironic, given that urban missionaries also saw cities like Naples as veritable cesspools of vice and debauchery and focused great efforts on evangelizing among the urban poor. Nevertheless, Acosta's attitude reflects a wider consensus (for this period, at least) that cities could at least provide some hope for civility and promoting Catholic orthodoxy.

The missionary relations for the Neapolitan Province also make frequent mention of just such 'uncivil' communities, arguing for a clear link between the complexity of social organization and the level of Christianization. In one early seventeenth-century missionary report from the interior province of Basilicata, Padre Antonio Cusola remarks upon the supposedly bestial nature of the people whom he encounters and their unhealthy reliance upon superstition and magic: '[Having just] arrived in these two places, upon first sight I was dismayed, finding them [the people] living more like herds of animals than in the homes of Christians . . .'. Cusola notes that the shepherds he meets are just nominally Christian, 'not having anything worthy of this name except baptism' and are 'given to sorceries and spells, and, in addition, to dishonesty.'[68]

By implication, then, for Cusola as for Acosta, the missions became essential aides, because they could provide a bulwark against the 'natural' tendencies for uncivil communities to continue in their backward practices and remain outside of the Catholic Reformation ideal: a universal, Christian community which promotes Catholic orthodoxy and recognizes established social and political hierarchies.

Nor were such descriptions merely the province of the rural missionary reports. As we have seen, the Neapolitan poor were regularly characterized as bestial. In *Il Forastiero* (1634) Giulio Cesare Capaccio vigorously decries the supposed state of debauchery and incivility among Neapolitans, not unsurprisingly placing the burden of responsibility for such a state of affairs upon women. According to Capaccio, superstitious beliefs and practices are 'as ever the offspring of these vanities among

---

[67] For a discussion of cultural attitudes toward nomads, see Pagden, *The Fall of Natural Man*, 195-7.

[68] ARSI, *Neap.* 73 (1613-39), Doc. XII, No. 6, ff. 113-114V, 'De Missione Basilicata,' Padre Antonio Cusola, 25 June 1618. For a similar reference to the 'savagery' in remote parts of southern Italy, see Saverio Santagata, *Istoria*, 3: 18-19. In his discussion of the Jesuit Silvestro Landini's mission in Corsica in 1553, Adriano Prosperi also raises the complexities of parallel references to Amerindian savages and 'selvaggi europei.' See Prosperi, *Tribunali della Coscienza*, esp. 551-7.

130   A PARADISE INHABITED BY DEVILS

the simple and ignorant women, and sometimes in [the] cruel and bestial
men that I have met, who have only the appearance of men and are
worse than oxen.'[69]

In his discussion of the institution of a new Jesuit college in the
Mercato district of Naples in 1612, the Jesuit historian Saverio Santagata
makes a similar argument, although with a decidedly different intention.
He notes that the impetus for the founding of first a college and later a
Jesuit residence in this poor, densely populated market district was in
response to the dire conditions which prevailed there. Santagata
describes the disorder which was unleashed in the Mercato upon the
departure of a popular Jesuit priest, Padre D. Francesco Romano:

> [W]ith the departure of that man [Romano], who was so zealous in
> honoring God and in the aid of his neighbors, that lowest part of
> the city, which is called the Mercato and contains at least seventy
> thousand people [who are] extremely needy of spiritual assistance,
> remained completely abandoned ... Therefore no longer having
> any check, those vices which in the past had been frightened away
> by the fervent work of the aforementioned priest, made a terrible
> inroad, and would have contaminated all those people with the
> most distressing depravation of custom: from the inundation of
> hatreds and of tricks, cursing, concubinage, and other more horrible
> excesses.

Tellingly, the Society's solution to this example of disorder was to
provide a permanent and consistent missionary presence, in order to
'give methodical and stable culture to the coarse and licentious people
of those districts.'[70]

The only solution for such communities, the Jesuits believed, was the
active intervention of well-trained clergy. Only civil life could produce
true Christianization, whether it was in a bustling European metropolis
like Naples or in the New World. For his part, Acosta urges that the
most 'savage' Amerindians be evangelized by 'bring[ing] them together
to teach them so that they learn to be men and instruct them as [you
would] children.' Although Acosta cautions restraint in such efforts, he
condoned the use of force to 'civilize' this third group of barbarians, if
they did not voluntarily submit to such instruction: 'And if by attracting
them with enticements, they permit themselves to be taught voluntarily,
so much the better; and if they resist, not for that should they be
abandoned, *but if they rebel against their own good and salvation, and
rage against the doctors and masters, it is necessary to restrain them*

---

[69] Capaccio, *Il Forastiero*, 72.

[70] This intervention began in 1610, upon the transfer of Padre Romano from the
Mercato, culminating in the founding of the College of St Ignatius in 1612 and a professed
house in 1613. See Santagata, *Istoria*, 3: 470-71.

REVERBERATIONS FROM THE NEW WORLD 131

with force and proper authority [. . .] in order to avoid obstacles to their salvation.'[71]

For Acosta, as for the Society of Jesus as a whole, the advocacy of a pedagogical role for missionaries was not inconsistent with an acceptance of the use of coercion to compel subjects, when necessary. Part of this ambiguity grew out of the Jesuits' understanding of the nature of 'incivility.' Those who did not possess 'right reason' (and in the world of early modern cultural elites, this included the urban poor, the peasantry writ large and New World 'savages') required different handling to their more 'civil' counterparts. Just as Acosta had argued that more 'advanced' barbarians like the Chinese might be evangelized in the manner employed by the Apostles in their dealings with pagans in the Ancient World, so he insisted that those who either lacked 'right reason' or were plagued by unseemly habits and cultural practices could expect tougher medicine.[72]

The Society's acceptance of compulsory methods of evangelization was by no means unique to the Indies, even if it took somewhat different forms in the context of southern Italy. In a curiously off-handed reference, a 1576 missionary report from Teramo d'Abruzzo (a small town near the Adriatic coast, northeast of Rome) brags about the large number of confessions heard during the Jesuits' visit to the area, while admitting that many may have been compelled by fear. According to the anonymous missionary chronicler, '[t]he people came from all the dioceses to make confession, especially those who feared excommunication, because it had been declared [mandatory] by the Bishop (as we were told by some of them upon our departure) for those who had not confessed for a long time.'[73]

What is interesting about this report is not the immodesty or *braggadocio* of its author's tone, which is actually mild, but rather the casual

---

[71] Acosta, 'Proemio,' *De Procuranda*, 69; cf. Pagden, *The Fall of Natural Man*, 159 (emphasis mine.)

[72] On Acosta's acceptance of the use of violence to compel 'civility' among 'savages,' cf. Pagden, *The Fall of Natural Man*, 159–61. I agree with Pagden when he notes that although Acosta argued that the use of force might be appropriate, he also stressed the educability of New World barbarians who, like Castilian peasants, were plagued by the persistence of unhealthy customs and 'perverse' habits. Acosta also stresses elsewhere in the text that true conversion can only be voluntary. See Book 1, Ch. 13, 197.

[73] ARSI, *Neap.* 72, Doc. V, 'Relation of Mission to Teramo d'Abruzzo,' 1576, ff. 14–14v, esp. f. 14. Although the Abruzzi (a mountainous area due east of Rome) was geographically closer to the Roman Province, it remained part of the vast Neapolitan Province during the period under discussion. The purpose of this comparison is not to equate the threat of excommunication with the use of armed force, but to demonstrate that, despite their insistence that 'conversions' needed to be voluntary, the Jesuits found a range of methods of Christianization permissible.

132 A PARADISE INHABITED BY DEVILS

reference to the Bishop's threat of excommunication to parishioners. In contrast to the threats of physical violence that might be invoked in missionary accounts from colonial America, here the anonymous author poses a less corporeal discipline: the possibility of excommunication. Still, this can hardly be viewed as mild. Within the context of sixteenth-century European life, to be excommunicated was to be a social pariah, with a range of legal and cultural proscriptions added into the mix.

Acosta expands upon the Jesuits' ambivalent approach to evangelization in Books One and Two of *De Procuranda*, considering the difficulties facing would-be missionaries in the evangelization of the Americas, particularly given the legacy of the Spanish conquest. These sections of his study reinforce two pillars of Acosta's complex, seemingly contradictory thinking: the educability of even the most 'savage' of missionary subjects with the use of appropriate methods and diligence, alongside an acceptance of the deployment of Spanish political and military authority to subdue resistance to evangelization.

In Book One of *De Procuranda*, Acosta takes on the Sepúlvedan argument that the Amerindians were 'slaves by nature' and therefore not proper subjects for effective Christianization. Juan Gínes de Sepúlveda was an official in the court of Emperor Charles V and the infamous opponent of Bartolomé de las Casas in the Valladolid debates over the legitimacy of the Spanish enslavement of the Indians (1550–51). He had been a vocal opponent of the civilizing mission, believing that only forcible conversions could secure the pacification of the Indies.[74] In response to this way of thinking, and in harmony with the theory of the educability of all human societies, Acosta followed Las Casas by advocating a belief in the basic sameness of the human mind and the importance of environment for the shaping of social values and practices.

In a manner that would become common to the writers of Jesuit instructional manuals, Acosta cites those difficulties that missionaries can expect to encounter in the field before presenting effective solutions to these challenges. This kind of discussion is warranted, Acosta argues, if it will prevent missionaries from making rash decisions or taking unnecessary risks: 'Remembering the difficulties that occur in the preaching of the word of God is useful, [especially] if it is carried out with prudence, in order to temper youthful ardor and to rein in its audacity; as Aristotle said very well, although one immediately confronts unknown dangers, with even greater speed [one] flees from suffering

---

[74] Juan Ginés de Sepúlveda, a Spanish humanist, advocated the idea that Amerindians were 'natural slaves.' Sepúlveda is probably most famous for his highly charged debate with Bartolomé de Las Casas on the very question of whether it was licit to enslave Amerindians. He also served as chaplain and royal chronicler in the court of Charles V.

them.'[75] Echoing the recommendations of the Neapolitan Provincials, Acosta urges his Jesuit brethren not to look to the civilizing mission in the Indies as an opportunity to achieve glory, but rather insists that their goals be selfless: 'among all the virtues necessary for this office, the most important one is humility.' The conversion of Amerindians will not be easy, Acosta admits, but reminds his readers that Christianization has never been an easy enterprise, especially since it requires not only a faith which 'exceeds human understanding,' but also calls for a transformation of well-established habits and practices.[76]

But in a curious twist which reveals the ambiguity of his representation of New World 'barbarians,' after comparing the tasks facing missionaries to those encountered by the early Apostles, Acosta draws a distinction: '[W]e are combating the timidity and the ignorance of the barbarians, while for the apostles, on the contrary nothing [hindered] them as much as the inflated and arrogant wisdom of the Jews, Greeks, and over all of the Romans [. . .].' Thus, according to Acosta, while the Apostles had to contend with the formidable power of Jewish, Greek and Roman civil and religious institutions, and the richness of existing traditions, sixteenth-century missionaries could, at least theoretically, rely upon the protection of Spanish forces and civil institutions. Amerindians had been subjugated by Spanish colonialism, Acosta argues, leaving missionaries 'suffering the inconstancy and natural imbecility of the Indians.' If the Apostles felt as though they were planting the seed of Salvation in rock, Acosta compares the work of the modern apostles in the Indies as working in 'sandy earth,' without, however, fearing for their lives as the original Christian Apostles had done.[77]

Whatever truth there may have been to this characterization of the relative safety of the missionary vocation in the Americas (and the number of missionaries who lost their lives in efforts to Christianize Amerindians casts doubt upon this representation), Acosta's comments again suggest both his confidence in the missionary enterprise and his conviction that distinctive methods are required, depending upon the 'level of civilization' which a given society had attained. The sub-text here is a recognition that the colonial enterprise provided certain protections for missionaries which they might not enjoy in other contemporary sites of evangelization such as China and India, with direct implications for the kinds of missionary methods which might be employed.

Aside from any other problems, however, Acosta insists that there are

---

[75] Acosta, *De Procuranda*, Book One, Ch. 3, 97. Many thanks to Julia Rodriguez for help with this translation.

[76] Acosta, ibid., 99. See also Burgaleta, *José de Acosta*, 80.

[77] Acosta, *De Procuranda*, Book One, Ch. 4, 107.

134   A PARADISE INHABITED BY DEVILS

no human societies that are incapable of receiving Christian instruction. He points to the many successes which had already been achieved, 'as much in the East Indies as in ours of the West,' in converting numerous people to Christianity, remarking upon the more 'miraculous' of these to show the work of the divine spirit in this enterprise.

The Jesuits presented examples of the 'miraculous' conversions of inveterate infidels, embodying an emergent narrative category of Jesuit missionary relations, whether in southern Italy or the Indies, wherein a recalcitrant sinner is brought around to the true faith shortly before her/ his death. The purpose of these stories was surely to emphasize the power of the Gospel to soften even the hardest hearts, but they also served the equally important role of demonstrating the efficacy of missionary activity in producing tangible results. Interestingly, such examples were frequently of recalcitrant female sinners, suggesting that for both members of the Society and the greater reading public, the image of missionaries' taming of women was particularly compelling.

In one of Acosta's tales, an old Indian woman who was the only member of her family not to accept baptism calls a priest to her deathbed to baptize her so that she might have a 'good death.' In her story, as in the myriad recited in the missionary relations from the Kingdom of Naples, and elsewhere, the woman is moved by a vision (in this case, of a young man, dressed all in white) who exhorts her to accept Christianity. And, in a suggestive example of the powerful calculus linking race/ color to virtue/sin, the woman also relates being visited by 'a black Ethiopian [. . .] who encouraged her to remain [faithful] to her superstitions.' As might be expected, the Indian woman chooses the path of virtue, rejecting the 'Ethiopian's' counsel, and impresses the priest with her death-bed conversion.[78]

In other instances, however, a (frequently) female sinner refuses the aid of missionaries until it is too late. Such stories, which can be found in the missionary reports and popular Jesuit histories from the Kingdom of Naples, serve as cautionary tales. In one such incident, a woman who had led her daughter to commit a 'mortal sin of the flesh' refuses to confess to the Jesuit fathers during the first night of the mission and dies a terrible death. But her death is not in vain, we are told, since it encourages her daughter to confess and, one can infer, leads her toward the straight and narrow path:

---

[78] Acosta, *De Procuranda*, Book One, Ch. 6, 133–5. In an interesting variation on the deathbed conversion, Xavier presents a story of an East Indian woman facing a difficult childbirth whose conversion and baptism leads to the rapid and healthy birth of her baby. See Xavier, 'To Father Ignatius of Loyola, in Rome' (Document 19), Tuticorin, 28 October 1542, pp. 61–2.

It was discovered among the audience a woman who, it was said, allowed her own daughter to commit sins of the flesh. This unfortunate mother still had not resolved herself to confess that evening . . . and perhaps was waiting for the morning to do it. But the poor woman died that night without either being able to confess, nor to give the sign of her salvation . . . [but] *at least her death was a warning to the daughter, who remained alive, so much so that she left her sin* [behind] *making herself holy.*[79]

Whether successful in promoting such conversions or not, authors as diverse as Acosta and the southern Italian Jesuit Father Prella included these stories as staples in missionary accounts. Like the ritualized enumeration of the numbers of souls who had made confession, or received communion, tales of deathbed conversions offered apparent evidence that Jesuit missionaries were accomplishing great things and, especially when included in published accounts, such as Scipione Paolucci's *Missioni de Padri della Compagnia di Giesù nel Regno di Napoli* (1651), served to publicize the order's triumphs in the name of the Roman Catholic faith. By focusing on efforts to convert recalcitrant women, these accounts both reinforce the notion that women presented particular challenges to missionaries and celebrate a taming of potentially disorderly and disordering womanhood.

Beyond introducing the concept of the 'levels of civilization' among potential converts and the methods appropriate to their evangelization, and serving to further Jesuit propaganda, one of Acosta's most vital contributions in *De Procuranda* is his discussion of the spiritual ministry which the Jesuits must forge in the New World. As in other sections of this work, Acosta poses a series of challenges facing would-be missionaries, and then proffers solutions. In Books 4, 5 and 6, he fashions a missionary manifesto of sorts by discussing the skills necessary for the clergy to be successful, the best methods to effect conversions, the significance of teaching the catechism, and urging frequent and 'correct' confessions to improve the moral fiber of Amerindians and correct unorthodox practices, and the dissemination of the sacraments among indigenous communities.

In order to overcome a whole range of obstacles to effective evangelization at home, the Jesuits in the Kingdom of Naples, like Acosta, took up a deliberate, pragmatic approach to missionizing. They stressed the need to accommodate to local conditions while remaining true to their order's apostolic vision. They sought to attract community members to

---

[79] ARSI, *Neap.* 74 (1640–1649), 'Missioni di Padre Prella,' 1645–1646, ff. 137–152v, esp. f. 138. Compare Paolucci's dramatic tale of a prostitute whose deathbed repentance comes too late for the Jesuit missionary to save her, in Paolucci, *Missioni*, 253–7 (emphasis mine.)

136   A PARADISE INHABITED BY DEVILS

their popular missions through a variety of methods, and to articulate their strategies in instructional manuals. In this way, Acosta, like Xavier before him, offered an important model (though by no means the only one) for the development of a set of distinctively Jesuit missionary strategies. These parallel visions point toward a growing sense of common purpose and practice in the Society of Jesus by the turn of the seventeenth century.

Toward a collective missionary identity

During the latter part of the sixteenth and the first half of the seventeenth centuries, an institutional missionary identity was forged in the Society of Jesus. Strongly influenced by the promotion of heroic missionary models such as that of Francis Xavier, the 'Apostle of the Indies,' and the dissemination of news of their brethren in remote mission fields, Neapolitan Jesuits enthusiastically sought placement in missions in the Indies.

Through their letters, the *Indipetae*, we can appreciate the lure of the Indies – a primary locus for the battle between Roman Catholicism and idolatry – but also an exotic magnet for those weary of teaching grammar and Christian doctrine to groups of unruly southern Italian schoolboys. By tracing shifts in style and content, as well as assessing the comments of Provincials that occasionally annotated these requests, we witness the self-conscious development of certain themes. While early letters remained largely formulaic in their authors' recitation of personal virtues and (especially) proclamations of divine calling, over time Jesuit novices became far more savvy about identifying areas of strength, training and experience. Some also learned to invoke the patronage networks that were always crucial in facilitating advancement within the Society of Jesus.

For their part, Provincial superiors' annotations to the *Indipetae* hint at the institutionalizing of the 'ideal' missionary type. This type would be elaborated upon by both Jesuit superiors in places like Naples and important New World commentators like José de Acosta. Ideal missionaries combined a range of personal qualities such as robust health, good judgement and flexibility with a strong obedience to the authority of superiors and a willingness to work for the greater good of the Society and, more generally, for the Catholic faith.

Finally, the *Indipetae*, as well as missionary letters, reflect the growing sense that Jesuit novices were encouraged to view their missionary vocation as universal in scope. When Giuseppe Cocollo enthusiastically relates his superior's promise that if he proves himself worthy in the

'Indies down here' he might improve his chances of being sent to a more distant mission field, he is indirectly affirming Miguel Navarro's earlier suggestion that the Society take seriously the need to use southern Italy as a training ground for the Indies.

Carlo D'Orta's letters home from Colombia close the circle: by addressing members of his congregation back home in Aversa, D'Orta suggests that his own work in the Indies – clearly influenced by the 'heroic' model of Francis Xavier – might have some relevance to the tasks facing missionaries in Naples. Had he lived to return to Aversa, perhaps D'Orta might have reversed Navarro's suggestion by viewing the Indies as a training ground for the ambitious reforms that the civilizing mission in southern Italy sought to achieve.

Acosta's model of a flexible yet comprehensive missionary program in the Indies that could accommodate a range of 'levels of civilization' had enormous implications for the elaboration of a missionary strategy in the Kingdom of Naples and the strengthening of the Jesuits' collective identity as a missionary order *par excellence*. Even while Acosta was composing *De Procuranda*, Neapolitan Jesuits were identifying parallel problems closer to home.

Ultimately, the creation of this missionary identity in the Society of Jesus, one that committed members to building a universal Christian community, and forging thoroughgoing moral reform in troubled areas like Naples, required something further of the still-young religious organization. For the civilizing missions to be successful, the Jesuits composed a variety of instructional manuals that identified uniform areas of activity, rules of decorum for missionaries and solutions to the thorny challenges that might be faced in the 'Indies down here.'

CHAPTER FOUR

'Use every means that you will judge opportune': Instructions to Jesuit missionaries

As much as Jesuit institutional character was forged through the 'heroic' models offered by missionaries in the Indies in the late sixteenth and early seventeenth centuries, the Jesuits' self-consciously constructed collective identity was also articulated through the development of instructional manuals that served to train novices in the science of conducting missions and to publicize the order's work to a broader public. The composition of these instructional documents facilitated the development of the Society's distinctive missionary approach in Naples and throughout the global reach of the order. In order to understand the significance of the Jesuits' broader approach to missionary methodology, and given the importance of the circulation of ideas and approaches to the Society of Jesus' corporate identity, I offer a comparative analysis of instructional manuals in the Neapolitan Province and in other parts of Italy.

Jesuit instructional documents reveal a gradual shift in emphasis across the seventeenth century. Over the course of the century, the instructions offered to missionaries grew not only more detailed and elaborate, alongside the Jesuits' increasingly well-defined institutional identity, but also shifted according to broader social and cultural patterns. For as much as the Society's members sought to be culture bearers and shapers, they were also affected profoundly by prevailing winds. This is nowhere clearer than in the discussions of strategies to combat sexual immorality and resolve marital disputes. In these instructions, we find the Jesuits grappling with a complex elaboration of proper post-Tridentine sexuality and appropriate gender relations. In particular, the definition of what was *prudent*, a major preoccupation for an organization that needed to balance its ambitious reform goals with the practical conditions in which it operated, evolved over the course of the seventeenth century. In the case of attitudes toward female sexuality and marital disharmony, for example, it is possible to trace a decided move away from stressing exclusive female culpability to a somewhat more balanced approach.

140   A PARADISE INHABITED BY DEVILS

The Jesuits' missionary science,[1] which found parallels in the order's comprehensive approach to education (outlined in the *Ratio Studiorum*), was based on five key principles. First, it consisted in the self-conscious elaboration of deliberate missionary strategies. Secondly, it involved the articulation of ideals of missionary decorum. While these ideals were suggested in the order's foundational documents, and reinforced in Claudio Acquaviva's early directives for the conduct of internal missions and in missionary manuals such as Acosta's *De Procuranda*, they became increasingly formalized through the composition and dissemination of instructional documents over the course of the seventeenth century. The third distinctive principle of the Jesuits' emerging missionary methodology lay in their emphasis on cultivating techniques for information gathering and stressing the benefits to be gained by the use of informants. While such a practice may have contributed to stereotypes of the order as a band of spies, it also reflects the high degree of pragmatism in the order. In fact, the Jesuits' instructional documents from Naples and elsewhere demonstrate a sensitivity to the suspicions which the order's information gathering efforts might arouse. While authors do not shy away from endorsing the practice, they spend considerable time recommending that missionaries do all they can to assuage fears and 'demonstrate every kindness' toward parish clergy and prelates.[2] Finally, and most important, the Jesuits' instructional manuals reflect efforts to strike a workable balance between accommodating to immediate circumstances and remaining faithful to a core theory of conducting missions, and thus remaining true to the order's 'calling.' As the Jesuits honed their tactics for effecting the civilizing mission in Naples over the course of the seventeenth century, they also demonstrated a sensitivity to the changing social and cultural milieu in which they found themselves.

The Jesuits' elaboration and formalization of instructions did not happen in a vacuum. Taking a cue from their mendicant predecessors, particularly the Franciscans, the Society of Jesus outlined its missionary vocation in foundational documents such as the *Constitutions*. But

---

[1] For one of the best introductions to the Society's educational program, see *La 'Ratio Studiorum.' Modelli Culturali e Pratiche Educative dei Gesuiti in Italia tra Cinque e Seicento*, ed. Gian Paolo Brizzi (Rome: Bulzoni, 1981). The literature on Jesuit science is vast indeed. For an excellent critical examination of Jesuit science and of its rich historiography, see Rivka Feldhay, 'The Cultural Field of Jesuit Science,' in *The Jesuits. Cultures, Sciences, and the Arts*, 107–30. On the Jesuits' voracious pursuit of scientific knowledge, see also Steven J. Harris, 'Mapping Jesuit Science: The Role of Travel in the Geography of Knowledge,' in ibid., 212–40.

[2] ARSI, *F.G.* 720A/I/1/9 (*c.* 1600) unfoliated, Fabio Fabi, 'Instruttione per li Padri che vanno à fruttificare nella Sabina' (Roman Province).

INSTRUCTIONS TO JESUIT MISSIONARIES   141

where the late medieval mendicants had made only general reference to the apostolic calling which motivated their actions, the Jesuits composed increasingly detailed and comprehensive instructions to guide the actions of the order's rapidly expanding membership.[3] Far more than their forebears (and contemporaries, for that matter), the Jesuits sought to systematize the missionary vocation, anticipate potential obstacles to success and draw the necessary lessons from past mistakes.

How did missionary instructions evolve over the course of the seventeenth century and with which areas were they centrally concerned? Besides institutional directives, such as General Acquaviva's order for members to engage in internal missions, there were at least four distinct instructional genres: internal forms such as missionary relations, circular letters and unpublished instructional manuals, as well as instructions earmarked for a wider audience, such as those included in published accounts of Jesuit missions.

Jesuit instructional manuals might touch on a vast range of topics, but were principally concerned with three important areas. First, authors considered logistical concerns such as when, where and how to conduct missions. Over the course of the seventeenth century, logistical instructions became increasingly more elaborate as the civilizing mission became more institutionalized and experience dictated certain strategies over others. A second area of emphasis for the Jesuits was in establishing and maintaining cordial relationships with clergy and secular elites. This was always a tricky matter, particularly given that the internal missions were often conducted with an awareness and conviction that local clergy were inadequate to the task of providing quality pastoral care, or that local elites might be guilty of irreligiosity

The third, and most amorphous category of instruction, was in the extirpation of idolatries and the reform of immoral behaviors. Taking a cue from their colleagues in the Indies (especially Acosta and Xavier), authors of the Jesuits' instructions offer suggestions for dealing with idolatrous parishioners and their unorthodox practices. Perhaps more pressing still were the apparently widespread examples of immoral behavior. The instructional documents provide missionaries with explicit instructions to address illicit sexuality, resolve marital disputes and combat other supposedly 'unchristian' practices. The instructions on

---

[3] For literature available on the missionary methods and orientation of the medieval mendicants, see, for example, E. Randolph Daniel, *The Franciscan Concept of Mission in the High Middle Ages* (Lexington, KY: University of Kentucky Press, 1975), and Noe Simonut, *Metodo d'evangelizzazione dei francescani tra musulmani e mongoli nei secoli XIII–XIV* (Milan: Pontificio Instituto Missioni Estere, 1947). (I thank Pauline Moffitt Watts for bringing the latter source to my attention.)

142 A PARADISE INHABITED BY DEVILS

combating illicit sexuality and resolving marital disputes offer a fascinating window onto shifting views of female sexuality during this period. From Francis Xavier's seemingly callous acceptance of marital violence in the mid-sixteenth century to Paolo Segneri's late seventeenth-century calls for encouraging family stability and mutual respect between spouses, we can see a broader transition in the missionaries' view of gender relations.

Institutional directives and the varieties of instructional documents

Instructions to missionaries might take a variety of forms in the Society of Jesus. Following Claudio Acquaviva's institutional directives for Jesuits to participate in the popular missions at the end of the sixteenth century, other leading members of the Society sought to expand or better organize this pastoral activity in keeping with the order's diversified interests, commitments and perpetually over-taxed personnel. For example, Acquaviva's successor as General of the Society, Muzio Vitelleschi (1617–42), seems to have been an enthusiastic supporter of the internal missions.[4]

Nevertheless, it seems the major institutionalization of the internal missions occurred during the brief generalate of Vincenzo Carafa (1646–49). Carafa, the seventh General of the Society and a member of a powerful and prominent Neapolitan family, believed that missionary activity was an essential component of Jesuit institutional identity and endorsed 'apostolic incursions' as ideal vehicles through which to fulfill the Society's missionary vocation.[5]

Carrying forward Acquaviva's earlier impulse to expand the internal missions, Carafa's directives also responded to an apparent gap between missionary ideals and the realities on the ground. By insisting on the value of the missions not only for the salvation of souls, but also for the 'personal perfection' of missionaries, Carafa urged his fellow Jesuits to apply themselves more consistently to the apostolic vocation.

---

[4] Santagata, *Istoria*, 4: 49–50; 388. Santagata indicates Vitelleschi's overall support for the internal missions, but pays special attention to his initial interests in expanding activity in the Indies. Later in his generalate, however, Santagata chronicles the expanded activities in and around Naples following the Jubilee year of 1625.

[5] For Carafa's philosophy of missionizing, as well as his directives for the institutional reorganization of the order's missionary activity, see Giuseppe Orlandi, 'S. Alfonso Maria de Liguori e l'ambiente missionario napoletano nel settecento: La Compagnia di Gesù,' *Spicilegium Historicum* 38 (1990), 5–195, esp. 14–16; cf. Armando Guidetti, *Le Missioni Popolari*, 100–102. On Carafa's life and work as a Jesuit, see Daniello Bartoli, *Della Vita del P. Vincenzo Carafa*, 2 vols (Turin, 1825).

INSTRUCTIONS TO JESUIT MISSIONARIES 143

Carafa formally initiated the office of the *Province Prefect of Missions* in 1647 in response to the inconsistent application of mission principles and to standardize the practices of missionaries across the order's European provinces. Writing to the Jesuits' five Italian Provincials in 1646, Carafa argued that the Society had taken up so many and such divergent activities that it was beyond the capabilities of the Provincials to satisfactorily attend to all of these obligations. Therefore, Carafa reasoned, the duties associated with the local missions should be separated out from the overall responsibilities of each Province's superior by creating the post of Missionary Prefect for each of the Society's provinces:

> Consequently, I have considered, in the sight of God and in light of our *Constitutions*, and with the advice of my assistants, to establish and fashion in every province a prefect of missions, whose office it would be to provide for the Provincial all that pertains to the missions of that Province [and] who, however, should also have a list of the colleges that have made obligations to the missions, and also a list of the Prelates and principal people of the Province, making sure that they are satisfied when they ask for some mission. Beyond this, he [the Prefect] will inform the Father Provincial which missionaries could be assigned to this or that mission, what kinds of help they would need . . .[6]

By creating this new office, Carafa indirectly acknowledged that the Society was having difficulty in applying its missionary vision in practice. This difficulty had been noted much earlier by Fabio Fabi (1542–1615). A prominent member of the Society of Jesus, Fabi held several posts in both the Neapolitan and Roman Provinces, became Assistant for Italy in 1605 and wrote a number of instructional documents for missionary novices. During his time as superior of the Neapolitan Province (1600–1602), Fabi composed a fascinating document which essentially laid bare the difficulties which the order was facing in living up to its missionary vocation.[7] Responding to Acquaviva's directive for each Province to provide for ten to twelve missionary priests to be involved in establishing missionary residences, Fabi offered a number of concerns before ultimately endorsing a modified version of the plan.

First, Fabi cautioned his superiors that there were not enough workers

---

6 Vincenzo Carafa, 'Copia di una lettera di N.P. Vincenzo Carafa al P. Valentino Mangione Visitatore, del Prefetto delle Missioni (1646)', reproduced in Carla Faralli, 'Le missioni dei Gesuiti in Italia,' 101.

7 ARSI, *Neap.* 73, Fabio Fabi, Document V, 'Delle Residenze et Missioni della provincia de Napoli' (no date given, *c.* 1600–1602), ff. 22–23v; cf. Mario Rosa, *Religione e Società nel Mezzogiorno*, 261–4. Rosa is quite right to indicate that Fabi's stringent criticisms of the plan to institute permanent missionary residences suggest his firm opposition to the plan, yet he does not account for Fabi's ultimate endorsement of the plan (at least on the rhetorical level).

144 A PARADISE INHABITED BY DEVILS

to fulfill the various duties required of the Jesuits in the colleges. In addition, many members of the order were either too old or too ill to be actively involved in the rigors of the missions. Despite the economic incentive to conduct missions (for example, the hope that wealthy benefactors in far-flung regions would be grateful for the order's attentions), Fabi noted the limitations of this approach given the vagaries of weather and distance, and the financial limitations of often impoverished citizenries far from the capital city.

In terms of the specific impact associated with initiating missionary residences, Fabi worried over the deleterious effects that such a commitment might have on the colleges. The loss of essential personnel would damage the educational institutions which were clearly the 'bread and butter' for the order. Fabi feared that it would be harder for the Jesuits to raise funds where they were already active because people would fear that the Society was 'abandoning them' and would get the impression that the order was not very stable ('it would seem difficult for them to give alms to those who were not stable in that land, but went away to serve and fructify elsewhere'). Discipline would be more difficult to maintain with members going away so often and having so much contact with the public.[8]

Despite all these criticisms, however, Fabi acknowledged the value of the missions and offered a compromise plan which, he argued, would achieve the desired goal of increasing missionary activity while preserving the integrity of the colleges and not unduly taxing their finite resources. Fabi suggested that those colleges with adequate personnel and resources choose appropriate individuals to initiate missionary centers near the colleges, and called upon those institutions' superiors to take up the task of selecting appropriate individuals to run these locales.[9] Fabi's concerns may have proved prophetic, because, despite good intentions, two years after Acquaviva's death in 1615 there were still no permanent missionary centers in the Kingdom of Naples.[10]

Thus, Carafa's institutional reform efforts were a direct response to an objective failing in the order, and particularly in the Neapolitan Province where the Society had focused a great deal of its initial missionary activity. Although subsequent generals would express sup-

---

[8] Fabi, 'Delle Residenze.'

[9] Fabi, ibid., f. 23v.

[10] Cf. Orlandi, 'S. Alfonso Maria de Liguori,' esp. 13. Orlandi notes that although the Society did maintain two residences that they referred to as 'missions,' they recorded having only two missionaries in one of these and one in the other. In addition, neither 'mission' is mentioned in the biannual catalogue for the Province in 1619, indicating their fleeting, and probably unsuccessful, tenure.

INSTRUCTIONS TO JESUIT MISSIONARIES 145

port for the Society's internal missions, the kind of instructional directives articulated by Acquaviva and Carafa would not be repeated. Instead, the Jesuits' instructions to missionaries became the purview of other members of the order, taking on a more unofficial form throughout the seventeenth and into the early eighteenth century.

These 'unofficial' Jesuit instructions to missionaries could be found in missionary relations, circular letters, unpublished instructional documents or instructions included in published materials. Not surprisingly, these genres were not always mutually exclusive. For example, Scipione Paolucci's popular history of the Jesuit missions in the Kingdom of Naples (1651) was a published account, presumably aimed at a broad reading public beyond the Society of Jesus, but heavily based upon his reading of missionary relations from the Neapolitan Province in the second quarter of the seventeenth century.

The missionary relations provide the most extensive record of the Jesuits' extensive and variegated missionary activity throughout the history of the order. Numbering in the hundreds for the period between *c.* 1550 and 1700, the relations provide first-hand reports on the conduct of internal missions, the methods employed by Jesuit practitioners, their successes and (less frequently) failures to win souls and the lessons that might be drawn from such experiences. Although the reports generally were addressed to the Society's General in Rome, or passed along to him via the Provincial Superior, the relations were evidently shared among other members of a Province, especially novices residing in the colleges and those living in professed houses.[11] Still, the missionary relations were not primarily conceived as training manuals for new members of the order, and the very fact that they were directed to the order's superiors often lends them a triumphal tone which does not necessarily permit a hard-nosed assessment of missionary methodology.

Aside from the relations, another genre gained early currency among members of the Society: the circular letter. In such letters, made famous by notable Jesuits like Francis Xavier in his travels in the Indies, we can find a wide range of concerns, including the dissemination of instructions to missionaries. We know that Xavier's letters had a tremendous impact upon members of the Society, and he is cited countless times in the *Indipetae* and in other correspondence by members of the

---

11 The question of how the missionary relations and other instructional documents were disseminated among members is a fascinating one which has not (to my knowledge) yet been addressed. We know only anecdotally that missionary relations were read widely to (or by) members of the order, as in numerous comments in the *Indipetae*, and Francesco Schinosi's description of the impact of letters/reports from the Indies impact upon novices' interest in pursuing a missionary vocation there. See Schinosi, *Istoria*, 2: 54.

146   A PARADISE INHABITED BY DEVILS

Society.[12] In Xavier's case, his descriptions of exotic locales and unfamiliar cultures must have played a part in the subsequent publication of such letters for popular consumption, but Xavier also wrote instructions to members of the Society of Jesus that reflect his missionary philosophy, sometimes speaking to broader social concerns of the mid-sixteenth century such as marital violence and gender relations. In these letters, then, prominent members of the Society could find a ready institutional audience for their concerns and their rapid dissemination within the order suggests a potential for exerting significant influence upon members.

The third genre in which we find an expression of missionary science is the actual instructional, or training, manuals. Varying in size from one or two folio pages to Antonio Baldinucci's more extensive, 67-folio *Avvertimenti a Chi Desidera impiegarsi nelle Missioni* (*c.* 1710),[13] these instructional manuals provide the most concrete evidence that the Society took seriously the business of training members to be effective in their apostolic vocation. In their manuscript form, it is difficult to ascertain how such documents might have been disseminated among members. Curiously, the bulk of the documents are written by and about activities in the Roman Province, suggesting perhaps the higher concentration of experienced members at the center of the organization's activities. Nevertheless, since their recommendations often match those prescribed in the missionary relations, and later, in published accounts of the missions, it is likely that these instructions were familiar to missionaries in the field in the Neapolitan Province and elsewhere. Besides Antonio Baldinucci, the instructional documents are the work of other prominent Jesuits such as Fabio Fabi and Cesare Croilo, first Prefect of Missions for the Roman Province (*c.* 1647). Especially in the case of Fabi, we know that he had an important role to play in the Neapolitan Province and can thus surmise that his instructions would have been equally valid in the southern Italian context.

Finally, published accounts of Jesuit missionary activity provide an additional avenue through which members of the order could discuss missionary methodology and propose strategies for dealing with the ever more complicated circumstances in which they found themselves working. In addition to Paolucci's account of missions in the Kingdom of

---

12 See, for example, Paolo Segneri, 'Letter to Muzio Vitelleschi,' 5 July 1641, in *Lettere Inedite del P. Paolo Segneri*, ed. Giuseppe Boero (Naples, 1849), 32. Antonio Baldinucci also cites Xavier's inspiration upon him for placement in the missions to the Indies. See Baldinucci, *Lettere inedite del P. Antonio Baldinucci della C. d. G. corredate di note per cura del P. Luigi Rosa* (Prato, 1899), esp. 118n.

13 ARSI, *Opp. Nn.*, ms 299, Antonio Baldinucci, *Avvertimenti a Chi Desidera impiegarsi nelle Missioni. Cavati dall'Esperienza di Quei che le Hanno fatte per Molti Anni, c.* 1710–17, 67ff.

INSTRUCTIONS TO JESUIT MISSIONARIES 147

Naples, both Francesco Schinosi's and Saverio Santagata's companion histories of the Jesuits in the Kingdom of Naples offer anecdotal discussions of missionary methodology and hint at the primary categories for missionary instruction: logistical considerations, dealings with clergy, and efforts to reform illicit sexual practices and family disputes. Far more detailed information, however, is offered in Paolo Segneri and Fulvio Fontana's *Pratica delle Missioni del Padre Paolo Segneri della Compagnia de Giesù* (1714), a comprehensive assessment of Segneri's missionary methodology that includes excerpts from sermons, daily schedules for missionary activities, specific strategies for dealing with a wide range of religious and cultural imperfections and advice for overcoming popular resistance to the missions. It is here that one finds an expression of the Jesuits' mature missionary science, confidently describing the Society's highly articulated yet accommodating formula for apostolic activity for the benefit of neophytes and a curious reading public. While Segneri never worked in Naples or southern Italy, it seems clear that the most famous seventeenth-century Jesuit missionary innovator was influenced at least in part by his Neapolitan confrères.[14]

Logistical concerns in the instructional manuals

A central concern in the training manuals, and a fundamental demonstration of the Jesuits' emerging missionary science, lay in the elaboration of logistical instructions to missionaries. Seemingly mundane issues such as the best time of the year in which to conduct missionary interventions, what kind of entrance to make in a new town or village, where Jesuits should lodge while in a new mission field, when and how to conduct activities and how to anticipate resistance from the laity offer evidence of the emergence of a systematic Jesuit missionary approach across the seventeenth century. A consideration of these logistical instructions highlights the delicate balance that the Society of Jesus tried to strike between systematizing its missionary methodology and remaining open to accommodating to specific situations.

---

[14] The full title of the text is *Pratica delle Missioni del Padre Paolo Segneri della Compagnia de Giesù predicatore Pontifico continuata dal P. Fulvio Fontana della Medesim Religione, per lo spazio d'anni ventiquattro, per una gran parte d'Italia, e di là da monti, nella Elvezia, Rezia, Valesia, e Tirolo. Con l'aggiunta delle Prediche, Discorsi, e Metodo Distinto Tenutosi nelle Funzioni Sacre*, Parts I and II (Venice, 1714); cf. Elisa Novi Chavarria, 'Le Missioni dei Gesuiti in Calabria,' 113–39, esp. 131. Novi Chavarria suggests that Segneri borrowed notions of penitential practice from the Neapolitan missionaries, but I would extend this point to include a wider range of missionary methods adapted throughout the seventeenth century.

148   A PARADISE INHABITED BY DEVILS

The emphasis on logistical instructions, like so much of the Society's practice, found embryonic form in the Jesuits' *Constitutions*. There, Loyola took great care to outline the duties of Jesuits to carry out their apostolic vocation in accordance with both their 'Special Vow' to the papacy and in the interests of the ever-expanding Society. For this reason, Loyola separated chapters dealing with 'Missions from the Holy Father' from those missions 'received from the superior of the Society.'[15] Even in this early document, the Jesuits' preoccupation with balancing practical concerns and their 'first principles' is evident. Superiors are enjoined to 'keep the greater service of God and the more universal good' foremost in mind, but also are offered a number of scenarios in which difficult choices must be made. In such cases, pragmatism rules the day. This can be seen in Ignatius' recommendation to superiors on the question of sending more than two Jesuits on mission, thus deviating from standard practice:

> To send more than two when the importance of the work intended in the service of God our Lord is greater and requires a larger number, and *when the Society can provide more laborers without prejudice to other things conducive to greater divine glory and universal good*, is something which the superior will have the authority to do.[16]

Although those 'other things conducive to greater divine glory and universal good' are not identified here, this comment refers to other areas of Jesuit activity deemed useful to the Society. In other words, in determining logistical questions regarding the conduct of missions, superiors had always to weigh which choice would bear the most fruit for the Society in its multifaceted endeavors.

It is difficult to unravel Loyola's preference in these matters. Although he cites a number of logistical issues with which a superior must concern himself, such as the manner in which missionaries should be sent on mission ('whether he will send them in the manner of the poor, so that they would go on foot and without money, or with better facilities'), or how to inform local ecclesiastical and secular officials of a prospective mission ('whether with letters to be helpful toward winning acceptance and benevolence at their destination . . .'), he is careful to frame such discussions of tactics in terms of considering what will reap 'the greater edification of the neighbor and the service of God our Lord.'[17] Nevertheless, the very attention that Loyola paid to such details provided his successors with a model for issuing instructions to members.

---

[15] See Ignatius Loyola, *Constitutions*, Part 7 (Chapters One and Two), 267–80.

[16] Ignatius Loyola, *Constitutions*, 276; 278.

[17] Ibid.

INSTRUCTIONS TO JESUIT MISSIONARIES

In his directives toward institutionalizing the internal missions, Claudio Acquaviva made a strong case for the urgency of conducting a civilizing mission among urban and rural dwellers, although he said little about the logistical concerns that missionaries might face. Early instructional manuals from the Roman Province, however, pay a great deal of attention to the nuts and bolts of conducting missions. These manuals are very valuable for understanding the strategies that the Jesuits in southern Italy sought to implement, although they come from work in a neighboring province because the work of the Society of Jesus in one locale was never conducted in isolation; rather, it was intended to be instructive to members of the Jesuit order as a whole. Just as the Jesuits working in Italy gained inspiration and concrete lessons from their brethren working overseas in foreign missions, so lessons gleaned from work in the Roman Province would have significant usefulness in the proximate Jesuit Province of Naples. This was particularly true because of the proximity of Naples to the heart of Jesuit activity in Rome, but even more due to the frequent exchange of personnel.

One crucial area of focus within the logistical instructions was the best time of year to arrive in a mission field. Although it might appear obvious, the Jesuit instructional manuals were explicit in recommending that missions take place in the late spring, before the heat of summer made such journeys more arduous. An anonymously written instructional manual from the Roman Province, probably from the early seventeenth century, offers the following advice: conduct the popular missions in the Lazio countryside between Easter and the end of May to avoid the hottest weather and to catch the shepherds before they return to the mountains for the summer. Start in the hottest places first, while the weather is still temperate, working your way toward the mountains as the weather warms up.[18] In this seemingly mundane example, we can see the extent to which Jesuits' instructional documents sought to anticipate potential obstacles to effective missionizing and to avoid them.

Besides considering the ideal time of year during which to conduct the popular missions, the Jesuit manuals also suggested the most appropriate days to begin missionary activities and considered whether it was more efficacious to enter a community during daylight hours or the

---

[18] ARSI, *F.G.* 720A/I/1/13, unfoliated. Although these instructions were directed toward missionaries in the Roman Province, a relatively similar climate, conditions and predominantly rural/pastoral population would have made such suggestions useful in the rural outposts of the Neapolitan Province as well.

150 A PARADISE INHABITED BY DEVILS

darkness of night.[19] Cesare Croilo, the Prefect of Missions for the Roman Province, stressed that missionaries arrive on festival days to obtain the best results. The choice of weekends or festival days made sense because, presumably, the laity would be more accessible at such times, and thus the missionaries could make positive first impressions. In this case, according to Croilo, the people should be informed of the imminent arrival of the Jesuit missionaries and prepared to participate in the missions. If they were not informed, Croilo warns, 'many, for not having heard [of the mission], would not participate, due to the inconvenience and would not respond [to the mission].'[20]

But, demonstrating some divergence of opinion among missionary commentators, Scipione Paolucci disagrees, arguing that it is better for the Jesuits to make their presence known only to the local ecclesiastical hierarchy in order to seize the most appropriate moment: 'This solicitude is useful in order to make a greater impression upon souls, that for the novelty and for the frightened fervor [inspired by the missionaries], almost cultivated on the spot, and without having time to guard against [it], [will] more fully receive the impression.'[21]

Likewise, authors of missionary instructions were not unanimous in arguing whether it was more effective (and dramatic) for the missionaries to make their presence in the daylight or evening. Implicit in this consideration was the question of what time of day or night would produce the desired effects upon the laity and local clergy. The early instructional manuals do not specify the ideal time of day when missionaries should arrive in a new locale, but instructions embedded in the missionary relations and in published accounts such as those of Scipione Paolucci and Paolo Segneri are quite explicit in their respective recommendations.

One way to make a strong impression upon a community was to take great care in the manner of arrival. Like some of the mendicant orders then conducting missions in the New World, the Jesuits placed great importance upon ritual gestures in their evangelizing

---

[19] For an interesting comparative discussion on the missionary methods of four of the Jesuits' contemporaries in the southern Italian context – the Congregation of the Pii Operai (f. 1602), the missionaries of St Vincent de Paul (1627), the Apostolic Missions (f. 1626) and the Redemptorists (1732) – especially concerning strategies for the first day of the mission, see Maria Gabriella Rienzo, 'Il processo di cristianizzazione e le missioni popolari nel Mezzogiorno. Aspetti istituzionale e socio-religiosi,' in *Per la Storia Sociale e Religiosa del Mezzogiorno d'Italia*, 1, 441–81, esp. 452–7.

[20] ARSI, *F.G.* 720A/I/1/6, unfoliated, Cesare Croilo, 'Istruttioni per li Missionanti delle Missioni Nella Provincia Romana.'

[21] Paolucci, *Missioni*, 11.

INSTRUCTIONS TO JESUIT MISSIONARIES   151

efforts.[22] First impressions *did* matter, as the Jesuits well knew, and their highly developed sense of theatricality (honed in the Jesuit colleges where theater was a staple of the educational program) became vitally important in the elaboration of techniques for effective missionizing.[23] While the early instructional manuals from the Roman Province do not emphasize the manner in which missionaries should arrive at a new site, missionary relations from the Kingdom of Naples instead make frequent references to how Jesuits should appear to prospective subjects.

In a mid-seventeenth-century pamphlet detailing the Jesuits' mission to Bitonto (near Bari), Giovanni Battista Di Elia opens with a highly dramatic account of the missionaries' entrance into the town during a public demonstration of military exercises. Here, rather than emphasizing the Jesuits' immediate impact upon the community, Di Elia presents the anecdote to demonstrate the humility and piety of the Jesuit fathers, in contrast to the apparent bombast and worldliness of the military parade. While this published account would not have been expressly intended to edify the public about the Jesuits' calculated, systematic approach to missionizing (in the manner of instructional manuals), the

---

[22] Numerous authors have highlighted the Jesuits' use of ritual and theatricality in their missionary methodology, especially in reference to making strong 'first impressions.' See, for example, Gentilcore, '"Adapt Yourselves to the People's Capabilities,"' 275–6; Carla Faralli, 'Le Missioni dei Gesuiti in Italia (sec. XVI–XVII): problemi di una ricerca in corso,' *Bolletino della Società di Studi Valdesi*, 82, No. 138, 97–116, esp. 108–109; Giuseppe Orlandi, 'Missioni Parrocchiali e Drammatica Popolare,' *Spicilegium Historicum Congregationssmi Redemptoris* 22, No. 2 (1974): 313–46, esp. 320–21; and Elisa Novi Chavarria, 'L'Attività Missionaria dei Gesuiti nel Mezzogiorno d'Italia tra XVI e XVIII Secolo,' in *Per la Storia Sociale e Religiosa del Mezzogiorno d'Italia tra XVI e XVII*, 1, 159–85, esp. 162–4. For a suggestive consideration of the application of ritualized behavior in the Franciscan missions in the New World, see Pauline Moffitt Watts, 'Languages of Gesture in Sixteenth-Century Mexico,' in *Reframing the Renaissance: Visual Culture in Europe and Latin America*, ed. Claire Farago (New Haven: Yale University Press, 1995), 225–47. For a fascinating discussion of the Franciscans' deliberate emphasis on recreating the ritualized arrival of the first twelve Franciscan friars in subsequent missions in seventeenth-century New Mexico, see Ramon Gutiérrez, *When Jesus Came, the Corn Mothers Went Away: Marriage, Sexuality, and Power in New Mexico, 1500–1846* (Stanford: Stanford University Press, 1991).

[23] For the role which theater played in the Jesuit colleges, see Marc Fumaroli, 'Il Crispus e la Flavia di Bernardino Stefonio,' in *Eroi e oratori. Retorica e drammaturgia secentesche* (Bologna: Il Mulino, 1990), 197–232. Three fascinating discussions of theatricality in Jesuit activities are: Giovanna Zanlonghi, *Teatri di Formazione. Actio, parola e immagine nella scena gesuitica del Sei-Settecento a Milano* (Milan: Vita e Pensiero, 2002); Bernadette Majorana, 'Lo pseudo-Segneri e il Teatro celeste: due tracce secentesche,' *Teatro e Storia* 9 (1994): 357–88; and Giuseppe Orlandi, 'Missioni Parrocchiali e Drammatica Popolare,' *Spicilegium Historicum* 22, No. 2 (1974), 313–46. Unfortunately, Zanlonghi's publication is too recent to have been examined critically in this work.

152 A PARADISE INHABITED BY DEVILS

following passage does indicate the missionaries' highly self-conscious approach to conducting their missionary entrance:

> Said Fathers, imitating the Apostle of the Indies St. Francis Xavier in the habit of pilgrims, arrived from Bari on foot, all of their faces covered with perspiration from the great heat of the season, but even more burnt in the heart of holy zeal. In entering the city so unnoticed, and all alone, they met up with a large crowd of people who were spectators at a military demonstration that was being conducted: wherefore they [the Jesuits] were forced to pass by everyone timidly, and with eyes on the ground to get through that crowd, which was very uncertain about their garb, not knowing who they were. But still, the Fathers said amongst themselves: who knows whether all these people will become like wax in our hands within a short time, and this Militia will see itself more ardently fighting against the Inferno![24]

In this instance, the rather innocuous and humble arrival of the Jesuits is contrasted with the implied pomp and pageantry of the profane military parade. The very fact that the citizens of Bitonto seem preoccupied by non-sacred matters sharpens the rhetorical purpose of this passage. Perhaps now the people are taken with secular concerns, Di Elia seems to be saying, but the missionaries have other plans for them. The juxtaposition between the apparent meekness of the 'pilgrims' and their intention to mold the parishioners like so much 'wax in our hands' also reconfirms the Society's dissimulating approach. Just as the Jesuits permitted the practice of 'mental reservation' in certain cases, here the author seems to be endorsing the strategy in a more gestural context.[25]

In contrast to Di Elia's recommended means of arrival, Scipione Paolucci maintains that the mission should begin at night to 'impress' the people with divine fear. This strategy not only insures making a successful first impression, but also bodes well for continued good attendance at various missionary activities. Paolucci argues that:

> the darkness of night is useful to the compunction of hearts, frightening souls with native horror and disposing them more surely to the blows of divine fear . . . [S]o it is that these so-called night-time incursions frequently are practiced after the beginning of the

---

[24] ARSI, *Neap.* 73, Giovanni Battista Di Elia, 'Relatione di Una Missione fatta da due Reverendi Padri della Compagnia di Giesù nella Città di Bitonto del Regno di Napoli, Nell'Anno 1646' (Trani, 1646, 31pp.), ff. 163–78; f. 165.

[25] Perez Zagorin, *Ways of Lying. Dissimulation, Persecution, and Conformity in Early Modern Europe* (Cambridge, MA: Harvard University Press, 1990), 163–4. Zagorin defines 'mental reservation' as the practice of holding back some aspect of the truth known only to the speaker. Although this approach was suggested primarily in casuistry, or determination of cases of conscience, its appeal was obviously much wider and consistent with the order's overarching strategy of accommodation.

INSTRUCTIONS TO JESUIT MISSIONARIES   153

mission[,] greatly inspiring the people with fervor and disposing them to more frequent concourse.[26]

While they may not have agreed on whether a nocturnal or daylight arrival was most useful, the authors of instructions were universal in stressing the importance of the first day of the new mission. In his 'Instructions for the Fathers who go to fructify in Sabina' (a rural area northeast of Rome), Fabio Fabi suggests that missionaries utilize the first day to convince the people of the value of the mission. Whether they arrived in the morning or evening, Fabi argues, Jesuits should make an exhortation 'in which, firstly, one deals with the necessity of knowing Christian doctrine and of evils, what constitutes mortal sin ... the necessity of Confession ...'.[27] In other words, regardless of whether resident clergy had paved the way for the Jesuit fathers, the missionaries needed to assert the value of their endeavor to a potentially skeptical community. But this was not always an easy task, since not all communities appeared equally enthused by the prospect of a Jesuit mission.

The missionary relations, in particular, offer examples of initial apathy, or resistance to missionary efforts. In fact, by their very nature, the relations tend to highlight the various stages of the mission in order to increase their own dramatic flavor and to accentuate victories won in even in the most initially hostile environments. Sometimes, missionaries cited bad weather as an obstacle that they must overcome. Other times, it was a lack of planning or community support which must be mitigated. Both of these concerns are addressed in an early seventeenth-century relation by Bernardo Da Ponte.[28]

Da Ponte begins his report by admitting that he was worried over whether the mission in question had any chance for success when missionaries arrived to find that no arrangements had been made for them: 'It occurs to me to say that this mission was made by extreme divine providence because there was no disposition nor provision made for keeping us in the city.'[29] According to the author, had it not been for the intervention of a devoted local, a layperson who belonged to one of

---

[26] Paolucci, *Missioni*, 14.

[27] ARSI, *F.G.* 720A/I/1/9 *c.* 1590), Fabio Fabi, 'Instruttione per li Padri che vanno à fruttificare nella Sabina' (unfoliated).

[28] ARSI, *Neap.* 72, Doc. XXI, Bernardo Da Ponte, 'Relation of a Mission to Cava' (1612), ff. 221–2. Da Ponte is an interesting example of a relatively unknown seventeenth-century Neapolitan Jesuit missionary whose discussion of strategies for overcoming technical problems faced by missionaries, such as overcoming great distances among hamlets, anticipates the more famous contributions of Paolo Segneri in the latter part of the century. For a brief biographical sketch of this Jesuit who served as Master of Novices in the Neapolitan Province, see Armando Guidetti, *Le Missioni Popolari*, 83–4.

[29] Da Ponte, ibid., f. 221.

154   A PARADISE INHABITED BY DEVILS

the Jesuits' local congregations, the missionaries would not have been able to find lodging, nor purchase foodstuffs.

An additional problem which Da Ponte cites was the relative indifference of the residents of Cava: 'The other [problem] was moving [the emotions of] such a people who applied themselves [mostly] to business and to earning money . . . [A]nd since the Society is not noted for this, they did not offer much cooperation in the beginning.'[30] In this passage, Da Ponte highlights his discouragement at the business-oriented disposition of this community, but his comment is highly ironic, given the Jesuits' well-known business ventures, both in European outposts like the Kingdom of Naples and far afield, and the opposition that such practices could sometimes elicit from the laity.

Finally, Da Ponte notes the logistical difficulties involved in conducting a mission in a town 'divided into distant hamlets, one, two, and three miles [apart] so that it was not convenient to bring them together.' To overcome this crucial problem required ingenuity and a willingness to endure, despite initial doubts:

> For these reasons, [those cited above] we were given little confidence and I thought that it [the mission] could not succeed. Beyond this, I thought that if things continued to go this way, it might be better to leave it [the mission] for another time. But God gave us perseverance, because all the things of Christ, as a rule, are [difficult] in the beginning and then succeed well. And from this achievement, I have learned to be more courageous in the future.[31]

Although he is careful to cite God's necessary inspiration in all the successful decisions made during the mission, Da Ponte also uses the opportunity to demonstrate his own technical innovations in organizing the popular mission. Anticipating Paolo Segneri's far more famous contribution of the 'central mission' by nearly half a century, Da Ponte describes the careful organization of the mission to accommodate to the decentralized layout of Cava, highlighting the furious pace of activities required of the (usually) two missionaries:

> God inspired us to go hamlet by hamlet among the more principal ones, and in each one, I would spend about a week, beginning with a sermon. And this was a good idea and it succeeded, as a result of which we divided our forces with preaching in the Cathedral in the morning, and during the day went to the hamlets, and [attended] to the Sabbath cults during the evening, and then, stopped to confess

---

[30] Da Ponte, ibid., f. 221.
[31] ARSI, ibid., f. 221.

INSTRUCTIONS TO JESUIT MISSIONARIES 155

[people] during the day, returning home in the evening. And this was our exercise for about five weeks . . .'[32]

Da Ponte uses his missionary relation to highlight the extent to which the Jesuits' arrival in a new mission field set the tone for the entire mission, even if it was a rocky start. His consideration of how to organize one's time most effectively, and also when and how to schedule the various activities associated with the popular missions, signals the deliberateness which characterized the Jesuits' emerging missionary science.

This highly articulated approach to conducting the civilizing mission, first experimented with in the southern Italian context, was later refined and formalized in the writing of the seventeenth century's most noted Jesuit orator and missionary, Paolo Segneri (1624–92).[33] Born in Nettuno (near Rome) in 1624, Segneri joined the Society in 1637. After being refused a mission vocation in the Indies (for which he vigorously campaigned), he turned his attentions instead toward the popular missions.[34] From 1665 to 1692, Segneri was actively involved in internal missions throughout much of northern and central Italy, gaining notoriety for both his fiery preaching style and his innovative missionary methods. According to one account, Segneri's vigorous missionary itinerary led him to conduct between twenty and twenty two missions each year, between Easter and autumn, for a total of 540 missions during his 27-year tenure in the field.[35]

In terms of envisioning a comprehensive philosophy and practical roadmap for conducting popular missions, Segneri was without peer. Clearly utilizing the experiences of numerous missionaries who had come before him, Segneri's primary contribution was to synthesize the lessons which had been indicated in the missionary relations and earlier

---

[32] ARSI, ibid., f. 221. Paolo Segneri, the noted late seventeenth-century Jesuit orator and missionary innovator, is usually credited with devising the 'central mission' in the second half of the seventeenth century. But Da Ponte is just one among several Neapolitan missionaries who anticipate Segneri's strategies. For a brief description of the 'Segnerian mission,' see Armando Guidetti, 'Il Metodo Missionario del P. Segneri,' *Appunti di Spiritualità* 31 (1991): 27–45.

[33] Giuseppe Orlandi, 'Missioni Parrocchiali,' 324. Orlandi argues, 'Father Paolo Segneri . . . systematized and perfected the penitential mission already in vogue among the Jesuits of South-Central Italy.'

[34] On Segneri's thwarted efforts to gain a vocation in the Indies, see *Lettere Inedite*, 29–37.

[35] For an interesting account of Segneri's highly active missionary career, see Armando Guidetti, *Le Missioni Popolari*, 104–106. A prolific writer, Segneri's collected works include his more famous methodological writings, such as *Il Cristiano Istruito nella sua Legge. Ragionamenti Morali* (1686). The edition of Segneri's *Il Cristiano* that I consulted is from 1745.

156   A PARADISE INHABITED BY DEVILS

instructional manuals in order to develop a uniform approach, designated the 'central mission.'

The 'central mission' was essentially the more evolved solution to a longstanding problem that Bernardo Da Ponte and other Jesuits had encountered several years earlier: how best to achieve effective interventions among the largest number of people despite logistical problems such as great distances between communities, dioceses or even villages. Segneri argued that a 'central mission' allowed missionaries to begin in one particular part of town and then methodically work their way out to all the adjacent dioceses or surrounding villages. To aid them in their work, Segneri suggested that missionaries familiarize themselves with topographical maps so that they could determine the length of time required to spend in each district and the number of priests required to achieve their goals.[36] To avoid wasting precious time, Segneri scheduled the missions back to back, so that just as one was finishing, a mission in an adjoining area was about to begin. He justified this approach by arguing that to allow a break between missions would interrupt the momentum that the missionary might build. But in a more positive light, he claimed that a continuous round of adjacent missions would allow maximum potential contact with sinners and a greater possibility to save souls: 'Distribute [the missions] in such a way that they are not too great a distance from one another, which will provide a great advantage to Souls in that it will permit more people to intervene in the functions [of the mission], and so dispose them to a true Confession, which, when it is not convenient to make in one place, can well be conducted in another.'[37]

Another crucial part of Segneri's methodology was to outline the specific days and times for the various activities that formed the core of the missionary experience. Here, his suggestions went well beyond the earlier instructional manuals in the level of detail provided, and in the novelty of his recommendations for how missionaries might involve even the most unwilling participants.

Well before Segneri's time, the Jesuits' instructional manuals had suggested the kinds of activities in which missionaries should engage, although they had not yet systematized a conventional schedule for missionaries to follow. After arriving in a new community and advising local clergy of their intentions, missionaries should attend to their principal duty of providing instruction in Christian doctrine. This

---

[36] The following discussion is based heavily upon *Pratica delle Missioni del Padre Paolo Segneri*, Part 2, 5–27. See also Guidetti, *Le Missioni*, 114–25. Cf. Antonio Baldinucci's advice for promoting 'good order in the missions,' in 'Avvertimenti,' ff. 17–18.

[37] Segneri and Fontana, *Pratica delle Missioni*, Part 2, 5.

INSTRUCTIONS TO JESUIT MISSIONARIES

instruction should be presented in a clear and simple manner, accommodating to the diverse needs and levels of understanding among parishioners.[38] In general, the authors of these instructions suggested, sermons should consider the most commonly practiced sins, the sacraments, the 'correct' means of making confessing and taking communion, mental and vocal prayer, examining one's conscience, correct use of the rosary and proper ways of listening to the Mass.[39] Beyond accommodating to the abilities of the laity, missionaries should also accommodate to their schedules. Thus, Cesare Croilo suggested that missionaries avoid preaching in the mornings, while many parishioners were occupied with labors in the fields, but instead find the most convenient times to pursue such activities.[40]

Even in some of the earliest instructional manuals, there is an effort to identify the most suitable times of the day and night for the central activities associated with the mission. According to Croilo, men could make confessions in the morning (presumably before work), while women were required to do so in church, and always in a well-lit place. Similarly, according to Croilo and others, men and women should meet separately to receive instruction in Christian doctrine. Women (and children) could be taught after lunch, and their learning could be aided by conducting processions and presenting them with holy images.

Men, on the other hand, should be convened in the church in the evening to receive their instruction. In such instances, Croilo is explicit in 'prohibiting that no woman' enter the church.[41] With this greater specificity came a more explicit concern to promote greater discipline, made evident by the greater emphasis on references to penitential activities and the necessity of maintaining a gendered division of devotion.

All of these logistical suggestions found fuller form and articulation in Segneri's later seventeenth-century missionary program. Segneri considered each detail of the missionary schedule, from the entrance that missionaries should ideally make (arriving on a Monday morning, to be greeted by a procession of the people, assembled outside of the parish

---

[38] Acquaviva, 'Lettera di Nostro Padre Claudio Acquaviva,' f. 32. Acquaviva had stressed this point in one of his early directives for the conduct of popular missions, cautioning missionaries: 'In preaching, be even more careful than usual to guard against using pomp or doctrine, but only resolve to invite men to penitence and to the hatred of sin.'

[39] ARSI, F.G. 720A/I/1/1, 'Instruttioni' (1590). Cf. the far more detailed late seventeenth-century account of Antonio Baldinucci, 'Avvertimenti,' ff. 27–30.

[40] ARSI, F.G. 720A/I/1/6, Croilo, unfoliated.

[41] Croilo, ibid.

158 A PARADISE INHABITED BY DEVILS

church, singing litanies)[42] to the introductory sermon, which would exhort the people to view the mission as an opportunity to regain their spiritual health: 'You should know that as God has eternally ordained, and determined the end of your salvation, so too he has determined the means; and what more efficacious means can he offer you than a holy mission, which has come to rest in your native land? Now, if you refuse it, couldn't you with good reason fear for your salvation?'[43] Segneri outlined the daily exercises through which the evangelical experiment would be effected, designating the mornings for the singing of spiritual songs, processions to the church and preaching on a different theme each day. In the afternoons, after lunch, one of the missionaries would teach Christian doctrine to men and women (presumably in separate quarters, in keeping with the vigorous emphasis on the gendered separation of devotional practice). This would also be followed by a brief sermon. The evening was reserved for the highly theatrical penitential processions for which Segneri was famous. These processions would not begin during the first few days of the mission, but should rather be seen as vehicles to further energize a community and encourage greater enthusiasm for the whole range of exercises associated with the mission.[44]

Beyond detailing the schedule of missionary exercises, Segneri provided specific suggestions on the ideal seating arrangement of the laity during sermons. He discussed where and how to set up an altar in the countryside, and how many priests and/or secular assistants would be required to aid the missionaries in their duties.[45]

Finally, Segneri's instructions to missionaries provided a thoroughgoing discussion of how to contend with nay-sayers and resistance to the missionary effort. Certainly, earlier Jesuit commentators had noted resistance to the missions and advised 'patience' in dealing with recalcitrant sinners. One late sixteenth-century instructional manual, for example, reminded novices 'not to be dismayed' if they did not instantly win over their charges. Instead, the author urged them not to 'immediately cede to the impediments which the Devil could pose.'[46]

Somewhat later, in another anonymously written instructional manual from the Roman Province, the author advised a more aggressive approach to winning over souls: 'On the day that one teaches Christian Doctrine, the instructor noted, assemble the people together by [ringing]

---

[42] Segneri and Fontana, *Pratica delle Missioni*, Part 1, 2.
[43] Ibid., Part 1, 4.
[44] Ibid., Part 1, 8.
[45] Segneri and Fontana, *Pratica delle Missioni*, Part 2, 9–10; 13, 14–15.
[46] ARSI, *F.G.* 720A/I/1/1, 'Instruttioni' (1590).

INSTRUCTIONS TO JESUIT MISSIONARIES

a bell across the land, and if they are negligent in coming, go throughout the public squares and the streets to find them, making the sermons [along the way] as best as you can.'[47]

In Bitonto, according to Di Elia's missionary report, the Jesuits had to show ingenuity to draw people away from their preferred, 'demon-inspired' recreations, in order to get them to participate in an outdoor sermon. To inspire awe in the people, the orator climbed to a high place above the town (presumably the church tower), and called out to the people in a loud voice, exhorting them to put aside their frivolous pleasures and 'follow the Crucifix . . . a meal more flavorful than that provided by the Devil, who governed all forms of human recreation.'[48]

When human efforts appeared to be ineffective, or the power of 'demonic' influence too great, a natural disaster might provide the most fruitful ally to a poorly received missionary endeavor. Scipione Paolucci offers an interesting story of how an earthquake drew an uninterested town toward the Jesuits' entreaties. He recalls that the evening arrival of the Jesuit fathers was greeted 'coldly' by the people of an unnamed southern Italian village. That same night, however, the town was visited by 'earthquakes so horrible they shook the entire city.' By morning, Paolucci happily reports, 'all the citizens went to Church to confess,' apparently insuring the success for a mission that had initially appeared to be a lost cause.[49]

In brief, then, discussions of strategies for dealing with opposition to the missions were included among the range of instructional documents, but they were presented quite differently, depending upon the genre. In the instructional manuals, suggestions for dealing with potential resistance were generally discussed with far less fanfare and dramatic flourish. In the missionary relations, by contrast, especially those destined for a non-Jesuit audience (such as Paolucci's), the discussion of missionary strategies was often embedded in an edifying tale of the Jesuits' heroic battle with demonic forces.

By the late seventeenth century, Paolo Segneri's missionary writings provide a comprehensive articulation of a maturing Jesuit missionary methodology. Here, members of the Society of Jesus were instructed to anticipate any and all *specific* excuses for non-participation in the

---

[47] ARSI, *F.G.* 720A/I/1/12, 'Instruttioni per li Padri della missione delle Campagne di Roma' (1615 or 1622).

[48] ARSI, *Neap.* 74, Giovanni Battista Di Elia, 'Relatione di una Missione fatta . . . nella Città di Bitonto,' (1646) f. 165v.

[49] Scipione Paolucci, *Missioni*, 228. On the power of demonic forces to detract from the efficacy of a mission, see 197–208.

160 A PARADISE INHABITED BY DEVILS

mission's exercises and to devise a pragmatic plan to proffer *specific* solutions to such challenges. Among the many novel contributions of the Segnerian mission, none demonstrates this calculated, deliberate approach to the apostolic enterprise better than the Jesuit orator's identification of the most common excuses offered by parishioners for failure to attend missionary functions. Anticipating the sorts of excuses that people might extend, he suggests how clergy can best respond to such rationalizations, providing a kind of early modern 'how to' manual for would-be missionaries and parish clergy.

First, Segneri refers to those who argue that they cannot attend missionary functions due to their labors. He responds by promising them that they will have ample time to attend to their labors in the field and return home to rest before being called to evening exercises. Segneri promises these laborers that not only will the missionary functions not interfere with their work, but that they will benefit by such activities: 'Assure them that, in the twenty-two years that I have been leading missions, I have always heard it said by the public that they have never succeeded better, nor found their efforts in the countryside more fruitful, than during the time of the missions.'[50] To the second excuse, that individuals were wont to participate in the missions because they could not attend all the penitential processions, Segneri assures his followers that in order to obtain a papal benediction (one of the coveted fruits of the mission), an individual need not attend all such functions, but attend at least one per day, allowing other members of the family to alternate at other activities. He cajoles family members to commit themselves to each attend two functions, dividing the burden of the mission among them so that no one need feel overtaxed. This bare minimum attendance was also aimed at those who presented the third excuse: that they would be out of town during the mission.

An additional tactic that Segneri employs is to try to convince parishioners to attend functions for those who were too ill or otherwise physically unable to participate. Stressing the community orientation of the mission, Segneri urges people to avail themselves of the 'golden opportunity' that the mission presented to them. He encouraged the missionaries to:

> Make the people understand that if they do not participate in the Mission each day with a Procession, they will be doing very great damage to all those who are either too sick, or crippled, or due to some legitimate impediment, whether care of animals, or of children, cannot come to the place of the Papal Benediction ... But if they come to the Procession each day, as a member of that body ...

---

[50] Segneri and Fontana, *Pratica delle Missioni*, Part 2, 18–19.

INSTRUCTIONS TO JESUIT MISSIONARIES 161

then those who remain at home, legitimately impeded, will obtain the same treasure, as if they were at the place of the Mission.[51]

Finally, Segneri instructs the local clergy to silence those who 'badmouth' the mission. Here, he seems to be responding to growing criticisms of the Jesuits' penitential missions by admitting that there were those who 'opposed themselves to the Holy Missions; blamed the external penitence; [and] who sowed [the seeds] of diabolical superstitions . . .'.[52] By drawing in clergy to defend the Jesuits' efforts, Segneri affirms the vital role which local clergy were seen to play in insuring the success of the missions. But as we shall see, the Jesuit relationship to diocesan clergy was never quite so straightforward.

Maintaining good relationships with fellow clergy

In addition to offering logistical instructions, the authors of the Jesuits' missionary manuals stressed the need to maintain cordial relationships with fellow clergy. This was especially important because implicit in the Society's missionizing impulse was a conviction that many parish clergy were neither adequately trained nor morally capable of providing a positive example for parishioners. This was, after all, one of the determinations made at the Council of Trent that led to calls for seminary education and episcopal residency requirements. For southern Italy, the problem was deemed that much more severe, particularly in rural areas outside of metropolitan Naples.

Without exception, the authors of Jesuit instructional tracts recommended that missionaries establish contact with local ecclesiastical officials before conducting missions, or immediately upon their arrival in a village or town. One early document directed missionaries to make contact immediately: 'In the beginning of the mission . . . the first thing, [the missionaries should] go to find the Bishop, or the Vicar and report to them on the Apostolic nature of the missions.'[53]

Fulvio Fontana, one of Paolo Segneri's missionary colleagues, provided a model form letter to be sent to local Bishops or Curates to inform them of the imminent arrival of the Jesuit mission and to ask them to prepare the people:

---

[51] Ibid., 19.

[52] Ibid.

[53] ARSI, F.G. 720A/I/1/1, unfoliated, 'Istruttioni per quelli che vanno à Missione per la Provincia [Roman] fatta nell'anno 1590.'

162   A PARADISE INHABITED BY DEVILS

Sir:

Would you please lead, or send your People in procession to _____ where on the _____ of the month _____ at the Church _____ the future mission of Father Fulvio Fontana, of the Society of Jesus, will begin. Try to see that everyone is there at _____ o'clock. And so, [this mission] will continue for several days; [and] such is the precise order of the Most Eminent Archbishop that this [request] be executed with great haste.[54]

Beyond merely announcing their imminent arrival, however, Jesuit missionaries were also advised to take great care in assuaging any concerns aroused by their visit. As Fabio Fabi counseled fellow missionaries: 'With the [P]arish priest or the head of the clergy, demonstrate every kindness without giving the slightest sign of making a visitation,' thus reassuring locals that the missionaries' only purpose 'is to teach Christian doctrine, to confess, to make peace, and in particular to give every satisfaction to the Clergy.'[55] Bernardo Da Ponte stressed the need to show a positive public face toward the clergy, while remaining ever mindful that the Jesuits' intervention could only serve to improve the spiritual climate: 'Because we have always tried to win over the Prelate and the clergy, we are constrained to never offend them in any way, and particularly in sermons, and to the Prelate we must always promise not to serve any authority without his consent, and seek to honor him . . . [and] his authority without limiting it in any way.'[56] Another instructional manual echoes Fabi's advice, but is even more explicit in suggesting that Jesuit missionaries do all they can to overcome the perception that they are spies: 'Don't appear to be spying on the priests nor the parishioners, nor speak in a sinister way in public.'[57] Such attitudes echo early Jesuit advisements to avoid giving offense or engaging in local controversies. On the eve of Diego Laínez and Alfonso Salmerón's participation in the Council of Trent, for example, Loyola instructed his confrères: 'Anyone of ours should be slow to speak and show consideration and sympathy' when considering matters of doctrine. He added: 'Along with his reticence, he should rely on a readiness to listen, keeping quiet so as to sense and appreciate the positions, emotions, and desires of those speaking. Then he will be better able to speak or to keep

---

[54] Segneri and Fontana, *Pratica delle Missioni*, 6. This form letter, devised by Fulvio Fontana, was entitled: 'Formula dell'Avviso, che si manda a' Signori Curati.'

[55] ARSI, F.G. 720A/I/1/9, unfoliated, Fabio Fabi, 'Istruttione' (*c.* 1600), (emphasis mine).

[56] ARSI, *Neap*. 72, Doc. XXI, No. 2, f. 222.

[57] ARSI, F.G. 720AI/1/11, unfoliated (no date given), 'Avvisi per le Missioni.'

INSTRUCTIONS TO JESUIT MISSIONARIES

silent.'[58] Although this advice was proffered in anticipation of the high visibility that Jesuit theologians would have at Trent among other leading members of the Church, it applies just as well to the Jesuits' broader notion of prudent dealings with fellow clergy in the missionary context.

The Jesuits were highly sensitive to the charges that they engaged in duplicitous and dissembling activities. This view, held by some clergy and laity, began to plague the order from the late sixteenth century, and only escalated during the seventeenth and eighteenth centuries.[59] According to Perez Zagorin's useful definition, '*Dissimulatio* signified dissembling, feigning, concealing, or keeping secret ... In a strict sense dissimulation is pretending not to be what one actually is ...'[60] My purpose here is not to suggest that the Jesuits were dissemblers, but that perception existed, and it troubled members of the order.

Despite their protestations to the contrary, several Jesuit documents betray the order's belief that many local clergy were responsible for the widely perceived dissolution of the people. As one missionary report from Salerno concluded, where the clergy do not adequately 'apply' themselves to their tasks, 'so is born in the people a great clumsiness [in understanding] of the things of God. . .'.[61] Scipione Paolucci was more blunt. Referring to missionary activity in some of the more remote villages of southern Italy, Paolucci cites the value of major efforts toward 'cultivating the clergy,' but added that, in his view, some local priests were 'in truth little better than the people.'[62] And, in one late seventeenth-century missionary relation from Lecce, the author bemoans the supposed laxness of local priests as a contributing factor in the prevalence of 'superstitious practices':

> Due to the carelessness of the Confessors, the superstitions in [these] two lands were infinite, committed by everyone without hesitation, and around every kind of business, whether it be marriage, or sin, or remedies, or Lawsuits, they resorted to Superstitions, sorceries, and other diabolical things.[63]

---

[58] Ignatius Loyola, 'Instructions for the undertaking at Trent' (1546) *Saint Ignatius Loyola. Personal Writings* (London: Penguin, 1996), 164.

[59] For a fascinating discussion of anti-Jesuit criticisms in the late sixteenth and seventeenth centuries, largely based on the order's association with casuistry and promotion of dissimulation among English Catholics in particular, see Zagorin, *Ways of Lying*, esp. 153–85; 201–204; 215–16.

[60] Zagorin, *Ways of Lying*, 3

[61] ARSI, *Neap.* 72, Doc. XXIV (7 May 1613), 'Mission to Salerno,' ff. 254–5v, esp. f. 254.

[62] Paolucci, *Missioni*, 17.

[63] ARSI, *Neap.* 76, Document VII, 'Brevissima Relatione d'alcune Missioni fatte l'anno 1667 nella Provincia di Lecce,' ff. 39–42V, esp. ff. 40–40v.

164   A PARADISE INHABITED BY DEVILS

In response to this generalized perception of an ill-prepared clergy, the
instructional documents emphasize the value of the Jesuits training local
priests and monks in Christian doctrine, alongside their training of the
laity.[64] In this way, the Jesuits articulated an institutional role for
themselves as the bearers of 'correct' Catholic Reformation theology,
while also remaining keenly aware of modifying their behavior toward
clergy to demonstrate respect for local hierarchies and appear to present
a united front with any ecclesiastical community. Critics might deem
this approach duplicitous, but to the Jesuits it was merely a pragmatic
approach to achieving their declared goal of promoting religious and
social reform. From the Jesuits' perspective, the many uneducated or
morally lax clergy required a bit of civilizing themselves, but they also
needed to be convinced of the value of further education. Thus, it would
not do to alienate fellow clergy, regardless of their apparent inadequacies
or suitability to provide the laity with spiritual guidance.[65]

Significantly, the range of instructional documents caution missionaries to avoid involving themselves in disputes either among members of
the clergy, or between clergy and laity. As with so many other areas of
instruction, such advice garnered varying levels of definition and articulation across the seventeenth century, depending upon the specific circumstances which missionaries faced at any given time. One theme,
however, is constant: the need for Jesuit missionaries to demonstrate
great prudence in negotiating such delicate matters. One early manual
stressed the need for Jesuits to remain neutral in the face of conflicts,
especially those involving 'prelates, or principal persons.' When such
conflicts arose, and requiring immediate attention, the manual advised
missionaries to do their negotiating in private, presumably to avoid
scandal.[66] Antonio Baldinucci concurs, urging missionaries to refuse to
take sides, if one finds the people or the clergy 'in grave discord' with
their bishop.[67]

Besides remaining neutral in disputes, the Jesuits apparently believed
that the involvement of secular clergy in all aspects of the mission would
be an invaluable way to win their support. Since the long-term goal of
the missions was to effect real changes in a community, the training of
local clergy was viewed as indispensable to the Jesuit endeavor. This

---

[64] Numerous historians have noted the problem of ill-equipped clergy, especially in the
Kingdom of Naples. See, for example, Gabriele De Rosa, *Vescovi, Popolo e Magia*; cf.
Gentilcore, *From Bishop to Witch*, esp. Ch. 2.

[65] I thank Mark Lewis for encouraging this more nuanced assessment of the Jesuits'
approach to fellow clergy.

[66] ARSI, F.G. 720A/I/1/1, 'Instruttioni' (1590).

[67] Baldinucci, 'Avvertimenti,' f. 15.

could be accomplished in three primary ways: first, by instructing clergy in basic Christian doctrine (especially the sacraments), strategies for educating the laity, and how to elicit 'proper' confessions; second, by recruiting secular clergy to aid in missionary exercises; and finally, by stressing that Jesuit missionaries model proper behavior. The early instructional manuals urged Jesuit missionaries to accept the assistance of secular clergy, but also mentioned the usefulness of teaching them Christian doctrine.[68] This was a potentially difficult tightrope to walk, since the implicit message of Jesuits' instructional manuals was that secular clergy were not up to the task of ministering to the laity, yet the Jesuits needed to avoid alienating them in any event.

Paolo Segneri paid particular attention to the value of utilizing the missions as a way of training secular clergy. He offered specific methods for involving clergy at the widest possible level from the very beginnings of a mission. Segneri urged Jesuits visiting new community missionaries to hold a 'conference' at the outset of their missionary intervention with local clergy and secular notables to convince them of both the spiritual and 'patriotic' value of the mission. He advised choosing one secular priest and two members of the laity to offer special assistance to the missionaries.[69]

The secular priests had a variety of functions that they were expected to perform. They could provide essential logistical support throughout the mission, particularly in making arrangements for the use of facilities, advising people of the proper order in which they should march in procession and what kind of disciplinary attire to wear. They could make religious standards that would be held aloft during processions, as well as announcing indulgences and counting the numbers of parishioners who attended missionary exercises each day. But these practical duties did not preclude them from fulfilling basic pastoral functions such as offering communion, hearing confessions and teaching spiritual songs.[70] Similarly, the secular clergy were expected to assist the missionaries in insuring the widest possible presence at all missionary functions and to inform the visitors of 'the dissensions that exist [. . .], of the animosities, and discord,' so that reconciliations might be facilitated.[71]

---

[68] See, for example, ARSI, *F.G.* 720A/I/1/6; *F.G.* 720A/I/1/9.

[69] Segneri and Fontana, *Pratica delle Missioni*, Part 2, 8. On the duties expected of secular notables, including working with secular priests to ensure 'good order,' helping women in their activities (because of their supposed helplessness) and bringing people along to confession, see 22–23.

[70] Segneri and Fontana, *Pratica delle Missioni*, Part 2, 11–15; 20–21. Cf. Antonio Baldinucci, *Avvertimenti*, ff. 19–20; 35–7.

[71] Segneri and Fontana, *Pratica delle Missioni*, Part 2, 19–20.

166   A PARADISE INHABITED BY DEVILS

Finally, a further means of training the secular clergy was for the Jesuits to serve as models. The instructional manuals present ideals of missionary decorum through which Jesuit novices could learn to mold proper clerical behavior. The manuals stress that missionaries must possess moral seriousness and a judicious nature. This was especially important given the climate of the Catholic Reformation where the Church was reeling from both Protestant and internal criticisms of the immorality of many clergy. Indeed, the Jesuit instructions are careful to warn missionaries to avoid any hint of indiscretion, particularly in dealings with women, but also with young boys.

Jesuits might prevent even the hint of scandal by only meeting with women in the context of hearing confessions. 'Women always confess in Church in a well-lit place.'[72] Antonio Baldinucci was still more direct, advising his brethren to 'never look a woman directly in the face,' nor speak with her even in church (beyond confessional duties).[73] This approach certainly fit in with the Society's overall goal of acculturating Jesuit novices to an institutional culture that stressed virtue and sought to protect members from the stain of scandal, but it also reflected a wider goal of combating clerical immorality through example.[74] Not surprisingly, such comments likewise reveal a wider cultural attitude that viewed women with suspicion.

Reforming illicit behaviors

The Jesuits' self-defined apostolic calling encouraged members to intervene in reforming a vast range of social and cultural beliefs and practices that might not immediately appear 'religious.' From its earliest missions in Naples, as we have seen, the order was especially concerned with illicit sexuality and sexual commerce (concubinage and prostitution). But the Society of Jesus also became increasingly involved in the

---

[72] ARSI, *F.G.* 720A/I/1/9, Fabi, 'Instruttione.'

[73] ARSI, *Opp. Nn.* 299, Antonio Baldinucci, 'Avvertimenti,' f. 13.

[74] The self-conscious articulation of ideals for missionary decorum finds a parallel in considerations of 'ideal' decorum for students in the ever-expanding Jesuit colleges of the mid- to late sixteenth century. See, for example, Giuseppe Cortesono's recommendations for dealing with numerous 'disorders' in the Collegio Germanico in Rome in *Constitutiones seu monita ad eorum usum qui Collegio Germanico praesunt*, written *c.* 1570, cited in Gian Paolo Brizzi, *La 'Ratio Studiorum'*, 26–34, esp. 30–31. Cortesono, Rector of the German College, presents an exceedingly detailed assessment of the many problems plaguing colleges in the late sixteenth century, and stresses the need for superiors to be judicious in the kinds of students whom they admit and in setting high standards for behavior among their charges.

INSTRUCTIONS TO JESUIT MISSIONARIES

regulation of family life across the seventeenth century. Their instructional documents help us to unravel the complex shift in attitudes toward gender, marriage and sexuality during this volatile century, as well as highlighting the order's increasingly detail-oriented approach to its civilizing mission in southern Italy and elsewhere.

Obviously, efforts to reform behaviors, which formed a significant part of the Jesuits' apostolic vocation, were nothing new within the Catholic Church. Still, the Society of Jesus distinguished its approach to this work in two key ways: first, by the self-consciously methodical way in which it gathered information on prevalent vices and/or disorderly practices in particular communities; and second, through its equally deliberate and systematic manner of prescribing specific remedies to the range of problems which missionaries might encounter.

The Jesuits' interest in extirpating vices and reforming 'illicit' behavior originated in the organization's *Constitutions*. There, Loyola recommended that members direct their studies of Scripture and the sacraments toward the practical needs of the order in its varied apostolic work. Members should anticipate specific biblical passages, 'for purposes of lecturing; likewise, to have considered in advance what pertains to the vices and leads to abhorrence of them and to their correction.'[75]

One crucial aspect of the Jesuits' emerging missionary methodology that was geared toward identifying specific vices more effectively was to instruct missionaries to gather as much information as possible before embarking on a mission. Cesare Croilo advised would-be missionaries to treat each locale as an individual entity, recognizing that 'not all people have the same vices. Therefore, it is a good idea to inform oneself of the vices of each village or diocese . . .'[76] Fabio Fabi, drawing upon his observations of both the Roman and Neapolitan Provinces, suggested that local clergy (whatever their failings) might prove to be excellent informants about which sins were most prevalent among a particular group of people. In this way, Fabi offers, missionaries 'can apply their arguments and efforts with greater understanding, and usefulness to souls.'[77]

Once missionaries had identified the particular vices which were prevalent in a community, they then had to set about correcting such behaviors. How did the instructional manuals propose to respond to these problems? The missionary relations, in particular, served as an ideal vehicle to convey the specific kinds of so-called illicit behaviors that missionaries were encountering and the strategies they had devised

---

[75] Loyola, *The Constitutions*, Part 4, Ch. 8, 201–202.
[76] ARSI, *F.G.* 720A/I/1/6, Cesare Croilo, 'Instruttioni.'
[77] ARSI, *F.G.* 720A/I/1/9, Fabio Fabi, 'Instruttione.'

168   A PARADISE INHABITED BY DEVILS

to combat these practices. One common method for countering the prevalence of such vices as gambling, card-playing or the possession of 'illicit materials' was to urge community members to confess to their impious habits and to publicly renounce and destroy the forbidden materials. One anonymous missionary in Capua, just north of metropolitan Naples, describes just such a scene in his report:

> Likewise notable, and worthy of not passing over in silence were the number of obscene, and prohibited books, witchcraft paraphernalia, lascivious letters . . . silk ribbons, and similar things . . . with which the Devil kept always lively the fire of sensuality in the souls of many, miserably sullied in vice, and carnal pleasure. From all of these things, the Father made a great bundle, carried it to the pulpit, where at the end of the sermon, he burned part of it in view of everyone, and saved part to burn the following day.[78]

He confidently assures his readers that the Capuans benefitted mightily from this ritual 'bonfire of the vanities' because they had expelled the Devil from their midst by symbolically casting their sins into the flames.

As this example indicates, among the numerous vices with which missionaries might contend, illicit sexuality was one area of special concern. In the mid- and late sixteenth century, when the earliest instructions were offered, the Society of Jesus shared a more generalized cultural suspicion toward women and female sexuality, evident in their many examples of unrepentant female sinners who faced violent deaths. While an examination of the development of this category of instruction from the mid-sixteenth to early eighteenth centuries in no way represents a model of progressive thinking, it does reveal important shifts in early modern attitudes toward gender and sexuality.[79] Although the instruc-

---

[78] ARSI, *Neap.* 74, 'Relatione d'una Missione fatta in Capua . . .' (1649), ff. 260–84, esp. 267–267v. For an example of Segneri's oratorical invocations against superstition, cf. Segneri and Fontana, *Pratica delle Missioni*, 35; 50.

[79] There is no clear unanimity on the question of women's 'improved' status in seventeenth-century Italy (or elsewhere, for that matter), but a few works do suggest an opening. For a discussion of changing representations of women's virtues and potential 'equality,' see, for example, Constance Jordan, *Renaissance Feminism. Literary Texts and Political Models* (Ithaca: Cornell University Press, 1990), esp. 250–69. In terms of women's shifting religious roles, see especially Gabriella Zarri, *Recinti: donne, clausura e matrimonio nella prima età moderna* (Bologna: Il Mulino, 2000), and her 'From Prophecy to Discipline, 1450–1650,' in *Women and Faith. Catholic Religious Life in Italy from Late Antiquity to the Present*, eds Lucetta Scaraffia and Gabriella Zarri (Cambridge, MA: Harvard University Press, 1999), 83–112; cf. Ruth P. Liebowitz, 'Virgins in the Service of Christ: The Dispute over an Active Apostolate for Women During the Counter-Reformation,' in *Women of the Spirit: Female Leadership in the Jewish and Christian Traditions*, ed. Rosemary Ruether and Eleanor McLaughlin (New York: Simon and Schuster, 1979), 131–52. Although she demonstrates the continuing legacy of clerical misogyny, Liebowitz's still useful survey of female religious activism in the post-Tridentine period also shows that

INSTRUCTIONS TO JESUIT MISSIONARIES 169

tions to Jesuit missionaries issued in the late seventeenth century unsurprisingly perpetuate a more generalized suspicion toward women and insistence upon their inferiority, they also reveal a more vigorous concern with male culpability in sexual immorality and the need to foster matrimonial stability than one finds in earlier discussions:

> '. . . there is absolutely not a place in women in which there has not been set a snare to entrap the eyes of men . . .'[80]

As with almost all aspects of Jesuit missionary practice and institutional philosophy, Ignatius Loyola set the standard for his companions. Even before founding the Society of Jesus, while still early in his career as a spiritual director in Spain, Ignatius developed a strong following among women of varying social groups. This following seemed both natural to the former courtier who had written frankly of his many dealings (and dalliances) with noble women, but also troubling. His spiritual work among women of 'dubious occupation' in Alcalá during 1526–27 contributed to a certain amount of scandal and brought Ignatius unwanted attention from ecclesiastical authorities.[81]

---

the old view that the Catholic Reformation was unequivocally negative for women is far too simplistic. For Naples, see Giuseppe Galasso and Adriana Valerio, *Donne e Religione a Napoli: secoli XVI–XVII* (Milan: Angeli, 2001). Natalie Zemon Davis has taken up the complex lives and opportunities of three seventeenth-century European women in *Women on the Margins: Three Seventeenth-Century Lives* (Cambridge, MA: Harvard University Press, 1995). See especially her investigation of Marie De L'Incarnation, 63–139. In terms of the role of Jesuits and other clergy in this shift in perceptions of gender roles and family dynamics, one of the best sources is Elisa Novi Chavarria, 'Ideologia e comportamenti familiari nei predicatori italiani tra Cinque e Settecento. Tematiche e modelli,' *Rivista Storica Italiana* 100, No. 3 (December 1988): 679–723. This essay is now available in *Il Governo delle Anime*, 183–229. On the eighteenth-century preoccupation with promoting marital stability as part of broader concerns with the social order, see Luciano Guerci, *La Sposa obbediente. Donna e matrimonio nella discussione dell'Italia del Settecento* (Turin: Tirrenia, 1988).

[80] Gian Matteo Giberti, *Constitutiones Gibertinae* (1527), Book One, Ch. 29, as cited in *The Catholic Reformation: Savonarola to Ignatius Loyola. Reform in the Church 1495–1540*, ed. John C. Olin (New York: Harper & Row, 1969), 133–48, esp. 144.

[81] For a broad, if self-consciously hagiographic, account of Ignatius's work with and attitudes toward women, see *Saint Ignatius Loyola: Letters to Women*, ed. Hugo Rahner, trans. from the original German by Kathleen Pond and S. A. H. Weetman (Edinburgh and London: Nelson, 1960), 1–26, esp. 9–14. Rahner notes both Ignatius's general ambivalence toward women and the juxtaposition between his insistence that the Jesuits orient their pastoral and reform labors toward lower-class women and his profound distrust of such women. A more recent, if brief, examination of these letters is Charmarie J. Blaisdell, 'Calvin's and Loyola's Letters to Women: Politics and Spiritual Counsel in the Sixteenth Century,' in *Calviniana: Ideas and Influence of John Calvin*, ed. Robert V. Schnucker (Kirksville, MO: The Sixteenth Century Journal Publishers, 1988), 235–53. A more thorough critical study of Loyola's complex relationships with women is certainly needed.

170　　A PARADISE INHABITED BY DEVILS

No doubt these kinds of experience, placed squarely within the chaotic social and cultural milieu of mid-sixteenth-century Europe, had a profound influence upon the Society's founder and shaped the order's wariness of women in general, and women of the lower orders in particular. But once again, the Jesuits were in no sense unique in this perspective. Misogynistic attitudes toward female culpability were evident in such fifteenth-century tracts as Heinrich Krämer and Jacob Sprenger's notorious witch-hunting manual *The Malleus Maleficarum* (1486). In the first half of the sixteenth century, we find echoes of these attitudes in the broadly conceived general instructions to members found in the Capuchins' 'Constitutions' of 1536. For example, in Chapter Eleven, friars are admonished to minimize contact with women, in imitation of the early Church fathers: 'According to the opinion of the holy Doctors, especially St. Jerome, familiarity with women, *however holy*, should be avoided with seraphic prudence, by the servants of God.' Such avoidance was not intended solely for interactions with lay women, but with female religious as well:

> As it behooves true religious and servants of Christ to avoid not only what is manifestly evil and sinful, but even whatever might have the appearance thereof; we desire that the Friars should not frequent any convent or other houses of religious women without the permission of the Vicar Provincial. The Vicar Provincial shall take heed not to grant such permission readily to anyone, save tried and mature Friars, and in cases of necessity or charity, because, as our father, St. Francis was want to say, God delivered us from a wife and the devil has provided us with the nuns.[82]

Indeed, the Jesuits did permit more extensive interactions with female laity and religious than their mendicant counterparts advised, but as we shall see, they might well have echoed St Francis' galling sentiments.

It is no exaggeration to say that Francis Xavier epitomizes a Jesuit variation on this kind of clerical misogyny. This is certainly evident in his instructions to missionaries, written during his years in the East Indies. Unlike later Jesuit missionary methodologists, Xavier remains wedded to a late medieval conceptualization of female blameworthiness. For him, social disorder has a decidedly female face and form. The potentially greater disorder posed by male debauchery (such as sexual aggressiveness, drunkenness or domestic violence) does not appear to concern Xavier to the extent that it will future missionary commentators. These attitudes are all the more significant because Xavier was viewed as an important model to future generations of Jesuit missionaries,

---

[82] The Capuchin *Constitutions* of 1536, cited in *The Catholic Reformation*, 149–81, esp. 177 (emphasis mine).

INSTRUCTIONS TO JESUIT MISSIONARIES

particularly in the Kingdom of Naples. Among the wide-ranging instructions and missionary reports that Xavier issued from the Indies, we find recurrent themes which reflect the extremely harsh, misogynistic views of sexuality and the married state which prevailed in the period.[83]

Following a time-honored tradition of placing primary blame upon women for the general state of sinfulness which the Jesuit fathers felt it was their calling to combat, Xavier reveals himself to be a man of his times. A curious incident while the young Jesuit was still in Rome may shed some light on his profound hostility toward women. In 1537, Xavier was involved in a scandal when a woman whose confession he had heard became pregnant.[84] While the stain of scandal did not appear to hamper his career in any way, it probably merely confirmed his apparent conviction that women were not to be trusted. To fully understand the significance of the Jesuits' shift in attitude toward female parishioners and the degree of female culpability in sexual transgressions, it is invaluable to begin with Xavier.

In his most extensive discussion of how Jesuit missionaries should ideally deal with women, written in 1552, Xavier instructs a fellow Jesuit, newly deployed in the Indies, on avoiding scandal. Initially, Xavier recites the familiar recommendation that the missionary use great prudence in meeting with women in their homes, or unaccompanied by a spouse or some 'good person who is known in the neighborhood.'[85] Xavier's primary purpose here, however, is not simply to re-state the familiar, but to articulate a philosophy of missionizing that Father Barzaeus could put to good use. At the heart of this philosophy, in keeping with the Jesuits' pragmatic orientation, was a commitment to pursuing those activities likely to bear the most fruit. Within this context, according to Xavier, undue attention to women did not seem a wise use of limited resources: 'Since women are generally inconstant,

---

[83] There were numerous misogynist tracts composed during the late fifteenth and sixteenth centuries, such as the more infamous Krämer and Sprenger's *Malleus Maleficarum* (1487) and John Knox's *The First Blast of the Trumpet Against the Monstrous Regiment of Women* (1558). While these more obviously hostile tracts sought to locate specific examples of unnatural female behaviors, there are a number of apparently more ambiguous humanist works written during this period, such as Juan Luis Vives's *De institutio foeminae christianae/Instruction of a Christian Woman* (1523), that both reflect conventional anti-female biases and subvert them. Each of these works had distinctive purposes, and one needs to be cognizant of the specific historical contexts within which they were composed.

[84] Rahner, *St. Ignatius Loyola, Letters to Women*, 14. Rahner's account of this incident is rather cryptic, and I have not yet been able to find a more detailed account.

[85] Francis Xavier, 'Fifth Instruction for Father Barzaeus, on Avoiding Scandals' (from Goa, between 6 and 14 April 1552), Document No. 118, *The Letters and Instructions of Francis Xavier*, 411–13.

172   A PARADISE INHABITED BY DEVILS

lacking in perseverance, and take up much time, you should deal with
them in the following way: if they are married, take great care to work
with their husbands so that they come to God; and spend more time in
producing fruit among husbands than among wives ... in this way
numerous scandals are avoided and more fruit is gained.'[86]

But Xavier's philosophy was not simply an endorsement of pragmatism. Like so many other manifestations of the Jesuits' burgeoning
institutional identity, Xavier's instructions reveal an effort toward balancing the practical with more deeply-rooted principles founded on both
theology and prevailing social values. Xavier's discussions of the missionary's proper response to marital disputes and domestic violence are
crucial indicators of his critical position as a hinge between the late
medieval clerical misogynists and the somewhat more measured, moderate Jesuit moralists of the seventeenth and eighteenth centuries like Paolo
Segneri.

At the heart of Francis Xavier's instructions to Barzaeus lies a world
view that castigates women as untrustworthy, manipulative and disorderly. Although he is directing his suggestions specifically to the culturally unfamiliar context of sixteenth-century India, Xavier's views
bespeak a much broader perspective. In discussing the problem of
resolving marital disputes, a more common theme in later instructional
documents, Xavier urges great discretion in dealing with warring couples
and warns his fellow Jesuit not to 'believe the pious aspirations of
women who say that they would serve God better if they were separated
from their husbands instead of living with them.' In making this
comment, Xavier is both echoing the commonly held notion that women
are inherently dishonest and cautioning Barzaeus to not be taken in by
their feminine wiles.[87] Just as many sixteenth-century commentators
placed the onus for sexual immorality squarely upon women's shoulders,
and Jesuit missionary chronicles are replete with incidents of unrepentant
female sinners meeting violent ends, so Xavier engages with the prevailing misogynist characterizations of female culpability in his approach to
domestic conflict.

This confident assertion of female culpability is obvious in Xavier's
recommendation that Barzaeus be careful not to offend the husband by
exposing his behavior publicly ('even though he is at fault'), because
greater damage arises from encouraging women to indulge their vengeful
instincts:

---

[86] Xavier, *Letters*, 411–12.

[87] Ibid., 413. Xavier goes on to advise Barzaeus that women's 'pious aspirations' are
'of short duration, and they are seldom effected without scandal.'

INSTRUCTIONS TO JESUIT MISSIONARIES   173

> Take care, as I say again, never to blame the husband in public, even though he is at fault, for women are so indomitable that they look for occasions to belittle their husbands, alleging to religious persons that their husbands are to blame and not themselves ... Even if the wives are not to blame, do not excuse them as they excuse themselves, but rather show them the obligation they have of putting up with their husbands, for they are frequently disrespectful to them and thus deserve some punishment; and that they should patiently accept their present difficulties and be induced to be humble, patient, and obedient to their husbands.[88]

For Xavier to stress that Barzaeus should use great prudence in publicly chastising the husband in a marital dispute was no great deviation from standard Jesuit practice. One universal characteristic of all instructional manuals produced by the Society was an emphasis on discretion and an avoidance of publicizing specific examples of sinful behavior in a community or among select individuals. This idea rested on the belief that to expose certain behaviors to public scrutiny might both encourage such behavior and foster mistrust and bad blood. But here, Xavier's meaning is much more focused. It is the problem of women's 'indomitability' that must be confronted, not necessarily the violence or mistreatment meted out by the husband.

Xavier's conceptualization of female culpability certainly reflects an early example of the Jesuits' frequent use of the image of the unrepentant female sinner in their missionary accounts, and the expressed need to deal sternly with sexually 'immoral' women. Citing examples culled from the Neapolitan Province's missionary relations through the mid-seventeenth century, Scipione Paolucci addresses this problem in his published account of the Jesuits' missions in the Kingdom of Naples. He cites Jesuit missionaries' suggestion that the *donnicciuole* ('weak little women') not be permitted to receive the sacraments until they had changed their ways (preferably by agreeing to 'public offerings of punishment, whether corporal, or pecuniary') and agreed not to sin in the future. Paolucci refers to the symbolic 'cleansing' of sins, such as cutting the hair of immoral women, or disposing of their jewelry.[89]

Another sign of the Jesuits' methodical approach to their missionary activity lay in their enumeration of the successful conversions or confessions of prostitutes and other 'unrepentant sinners.' Enumerating confessions and those taking part in communion was a standard feature of the missionary relations, but in the context of the Society's special concern to combat sexual immorality and reform 'fallen women,' this practice took on added importance. As we have seen, it was an early

---

[88] Xavier, ibid.
[89] Paolucci, *Missioni*, 170–76.

174   A PARADISE INHABITED BY DEVILS

modern commonplace to believe that the reform of prostitutes was
critical to a broader cleansing of society. Missionaries cited such figures
to offer evidence of their apparent success in countering vices, but also
as examples for neophytes to follow. The missionary relations might
offer dramatic examples of the repentance and conversion of prostitutes
to embolden novices in their efforts. In his published account of a
mission to Bitonto (1646), Giovanni Battista Di Elia, for example, offers
a vivid image of sixteen prostitutes prostrating themselves before the
missionaries: 'In imitation of [Mary] Magdalen they ran to the feet of
the Fathers (who had) now arrived in the room, dragging their tongues
along the ground by the door, where the Fathers stood ... and there
they prostrated [themselves], shedding bitter tears for their many sins,
[about] which they had confessed in public.[90]

Increasingly, the Jesuits offered cautionary tales meant to instill a
proper fear and respect for divine wrath in their missionary subjects, but
also to provide other Jesuits with models for facilitating behavioral
reform. While such images continue to provide creative fodder for their
efforts to publicize their reform activities, the intense scrutiny upon
female guilt was mitigated to some extent by the mid-seventeenth
century.

Scipione Paolucci himself is exemplary of this transition. While
Paolucci's account of Neapolitan missions perpetuates many of the
prevailing stereotypes of female culpability, he also offers edifying
examples of male misdeeds. In one perhaps unintentionally humorous
story, a peasant experiences a rude shock while attempting a late-night
rendezvous with his lover in the fields outside a country village. In this
story, the very fervency of the parishioners' response to the Jesuit
missionary's preaching creates such a racket that the unknowing peasant
is inspired to repent and interrupt his sinful dalliance:

> and in another case, a single echo and reverberation was enough to
> effect Divine Grace ... in a little village in the countryside, while
> souls were being inspired to penitence with fervent noises, someone
> had retired to a nearby little valley and, favored by the cover of
> night, was amusing himself with his woman. [W]hen suddenly, he
> was astonished by an unexpected reverberation, and without hear-
> ing the sound of voices, he was penetrated by a feeling (at that point
> just like [hearing] a roar from Heaven without seeing the thunder-
> bolt) enough to frighten him to not only abandon his dishonest
> business at once ... but to draw away from it entirely. [A]t that

---

[90] ARSI, *Neap.* 74, Di Elia, 'Relatione di Una Missione ... nella Città di Bitonto,' f.
166.

INSTRUCTIONS TO JESUIT MISSIONARIES 175

very moment, he went and asked to confess and a little while later, made a serious emendation of his life.[91]

While Paolucci no doubt includes this example more to demonstrate the miraculous effects of Jesuit missions than to suggest a greater scrutiny of male sexual misconduct, its very inclusion does indicate a shift in emphasis which finds expression in other seventeenth-century texts. Here, the onus for sexual misconduct is placed on a man.

As Constance Jordan, among others, has shown, seventeenth-century Italy was rife with learned debate over the proper place of women in society, with feminists and anti-feminists trading rhetorical jabs. Often, such debates centered around the proper role of women in statecraft, but broader discussions of gender and morality were also prevalent. On the question of society's condemnation of women for their supposedly more insatiable lust and voraciousness, the Venetian author Lucretio Bursati, in *La Vittoria delle Donne* (Venice, 1621), challenged a societal double standard which placed greater responsibility upon women's shoulders:

> If a woman gives herself imprudently to a man, she is pointed at by everyone ... and considered ... to be deserving of poison, or the stiletto. The adulterous man, who commits a thousand other worse acts of dishonesty, does not lose honor, his dissolute life does not matter, no one rejects his company or refuses to speak with him; he is like the other men of the city: honored, appreciated and valued. And why ought a woman to be in a worse condition than a man? If the crime is the same, why does not a man suffer the same infamy?[92]

Undoubtedly, Bursati's view represented an unusually forthright criticism of early modern sexual morality, yet one finds a more general reassessment of such values in a wide range of secular and religious tracts of the period. Far from advocating gender equality, however, many of these writers (among them a number of Jesuit commentators) emphasized the need to promote family cohesiveness and to combat sexual commerce as tools to promote social order. Beyond decrying men's sexual aggressiveness in more explicit terms, a number of seventeenth-century commentators re-evaluated the dangers posed by marital violence and disorder.

Such concern found expression, for example, in an early tract by the Neapolitan chronicler Giulio Cesare Capaccio. In a published work that deals primarily with emblems, Capaccio argues that male brutality actually represents a threat to social and civic order because it threatens

---

[91] Scipione Paolucci, *Missioni*, 16.

[92] Lucretio Bursati, *La Vittoria delle Donne* (Venice, 1621), 3v–4; cf. Jordan, *Renaissance Feminism*, 261–6, esp. 263.

176   A PARADISE INHABITED BY DEVILS

the bonds of marriage and encourages women to rebel against their
natural state of subjection to male authority. Capaccio writes:

> the serpent leaves its poison when it mates with the female [but] the
> husband does not know enough to forget his pride when he deals
> with his wife. She, on the other hand, stubbornly refuses to endure
> the brutal habits of her husband . . . Instead of love there is hate,
> instead of making his wife his subject, he makes her recalcitrant,
> instead of a lover, she is so full of dislike that she cannot stand him.
> Then, he decides to be high-handed with his wife, as if he were
> dealing with an armed enemy.[93]

While this passage by the conservative Capaccio in no way endorses
female rebellion against an oppressive gender hierarchy, it places the
blame for social disintegration upon men for their callous treatment of
their wives. Inherent in Capaccio's analysis is a recognition that marriage
plays a vital role in upholding social order, and that any threat to this
institution might suggest a broader state of social decay. Certainly, early
seventeenth-century Naples, with its economic troubles, ever-increasing
population, natural disasters and grave social inequalities, was a prime
example of a highly vulnerable polity where family cohesion could play
a vital part in preventing further disorders.

Within this context, the shifting view of female responsibility for
sexual (and thus, social) disorder indicated a begrudging acceptance of
women's potentially positive role in promoting Catholic orthodoxy in
the home and in the community.[94] Given the social and economic
upheaval in seventeenth-century Italy, particularly in Naples, missionaries may have come to realize that pious women could be allies in the
defense of social and religious orthodoxy.

Beyond their acknowledgment that women might serve as able part-
ners in promoting moral reform, the shift in Jesuit attitudes toward
gender and sexuality also reflected a reassessment of the practical
problems that missionaries were encountering on a day-to-day basis.
According to Schinosi, the Jesuits in early seventeenth-century Naples,
the Society increased its activities in southern Italy significantly during
the first quarter of the century. This increase in activity coincided with
growth in the Society's population in the Province as a whole, but

---

[93] Giulio Cesare Capaccio, *Il Principe . . . tratto da gli emblemi dell'Alciato, con
duecento e più avvertimenti politici e morali* (Venice, 1620), cited in Jordan, *Renaissance
Feminism*, 252.

[94] Elisa Novi Chavarria, 'Ideologia e comportamenti familiari,' 685. Novi Chavarria
cogently argues: 'tra la fine del XVI e gli inizi del XVIII secolo, il ruolo riconosciuto dalla
morale ecclesiastica alla donna all'interno della famiglia venga a poco a poco emancipan-
dosi da alcuni tradizionali stereotipi e circondato, di contro, da un'aurea di dignità e di
rispetto.'

INSTRUCTIONS TO JESUIT MISSIONARIES

paradoxically, the broadening of activities beyond the context of urban Naples occurs simultaneously with an increasing centralization and urbanization of the Society's members.[95] The year 1625 was significant in this development, as Rome had declared this a Jubilee year, and the following years witnessed an increase in both the scope and scale of the Society's apostolic activities.[96] By the mid-seventeenth century, the breadth of activity and the growing awareness of the obstacles that missionaries were encountering led to a centralized reorganization of the way in which missionary activity was conducted.[97] Of equal significance to this institutional reorganization was the greater emphasis placed upon standardizing a pastoral approach to common problems, such as family disharmony.

More than any other member of the Society of Jesus in seventeenth-century Italy, Paolo Segneri contributed to a comprehensive vision of the Jesuit missionary vocation and outlined a pragmatic approach to realizing the order's reform goals. Beyond his invaluable contributions in the area of logistical instructions to Jesuit missionaries, Segneri was no less significant in his articulation of concrete strategies for addressing pressing social and religious concerns through a methodically presented catalogue of sermons and ritualized activities. On the question of sexual morality and combating familial disorder, Segneri played a pivotal role. Elisa Novi Chavarria considers his contributions to a re-evaluation of female culpability indicative of a broader shift in the late seventeenth century. Novi Chavarria argues:

> Segneri's *Quaresimale* [1679] signaled a decisive turn. The woman to whom he addressed himself was no longer the instrument of the inferno, ruining even the greatest of men, the instigator of scandals and sins, difficult to govern because [she was] obstinate, diffident, irritable, stupid, voluble . . . Compare in the preaching of Segneri . . . the image of the 'new woman', [who had] become an emissary of the Church in comparison to her husband and a transmitter of virtues, as she will [become] even more clearly in the eighteenth and nineteenth centuries.[98]

---

[95] The Society's membership in the Neapolitan Province increased from 531 to 579 between 1611 and 1620, while the number of colleges and 'houses' increased from 10 (1592–93) to 18 (1611) to 28 (1622) (*Neap.* 73). Although the Society expanded its activities throughout the Province during the second and third decades of the seventeenth century, it also became increasingly situated in Naples. Cf. De Rosa, Appendix 1, *Religione e Società nel Mezzogiorno*, 271; 252–3.

[96] Santagata, *Istoria*, 4: 388.

[97] Recall that in 1647, General Vincenzo Carafa's created the new post of Prefect of Missions in each of the Jesuits' Italian provinces.

[98] Cf. Novi Chavarria, 'Ideologia e comportamenti familiari,' 685–6. Novi Chavarria also argues cogently that the Jesuits moved away from a more typical late medieval

178   A PARADISE INHABITED BY DEVILS

The *Quaresimale*, like other popular works of Segneri, was fashioned as a moral guide to lay Christians. A collection of Segneri's sermons, this important work reveals a fascinating transition in the depiction of female sexuality and of a late seventeenth-century vision of the married state. One finds echoes of this new philosophy in the excerpts of sermons, edifying tales and instructions to missionaries collected in *Pratica delle Missioni del Padre Paolo Segneri* (1714), which details Segneri's work in the latter part of the seventeenth century.

Following the gradual break from depicting women as the sole (or even primary) instigators of illicit sexuality and sinfulness, Paolo Segneri instead presents several images of young women being betrayed by men's lust and left to fend for themselves. In one such stock sermon, Segneri represents the female as the 'more timid and more devout sex' who can easily be led astray by a selfish man. He warns young girls to beware of false promises and to protect their chastity, even in the face of charming entreaties, because 'after having experimented [with him] that Lover is a thief of your salvation, of your honesty.'[99] Still another passage sounds surprisingly modern in its impassioned plea for young women to avoid obtaining a 'bad reputation' and ending up as 'damaged goods.'[100]

But despite this rather familiar invocation of the classic double standard, Segneri also provides exemplary, even spiritually heroic young women who defend their honor, and so honor God in the process. In one such highly dramatic tale, a pious young woman is being hotly pursued by a 'dishonest' young man who refuses to take 'no' for an answer. As the Jesuit orator tells us, she has tried 'prayers, made use of warnings, mixed in threats; but all was in vain.' One day, while the young girl is alone in her house, she is visited by this unwelcome pursuer in a scene which can only be described as an attempted sexual assault. But Segneri's primary purpose here is not to titillate his listeners. Instead, he wants to demonstrate the power of faith and the heroics of the young

---

misogyny before clerical counterparts such as the Dominicans and Theatines, though she offers no reason for this distinction. For a less sanguine view of Segneri, cf. Luciano Guerci, *La Sposa obbediente*, 16–25. Guerci finds Segneri's views of women (especially in the context of marriage) much more ambivalent than the image offered by Novi Chavarria. While it is obviously important to document such continuing ambivalence, for the purposes of my discussion of the development of Jesuit instructions to missionaries on coping with sexual immorality and family disorder, Novi Chavarria's arguments are more persuasive, because she traces this significant shift without necessarily glorifying Segneri's more moderate approach.

[99] Segneri and Fontana, *Pratica delle Missioni*, Part 1, 32.
[100] Ibid., 35.

INSTRUCTIONS TO JESUIT MISSIONARIES 179

woman's religious convictions in overcoming the lustful designs of her assailant.

In this highly dramatized account, when the young woman is pursued in her room by the intruder, she looks heavenward, praying for some aid in fending him off. She then spies a large crucifix, which she brings down and carries with her, extended outward like a talisman. Standing at the door of her bedroom, she dares the young man to cross her path and thus incur Divine wrath: '[T]hence with her face inflamed, with a dark look, [and] with a voice more than female, full of such daring she cried: 'Come on then, come on, and get me, oh you scoundrel; but here is what you must pass beyond, this Christ.''[101] Naturally, her bold actions confuse and shame the young man, and Segneri approvingly notes her spiritual victory.

While this example in no way indicates an approving view of female sexuality – such would be unthinkable for Catholic Reformation missionary oratory in seventeenth-century Italy, or elsewhere at that time – the example of female heroic behavior in the face of evil-doing harkens back to legendary female figures from classical antiquity, like Lucretia, whose rape became part of the foundational myth for the Roman Republic.[102] This is particularly the case given the equally significant shift in views of marriage which find voice in Segneri's orations.

In Paolo Segneri, as with a growing number of Jesuit and other clerical commentators of the late seventeenth century, there is a re-evaluation of the married state and more equanimity in assessing women's role in transmitting morals and upholding social norms. While Francis Xavier unwaveringly advised Father Barzaeus to remain suspicious of women's complaints about their husbands, including those involving well-documented violence, Paolo Segneri and others take a new approach. In one sermon, Segneri implores men not to do violence to their wives, but to view them as companions:

> I remind the Husbands, not to mistreat your poor consorts, you know that you are not [their] Masters to beat them, they are your companions, not slaves, not servants. In creating the Woman, God did not form her from the head of Man, because she should not be his superior, neither did he form her from the feet, because neither should she be subjected, but instead from the rib, because she should be his companion.[103]

---

[101] Ibid., 52.

[102] For a fascinating examination of the literary representations of Lucretia, especially in Humanist Florentine thought, see Stephanie Jed, *Chaste Thinking. The Rape of Lucretia and the Birth of Humanism* (Bloomington, IN: University of Indiana Press, 1989).

[103] Segneri and Fontana, *Pratica delle Missioni*, Part 1, 34.

180   A PARADISE INHABITED BY DEVILS

In this analysis, Segneri departs from much of the prevailing clerical ideology of the previous period. Compare, for example, the arguments of the late sixteenth-century Dominican Serafino Razzi. While Razzi, like Segneri, had counseled men not to beat their wives, he insisted that they should 'correct' their defects and offer moral and material protection to them.[104] Segneri's implicit argument suggests that there is no necessary reason to expect that husbands will be any more morally fit than their wives. And, if we take his broader comments about spouses and family morality into consideration, we might expect quite the opposite. By the seventeenth century, then, women' s potentially positive role as moral educators was being noted, and the new period provided more consistent examples of this phenomenon.[105]

In tandem with this somewhat ameliorated view of female sexuality and women's value as wives and mothers, the Jesuits, in particular, saw the dangers presented by male debauchery, particularly that of husbands and fathers. But we should not simply assume that the missionaries took a harsher view of men's sinfulness out of solidarity with women. Rather, especially on the heels of the social unrest that characterized the mid-seventeenth century and the Society of Jesus' increasing interest in expanding the scope of its missionary efforts to the most intimate realms of life, one can see this shift as indicative of the Jesuits' maturing civilizing mission. Foreshadowing nineteenth-century moral entreaties to newly proletarianized workers, Paolo Segneri implores husbands not to drink their earnings in the *osterie*, while their wives are left to fend for themselves and struggle to provide food and clothing to the children.[106] Implicit in this and other critiques of male violence was a strong conviction that incivility, combined with poor Christian education, would lead to social disintegration.

These evolving attitudes and approaches toward challenging sexual immorality and family violence – bound up as they were with at least nominally shifting cultural attitudes toward gender, female sexuality and moral reform – demonstrate well the solidifying of an institutional identity within the Society of Jesus across the seventeenth century. This maturing collective identity was built upon both heroic images of missionary practitioners and the development of a methodologically sophisticated approach to conducting missions, as exemplified in the instructional manuals. Through the articulation and dissemination of instructions to members of the order, and sometimes to a lay reading

---

[104] Serafino Razzi, *Sermoni ... per le più solenni, così domeniche, come feste de'Santi ...* (1590), cited in Novi Chavarria, 'Ideologia e comportamenti familiari,' 686–7.

[105] Novi Chavarria, 'Ideologia e comportamenti familiari,' 689–92.

[106] Segneri and Fontana, *Pratica delle missioni*, Part 1, 34.

public, the Jesuits defined in ever bolder strokes their unique vision for Catholic reform. One major category of instruction that has not yet been considered – social reconciliation and peace-making – became central to this burgeoning institutional identity and a hallmark of Jesuit missionary activism in southern Italy throughout the seventeenth century and into the eighteenth century.

CHAPTER FIVE

Taming the beast:
Confronting discord in early
modern Naples

In 1621, the newly appointed Neapolitan Viceroy, Cardinal Gaspar Borja, ordered that a mission be conducted in the dioceses of Aversa, just outside Naples. According to Jesuit sources, the area had long been the site of vicious factionalism, discord and apparent decline in attention to religious devotion. Just a few years earlier, the Jesuit missionary Carlo D'Orta had written an impassioned letter from Colombia to members of his congregation back in Aversa, imploring them to 'escape the dangers of sinning, embrace positive occasions, easily pardon those who offend you, and do not pay too much attention to that which will soon pass and be over.'[1]

The Jesuit historian Saverio Santagata provides a vivid description of the apparent motives behind the mission, the significance of its ecclesiastical support, the missionaries' 'heroic' efforts to overcome initial resistance and their use of theatrical methods to assure the mission's success. Santagata tells us that 'the motive for doing [the mission] was this: for various reasons an implacable discord had been stirred up in the City. Acts of violence very soon degenerated into cruel factions, and the Plebe, and the Nobility divided into parties, eager for mutual destruction. The blood of the many murder victims had obliged the Courts of Justice to make rigorous executions, [but] all that did not put an end to the raging of the citizens toward one another.'[2]

In response to this difficult situation, Cardinal Borja called upon the Jesuits to conduct a mission that might placate the warring factions and restore order to the chaotic situation. As was so often the case in these representations of the Jesuit missions (or at least in the representations that filled published histories like Santagata's), missionary fathers faced initial disinterest among parishioners, only to ultimately triumph over

---

[1] An earlier version of this chapter appeared as 'Angels of Peace: The Social Drama of the Jesuit Mission in Early Modern Southern Italy,' in *Beyond Florence: The Contours of Medieval and Early Modern Italy*, eds Paula Findlen, Michelle Fontaine and Duane Osheim (Stanford: Stanford University Press, 2003), 160–75.

[2] Santagata, *Istoria*, 4: 202–203.

184 A PARADISE INHABITED BY DEVILS

the resistance, thus increasing the dramatic flavor of the missionary endeavor. In this instance, local ecclesiastical officials also provided much-needed assistance at the outset. Santagata continues: 'Our fathers went [to Aversa], and at the beginning had no listeners of any kind. After the action of the Bishop, and of some zealous priests, a suitable audience was assembled, but [it was] full of shadows, and of suspicions, so that [with] everyone fearing traps, they brought to the Church almost a perfectly armed battlefield.'[3] This suspicious atmosphere was so strong that the member of the missionary team whose job it was to preach found that 'as much as he toiled, no one gave a sign of wanting to cast off the bitterness of the contest.'[4]

All of the normal channels of persuasion appear to have failed to move this decidedly unyielding community, so that after several days, the Jesuits turned to the use of props and exercised their theatrical training to effect the desired reconciliations. Once he had assembled the parishioners, the missionary preacher carried two death skulls into the church, asking the people assembled to imagine that these two skulls represented the heads of the two factions. He then proceeded to have the two skulls carry on a discussion of the 'bitter fruit brought forth by the obstinacy of their hatreds.'[5]

This 'funereal demonstration' appeared to have had the desired effect. The congregants were greatly moved by the missionary's example to renounce past rivalries, and insisted that they no longer had any enemies. Crucially, the reconciliation drama ended with former enemies embracing one another, promising to do penance, and foreswearing future acts of violence and dissension.

Santagata's narration of the Jesuit mission to Aversa is instructive for a number of reasons. First, it demonstrates that the Jesuits appeared to take their peacemaking function very seriously. Although the mission was not successful at the outset, and indeed reconciliation appeared very unlikely, the missionaries demonstrated perseverance and flexibility in finding effective means to win over their subjects. But the mission to Aversa had a broader lesson. In its vivid description of a community torn apart by unnamed but acutely felt divisions among its populace, we see a glimpse of the broader violence and social conflict that characterized seventeenth-century southern Italy.

In the seventeenth century, peace-making became central to the

---

[3] Ibid., 202.
[4] Ibid.
[5] Ibid.

CONFRONTING DISCORD IN EARLY MODERN NAPLES 185

emerging Jesuit institutional identity.[6] Although reconciling individuals, families and whole communities had long been a conventional activity for Roman Catholic clergy, rooted in theology and Church tradition, the Society of Jesus made it an important facet of its ambitious apostolic agenda. The Jesuits' peace-making endeavors represent both an institutional response to growing social tensions (highlighted in places like Naples, but characteristic of much of Europe) and a concrete expression of the heroic missionary identity being forged during this period.

As we have seen, this emerging collective missionary identity in the Society of Jesus was based very much on a triumphal vision of the civilizing mission. In the narratives of these missions, intended to serve as an inspiration to novices and the public at large, and sometimes as instructional devices, model missionaries combined such essential personal qualities as integrity, enthusiasm, prudence and perseverance with an ability to accommodate to specific situations and unforeseen obstacles. The heightened tensions of the 'long' seventeenth century provided the Jesuits with greater opportunities to demonstrate 'heroic' missionary intervention, and the social drama of peacemaking and reconciliation only served to sweeten the victory.

In the mission to Aversa, this 'social drama' was enhanced by the Jesuits' employment of theatrical techniques to aid them in winning over the most recalcitrant sinners and combatants. The use of props, special effects, dramatic dialogue and audience participation played a crucial role in the order's peacemaking activities, and in the rituals of penitence that inevitably accompanied the reconciling of warring parties.

The Jesuits styled themselves as 'Angels of Peace,' self-consciously articulating an important part for members in combating a whole range of disagreements among individual parishioners, religious men and women, and whole communities which were riven by dissension, such as in the case of Aversa. An examination of the significance of peacemaking to the Jesuits' institutional identity, and its growing in the face of rising social tensions, especially by the mid-seventeenth century, further highlights the order's complex relationship to the broader events convulsing European society in the early modern period.

---

6 Cf. Novi Chavarria, 'Las Indias Por Açà," in *Il Governo delle Anime*, esp. 145 and 153–6. As part of a broader argument about the multiple valences of the Jesuit missionaries' desired role as 'culture bearers,' Novi Chavarria cites their part in 'elaborating a language of mediation' that might reduce community tensions.

186   A PARADISE INHABITED BY DEVILS

'Blessed are the Peacemakers for they Shall be Called the Sons of God' (Matthew 5:9)

The practices of reconciliation and peacemaking had deep roots in the Roman Catholic Church. At the broadest level of definition, 'reconciliation' was inextricably bound up with the sacrament of penance and confessional practice. While the Church had historically placed varying degrees of emphasis on confession, as an individual and collective activity, the notion that it was essential for all sinners to 'reconcile' themselves with their God, and their neighbors, was intrinsic to Roman Catholicism, particularly by the late Middle Ages.[7]

Late medieval popular preachers like San Bernardino di Siena, an Observant Franciscan, also placed peacemaking among their most important activities.[8] Responding to the epidemic of violence in medieval Italian cities, mendicants sometimes worked alongside secular authorities to reduce factional violence and to forge 'instruments of peace' – legally binding oaths taken by feuding parties which included the signing of a peace document, the gathering of witnesses, the 'kiss of peace' and financial sanctions should the parties break their promise to one another and to the community at large. As one historian has noted, religious and secular peacemaking rituals 'were often intertwined.'[9]

While secular authorities took a growing interest in the factional battles that plagued their communities, it was impassioned preachers like San Bernardino, and many of his fellow Franciscans, who took on the task of achieving mass, community-based reconciliations by the early fifteenth century. They are, in many ways, the apostolic forebears of seventeenth-century missionary peacemakers like the Jesuits, though the

---

[7] There is remarkably little discussion of the historic role of peacemaking/reconciliation in the Roman Catholic Church. For a consideration of the theological basis for reconciliation, see Kenan B. Osborne, *Reconciliation and Justification. The Sacrament and its Theology* (New York: Paulist Press, 1990). One fairly recent volume, though not specifically relevant to the case of southern Italy, is John Bossy, *Peace in the Post-Reformation* (Cambridge, UK: Cambridge University Press, 1998).

[8] For an excellent study of San Bernardino's role as popular preacher and peacemaker, and of his early fifteenth-century milieu, see Cynthia Polecritti, *Preaching Peace in Renaissance Italy: San Bernardino of Siena and his Audience* (Washington, DC: Catholic University Press, 2000). Cf. Franco Mormando, *The Preacher's Demons: Bernardino of Siena and the Social Underworld of Early Renaissance Italy* (Chicago: University of Chicago Press, 1999). For a discussion of a different set of medieval peacemakers, see Diane Webb, 'Penitence and Peace-making in City and Contado: The Bianchi of 1399,' in *Studies in Church History: The Church in Town and Countryside*, ed. Derek Baker (Oxford: Oxford University Press, 1979), 243–256.

[9] Polecritti, *Preaching Peace*, esp. 92–6.

CONFRONTING DISCORD IN EARLY MODERN NAPLES   187

mendicant vocation bears marked differences with the more 'active' ministry of the Jesuits.

By the late fifteenth century, on the eve of the Protestant Reformation, the Catholic Church gave growing attention to the infrequency of confession among the vast majority of Christians and the problems of a clergy largely ill trained to facilitate 'good confessions.' Penitential handbooks were published for confessors, while members of the religious orders and the episcopacy vied for confessional privileges.[10] In addition to his theological quarrels with the Church, Martin Luther's objections were driven by his disgust at the Church practice of selling indulgences through which the laity could remit their sins and gain a 'ticket' to salvation.

Among its numerous agenda items, the Council of Trent took up the question of penance in 1547, but did not issue a refined definition of the sacrament until four years later. Broadly speaking, the Tridentine bishops focused on: 1) defending the sacramental nature of penance against Protestant dissent; 2) distinguishing this sacrament from that of baptism; 3) clarifying that the remission of sins involved 'acts of the penitent' (contrition, confession and satisfaction); 4) asserting the centrality of the priest's sacramental role in the absolution of sins, and in so doing, confirming Church authority in this, as in other matters of faith and practice.[11]

For their part, the Jesuits explicitly noted peacemaking and reconciliation as distinctive components of their apostolic vocation in their foundational documents. In the 'Formula of the Institute' (1550), for example, Loyola comments: 'Moreover, this Society should show itself no less useful in reconciling the estranged, in holily assisting and serving those who are found in prisons and hospitals, and indeed in performing any other works of charity, according to what will seem expedient for the glory of God and the common good.'[12] In his instructions on 'The Ways in Which the Houses and Colleges Can Help their Fellowmen,' he reiterates this theme of helping the needy, stressing that members can and should 'reconcile the disaffected,' along with the poor and prisoners, 'both by their personal work and by getting others to do it.'[13]

Until the latter part of the sixteenth century, of course, these broad

---

[10] Osborne, *Reconciliation*, 157–9.

[11] For a through discussion of these deliberations during the Council of Trent, including complex doctrinal debates among Catholic clergy, see Osborne, *Reconciliation*, Ch. 8, 157–97, esp. 159–84.

[12] Loyola, 'Formula of the Institute of the Society of Jesus,' in *Constitutions*, 67. For a brief but helpful discussion of peacemaking, cf. O'Malley, *The First Jesuits*, 168–70.

[13] *Constitutions*, 282.

188   A PARADISE INHABITED BY DEVILS

pastoral goals remained fairly vague. It was only when the early instructional manuals began to be produced by the Society that peacemaking was mentioned as one important area of focus. Even then, however, missionaries were urged to remain above the fray as much as possible. Positive examples of reconciliations were balanced by a cautionary note that missionaries should remain neutral in matters of conflict, particularly among the religious, and avoid involvement in secular matters.[14]

In practice, of course, this suggestion was not always followed. For example, in the case of the 1585 Revolt of Naples, Jesuit missionaries like Carlo Mastrilli apparently advocated an important role for the order in restoring peace to a strife-torn community, stressing the illegitimacy of revolt as an act displeasing to God, but also upholding the prerogatives of social elites. In a customarily triumphal manner, Schinosi's *Istoria* touts 'antagonisms eradicated' as among the Jesuits' successful achievements in the aftermath of the 1585 Revolt, alongside 'superstitions extirpated ... [and] conversions from the relaxed life to penitence.'[15]

Similarly, other Jesuit documents are replete with examples of missionary interventions in disputes among the religious. As the papal visitor Tommaso Orfini had noted in his reconnoiters through the Kingdom of Naples (1568), there was an urgent need to reconcile warring members of the clergy and the episcopacy. There were also notable conflicts between clergy and members of the lay community. Like San Bernardino di Siena before them, the Jesuits heartily embraced a peacemaking role as part of their apostolic vocation, but unlike San Bernardino and others, they made the image of the heroic Jesuit peacemaker a staple of the emerging institutional identity of the new religious organization.

The heroic image of Jesuit peacemakers

The reconciliation of disputes among the clergy and members of religious communities became among the first visible examples of the Jesuits' concerted efforts to extol the virtues of their members. Notably, the most vivid and detailed early stories of reconciliations involved the intervention of missionaries like Pierantonio Spinelli in female religious communities in and around Naples. These tales reflect a grave concern over the supposed disobedience among female religious, particularly where disputes involved local bishops, and they reinforce an image of

---

[14] See, for example, ARSI, F.G. 720A/I/1/1 (1590), unfoliated.
[15] Schinosi, *Istoria*, 2: 89.

CONFRONTING DISCORD IN EARLY MODERN NAPLES   189

the Jesuits laboring to shore up disordered social relations.[16] But these edifying stories also indicate the importance that such mediations held for the Society of Jesus' efforts to bolster its public image.

One specific anecdote involving Spinelli's apparently successful reconciliation of recalcitrant nuns in a conflict-ridden convent was apparently deemed exemplary, since it appears in at least two different Jesuit sources. In his *Missioni de Padri della Compagnia di Gesù nel Regno di Napoli* (1651), Scipione Paolucci makes reference to Spinelli's efforts as part of a broader discussion of peacemaking in a faction-ridden religious community. In this instance, the Jesuits were called upon to restore order after a resident bishop found himself unable to resolve the difficulties on his own.[17]

As Paolucci relates the story, after having been satisfied by Jesuit peacemaking activities in his dioceses, the bishop of an unnamed location ordered the members of an unruly convent to attend the ministrations of Father Spinelli, 'under pain of excommunication' from their Vicar and 'one after the other.' The Vicar's heavy-handed presence was deemed necessary, according to the author, owing to the greater 'obstinacy' of women, who 'cleave to [their beliefs] all the more tenaciously, given their female weakness.'[18] Initially, despite Spinelli's best efforts, the nuns only begrudgingly followed his requests, but, at least according to the account, the missionary doggedly persevered:

> They obeyed [him], but with such ill-will that for three continuous days he exerted himself to persuade them with exhortations, prayers, and other most tender entreaties . . . with little or no profit: wherefore, as a last attempt, the Father warmly beseeched them to grant him a pair of times to bring them all together just to hear him give two brief discourses.[19]

---

[16] For an interesting consideration of the 'problems' of female monasteries in southern Italy and attempts to reform them during the Catholic Reformation, see Carla Russo, *I Monasteri feminili di clausura a Napoli nel secolo XVII* (Naples: Istituto di storia medioevale e moderna, 1970). On the imposition of increased Church 'discipline' over the female monasteries beyond the Neapolitan context, see Gabriella Zarri, 'From Prophecy to Discipline (1450–1650),' in *Women and Faith. Catholic Religious Life in Italy from Late Antiquity to the Present*, eds Lucetta Scaraffia and Gabriella Zarri (Cambridge, MA: Harvard University Press, 1999).

[17] Paolucci, *Missioni*, 73–4. Although Paolucci never mentions Spinelli by name (nor the names of any other missionary practitioners), the story is nearly identical to one related by Antonio Barone in his biography of Spinelli. Although Barone's hagiography was published some fifty years after Paoluccii's (in 1707), as a member of the Neapolitan Province delegated to write the history of the missions, Paolucci surely would have had access to reports of Spinelli's activities. Cf. Barone, *Della Vita*, 112–13.

[18] Paolucci, *Missioni*, 73.

[19] Paolucci, *Missioni*, 73–4.

190 A PARADISE INHABITED BY DEVILS

In his first lecture, Spinelli spoke of 'the excellence of their vocation,' no doubt hoping to soften the nuns' resolve through an acknowledgment of their valuable service to God and their community. In the second speech, however, Spinelli focused upon the harmful effects of the conflicts raging within the convent. Here, he castigated those who 'correspond poorly' to the religious vocation by refusing to accept legitimate authority. After so much trouble, Paolucci reports, the victory was all the sweeter, as the nuns 'recognized their error,' accepted the Prelate's choice for confessor and asked 'to be punished according to his will for the past disobedience and resistance to his orders . . .'[20]

As this story suggests, Jesuit missionaries used their oratorical training and powers of persuasion to rectify seemingly irreparable situations. But reports of dramatic reconciliations remained fairly uncommon in accounts of late sixteenth and even early seventeenth-century missions. The missionary accounts from the second half of the seventeenth century, however, reveal the Society's growing preoccupation with itemizing the discrete components of the missionary endeavor. With this development, we see more frequent mention of the numbers and kinds of reconciliations effected.[21] For example, the Neapolitan Jesuit missionary Francesco De Geronimo (1642–1716) embellished his own image as a heroic missionary by following the Jesuit tradition of enumerating the confessed and reconciled in the civilizing missions in and around Naples. According to his own calculations, during a nearly ten-year period (1680–89) De Geronimo had confessed approximately 3774 souls.[22]

There were three major contributors to Jesuit missionary strategy during the late seventeenth and early eighteenth centuries: Antonio Baldinucci, Paolo Segneri and Francesco De Geronimo. Each offered important suggestions for Jesuit efforts to forge reconciliations and peace in the communities in which they traveled, though all took a slightly different focus. What they shared, however, in contrast to earlier religious peacemakers like San Bernardino, was a self-conscious attention to institution building. Despite the fact that all three were noted preachers who embodied (to a greater or lesser degree) the heroic Jesuit missionary image, Baldinucci, Segneri and De Geronimo each seemed committed to

---

[20] Paolucci, *Missioni*, 74.

[21] See, for example, ARSI, *Neap.* 72, Doc. XXIV (Salerno, 7 May 1613), f. 254V; *Neap.* 74, 'Missioni di Padre Prella' (1645–46), ff. 137–152V; Giovanni Battista di Elia, *'Relatione di Una Missione fatta da due Reverendi Padri della Compagnia . . .'* (1646), published pamphlet, 19–20; *Neap.* 76, Doc. IV (1666), ff. 23–28v.

[22] Francesco De Geronimo, *S. Francesco Di Girolamo e le sue missioni*, G. Boero, ed., (Florence, 1882), 98–104. This is an edited collection of De Geronimo's own missionary writings. Note that De Geronimo is sometimes referred to as 'Di Girolamo.'

CONFRONTING DISCORD IN EARLY MODERN NAPLES   191

disseminating their own successful strategies to fellow members of the order.

In *Avvertimenti*, his unpublished manuscript of advice for novice missionaries, Antonio Baldinucci notes that although peacemaking is potentially one of the great fruits of the mission, one must approach it gingerly, 'using great caution, in order to not cause a large disturbance.'[23] We have noted the importance of the timing of events associated with the mission, and this was all the more true for a delicate public ritual like peacemaking. Baldinucci recommends that missionaries not attempt reconciliations at the start of the mission, since people did not yet feel the sense of unity and cohesion that will allow for success.

In keeping with Jesuit tradition, Baldinucci suggests that missionaries secretly obtain a list of names of enemies, and the causes of their conflicts. When the people seem ready for reconciliation, he contends, the missionary should initiate a penitential procession, or some other 'fervent' activity, in order to prepare them for the rigors of peacemaking. If necessary, the missionary must be prepared to exert a little extra pressure, for example reminding the people that in order to receive official proof of God's benediction – one of the promises of the Jesuit missions – they must embrace their enemies: 'God does not wish to bless the people, if they do not first reconcile themselves with their neighbor.'[24]

Like Baldinucci, his rough contemporary, Paolo Segneri provided specific instructions to his brethren on how to effect successful reconciliations. Following earlier authors of instructional manuals, Segneri cautioned his fellow Jesuits to avoid any hint of impartiality in their endeavors. They should always avoid inserting themselves in disputes among members of confraternities or communities, no doubt because this could only damage the missionaries' reputations and not further the goal of social peace. But although this message implies an even-handed approach to all members of a community, Segneri subscribed to prevailing notions about the greater reliability and virtue of social elites by recommending the appointment of secular men and women 'of major authority' to assist in all aspects of the reconciliation/peacemaking process, and to help maintain order. Such elites would be delegated to determine 'all the disunions' and to do whatever they could to calm the opposing parties without relying upon the missionary fathers, unless they required their intervention.[25]

Many of Segneri's instructions on peacemaking are embedded in his sermons. For Segneri, the dramatic tension surrounding the missionary's

---

[23] Antonio Baldinucci, *Avvertimenti*, ff. 50–53, esp. 50.
[24] Baldinucci, *Avvertimenti*, f. 50.
[25] Segneri and Fontana, *Pratica*, 23–6.

192 A PARADISE INHABITED BY DEVILS

presence on the pulpit offered the ideal opportunity to convince members of a community of their duty to reconcile themselves. In one of the earliest sermons in the cycle of topical sermons which the Jesuit would present to a community, Segneri pleads with his listeners to repent, or face dire consequences: 'You poor people, you miserable sinners, since you want to be like [those] in Jerusalem, you should refuse the calls of God, after which you would still try destruction. Do you know what you are doing? You should fear for your souls, since you will not make peace with your enemies.'[26] As this sermon suggests, Segneri's conversational preaching style was sensitive to anticipating the recalcitrance of his listening audience. His cajoling and taunting was no doubt a rhetorical flourish, but as San Bernardino had no doubt known as well, such a direct style could help the preacher establish a direct connection with audience members. Like Bernardino, Segneri also remains attuned to the dominant cultural values of his contemporaries and realizes that he must address their preoccupations.

This is nowhere clearer than in a sermon on maintaining one's honor while still pardoning an enemy. Here, Segneri acknowledges the overwhelming cultural preoccupation with defending one's honor that permeated early modern Italian society. But Segneri is emphatic in arguing that although people often seek vengeance to restore a lost sense of honor, this behavior does not please God, who only honors those who pardon their enemies: 'Now this God is so great, and so potent, that he commands you to not hate your enemy, which means, do not plot his death; do not slander him; do not steal his things, or his reputation.'[27]

Often, however, the first step in effecting the reconciliation of communities involved convincing individual sinners to repent and reconcile themselves to God. Segneri adroitly raises this connection when he refers to the unrepentant sinner as an 'enemy' of heaven and earth, asking, 'Oh, miserable sinner! Do you have a hostility toward Heaven; what will you do? Call, if you can, the earth to your defense: except that you cannot because you have also opened antagonism with the earth and with Mankind through your mortal sin, which smolders in your breast.'[28]

One of those Jesuits most noted for the successful conversion and reconciliation of previously unrepentant sinners was Francesco De Geronimo (1642–1716), an Apulian missionary whom his primary

---

[26] Segneri and Fontana, *Pratica*, 5.
[27] Segneri and Fontana, *Pratica*, 59–60.
[28] Segneri and Fontana, *Pratica*, 37.

CONFRONTING DISCORD IN EARLY MODERN NAPLES   193

modern biographer refers to as 'the most popular orator of his time.'[29] De Geronimo was born in the village of Grattaglie in the region of Puglia and spent his formative years in Taranto, at the Jesuit college in the trading-port city, in Naples, where he took his degree, and finally in Lecce, where he spent his novitiate (1671–74). There, De Geronimo learned the missionary vocation which would consume most of his lengthy, active life as a Jesuit, and it was in Lecce that De Geronimo first made a name for himself as an urban preacher and peacemaker.

But Naples would be the city most closely associated with De Geronimo, and the site for the maturation of his highly public, theatrical style of missionizing. For forty years (from 1676 to 1716), De Geronimo conducted several tours of missionary duty in and around Naples, and it is here that we find many dramatic examples of the reconciliation of previously unrepentant sinners. De Geronimo's specialty was the conversion of prostitutes and concubines, and he was apparently a common (if sometimes dreaded) sight traversing the meaner streets of Naples with crucifix in hand.

Ideally, the reconciliations that De Geronimo effected resulted in marriage, signaling the close connection between a restoration of religious piety and the establishment of 'correct' social arrangements for early modern reformers. Such was the case, for example, of one young concubinary who, upon hearing De Geronimo's fervent preaching, not only resolved to 'leave his ugly concubinage,' but agreed to marry his lover, so that both of their souls might be saved.[30]

In another dramatic example of such idealized reconciliations, De Geronimo tells of a young prostitute who is equally moved to change her own life and the life of her male companion, despite his pleas to keep the illicit relationship intact. Finally, marriage is presented as the only viable solution:

> A prostitute in the Greek Quarter . . . determined to abandon the evil life, and when her friend, who was a jeweler, arrived that evening, as usual, she chased him away, saying: 'there is no more time, I am already conscience-stricken, I do not want to live my life any longer in the disgrace of God.' And although the youth begged her and begged her, nevertheless, she constantly refused him, so that

---

[29] F.M. D'Aria, *Un Restauratore Sociale. Storia Critica della vita di san Francesco de Geronimo da documenti inediti: Saggio sui suoi autografi. Le sue lettere inedite* (Rome: Edizioni Italiane, 1943), 3. For a brief assessment of the value of D'Aria's biography, including excerpts from his unpublished account of De Geronimo's missionary activities in the hinterlands of the City, see Filippo Iapelli, 'Missioni di San Francesco De Geronimo in Campania in un Inedito di Di Francesco D'Aria,' *Campania Sacra* 32 (2001): 311–24.

[30] De Geronimo, cited in D'Aria, *Un Restauratore Sociale*, 354–6, esp. 354.

194   A PARADISE INHABITED BY DEVILS

seeing himself so rejected, he went away, and then married her, liberating them both from the snares of the devil.[31]

Examples such as these remind us of the inextricable ties that bound individuals to the larger community in the early modern period. For the Jesuits, they serve as testimonials to the efficacy of their missionary agenda, adding luster to their self-conscious effort to publicize the order's concrete successes in reclaiming lost souls and restoring peace to the strife-torn society of southern Italy.

'Exhorting the people to live peacefully': The Jesuits and the Revolt of Naples, 1647–48

Although historians have vigorously debated the long-term significance of the so-called 'Revolt of Masaniello' (1647–48) – a violent uprising which bitterly divided the population of Naples (and many parts of the Viceroyalty), briefly threatening the power of the Spanish Crown – the impact of the revolt on the work of religious orders like the Jesuits has not been adequately considered.[32] Nevertheless, by any account, the Revolt of Naples posed both serious problems and possibilities for the Jesuits and other religious. On the one hand, in so far as they came to be closely identified with the despised members of the nobility and the mistrusted Viceroy, the Jesuits lost credibility in the eyes of many commoners. And yet, in the aftermath of the revolt, the Jesuits seemed to draw important lessons about the centrality of peacemaking and reconciliation to their apostolic work and institutional identity.

The Revolt of Naples was just one of several early modern popular uprisings which posed direct challenges to the prerogatives of regional nobilities, abuses of monarchical power and the wealth and influence of the Church. As Rosario Villari has suggested, these popular movements, whether in the Viceroyalty of Naples, Spanish Netherlands or England, gained inspiration from one another and were instrumental in establishing an 'international' network, particularly among would-be republicans. Villari cites the broad interest in political sea changes in England,

---

31 De Geronimo, as cited in D'Aria, *Un Restauratore Sociale*, 354.

32 See Aurelio Musi's *La Rivolta di Masaniello nella scena politica barocca* (Naples: Guida, 1989); for an excellent discussion of the historiographical debates surrounding the Revolt of Naples, see Rosario Villari, 'Afterword One: Masaniello. Contemporary and Recent Interpretations,' in *The Revolt of Naples*, 153–70. For brief considerations of the impact of the revolt on Jesuit missionary activity, see Carla Faralli, 'Le missioni dei Gesuiti,' 104–106; and Roberto Rusconi, 'Gli ordini religiosi maschili dalla Controriforma alle soppressioni settecentesche. Cultura, predicazione, missioni,' in *Clero e società nell'Italia moderna*, ed. Mario Rosa (Rome-Bari: Laterza, 1992), 207–74, esp. 246.

CONFRONTING DISCORD IN EARLY MODERN NAPLES   195

Naples, Catalonia and the Netherlands among gazetteers and chroniclers in many parts of Europe, producing a large volume of letters, eyewitness accounts and book-length narratives.[33]

This interest is nowhere more evident than in the rapid publication of James Howell's 1650 English translation of Alessandro Giraffi's *Le Rivolutioni di Napoli* (Venice, 1647). Howell, an interesting figure in his own right, had served with the British East India Company in Italy and Spain before producing his translation of the Giraffi account. This translation, entitled *An Exact Historie of the Late Revolutions in Naples* (1650), was reprinted twice more during the seventeenth century, along-side a continuation of the volume, based on new information that Howell had received from informants in Italy.[34] Beyond providing a lively sketch of the significant events that unfolded during the revolt, the work represents one of the few Italian accounts to present the popular forces in a relatively sympathetic light. It also sheds light on the suspicions which the popular classes held toward the religious orders, the Jesuits among them.

Giraffi begins his narrative by relating the background to the 1647 Revolt, informing the reader of Naples' long subjection to foreign powers, the heavy taxation under which the population suffered and the oppressive nature of local authority. In Giraffi's view, the revolution takes on a kind of inevitability, occurring because Neapolitans could not take it any more: 'For it is a clear case that there is engraven in the breasts of men by nature herself a detestation of slavery and how unwillingly they put their necks into the yoke of another.'[35] More immediately, the impetus to revolt was the exaction of a fruit *gabelle* that adversely affected local fruit vendors and consumers alike. Although the people had petitioned the Viceroy, Rodrigo Ponce De Leon, the Duke of Arcos, through the Neapolitan Archbishop Ascanio Filomarino, this had been ineffective. Giraffi argues that news of a successful tax revolt in Sicily emboldened the Neapolitan poor and set the stage for the spectacular confrontation that was to follow. The controversy of the fruit *gabelle* coincided with a move by the Neapolitan municipal government to lower the official weight for a loaf of bread, thus further alienating an already restive Neapolitan Plebe.

---

[33] Villari addresses this 'international' exchange in 'Afterword Two: Naples and the Contemporaneous Revolutions. Some Points of Convergence,' in *Revolt of Naples*, 171–88.

[34] Villari, 'Afterword Two,' 183.

[35] Alessandro Giraffi, *Le Rivolutioni di Napoli* (Venice, 1647), trans. James Howell as *An Exact Historie of the Late Revolutions of Naples; And of their Monstrous Successes, not to be Parallel'd by any Antient or Modern History*, 2 vols (London, 1650–52), 4.

196 A PARADISE INHABITED BY DEVILS

On 7 July 1647, a day devoted to the Virgin of the Carmine, a highly popular Neapolitan religious holiday, after a brief, angry altercation between local fruit sellers and the Elector of the People, Anaclerio, over the *gabelle*, a young fisherman named Tommaso Aniello (Masaniello) organized a group of young boys to join the fruit sellers in protesting the tax. Parading around the popular Mercato quarter of the city, they shouted: 'Let the King of Spain live, but let the ill government die!' Within a few hours, Masaniello had been joined by thousands of men, women and children who marched through the city burning the toll house which held all documents pertaining to the much-hated *gabelles*, freeing prisoners, and surrounded the royal palace, demanding to meet with the viceroy, who at first attempted to hide in a closet, but then escaped over a wall and out through an adjacent church.[36]

From this seemingly spontaneous beginning, the Revolt of Naples emerges as one of the most explosive and complex popular insurrections of the early modern era, full of picturesque incidents, colorful figures and high drama. In broad strokes, however, the popular phase of the revolt lasted just a few months. During the first tense weeks, the popular forces, nominally led by the iconic fisherman Masaniello and key members of the intelligentsia such as Giulio Genoino, sought to negotiate a number of demands with the Spanish Crown and the viceregal government, generally through the intercession of the popular Arch-bishop, Ascanio Filomarino.

Just a little over one week into the revolt, however, Masaniello was murdered, thus setting off a new round of recriminations, fears of betrayal and popular indignation. Although Peter Burke and many others argue that the popular phase of the revolt died along with its mythic leader, the 'barefoot, illiterate fisherman,' Rosario Villari has challenged this view, asking us to look beyond Masaniello to the broader forces that propelled the movement forward.[37] Clearly, the popular phase of the revolt continued throughout the summer and autumn of 1647 as the Plebe continued to arm itself, enforce the new laws which the Republic established and broaden its demands upon the Crown.

---

[36] Giraffi, *An Exact Historie of the Late Revolutions*, 10–17.

[37] Burke is convinced that the Revolt of Naples was largely a symbolic struggle, pointing to its impetus on the feast of the Virgin of the Carmine as evidence that we can understand the revolt within the context of a 'carnivalesque' matrix. See his 'The Virgin of the Carmine and the Revolt of Masaniello,' esp. 14–18. Although Burke is right to highlight the theatricality of the revolt, part and parcel of early modern Neapolitan society, Villari makes a cogent critique of his fellow historian's easy willingness to downplay the broader implications of the insurrection in the context of early modern social struggles. See Villari, 'Afterword One,' esp. 153–63. This essay is based on an earlier response to Burke, published in *Past and Present* (August 1985): 117–32.

CONFRONTING DISCORD IN EARLY MODERN NAPLES   197

Although the revolt would ultimately flounder in 1648 when the rebels placed undue faith in their French patrons, led by the Duke of Guise, and the Spanish would regain control by the summer of that year, the longer-term impact of the Revolt of Naples continues to resonate among scholars and the Neapolitan citizenry to this day.

For the religious, the impact of the Revolt of Naples cannot be understated. From Cardinal Filomarino's frantic missives to the Pope to the Jesuits' own troubled reports to Rome, we get an image of a city besieged and the threat of popular forces which do not appear easily quiescent. The ideal of social peace that the Church tried so ardently to promote appeared to be abandoned, and although individual clergy sided with the rebels, most found themselves the target of popular anger. Even Filomarino, apparently a well-loved and trusted ecclesiastical official, proved unable to negotiate effectively between the popular forces and the representatives of the viceregal court, thus largely failing in his role as the peacemaker *par excellence* for a number of months until order was once again restored in the Southern Italian capital and its environs.

Cardinal Filomarino's letters to Pope Innocent X evoke the delicate negotiations that the Archbishop attempted to foster during the early stages of the revolt and his many frustrations in contending with miscommunications and the suspicions which the people held toward the nobility and the viceregal government. Filomarino is careful to emphasize his own positive role in efforts to broker a peaceful resolution to the conflict, such as calming fears that the local water supply had been poisoned by publicly drinking a glass of water and offering benediction to the people in the name of Pope Innocent, 'exhort[ing] them to quiet themselves' and cease their pursuit of vendettas against their opponents.[38]

In his description of Masaniello, Filomarino has nothing but praise, commenting especially on the popular leader's respectful and 'obedient' demeanor toward the episcopal leader as a 'true miracle of God in this so arduous [a] business.' But with Masaniello's death, the Cardinal lost a direct connection to the popular forces, and, although he does not admit as much to the Pope, his sense of frustration is clear as he narrates the twists and turns in his negotiations between the government and the people, citing hopeful signs of forging a lasting peace, only to have his

---

[38] BAV, Ferraioli IV, 9186, 'Lettere al pontefice Innocernzio X salla Sommossa di Masaniello'. On Filomarino's place in the wider frame of mid-seventeenth-century Naples, cf. Clelia Manfredi, *Il Cardinale Ascanio Filomarino, Arcivescovo di Napoli nella Rivoluzione di Masaniello* (Naples: Istituto della Stampa, 1950).

198   A PARADISE INHABITED BY DEVILS

hopes dashed by some new intrigue.[39] In his sixth letter, dated 24 August 1647, Filomarino reveals what other eyewitness accounts had already confirmed: that the viceroy's hopes that efforts by the religious could placate the people were in vain. Describing his call for the people to assemble in front of the viceregal palace, and the flying of the white standard of peace in front of the castle, the Cardinal is forced to admit that his peacemaking mission has not succeeded: 'The entire city was stirred up again, crying: 'Betrayal, betrayal'; there where earlier it had been pacified by the white standard, and had celebrated the peace.'[40]

Filomarino's acknowledgment of failure is echoed in an anonymous account of the revolt where the author stresses the futile attempts of the secular authorities to use religious processions to quell resistance. The chronicler reports that the Viceroy, the Duke of Arccos, 'thought to avail himself of the Religious' when other options failed to produce the desired results. Dispatching Cardinal Filomarino throughout the city's churches, displaying the 'Most Holy Sacrament' in all the major churches, the viceroy also encouraged the Religious 'to go on many processions, praying for quiet and [for] the peace of the People, and many others preach in the same Piazza del Mercato and exhort the People to live quietly, and to leave behind the rebellions.' But such tactics, according to the author, proved ineffectual: 'this remedy was worth nothing, because the People were so inflamed with indignation from the betrayal of the Duke that they also directed some credit for this to the Religious, and trying to send them back to their monasteries, did not even allow them to preach.'[41]

Not only did the episcopacy and the religious orders face a cynical population in efforts to quell the revolt, but very soon the religious began to suffer popular hostility for their apparently close links to the nobility and the viceregal court. In an anonymously written Jesuit account of the revolt, dated 2 December 1647, the author notes damage to monasteries and churches, and the rebels' confiscation of grain stores held by members of the ecclesiastical community. Although he notes that the Jesuits themselves have not suffered any direct damage, he mentions that one of their buildings has narrowly escaped burning, although he does not identify the site. Others have not been spared: a Dominican monastery has been set ablaze and turned into a 'head-quarters' for the popular militia. The fighting between rival forces has

---

[39] Filomarino, 'Lettere,' 385.

[40] Filomarino, 'Lettere,' 391.

[41] BAV, mss *Chigiani* G. VII 210, 'Delle Rivolutioni di Napoli,' Vol. 1, 'Succinto Relatione della sollevatione di Napoli occorsa nel presente anno 1647 à 7' di Luglio giorno di Domenica sino alla mort' di Tomm'Aniello,' ff. 63–102, esp. ff. 79–80

CONFRONTING DISCORD IN EARLY MODERN NAPLES   199

also led to great damage among a number of Neapolitan churches. Both the tone and content of this letter differ greatly from the normally confident Jesuit missives. In closing, the unnamed author beseeches his superior: 'I pray, Your Paternity to continue to make orations as well as to bless us and to pray to Our Lord for my miseries.'[42]

Nor was popular hostility to privileges enjoyed by the clergy limited to sporadic acts of violence against religious houses. In the official concessions that the popular forces wrested from the Spanish Crown, we can see increasingly broader demands from the summer into the autumn of 1647. In the first charter of concessions, dated 13 July 1647, just one week into the revolt, popular demands dwell primarily on matters of taxation, criminal reform, and exacting general pardons for rebels. In keeping with one pre-modern aspect of the revolt, the insurgents demand recognition of their 'traditional' rights to concede the levying of *gabelles*, harkening back to the Aragon kings of Naples who preceded the Spanish Viceroyalty, and their promises to honor Neapolitan prerogatives. The charter also confirms the right of the people (male members of the Plebe) to choose their popular representatives to the local government – the Elector of the People and the 'Captains of the Street' – to garner equal votes for the people's representatives *vis-à-vis* those of the nobility, to ensure that the Crown would raise levies only in cases of urgent need and, with popular consent, to free prisoners held in local jails.[43]

But by early September, after Masaniello's assassination, the discovery of the popular betrayal of Giulio Genoino, the President of the rebel government, and increasing suspicions toward the viceregal government and some of its ecclesiastical patrons, the popular demands become noticeably more comprehensive. In a new charter, the rebels demand that the Crown deprive nobles of leading positions in the military, courts and all public offices, and insist that only native Neapolitans (with popular support) should hold office. But for the first time, the popular insurgents also seek to enforce certain restrictions on the ecclesiastical community and secularize control of key religious rituals and institutions. For a start, the charter demands that all 'foreign' monks and religious leave the city and the Kingdom of Naples, and that any

---

[42] ARSI, *Neap.* 74, 'Rumori di Napoli,' anonymous, 2 December 1647, ff. 370–371v.

[43] Giuseppe Donzelli, *Partenope liberata. Overo Racconto dell'Heroica Risolutione fatta dal Popolo di Napoli per Sottrarsi con Tutto il Regno dall'insopportabil Giogo delli Spagnuoli* (Naples: 1647); modern edn, ed Antonio Altamura (Naples: Fausto Fiorentino, 1970), 87–92. Donzelli, a Neapolitan nobleman and a physician, was one of those chroniclers most supportive of the Neapolitan revolt. A filo-French advocate, Donzelli dedicates *Partenope Liberata* to the Duke of Guise.

200 A PARADISE INHABITED BY DEVILS

positions of authority within the religious orders be held by native Neapolitans, or natives of the viceroyalty. The people also demand control over the Corpus Christi procession, requiring that it be centered on the newly named 'Piazza del Popolo,' and that the popular classes perform key functions in the annual ritual. Finally, in another example of asserting secular authority over the religious orders, the rebels maintain their right to occupy the strategically key monastery of St Elmo as a defense against possible incursions by noble armies, and seek to control the movements of the resident clerics.[44]

While none of these concessions relate specifically to the Jesuits, the order to expel non-native Neapolitans from the city had special resonance for an order with a pan-European membership. Other evidence, however, points to a more focused hostility toward the Society of Jesus. Rosario Villari cites a report received by the Dutch Consul in Venice (probably during the late summer or early autumn of 1647) and sent to the States General in Amsterdam, in which we see that the Jesuits had been an early target of the rebels' anger:

> Having discovered that the Jesuit fathers were conspiring with the nobility, citizens and merchants with the aim of oppressing the people, the latter went to the Very Eminent Archbishop Filomarino to remonstrate that if His Eminence did not put a stop to the affair, the people would expel all the Jesuit fathers from the Kingdom leaving them only their shirts and drawers.[45]

This comment, although not corroborated in any of the other chronicles of the revolt, nevertheless points to a very real credibility problem that the Jesuits faced. Although we should be cautious in accepting such conspiracy theories, given the widespread hostility toward the Jesuits already finding its way into official discourse (especially Protestant) in this period, the perception of the Jesuits' close ties to local elites is not hard to document. Despite the legacy of at least fifty years of popular missionary activity in the city of Naples and across the viceroyalty, the Jesuits remained very much linked to their elite patrons and supporters. Perhaps more important still, although they had advocated religious and cultural reform within the context of an increasingly articulated civilizing mission, this did not mean that the Society had any solutions for alleviating the very real social inequities and abuses of power which plagued the *Mezzogiorno*. What they could do, however, was strengthen their resolve to de-legitimize social revolt in the wake of the upheavals

---

[44] Donzelli, *Partenope Liberata*, 144–167.

[45] Reports of J. Van Sonnevelt, Dutch Consul in Venice, to the States General, July–December, 1647 (date not specified), as cited in Villari, 'Afterword Two: Naples and the Contemporaneous Revolutions,' in *The Revolt of Naples*, 171–88, esp. 184–5.

CONFRONTING DISCORD IN EARLY MODERN NAPLES   201

of 1647–48 and redouble their labors to effect lasting social peace and rebuild a unified Christian community.

After the Revolt: The social drama of peacemaking

> The past turbulence in the Viceroyalty has also offered frequent occasions to practice such Christian acts [as reconciliation]. Many lords amply mistreated, and offended by that violent power of their vassals, who had never been accustomed to rule ... will pardon with generosity that which they suffered with constancy ... Elsewhere, the multitude has been reunited in ancient affection and reverence toward the nobility and one can affirm [that] in many locales, a great number of the Plebe who had been stirred up, and in whose hearts still lives the sparks of the past anger, and the ambition from the power they enjoyed, [were] grieved by the missions, and let go of any violent design; revealed [it] to confessors, and showed distaste toward any sign of carrying it out by throwing away already prepared munitions and gunpowder.[46]

Despite their difficulties during the Revolt of Naples, the Jesuits appear to have emerged from the crisis with the renewed commitments to conducting the popular missions and publicizing the order's successes. This passage, from Paolucci's chronicle of the Neapolitan missions, published just three years after the end of the revolt, is one of the few direct mentions of the tumultuous event. In its idealized view of social harmony restored, it makes a fitting introduction to a section on the 'social drama' of reconciliation in the Jesuit missions.

Paolucci's description of the many examples of forgiving nobles and contrite vassals evokes a picture of a southern Italian society restored to its previous equilibrium. According to Paolucci's idealistic portrayal of the new mood in the southern Italian countryside, the lords represent 'nobility' in the truest meaning of the word, gladly 'pardoning' the anarchic Plebe for their illegitimate (and apparently inept) experiment with social power. It is the Plebe, according to Paolucci, who need to be subdued, to become quiescent. With the help of the Jesuit fathers, however, they not only abandon further plans for violent resistance, but 'throw away' the very weapons of destruction.

But if Paolucci's example suggests a long-term renewal of social peace, Jesuit missionary reports tell a very different story. In the aftermath of the Revolt of 1647–48, the fabric of society did not easily mend. Economic woes continued to plague the viceroyalty and the region was hit with wave after wave of famine, a major outbreak of the

---

[46] Paolucci, *Missioni*, 152–3.

202 A PARADISE INHABITED BY DEVILS

plague in 1656 and the range of natural disasters to which the region was all too tragically accustomed.[47]

Throughout the latter half of the seventeenth and into the eighteenth century, Jesuit missionaries labored to reconcile faction-riven communities, clergy, warring family members, murderers and their victims' families and inveterate sinners, such as prostitutes. In this respect, they were simply following a tradition which dated back to the order's founding, and, even earlier, to their mendicant predecessors. But something had changed. Although the Jesuit accounts of peacemaking had always highlighted the dramatic flavor of reconciliations, part and parcel of the intrepid image of the Jesuit missionary that they were publicizing, these later chronicles bespeak a more consciously theatrical approach to conducting missions.

The social 'drama' of reconciliation represented the missionary as but one (albeit the most important) of the actors in a complex enactment of social conflict and resolution, and formed part of a more standard means of chronicling Jesuit missionary efforts. Although a more thorough discussion of Jesuit missionary theater will be presented in the next chapter, it is useful to offer a broad sketch of how a dramatic reconciliation might proceed.

Initially, missionaries' efforts to effect reconciliations were often met with skepticism, or downright ridicule. In his discussion of a mission made in Capua in 1649, an anonymous missionary reports that a primary goal of the mission had been to reconcile two rival, noble families who had been locked in vicious blood feud that had engulfed the entire community. When the missionaries had arrived on the scene, members of the two families had made fun of the mission. But gradually, according to the author, the noblemen were moved by the example of others: 'At the beginning, these [men] had made fun of the work of penitence, and of mortifications, that in the time of the mission one saw done every day, first by the common people, and then by the heads of the more principal [families] of the City.'[48]

Far from merely overcoming the resistance of a few key players, however, the 'drama' of reconciliation in this mission involved spectacular ritual acts. Such was the zealous attitude of the community that the

---

[47] For an overview of the post-Revolt period, see, for example, Ghirelli, *Storia di Napoli*, 64–78. On the extent of the devastation wrought by the plague, Ghirelli estimates that nearly half the population of Naples was decimated, 73. For a more detailed assessment of the demographic impact of the plague, see also Claudia Petraccone, *Napoli dal '500 all '800*, 108.

[48] ARSI, *Neap.* 74, 'Relatione d'una Missione fatta in Capua,' (1649), ff. 260–84, esp. 264–267v.

missionary describes young noblemen, 'with ropes around their necks and without collar[s],' pleading with those assembled in church to pardon them for their scandalous behavior and 'bad example.' He presents vivid images of esteemed men in the community leaping onto the pulpit and spontaneously confessing their sins to the Jesuit father.[49]

Nor were such ritual acts limited to the laity. While earlier chronicles had illuminated Jesuit efforts to reconcile female religious, these later seventeenth-century accounts include the clergy as well. One missionary relation from 1666 offers the unusual sight of five clerics making a public apology to the bishop whom they had slandered. According to the author, these five troublemakers had written a 'defamatory missive' about their own bishop and then 'threw it into his room.' Yet apparently, the general atmosphere of penitence was too much for the restive priests, and they 'offered to do everything for the Prelate – penitence and giving him every satisfaction in order to obtain the pardon.'[50]

Francesco De Geronimo is also celebrated for his abilities in reconciling conflicts among members of religious communities. When it came time for the nuns of 'one of the most celebrated and noble' convents to receive the *Spiritual Exercises* from their Jesuit confessor, he became suddenly ill and was replaced by De Geronimo. But De Geronimo found the nuns bitterly divided into factions. As in other cases of factional conflicts, De Geronimo at first faced suspicion, then mere indifference, until finally, 'they passed over into devotion, and such was the concourse that it was commonly said in the convent that they did not remember a gathering so numerous [in the past].'[51]

According to De Geronimo, however, as gratifying as it was to have successful and enthusiastic attendance at the meditations associated with the *Exercises*, the real benefit of the mission was in the peacemaking ritual which he organized. Having gathered all the nuns and the *converse* (lay sisters, servants) together one evening, De Geronimo directed each one of them who 'had been offended with words or with uncomplimentary acts' to throw herself at the feet of her offender and reconcile herself with this person: 'As soon as that was said, one of them got up and approached another [woman] from the opposing faction, and prostrated herself, praising God to see that entire community of seventy nuns so moved in fervor of the spirit [that] . . . each one of them met with her adversary and with many tears and sobs they asked each other's pardon.'[52]

---

[49] ARSI, *Neap.* 74, 'Relatione d'una Missione fatta in Capua,' ff. 265–265v.

[50] ARSI, *Neap.* 76, Doc. IV (Anonymous, 1666), ff. 23–28V, esp. 25–25v.

[51] *S. Francesco di Girolamo e le sue Missioni*, 142–4, esp. 143. This is an edited collection of De Geronimo's own writings.

[52] *S. Francesco di Girolamo e le Sue Missioni*, 143–4.

204   A PARADISE INHABITED BY DEVILS

Such dramatic reconciliations are especially striking given the initial resistance to the missionary's labors, and yet they became an ever more common staple of missionary reports during the late seventeenth century. We may be skeptical of De Geronimo's claims that the peace was 'maintained until now.' Still, there is no reason to believe that these reconciliation rituals did not effect at least temporary peace in strife-torn communities. After all, early modern society was at home with ritualized, often theatrical gestures, particularly in the realm of religious practice.[53]

If factional disputes divided the monasteries and convents, there was also frequent enmity between secular clergy and the laity. Some parish priests were considered immoral, or driven more by financial incentive than pastoral concern for a community. In a small community on the outskirts of Naples called Casollo, Francesco De Geronimo celebrates this particular brand of reconciliation ritual by describing the conflict between a clergyman who was 'not very esteemed in this place' and the laity. After community members had made many 'tearful confessions and general communion,' they were ready to reconcile with their parish priest. De Geronimo led this peacemaking ritual from the pulpit with a rope around his neck and a chain in his hand:

> He carried the Crucifix to the high altar of the church where the parish priest came and took the rope from the Father [. . .] [P]lacing it around his neck, the priest asked the people's pardon. At this point the Father [De Geronimo] spoke according to what God suggested, ordering all the people to kiss the feet of their pastor. This was done with such fervor that the men not only kissed the [priest's feet], but even more, prostrated themselves on the ground and could not stop crying with bitter tears.[54]

In this example, the prescribed elements of the peacemaking ritual were all in place: the dynamic, divinely inspired missionary orator; a contrite cleric; and finally, an inflamed community, eager to perform the necessary symbolic gestures of forgiveness (the 'kiss of peace,' prostration). If the incident strikes some modern readers as too dramatic, or disturbing in its intensity, bespeaking an overly emotional religious devotion, such descriptions would not have shocked an early modern audience. Similar examples are offered for reconciliations between feuding siblings, fathers

---

[53] For an interesting discussion of this phenomenon, see Edward Muir, 'The Virgin on the street corner: the place of the sacred in Italian cities,' in *Religion and Culture in the Renaissance and Reformation*, ed. Steven Ozment, Sixteenth Century Essays and Studies XI, (Kirksville, MO: Sixteenth Century Journal Publishers 1989), 25–40.

[54] *S. Francesco di Girolamo e le Sue Missioni*, 146–7.

CONFRONTING DISCORD IN EARLY MODERN NAPLES   205

and sons, and whole families torn apart, frequently by disputes over property.[55]

If reconciliations were symbolically vital enactments for a strife-torn community, permitting a cathartic release of grief and anger, they also served a very real function in promoting social order. In a society where the criminal justice system remained relatively underdeveloped, and where violent feuding was rampant, restoring social peace was seen as an essential component of the religious vocation, particularly in an order committed to a civilizing mission, such as the Jesuits. De Geronimo cites cases where a series of homicides had left two communities in turmoil. Although in one case the two accused assassins were in the *Vicaria*, De Geronimo arranged for a member of one of the afflicted families to pardon the accused murderers in order to restore peace within the community. This action was most effective, De Geronimo notes. After having 'settled the civil controversies,' he met with the ministers of the tribunal of criminals and convinced them to pardon the incarcerated men, thus permitting a full reconciliation of the parties involved.[56]

Promoting social order, however, was not simply a question of reconciling criminals with their victims' families. Ongoing blights on the social landscape such as prostitution were viewed as reminders to the faithful that a unified Christian community had not been achieved and were viewed as threats to the well-being of all. Efforts to reconcile prostitutes continued to occupy the energies of missionaries like De Geronimo and Segneri, raising fascinating questions about the limitations of moral reform to address the more complex and troubling realities of a highly unequal and increasingly desperate southern Italian society.

In De Geronimo's accounts of his own travels through the popular quarters of Naples, the missionary speaks of himself in the third person, presenting a familiar image of bustling urban life, the people's indulgence in 'profane pleasures' and the wondrous effects of vigorous mission ary intervention in combating a range of social ills. He tells us that it was his custom to preach each Sunday of the year in a large *piazza*, typically frequented by 'innumerable [crowds of] people gathered out of curiosity to hear little farces put on there by companies of acrobats.' The spectators at such festive events, he argues, were composed of 'the laziest people – as much [natives] of this city, as of the many peoples and nations who gather[ed] there.'[57] But although people may have come together to enjoy some free entertainment, De Geronimo's intention was

---

[55] *S. Francesco di Girolamo e le Sue Missioni,* 147–9.
[56] *S. Francesco di Girolamo e le Sue Missioni,* 152–3.
[57] *S. Francesco di Girolamo e le Sue Missioni,* 68.

206   A PARADISE INHABITED BY DEVILS

to use the occasion to effect reconciliations of many inveterate sinners: 'That which one can say, generally, is that many sinners in that *piazza*, due to the confusion and compunction of their sins, were given to [shedding] bitter tears and at times came to the foot of the holy crucifix and publicly asked pardon, beating themselves with a chain on their shoulders.' Where the acrobats merely provided mindless diversion from the daily toils which people faced, De Geronimo's vigorous preaching 'caused great contrition and edification in the listener[s] and a great many of them, at the end of the sermon, attached themselves beside the Father, crying and saying: "Father, help me, I am damned."' Following these outbursts of renewed faith, the remorseful sinners would be taken to an oratory where they would practice penitential discipline and then make a good confession.[58]

In this instance, as in many which we will note in the following chapter, the Jesuits appropriated the theatricality of profane companies in order to captivate the 'audience' and turn them toward a more pious way of life. What is missing in such accounts is any discussion of what happens to the profane actors who are displaced by their sacred counterparts, or any acknowledgment that some members of the audience (not to mention the actors themselves) may have objected to this literal 'upstaging.'

F.M. D'Aria, one of De Geronimo's modern biographers, also evokes the Neapolitan Jesuit's highly ritualized, theatrical travels through the popular quarters of the city, seeking willing converts and souls to reconcile. Citing several of De Geronimo's contemporary biographers, D'Aria posits the missionary's dramatic impact upon his would-be subjects, 'women of the profession':

> Upon the arrival of the missionary in the zone . . . the great majority of those unhappy [women] disappeared from the streets, and closed themselves inside their homes, 'in order not to hear . . . the voice of the celestial charmer,' Father Francesco continued to roar, threatening the punishments of God to the obstinate and promising heavenly mercy to those who would submit. Whether out of feminine curiosity, or through supernatural influence, most [of the prostitutes] ended up standing at their windows listening to him.[59]

As in a conventional Jesuit narrative, the sinners are initially wary of the missionary reformer, but cannot resist his overwhelming persuasiveness. Whether they are drawn in by mere 'curiosity' or 'supernatural influence' does not really matter, according to such narratives: the end result is what is crucial. In De Geronimo's able hands, we are told, female sinners

---

[58] *S. Francesco di Girolamo e le Sue Missioni*, 68–9.
[59] F.M. D'Aria, *Un Restauratore Sociale*, 347–9.

whose very livelihoods had been shaped by their pursuit of illicit 'pleasures' (in this case, sexual commerce, most likely a means of economic survival) are made humble, 'transported as if by an irresistible force, all humble.' And, in a symbolic gesture of their true conversion, D'Aria tells us, the *convertite* would cut off their long, flowing hair and place it at the foot of a large crucifix like a 'trophy of victory.'[60]

This theatrical element in accounts of Jesuit-inspired reconciliations was not always so public, however. It could also involve extraordinary examples of individuals confronting sinful or inappropriate behaviors, and vowing to change their lives. In these cases, the drama was heightened by the degree of sin and the power of the missionary to intervene effectively to reverse its effects. For De Geronimo, the prostitute was a favorite subject for such miraculous reconciliations. He relates one story of a 'very famous' and formerly wealthy and well-connected prostitute who finds herself suffering from a 'horrendous' affliction.

This woman, whose customers had included 'the first names of that city,' had become impoverished due to her ever-worsening condition and, in desperation, was moved to call upon De Geronimo's aid after hearing him conduct one of his sermons. When he arrives at her bedside, the woman pleads with the Jesuit to advise her on how to proceed, and De Geronimo encourages her to leave her quarters and go to the 'Hospital of the Incurables,' where she might receive 'help for the soul and for the body.' At this advice, the prostitute is visibly disturbed, replying: 'Father, one such as me at the Incurables? I was almost the patroness of half the nobility of Naples and of Rome; and now to the Incurables?' But De Geronimo's purpose is to force the woman to give up any residual pride and accept her fate: 'Daughter, don't look at who you have been, but who you are now. It is better to go from the Incurables to paradise, than from this house to Hell.'[61]

In this example, which ends predictably with the former prostitute languishing in a hospital bed for several weeks, examining her past sins, confessing and finally dying a 'good death,' thanks to De Geronimo's timely intervention, we see a vivid example of how the Jesuit narratives represent moral reform as the best solution to pressing social concerns such as the widespread presence of prostitution in early modern Naples. Here, unlike in the previous example of poor street prostitutes, is an example of a formerly successful prostitute (perhaps more accurately called a courtesan, given her apparently high-level connections in Neapolitan and Roman society) facing divine punishment for her many years of 'illicit' behavior. Given the poor state of her health, placement in a

---

[60] Ibid., 349.
[61] S. *Francesco di Girolamo e le Sue Missioni*, 73–6, esp 74–5.

208   A PARADISE INHABITED BY DEVILS

monastery for *convertite*, or finding her a suitable marriage, would not have been an option, yet at least reconciliation can insure a good death for the woman.

In these and other examples from De Geronimo's wanderings through the prostitutes' quarters of Naples, we receive vague testimony of reconciliations, revealing the depth of a problem for which not even the dramatic, heroic fervor of the missionary could provide solutions. Moral reform made for powerful anecdotes about extraordinary conversions and reconciliations, but as the Neapolitan economy worsened and conditions for the urban poor remained desperate at best, such examples begin to sound formulaic and self-serving. Rather than challenging the veracity of De Geronimo's and his contemporaries' representations of miraculous reconciliations (impossible to prove, in any event), perhaps we should instead ask what purpose such edifying tales held for members of the Society of Jesus, or a lay audience interested in their activities.

There is no way to gauge whether reconciliations such as those effected by De Geronimo and others had any long-term impact on promoting social peace in Naples, but the renewed attention given to this aspect of the Jesuits' apostolic vocation in the period following the Revolt of Naples suggests that the Society acknowledged its central relevance in their work.[62] The hostilities that the order faced during the uprising no doubt served a cautionary note, encouraging greater attention to promoting peace at all levels of society. But the more theatrical, orchestrated missions of the latter seventeenth and early eighteenth centuries were not simply defensive responses to outside events. Rather, the social drama of reconciliation, coupled with the penitential exercises that came to provide a dramatic closure to the missionary encounter, epitomized the mature, highly articulated Jesuit civilizing mission of the period. More than a century after its founding, the Society of Jesus had constructed a well-defined and appealing identity for its missionary practitioners. Novices could call upon a range of 'heroic' forefathers from whom to gain inspiration, accessing the words and deeds of these

---

[62] It is important to point out that the Jesuits were not alone in this assessment. Many other religious organizations sought to promote peace, particularly in the Viceroyalty of Naples, such as the newly formed Congregation of Apostolic Missions, founded by Sansone Carnevale in 1646. This missionary order was especially active in the popular quarters of Naples, during the revolt and in its aftermath, trying to forge reconciliations and prevent further acts of resistance. The similarly named Congregation of Missions, founded by St Vincent DePaul in Paris, was brought first to Rome (1631) and later to Naples (1668) to conduct similar work. On both orders and their peacemaking activities, see Rienzo, 'Il processo di cristianizzazione;' on the latter, see Luigi Mezzadri, 'Le missioni popolari della congregazione della missione nello stato della Chiesa (1642–1700)', *Rivista di Storia della Chiesa in Italia* XXXIII (1979), 12–44.

innovators through their letters, sermons, missionary relations and instructional manuals which the order kept as part of a repository to collective memory. Through striking examples of prolific and skillful 'angels of peace' like Francesco De Geronimo, the Jesuits argued for their apparent efficacy in promoting social reconciliation and combating the 'vices' that plagued early modern Naples.

CHAPTER SIX

Perfecting one's craft:
Jesuit missionary theater in Naples

Just as reconciliations formed a vital part of the 'social drama' of the Jesuit missions, both reinforcing notions of missionary heroism and functioning as an important means of resolving local disputes, so penitential practice came to be a defining feature of the Society of Jesus' activities during the seventeenth and early eighteenth centuries. These ritualized acts of penitence were deftly woven into a sacred theater through which the Jesuits sought to promote an abhorrence of sinful behavior and a righteous fear of divine punishment. Paradoxically, the very dramatic nature of the Jesuits' missionary theater, particularly the fevered pitch which penitential exercises often reached, became a source of controversy, both within the order and especially among a growing chorus of external critics. By the eighteenth century, the Society of Jesus found itself on the defensive, accused of indulging popular notions of religiosity out of step with a new ecclesiastical mood, and charged with unleashing passions that might threaten social order.

In staging their missions, the Jesuits were mindful of the importance of winning missionary subjects away from their so-called profane competitors. By the early seventeenth century, their missionaries were self-consciously competing with secular theater troops for the attention and devotion of the people. The Jesuit colleges had long viewed sacred theater as an integral feature of the educational curriculum, and by the late sixteenth century institutions like the Collegio Romano had produced a number of popular theatrical productions.[1] Ironically, although

---

[1] For an overview of the development of Jesuit theater in the colleges, see William H. McCabe SJ, *An Introduction to Jesuit Theater*, ed. Louis J. Oldani SJ (St Louis: The Institute of Jesuit Sources, 1983), esp. 3–18; *The Oxford Companion to the Theatre* (3rd edn), ed. Phyllis Hartnoll (London: Oxford University Press, 1967), 508–14. See also Marc Fumaroli, *Eroi e oratori*, esp. 197–204. For a wide range of perspectives on Jesuit theater, cf. Maria Chiabò and Federico Doglio, eds, *I Gesuiti e i Primordi del Teatro Barocco in Europa* (Rome: Centro Studi Sul Teatro Medioevale e Rinascimenti, 1995). For a more recent and valuable monograph study of seventeenth- and eighteenth-century Jesuit theater and spectacle in Milan, see Giovanna Zanlonghi, *Teatri di Formazione. Actio, parola e immagine nella scena gesuitica del Sei-Settecento a Milano* (Milan: Vita e Pensiero, 2002). A relatively recent bibliographical guide to such works can be found in L.J. Oldani SJ and

212   A PARADISE INHABITED BY DEVILS

the Society produced stringent critiques of profane theater, it utilized many theatrical techniques in its productions, and paid close attention to theatrical elements in the popular missions.[2]

Jesuit accounts of the missions were theatrical representations in and of themselves, setting up a conventional, dramatic structure through which authors recounted the signal events associated with the missionary endeavor, often building upon initial obstacles or conflicts to highlight eventual successes. Within the larger drama of the mission, the penitential rituals served as a kind of 'final act,' providing the resolution of pre-existing tensions and the closure of the mission itself.

The so-called 'Schools of Mortification' – a series of penitential activities associated with the climax of the missionary endeavor – served a variety of functions. As in earlier, medieval practices, the penitential acts associated with Jesuit missions were viewed as collective re-enactments of the suffering of Christ. In this sense, they were meant to bring penitents closer to God and to expiate guilt. But the rituals also had social functions that are not immediately apparent from contemporary accounts.

In order to understand the role that missionary theatricality and penitential practice had in the development of Jesuit corporate identity in Naples, but also elsewhere in Italy, I focus on the work of two important seventeenth-century innovators: Francesco De Geronimo and Paolo Segneri. Their theatrical brand of conducting missions bore the distinctive stamp of the Jesuit order, while also accommodating to popular tastes and forms of devotion. Within these missionary endeavors, De Geronimo and Segneri exemplified the promises and dangers inherent in the penitential missions within the shifting religious and cultural climate of early eighteenth-century Italy.

Staging the missions

Theatrical considerations had always played a part in the construction of Jesuit missions. Authors of instructional manuals from the late sixteenth century stress the importance of missionaries making a dra-

---

M.J. Bredeck SJ, 'Jesuit Theater in Italy: A Bibliography,' *AHSI* 66, no. 131 (January–June 1997): 185–235.

[2] Jean Delumeau points to the widespread use of theatrical techniques in religious reform efforts, cutting across confessional lines. See Delumeau, *Sin and Fear*, trans. Eric Nicholson (New York: St Martin's Press, 1990), 333–7. Cf. Adriano Prosperi's valuable discussion of the use of theater as a 'tool' of post-Tridentine social disciplining, 'La Chiesa Tridentina e il Teatro: Strategie di Controllo del Secondo '500,' in *I Gesuiti e i Primordi del Teatro Barocco*, 15–30.

JESUIT MISSIONARY THEATER IN NAPLES 213

matic entrance into a new community. Similarly, historians of Jesuit missionary activity in the Kingdom of Naples highlight the value of spectacular techniques in converting recalcitrant sinners. For example, in Francesco Schinosi's eighteenth-century popular history of the Jesuits in Naples, he recounts Bernardino Realino's unorthodox methods for converting Muslim slaves to Roman Catholicism. According to Schinosi's account, Realino would try to work with the slaves for a few hours per day, for five continuous days, to encourage their conversion. But if such methods proved fruitless, the missionary would alter his tactics. In an effort to break their will, Realino would meet with his charges at night, proffering visions of demons and 'menaces' to encourage them further: 'Then, when he did not succeed with daily and personal diligence, God sought a remedy at nighttime, through the oration of this his servant [Realino]; now terrifying them with visions of demons, and with menaces of infernal punishments, and now ensnaring them with other mysterious apparitions.'[3]

In a similar example, Schinosi relates how an unnamed Neapolitan missionary used vivid imagery and hyperbole to effect the gallows conversion of a group of Muslim slaves who faced execution for killing their cruel master. Playing upon the slaves' deep-seated hatred for their slain overlord, the missionary evokes both the pains of hellfire – and, perhaps most fittingly, the horror that the accused killers would feel in spending eternity with their despised enemy – as dramatic gestures to win them over to Catholicism.[4]

Naturally, these sorts of theatrical methods were not unique to the Society of Jesus. As we saw in the last chapter, late medieval preachers like San Bernardino di Siena played upon the highly emotional climate which surrounded sacred oratory and the rituals associated with it to instill a righteous fear of damnation upon their audience. But it was not simply a question of employing spectacular *exempla* in sermons on Hell and damnation. A wide range of early modern missionaries also integrated more sophisticated theatrical techniques into their sermons and penitential orations. Among the most popular props was the death skull (*teschio*), which missionaries used frequently, and in a variety of creative ways. Jean Delumeau relates the example of a French Capuchin, Father

---

[3] Schinosi, *Istoria*, 1: 431–3. Novi Chavarria has suggested that this method of proffering visions and apparitions was a common strategy among Jesuit missionaries, both within southern Italy and the Americas. See 'L'Attività missionaria dei Gesuiti,' 168–71. For the Jesuits' use of this approach among Amerindians in New Spain, see Serge Gruzinski, 'Délires et visions chez les indiens du Mexique,' *Mélanges de l'École française de Rome* (Moyen Age–temps modernes) 86 (1974), 445–80.

[4] Schinosi, *Istoria*, 1: 433–5.

214   A PARADISE INHABITED BY DEVILS

Honoré de Cannes, who would adorn the death's head with 'a judge's cap, a military headpiece ... a doctor's wig, an Academy member's crown, or an abbot's hair grip,' apparently depending upon the object of his sermon.[5] Accounts of the Neapolitan missions also highlight the use of the death skull, as well as lighting and other visual aids to enhance the atmosphere of horror. Scipione Paolucci presents a vivid example of how Jesuit missionaries set the stage for penitential rituals, the dramatic climax of the popular missions:

> With mournful decoration and dolorous pomp, the chapel is dismally adorned so as to keep out sunlight, with only several oil lamps or candles. With a devout horror, the darkness is also held off, however weakly; stretched over the ground are pieces of mourning fabric and over these long strings of bones and death skulls, interrupted by thorns, ropes, and other penitential instruments, and at the end of the room, extended decorously over some black rug, the Holy Crucifix. Around this are provided small benches and other tables in order to allow the listeners places to sit.[6]

Although these extensive preparations were part of the wider deployment of theatrical technology that characterized much of Catholic religious culture in the early modern period, Paolucci's description reminds us once again of the Jesuits' methodical approach to the missionary vocation.

Indeed, although the Jesuits' sixteenth-century instructional manuals, source for such a wide range of guidelines for novice missionaries, do not place great emphasis on stagecraft, setting and the means for eliciting audience participation, later sources are quite interested in such concerns. This decisive turn toward greater theatricality no doubt reflected the maturation of the Jesuits' missionary methodology, but it also suggests the influence of Jesuit theater in the colleges, and the greater challenges that the order perceived in the seventeenth century, such as contending with the widespread social conflict that characterized the period and the need to forge peace and reduce factional violence. Further, the rise of secular theater companies meant that itinerant missionaries might not be the only 'novelty' in a small city or village, forcing the Jesuits to integrate theatricality more consistently into their missionary program.

Even beyond Naples, Jesuit missionary practitioners like Antonio Baldinucci focused on the critical role that the clergy could play in setting positive examples for the laity. He encouraged priests to use penitential props such as crowns of thorns or cords of rope at the throat

---

[5] Delumeau, *Sin and Fear*, 334.
[6] Paolucci, *Missioni*, 47–8.

JESUIT MISSIONARY THEATER IN NAPLES 215

to inspire the faithful to a greater abhorrence of sin.[7] Similarly, Paolo Segneri provided an elaborate discussion of the most efficacious use of theatrical techniques to effect conversions. Following upon his instructions in other aspects of missionary work, Segneri strove to anticipate any and all potential obstacles to resistance among his audience of laity and fellow clergy. Segneri and his missionary companion, Fulvio Fontana, noted that it was crucial to pay special attention to the placement of the preacher on the stage *vis-à-vis* his audience. Segneri sought to prevent visual and aural obstacles which might obstruct his holy theater, while also insuring that the placement of audience members conformed to the strict gender segregation which modeled conventional notions of order and decorum.

Whether the 'stage' was a pulpit or a proscenium built on a *piazza* or a makeshift stage out in the countryside, Segneri believed that it should be set up to facilitate the comfort of the faithful. When constructing a stage expressly intended for missionary theater, *al fresco*, Segneri suggests erecting it on top of a slope, 'because then the people have the ease of convenient seating, and seeing who preaches.' The seating area 'must always serve to divide the men from the women,' a goal easily accomplished by 'encircling the area with either a rope or with benches in such a way that they form either a nice square, or an attractive oval.' One of the missionaries' assistants (probably a member of the secular clergy, or a local notable) could then assist the men and women in taking their seats – benches for the clergy and principal members of the community, and the ground for the common folk.[8] It seems curious that Segneri would concern himself with such aesthetic considerations as the shape of seating areas, but perhaps less so when one considers the extent to which Jesuit theater had become quite technically sophisticated by the late seventeenth century.

Such strategies were not surprising, given the enormous popularity of profane theater in the early modern period and the emergence of new, potentially threatening forms of secular entertainment such as the *commedia dell'arte* companies that toured Italy.[9] But the adaptation of

---

[7] Baldinucci, *Avvertimenti*, 36.

[8] Segneri and Fontana, *Pratica delle Missioni*, 9–15, esp. 9–10.

[9] The development of the *commedia dell'arte* is, of course, an enormous topic. For a quick overview of this sixteenth-century innovation in profane theater, see *The Oxford Companion to the Theatre* (3rd edn), 487–91. On the origins of the *commedia dell'arte* companies, compare Ferruccio Marotti and Giovanna Romei, eds, *La Commedia dell'Arte e la società barocca. La professione del teatro* (Rome: Bulzoni, 1991), esp. xxv–lvi; Ferdinando Taviani and Mirella Schino, *Il Segreto della Commedia dell'Arte. La Memoria delle compagnie italiane del XVI, XVII, e XVIII secolo* (Florence: Casa Usher, 1982); for Naples, see Benedetto Croce, *I Teatri di Napoli*, ed. Giuseppe Galasso (Milan: Adelphi,

216 A PARADISE INHABITED BY DEVILS

secular theater was also fueled by missionaries' efforts to 'sacralize' the revelries of Carnival. The Jesuits made a conscious effort to reform Carnival rituals from the late sixteenth century, particularly through the institution of the 'Forty Hours' of religious devotion. They hoped to effect their desired civilizing mission and educate the public in Christian doctrine through this ritual, but substituting profane activities for religious ones was not quite so straightforward. As in so many other areas of their work, the Jesuits needed to accommodate to some extent to popular tastes and proclivities.

Initially, such efforts at 'substitution' appear successful, at least according to Jesuit chronicler Francesco Schinosi. Referring to this campaign, Schinosi comments approvingly:

> The Fathers set out to repel such ancient pernicious customs with a new one [. . .] of devout usage; calling a very considerable number of people, during those same days, to be devoted to the adoration and to communion with the ineffable Sacrament; in this way, given the efficacy of our missionaries, [the people] emptied the *piazze* and filled the Jesuit Church [. . .] so leaving behind that more licentious part of Carnival.[10]

But substituting profane for sacred rituals was evidently not enough. As the Jesuit sources contend, at least, some accommodation to theatricality and embracing of the spectacular nature of popular religious ritual became characteristic of Jesuit missionary practice in Naples and beyond.

The Jesuits developed their own sacred theater, sometimes referred to as 'sanctifed Carnival.' This sacred ritual was meant to serve as a 'devotional counterpoint to the profane and popular spectacles of the season.' Such theater was characterized not only by its use of some of the newest techniques in stagecraft, but also by the inclusion of pagan themes and characters in the service of post-Tridentine Catholicism. If sacred theater had the obvious objective of providing morally edifying entertainment to its audiences, it also held importance for members of the Society of Jesus as well. At the Roman College, as elsewhere in the order, the great labors required to mount a theatrical production required the efforts of many of the students. By keeping students

---

1992), esp. 41–55. Croce notes that the first Neapolitan comedy troupe was legally constituted in 1575.

[10] Schinosi, *Istoria*, 2: 89–90. There was some resistance on the part of the Spanish authorities to the shift toward Quarant'Ore in the Kingdom of Naples, perhaps due to larger disputes between local representatives of the Crown and the Church. On Schinosi's take on the broader dispute, see ibid., 90–91.

occupied with such productions, the Jesuits may have hoped to distract them from potentially corrupting influences on the streets.[11]

Jesuit theater in the colleges served a variety of functions that influenced the broader theatricality in the Society's missionary work. Within the context of the *Ratio Studiorum* – the Jesuits' educational curriculum – theatrical productions could be excellent vehicles to teach rhetorical principles. They also served a recreational function for students, as well as those audience members who were dazzled by these productions. With themes that often tried to bridge the gap between Greco-Roman Antiquity and biblical tales, the profane and the sacred, the worldly and the supernatural, and even the linguistic gulf between Latin and vernacular tongues, Jesuit theater could be accommodated to a range of tastes, local preferences and diverse purposes. These productions, like the Jesuits' theatrical missionary oratory, promoted notions of the Society's apostolic heroism by demonstrating members' virtuosity, and victories over heretics, infidels and inveterate sinners.[12]

Early Jesuit playwrights like Bernardino Stefonio (1562–1620) provided important models for the blending of the sacred and the profane, and took pride in elaborate use of stagecraft.[13] Inspired by humanistic themes in their work, these theater artists shared with later missionary theater practitioners a preoccupation with developing and utilizing sophisticated techniques to promote a morally edifying message and to overwhelm spectators, leaving them 'exhausted and convinced.'[14]

If college-based productions represented the 'high' end of Jesuit theater, they were certainly not the only response to the growing presence of secular theater in the late sixteenth century. Shortly after Stefonio's early productions, we find the first mentions in southern Italy of Jesuit theater with a decidedly missionary purpose. Once again, the impetus for these productions was the revelries of Carnival time. In 1605, the Jesuit College at Benevento presented a home-grown production to the public at large:

> Around the events of the other colleges, the zeal demonstrated by Ours at Benevento was notable for extirpating every sort of public

---

[11] Fumaroli, *Eroi e oratori*, 203–204.

[12] Cf. Michelino Grandieri, 'Della moderazione onesta. Introduzione al teatro dei Gesuiti in Italia,' *Storia dell'Arte* 32 (1978): 59–70, esp. 62–3.

[13] On Stefonio's contributions to Jesuit theater, see Fumaroli, *Eroi e oratori*, 198–214. Bernardino Stefonio was born on 8 December 1562 in Poggio Mirteto (Rieti), Italy, and died on the same day in 1620 in Modena. A professor of rhetoric for several years at the Collegio Romano, he became known for his classically based plays and their highly elaborate productions. Cf. *Diccionario Histórico de la Compañía*, s.v. 'Stefonio, Bernardino.'

[14] Grandieri, 'Della moderazione,' 65–7.

218 A PARADISE INHABITED BY DEVILS

> abuse and especially those of the improper Comedies [*Commedie scorrette*]. In order to prevent these [from being performed] our scholars presented a Drama composed by their Master, entitled the Prodigal Son, to be shown during Carnival [. . .] for the great profit and pleasure of the Public.[15]

As this example suggests, the Jesuits had real concerns about the presence of secular theater artists and their potentially harmful impact upon the faithful. In this fear, they were not alone, as other ecclesiastical and secular authorities shared anxieties about the potential for violence and social disorder that Carnival-related activities might ignite.[16] In 1639, for example, Jesuits on the island of Malta were themselves the target of Carnival rioting when they attempted to interfere with dramatic productions being organized by the elite Knights of St John. For their trouble, the Jesuits had their quarters looted and were temporarily driven off the island.[17]

Although overt discussions of the drawing power of the comedic artists is muted in sixteenth-century sources, by the mid-seventeenth century they become a more common feature of Jesuit missionary relations, as well as the object of pointed critiques. As we saw in the previous chapter, Jesuits like Francesco de Geronimo issued polemics against the presence of troupes of 'acrobats' on the streets of Naples, but this competition found its way to smaller locales as well.

In a missionary report from Nola, dated November, 1653, the author bemoans the fact that upon their arrival, he and his companion(s) had to contend with both bad weather and the unwelcome presence of a troop of comedians. Initially, the Jesuit preachers faced poor attendance, 'not only due to the continuously rainy weather,' but because 'a numerous company of comedians had arrived in Nola with their scenic and curious spectacles,' thus distracting the faithful and enticing them with an 'occupation completely alien, and directly opposed to sermons and other devout exercises' of the missionary fathers. Ultimately, however, the Jesuits prevailed, if only because they convinced the ecclesiastical and secular authorities to order the comics out of the city, post-haste.[18] It certainly may have helped that the Jesuits had long-standing ties with powerful residents of Nola through the Jesuit college there (founded in 1556).

---

[15] Santagata, *Istoria*, 3: 175.

[16] Due to fears that theater artists might spread heretical ideas, a diocesan synod in the Abruzzi (Kingdom of Naples) in 1581 imposed restrictions on the kinds of theatrical productions that could be performed. See Alberto Tanturri, 'Sinodi a Chieti all fine del secolo XVI,' *Campania Sacra* 28 (1997): 321–45.

[17] D.F. Allen, 'Anti-Jesuit Rioting by Knights of St. John During the Malta Carnival of 1639,' *AHSI* 65 (January–June 1996): 3–30.

[18] ARSI, *Neap.* 75, Doc. VIII (November 1653), ff. 53–53v.

Although they noted the presence of comedians as challenges to the successful initiation of their missions, Jesuit commentators also used these impediments to add dramatic tension to their narratives. The missionary relations were replete with examples of the many obstacles that the Society faced in its evangelizing efforts. On one level, the presence of secular comedians appears to be no more significant than the mundane difficulties that missionaries might experience, such as poor weather, indifferent parishioners, hostile clergy or inadequate lodgings. But the stringent diatribes that Jesuit missionaries like Paolo Segneri (and others) lodged against secular comics suggests a more complex picture.

The emergence of professional touring comedic troupes in mid-sixteenth-century Italy represented both a new twist on an earlier tradition of comic theater and something quite novel for the period. Up until the late fifteenth century, religious dramas were the dominant form of spectacle across the Italian Peninsula. From the mid-thirteenth century, with the rise of penitential movements such as the Flagellants, religious praise-singing gave way to dramatic presentations that devotional groups might enact in their processions. Medieval dramas were characterized not only by their largely liturgical themes, but also by the fact that the players involved were almost exclusively amateurs. Comedic characters began to infiltrate these fairly somber productions by the fifteenth century, while at the same time the rise of humanism inspired renewed interest in classical themes, such as those that found their way into the work of collegiate productions, like Stefonio's.[19] By the late fifteenth century, theater began to develop in two distinct, though not mutually exclusive, directions: tragedy and comedy. Before the *commedia dell'arte*, humanism had its impact on the revival of classical comedy (so-called *commedia erudita*), often through the patronage of Renaissance courts.

Commedia dell'arte was thus both a natural progression of playwrights' growing willingness to break free of formulaic strictures and the sign of a new, improvisational style and spirit in the theater. While there were some antecedents to this new theatrical style, the comedy troupes that emerged by the mid-sixteenth century were self-consciously professional.

That these itinerant comedy troupes should have posed such a perceived threat to Jesuit missionary culture is not so surprising when one considers the striking parallels between the two relatively new institutions. Like the Jesuits, some of the more learned, self-conscious proponents of *commedia dell'arte*, such as Giovanni Battista Andreini, developed notions of artistic convention and a precise craft, while many

---

[19] For a broad overview of this development, cf. *Oxford Companion to Theatre*, 481–2.

220 A PARADISE INHABITED BY DEVILS

other comics were itinerants who traveled from town to town, improvising and adapting their performances to inspire diverse patrons. Even on the rare occasions when actors worked from written scripts, they improvised in order to keep filling the theaters, sometimes switching characters or changing the plot to leave their audiences satisfied. Like the Jesuits, then, although for a pecuniary motivation, comic players accommodated to their audiences. And, as two scholars of the early modern *commedia* have commented, 'the system permitted [the players] to adapt the spectacle, from time to time, to a given audience, whether this was the Pope, or paying spectators in a comedy venue.'[20]

But the parallel between the efforts of professional comedy troupes and an evolving missionary order like the Jesuits is not simply a question of flexibility or a willingness to travel. Both groups developed specific strategies to enhance their opportunities for success, and both felt the need to justify themselves before a growing chorus of critics, albeit for quite different reasons. Just as the Jesuits recognized the necessity of having missionaries fluent in a range of dialects and languages, so the comic troupes tailored their dialogue and character development to a linguistically diverse early modern Italian society. Like missionary methodology, theatrical improvisation was not random, but allowed for variations on a standard theme to keep performances fresh and spontaneous, while remaining true to an increasingly well-defined set of thematic and stylistic conventions.

Both Jesuit missionaries and comics relied heavily on a highly physical mode of performance.[21] Performers struck a balance between improvisation and adherence to a set of core values and protocols. For example, the comic director (*capocomico*) planned the montage of scenes in order to play with language and plot, while relying upon 'expert professionals' to 'win the attention of the public' by dynamic displays of physicality, including demonstrations of acrobatic skill and dance.[22] While the Jesuits did not go quite so far in demanding extraordinary feats on the part of members, the penitential missions, in particular, required the missionary to undergo extreme conditions in the service of evangelization.

Finally, like their missionary counterparts, *commedia dell'arte* players faced criticisms of their work and found themselves in the position of

---

[20] Marotti and Romei, *Commedia dell'Arte*, xli.

[21] Cf. Marotti and Romei, *Commedia dell'Arte*, xli–xliii. On the need for missionaries to be physically robust, compare Antonio Baldinucci, *Avvertimenti*, 6; 10–11. Baldinucci concedes that missionary work is an 'arduous ministry,' requiring its practitioners to keep a prudent diet and get adequate sleep.

[22] Marotti and Romei, *Commedia dell'Arte*, xliii. Marotti, however, does not suggest any parallels between comic players and missionaries.

JESUIT MISSIONARY THEATER IN NAPLES 221

having to justify themselves and their profession. In a fascinating study of the efforts of several secular comics to defend the virtue of their craft in early modern Italy, Bernadette Majorana argues that by the early seventeenth century, comedy troupes became the target of numerous and wide-ranging ecclesiastical critiques. Writing in 1621, for example, a Theatine critic named F.M. Del Monaco blamed actors for widespread criminality and social disorder.[23]

The presence of female actors in several comedy troupes was an additional cause for grave concern for Jesuit polemicists. One 1602 polemic by the Jesuit Francisco Arias presented the female actor as a kind of lightning rod, exposing the dissolution that the theater might supposedly engender. For Arias, the theater was 'like the fire that inflames hearts to dishonest love,' a powerful force 'with its lascivious songs, making [individuals] yield to evil desires, [it] kills the soul.'[24] Writing at the end of the seventeenth century, Paolo Segneri's 'In detestazione delle Commedie Scorrette,' a lengthy critique of the profane theater of the comics included in Il cristiano istruito nella sua legge (1686) also focuses on the apparently deleterious effects of female performers. For Segneri, not only did the commedie scorrette depict the amorous adventures of wide-ranging social groups, inflaming the passions of lay audiences, but the troupes themselves compounded this abomination by the presence of women on stage, a practice long forbidden by custom and ecclesiastical proscription:

> Unfortunately, the other diabolical advantage [of these comedies], in order to more efficaciously encourage this same liberty in love affairs, is to have [female characters] represented by real women on stage [. . .] St. Paul did not want women to preach in the Churches, because of that danger which was run in listening to them [. . .] Now, if it cannot be tolerated among Christians to hear a woman speak to them from the pulpit of divine love, how can one tolerate her speaking on stage of profane love?[25]

For Segneri, the dangers apparently posed by secular theater went well beyond suspicions toward the actors themselves. Not only did the secular theater Segneri criticizes distract the faithful from their duties as Christians, but the theater seemed to mock the Church's own teachings, as in

---

[23] Bernadette Majorana, 'Un "Gemino Valor,"' 178–179n. Majorana notes the irony of Paolo Segneri's use of theatrical techniques borrowed from the comics, but she does not extend the comparison of the two institutions to consider broader questions of professional identity, or virtuosity.

[24] Bernadette Majorana, 'Un "Gemino Valor,"' 178–80; Francisco Arias, Profitto spirituale (1602), cited in Majorana, 180.

[25] Segneri, 'In detestazione delle Commedie Scorrette,' in Il Cristiano Istruito nella sua Legge, 3: 279–80.

222   A PARADISE INHABITED BY DEVILS

the case of permitting female performers to perform their craft in public. The very notion that the stage permitted a blending of the world of fantasy with episodes from daily life threatened the priorities of the post-Tridentine Catholic Church, particularly as it sought desperately to maintain its hold on the realm of the sacred. As Majorana thoughtfully suggests, for critics like Segneri the theater was viewed as 'a world of dangerous and dishonest passions,' where actors were merely the vehicles for a highly seductive but impious corruption of the community, writ large: '[T]hey came to be named as disciples and agents of the devil, the dissimulators, par excellence, materializations of diabolic phantasms that lie in wait for each of the faithful: subtly seductive, lustful, transgressive, drawing the spectator into a vortex of disorder [. . .].'[26]

It was the combination of the emotionalism of the theater, with its simulatory (or dissimulatory) features, that fed clerical polemics such as Paolo Segneri's. For Segneri, theatrical representations had an enormous potential to influence spectators, directing them toward 'malefice' and literally invading their very interiors. Citing the long-standing tradition of Church opposition to secular theater, Segneri notes that 'the spectators of profane Representations are very much Possessed, not in the body, that would not be so bad, but in the spirit. And that is why I want to make you aware of the abominations that are the improper comedics.' According to the noted missionary, the Devil 'allows you to go away from that theatrical enclosure where he wounded you,' assured that the demonic effects of the drama have penetrated the subject 'through the eyes, through the ears,' and like some 'pointed dart in the heart of the viscera.'[27]

As Segneri's moralizing commentary suggests, comics were dangerous not only for the impious content of their productions, the improper usage of female performers and power of profane fantasy to stir up inappropriate passions in spectators, but also because they appeared deceptive in their very enterprise. In this regard, at least, Catholic moralists like Segneri shared a common complaint with their Puritan counterparts in seventeenth-century Britain. As Jonas Barish argued some years ago in *The Antitheatrical Prejudice* (1981), Puritan polemicists in the late sixteenth century revived a long-standing Western tradition of castigating theater, precisely because they believed that it promoted insincerity and deception, and thus wider corruption. While Barish traces anti-theatrical attitudes in the West back to Platonic writings, he argues that the real roots of early modern Christian polemic against the theater were articulated early on by Augustine, who wrote:

---

[26] Majorana, 'Un "Gemino Valor,"' 179.
[27] Segneri, 'In detestazione,' 3: 278; 284.

JESUIT MISSIONARY THEATER IN NAPLES   223

'To the end that we may be true to our nature, we should not become false by copying and likening ourselves to the nature of another as do the actors and the reflections in a mirror.'[28] Here, the idea of mimicry is associated with deviating from one's true (and presumably God-given) nature.

Critics labeled theater artists as 'hypocrites' because some of the more self-conscious among these comedians pretended to offer people 'comedy as a source of well-being and of honest pleasure.' But two features of the professional theater – ironically, quite similar to that of the missionary endeavor – rendered such promises highly suspect among their critics: the requirement that comics 'sell' their craft to the public, and their nomadic existence.

Certain renowned comic artists like Giovan Battista Andreini (1576?– 1654), son of two of the most illustrious early *commedia dell'arte* practitioners, Isabella and Francesco Andreini, combated the opinions of critics like Segneri through polemics of their own. Andreini defended his profession against ecclesiastical criticisms by claiming, for example, that the 'fables' that were presented on stage allowed audience members to appreciate the ephemeral nature of daily existence and see their own parts as 'actors' in a celestial drama. Such stories, Andreini contended, 'allow us to see that our life is nothing but a fable' and 'remind us how the catastrophe of the brief course of our lives [. . .] will require us to discover [. . .] that there will be no greatness, nor honors and conveniences of fortune, nothing but dreams, shadows, dust, earth and ashes at the end.'[29] In other words, Andreini argues, in so far as the stage provided a mirror of earthly existence, it could help to reinforce the goals of religious reformers, rather than pervert them. Crucially, commentators like Andreini linked the apparent virtue of actors like himself with their professionalism, their mastery of craft. In this way, then, they were unknowingly echoing at least part of the Jesuits' own heroic ideal for missionaries: one based on both personal qualities and on the mastery of technical skills.

Within this context, Segneri's polemic against the profane theater was profoundly incongruous. More than any other Jesuit (or, for that matter,

---

[28] Jonas Barish, *The Antitheatrical Prejudice* (Berkeley, CA: University of California Press, 1981). Augustine, cited in Barish 56–7.

[29] Giovanni Battista Andreini, *La Ferza. Ragionamento Secondo. Contra L'Accuse Date alla Commedia* (Paris, 1625), reprinted in Marotti and Romei, *Commedia Dell'Arte*, 489–534, esp. 534. The date of Andreini's birth seems to be in some dispute, with possible dates ranging from 1576 to 1579. Although he does not draw out a comparison with the likes of Andreini, Barish argues that English defenses of the theater in the same period, such as that of Thomas Heywood, are generally weak and ineffectual. See Barish, *The Antitheatrical Prejudice*, 117–22.

224 A PARADISE INHABITED BY DEVILS

any other early modern missionary), Segneri's own reputation owed much to his adaptation of theatrical techniques and overt emotionalism to the demands of evangelization. And like Andreini's advocacy of a virtuous professional ideal for the secular performer, Segneri's detailed elaboration of a missionary science signaled the evolution of a high degree of professionalization and the desire to build a strong corporate identity within the Society of Jesus. In fact, the mastery of theatrical technique in the Segnerian mission was part and parcel of the heroic missionary identity towards which the order was striving.

In southern Italy, the scene of so much of the early experimentation with missionary forms and spheres of activity, missionaries were equally concerned with perfecting their apostolic craft in the seventeenth century. Although they explicitly disavowed monetary remuneration for their labors, would it be far-fetched to compare their itinerant apostolic excursions to the tours of early modern comic troupes? As the missionary relations from the Kingdom of Naples maintain, the arrival of a pair of Jesuit missionaries ideally aroused the same sort of enthusiasm and curiosity as a band of acrobats or comedians, representing a welcome diversion from the everyday concerns that preoccupied most commoners, rural and urban dwellers alike. The Society of Jesus recognized that it must directly compete with secular actors for the devotions of the crowd.

For evangelical practitioners like the anonymous author of a seventeenth-century Jesuit relation from Barletta, the mission itself was conceived of as a 'holy theater,' an opportunity to return the faithful to the apparent authenticity and devoutness of the early Church. The chronicler describes the re-enactment of a divine drama, whereby God and his clergy watch the faithful as if from 'a balcony projecting onto the inner hall of consciences,' like so many 'spectators of this copious fruit which the people render to God.' According to this spectacular representation, the Jesuit mission, like some 'unfailing miracle,' becomes the source of 'devotion, penitential acts, [and] Innocence.' Here, one sees the 'fervor of the most fervent primitive Church given new life in Christian communities.'[30]

In this missionary report, as in others, a secular comedy troupe provides a foil for the successful realization of the holy theater, and as elsewhere, this obstacle is incorporated skillfully into the dramatic narrative. In this case, however, the dramatic structure departs somewhat from the standard fare: mission begins badly, missionaries over-

---

[30] ARSI, *Neap.* 75, Doc. XIX, 'Missioni di Barletta' (January 1656), ff. 149–55, esp. 149.

JESUIT MISSIONARY THEATER IN NAPLES

come difficulties, people are universally won over. In the Barletta mission, instead, the conflict arises in what we might call 'Act II.'

Initially, we are told, the mission was greeted with 'universal consensus.' During the first two evenings, the Jesuit fathers led processions of hundreds of people through the city's streets. But then, as if by demonic intervention ('the rage of the Devil'), the faithful were lured from the holy mission by a troupe of comedians who proceeded to 'draw the people from the scene of devotion at the Pulpit, contaminating them with liberty.' It required a threat by the Jesuit fathers to leave the town if the comedians were not expelled to restore order, and produce the 'great fruit' to which the account above alluded.[31]

Francesco De Geronimo also reports having to resort to extreme tactics to displace comedy troupes that were frequenting a popular Neapolitan square and supposedly corrupting young men and boys with female performers, offering 'incentives to lechery in everyone.' Writing in 1690, De Geronimo described how a troupe of acrobats was drawing 'innumerable people' to its 'little farces,' including joining forces with a company of 'scandalous women, who in the public plaza, in the presence of many people, performed acts of love-making [and] marriage, with dishonest words, gestures, and signs.'[32] Recalling an earlier such incident where he had turned to ecclesiastical authorities to remove the 'offensive' company from the city's public squares, De Geronimo claims that he has used his own theatrical approach to steer people away from profane pleasures.

In that earlier example, De Geronimo had complained forcefully to the director of the comic troupe in question, urging him to clean up their act in order to prevent 'innumerable sins.' According to his own account, De Geronimo implored the man 'for the love of God' to alter their performance so that they would not scandalize the youth, but although the director apparently agreed to these terms, they were not carried out in practice, because, as De Geronimo derisively relates, such people 'value their own interests and [the things of this] world more than the soul and God.' Next, De Geronimo sought to shame the players into abandoning their profane performances by 'preaching often and at a time when they were performing their filth; but neither did this strategy prove profitable.' Finally, when he discovered that one of the young women with whom the troupe was performing was the mistress of the

---

[31] ARSI, *Neap.* 75, 'Missioni di Barletta,' f. 149v.

[32] *S. Francesco di Girolamo*, 94–7, esp. 94–5. For an interesting perspective on De Geronimo's notoriety as a 'popular preacher,' cf. Elisa Novi Chavarria, 'Francesco De Geronimo e Gregorio Rocco,' in *Il Governo delle Anime*, 269–90.

226 A PARADISE INHABITED BY DEVILS

director, De Geronimo used his influence to force them to marry, thus ensuring that the players left Naples.[33]

But despite his persistent efforts, De Geronimo reports, he again faced the pesky problem of an unruly ensemble of comic players in 1690, once again accompanied by female players. In this instance, however, De Geronimo reports that his efforts to employ ecclesiastical and secular authorities to drive out the comics proved unsuccessful, possibly, he suggests, because one of the female performers was a 'public and licentious prostitute,' and perhaps had friends among the Neapolitan officialdom. Failing all else, De Geronimo turned to what he knew best, a highly theatrical brand of penitential preaching in order to effect contrition among the Neapolitan laity. De Geronimo relates how he 'went to that place to preach with sentiments so bitter that the audience was moved by it, and he dragged out the sermon so long that he finished late at night, at such a time that it was no longer possible for [the comedians] to perform their trifles; and he publicly threatened them that he would continue to do this every evening during the festival days if the women continued to get up on stage.'[34] By De Geronimo's own estimate, this threat apparently worked, because the troupe's leaders agreed to carry on without the female performers, thus dooming their performances, since 'without the women, they could not attract many people.' Within a few days, De Geronimo reports victoriously, the comedians had left town.[35]

How might we interpret this apparently sudden presence of secular comedy troupes in the towns and villages where the Neapolitan missionaries traveled during the latter half of the seventeenth century? Obviously, the troupes had been a presence earlier on, but it does seem that the Jesuits had a heightened sense of concern over their missionary endeavors in the wake of the troubles of mid-century. Just as they placed greater emphasis on the heroic Jesuit missionary as a peacemaking force in the strife-torn *Mezzogiorno* after 1648, so the Society's fairly small cadre of missionary preachers in the South appear vigilant in their efforts to represent their abilities as equal, if not superior to, those of secular entertainers.[36] They stress the deployment of theatrical techniques capable of holding the public's attentions, while making the centrality of

---

[33] *S. Francesco di Girolamo*, 94–7.

[34] Ibid., esp. 96–7

[35] Ibid.

[36] Giuseppe Orlandi, 'S. Alfonso Maria de Liguori,' 16. Orlandi makes the important point that although the Jesuits made much of their popular missionary strategies, especially in the *Mezzogiorno*, by the mid-seventeenth century the order still devoted a few of its members to full-time missionary duties. By 1651, for example, out of 543 total members of the Neapolitan Province, only six are officially counted as missionaries.

their penitential activities ever more explicit. And here, in the growing emphasis placed on penitential exercises, we can see the increasingly paradoxical role which the Jesuits came to play in popular religiosity in late seventeenth- and early eighteenth-century southern Italy.

Schools of mortification

In the Kingdom of Naples, the Jesuits' sacred theater served a variety of functions not peculiar to the order, nor to southern Italy, but given a particular resonance by each. With penitential rituals at the centerpiece of a series of dramatic but by no means spontaneous moments in the missionary endeavor, this theatricality was part and parcel of a wider climate of ritualistic practice. For the Italian scholar Roberto Rusconi, the Jesuits' (and others') adaptations of such theatricality was simply 'a functional expression of the profoundly ritualized Catholicism of the Counter Reformation, in which a similar type of liturgical practice also has the direct purpose of absorbing within it other rites, behaviors and customs of a habitual nature and of folkloric origin.'[37]

Southern Italian religious culture was seen as especially well suited to the Jesuits' theatrical representation of Tridentine piety, since the Kingdom of Naples had always been a region renowned for its pronounced forms of worship and devotion. While the late medieval incarnation of penitential disciplining arose spontaneously from among the laity, later to be adapted, to some degree, by newly institutionalizing mendicant orders like the Franciscans, in the early modern period the missionary orders stage managed such rituals to a number of socio-religious ends.[38] Scholars have noted the greater emphasis on penitential disciplinary rituals in southern Italian religiosity, including such practices as tongue dragging (*strascinando la lingua*), crawling on one's knees to the altar of a revered saint or madonnine image while striking one's self, and other blood-letting rituals.[39]

On a fundamentally sacral level, the penitential rituals had always offered a concrete, collective expression for the expiation of guilt. With the missionary preacher leading the way, a community might participate

---

[37] Roberto Rusconi, 'Gli ordini religiosi maschili,' in *Clero e società nell'Italia moderna*, ed. Mario Rosa (Rome–Bari: Laterza, 1992), 207–74, esp. 248–9.

[38] On the distinctiveness of late medieval penitential culture, particularly *vis-à-vis* the early modern variant, see Ida Magli, *Gli uomini della penitenza. Lineamenti antropologici del medioevo italiano* (Milan: Garzanti, 1977).

[39] Michael Carroll, *Madonnas that Maim. Popular Catholicism in Italy Since the Fifteenth Century* (Baltimore and London: Johns Hopkins University Press, 1992), 129–37, esp. 133.

228 A PARADISE INHABITED BY DEVILS

in a violent re-enactment of Christ's suffering, in the hopes of making themselves worthy of the oft-promised redemption. The so-called 'Schools of Mortification' were another southern Italian innovation that stressed the missionary's role in modeling proper mortification to the generally male lay population that formed his audience. The term appears to have originated with Onofrio Saraco (1605–50), a Neapolitan Jesuit especially noted for his vivid preaching style and his missionary excursions through the regions of Abruzzi and Puglia. Like other seventeenth-century Jesuit orators, Saraco placed a high premium on employing theatricality in his sermons. A recent biographical sketch of Saraco provides this idealized image of his missionary style:

> He preached with a very simple and basic style, and his sermons had an incomparable force in persuading souls, making one marvel [at the fact that] such common arguments had such singular efficacy. In the missions, he used a death's skull in order to move souls on the nature of human frailty: he called it [the *teschio*] his companion and encouraged many numerous conversions, even among the most obstinate wrong-doers.[40]

But beyond the use of theatrical props like the *teschio*, Saraco also integrated ritualized penitential exercises into his sermons 'to excite [people] to penitence and to mortification, [Saraco] instructed a judicious cleric in the means by which he should abuse him.'[41] Apparently, Saraco's example was soon followed by other Jesuits in the southern Italian missions.

By the mid-seventeenth century, when Scipione Paolucci composed his history of Jesuit missions in the Kingdom of Naples, penitential activity had already become highly ritualized practice. As Paolucci describes it, the so-called 'School of Mortification' might take place during a penitential procession, or an outdoor sermon, but the contours of the ritual had not been greatly modified from Saraco's earlier example. With a death skull in hand, the missionary would make a 'fervent meditation, offering to the listeners various and very useful points on which to ruminate.' The sermons themselves had the object of 'encouraging a serious and true reform of customs,' but Paolucci believed that this was facilitated best through dramatic examples of mortification:

> Having convinced the mind and inspired affection with fervor, in order to give some test to the sentiments of the heart, everyone was invited to make some act of penitence in satisfaction of their errors. Sometimes, the father begins and is either struck on the cheek by some cleric, who has already been designated and instructed to this

---

[40] Guidetti, *Le Missioni Popolari*, 84–5.
[41] Ibid.

JESUIT MISSIONARY THEATER IN NAPLES 229

end, or ill-treated [like an] animal with injurious acts and words, and in various ways, reproaches himself for his malice and audacity in offending the common Gentleman.[42]

In this way, the dramatic quality of the mortification ritual aimed to overwhelm the senses of the viewers in a manner similar to the way that popular theater artists hoped to stir the hearts of audience members. Elisa Novi Chavarria draws out this analogy between sacred and popular theater in the penitential realm, arguing that the 'corporeal mortifications' were expressly intended to leave those assembled in 'emotional states of bewilderment' and 'collective excitement.' Within this frenzied atmosphere, the crowd 'slapped themselves in the face or beat themselves bloody with great ropes or with stones. Thus, the faithful contemporaneously assumed the role of spectator and of protagonist in the ceremony.'[43]

The act of involving the faithful directly in mortification suggests an additional function which the penitential rituals might perform: facilitating the internalization of the missionary message and, in this way, effecting true conversion. For Scipione Paolucci, the disciplinary exercises offered a sort of 'proof' that the missionary's message had been taken to heart, since 'the discipline is almost a practical confirmation of that which has been speculatively taught in the sermons.'[44] If the Jesuits' aim was for parishioners to literally purge themselves of their sinful tendencies, then disciplinary exercises, even the most violent, offered an effective vehicle. As Serge Gruzinski's work on the delirious dreams and visions of Amerindians who had been exposed to Jesuit evangelizing in Mexico suggests, this theatrical rendering of penitential exercises could have a profound effect on people's psyches.[45] Or, as Novi Chavarria aptly argues: 'The assimilation of the [Jesuit] message surpassed the stage of the conscious in order to penetrate into the depth of the human being.' In other words, the penitential rituals served to effect the 'acculturation of the unconscious.'[46]

Both theatricality and the self-conscious application of specific techniques for effecting successful penitential missions were essential features of the penitential processions that formed a staple of Jesuit missions. Although the processions often appeared spontaneous, especially given the boisterous and extremely volatile nature of penitential discipline, missionaries theorists like Segneri plotted out each detail of the proces-

---

[42] Paolucci, *Missioni*, 47–8
[43] Novi Chavarria, 'L'Attività missionaria dei Gesuiti,' 171.
[44] Paolucci, *Missioni*, 24–5.
[45] Gruzinski, 'Délires et visions chez les indiens du Mexique.'
[46] Novi Chavarria, 'L'Attività missionaria dei Gesuiti,' 171.

sion, from the chronology of events, where the missionary should stop to make short orations during the course of the promenade and which props he should utilize on those occasions. The deliberateness of Segneri's approach reinforces our image of Jesuit missionary 'science' in action.

Segneri, like his Neapolitan counterpart Francesco De Geronimo, viewed penitential processions as a sure-fire method to convert even the most hard-hearted sinner and thus effect changes in behavior that were the ultimate goal of the civilizing mission. But success required careful planning. First, it was essential that the people be prepared for penitential exercises by announcing the event ahead of time. In Segneri's case, he would follow his sermons each day with brief announcements (*ricordi*) about the mission itself. Typically, on the fifth day of a Segnerian mission, the preacher would announce to the assembled that a general penitential procession would take place on the following day. He would urge them all to attend and be prepared with proper penitential garb and accouterments, encouraging their penitential zeal, while also counseling some moderation:

> Tomorrow, I expect everyone in penitential dress; there should be neither men nor women who are not wearing a crown of thorns on their heads, and ropes hanging from the neck; I remind you [however] not to wear chains around your neck because sometimes it has happened that someone beats themselves immoderately, with damage to their families; [instead] carry the chains by dragging them with your feet, and have the ropes at your neck.[47]

In Naples, too, the penitential processions were represented as having had a spectacular effect on the community. Once again, while chroniclers attempt to highlight the apparently spontaneous nature of popular religiosity and fervor, they also suggest that the Jesuits had a major role in organizing and executing the rituals. In 1688, for example, in the aftermath of a devastating earthquake that leveled a number of towns and caused major damage to important structures in Naples itself, De Geronimo and his brethren sought to hold a series of penitential processions. Such acts of penitence were not unusual in the face of natural disasters like an earthquake, an all too frequent occurrence in southern Italy, after all.

For three consecutive days, we learn, the Jesuits led processions through various quarters of Naples, such that the people 'did not see anything but penitential processions of secular men, clergy and also women, especially fallen virgins.' Ultimately, De Geronimo acknowledges the dramatic impact that the earthquake had in facilitating his

---

[47] Segneri and Fontana, *Pratica delle Missioni*, 65.

JESUIT MISSIONARY THEATER IN NAPLES 231

evangelizing agenda, noting that 'the earthquake bore great fruit in making people confess who had not confessed for a long time.'[48]

The closure of the penitential procession might also require a strong, theatrical finish to reinforce the desired effects of penitential discipline and cement a sense of spiritual and social unity. This might include rituals such as covering penitents in ashes, igniting a bonfire of the vanities to immolate 'diabolical furnishings,' including such items as profane songbooks, playing cards and women's beauty items, but also suggest the expulsion of non-material demonic forces from the assembled laity.

In a passage surely meant to entertain readers, even while proving edifying, Paolucci offers a vivid story of an enraged demon that must be exorcized from one of the women in the penitential procession. According to Paolucci, the *spiritata* that 'possessed' the woman 'let out such screams, with such fury, that it well demonstrated the torment from those flames, so dear to Heaven, that was growing in that Demon, that had possessed the woman.'[49]

In these examples of spirit possession, the demonic presence seems almost a requirement in order to shock the penitents into a recognition of the drama of penitence and the continual threat posed by sin and evil in their daily lives. As a 'final act' in the processions, the purging of demonic forces was meant to reinforce group cohesion while allowing the missionary preacher, as director of the penitential drama, to banish such evil forces, order the *spiritata* to be silent, and thus demonstrate his virtuosity.

Sometimes, the impact and the theatricality of the penitential processions was not immediately felt, but could be invoked at a later time as a critical force in motivating a previously recalcitrant sinner to penitence and conversion. Such was the case, for example, with a young woman whom Francesco De Geronimo had confessed at Naples Hospital of the Incurables in 1693. According to De Geronimo, the woman related how she had been consumed by the attentions of numerous lovers, 'who had always kept me busy with amusements and diversions,' until one day, she happened to hear singing outside of her home and realized that it was a penitential procession, led by De Geronimo. After hearing the Jesuit preacher's sermon, we are told that she was filled with contrition

---

[48] *S. Francesco di Girolamo*, 103–104. On the more generalized practice of leading religious processions in the aftermath of disasters, cf. Mario Rosa, 'L'Onda che ritorna: Interno ed esterno sacro nella Napoli del '600,' in *Luoghi Sacri e Spazi della Santità*, eds Sofia Boesch Gajano and Lucetta Scaraffia (Turin: Rosenberg and Sellier, 1990), 397–413, esp. 397.

[49] Paolucci, *Missioni*, 46.

232   A PARADISE INHABITED BY DEVILS

and resolved to change her life. Ultimately, according to the chronicle, she took up orders as a nun, in order to escape temptations. After hearing the Jesuit preacher's sermon, she was filled with contrition and resolved to change her life. Ultimately, despite the entreaties of her boyfriends, she took up the religious life.[50]

Although the greatest beneficiaries of penitential discipline were the participants themselves, spectators might also internalize the message of contrition and be changed by such acts of mortification. In one example from his missionary accounts from late seventeenth-century Naples, Francesco De Geronimo describes a man haunted by dreams of the Virgin Mary imploring him to confess, after he has witnessed several penitential rituals. At first, the man explains, he had often been eager to seek out De Geronimo's services:

> Father, I was sent here by the Madonna. Do you know that it has been twenty seven years since I have confessed, even though I have seen many flagellants of God. Many, many times I have heard Your Reverence preach and, terrified and moved, I have made many resolutions to change my life and confess; but whenever I was coming to find you, I would change my mind, saying: 'Tomorrow, I will go there;' or else I found some friend who pulled me elsewhere.

Over time, always finding excuses not to confess, the man began to be tormented by dreams of remorse. In these dreams, he is visited by a beautiful woman who asks him why he has not confessed: ' "What are you doing? Why don't you confess? I command you to go first thing tomorrow morning and confess." ' But although this vision made a strong impression on the man, by morning he doubted the veracity of his dreams and went about his business as usual. A few days later, however, he was once again visited by the same image, but in the morning, a 'demonic' voice chides him to ignore what is, after all, merely a dream: 'By the morning, here again was a demonic thought, which told me: "Why are you giving credit to a dream? Don't you see that you have been dreaming? So, to what are you confessing?" '[51]

Finally, for the third time, the man was visited by the Madonna, but this time she is explicit in her advice to him, warning him that he must confess immediately if he hopes to 'merit these graces.' More specifically, she admonishes him to confess to De Geronimo himself, which he does. What this example demonstrates is the suggestibility of relatively unobservant individuals to the power of penitence in the broadest meaning of the term. The vision of the Virgin which tormented the man in this exemplary tale was not novel, nor was the dramatic battle

---

[50] *S. Francesco di Girolamo*, 107–108.
[51] Ibid., 108–11.

JESUIT MISSIONARY THEATER IN NAPLES 233

which ensued between her efforts to gain his confession and the nay-saying of the demonic morning voice which discouraged such penitence. But in the context of the Jesuits' employment of both theatricality and penitential exercises, the story reinforces the prescriptive notion that people internalized a message of contrition, although there is no way to verify this.

On another level, this case illustrates, albeit subtly, the heroic image of the Jesuit missionary. For the Madonna figure does not merely implore the unnamed sinner to confess his sins to any of her 'sons,' but specifically points him toward De Geronimo: 'Then the Mother of mercy benignly said to me: "Go to the house of my Son (and he knew that she said to the Gesù) and you will find the Father and be confessed by him." '[52] Thus, the Jesuits might utilize such examples of dramatic conversions, encouraged by examples of theatricality and penitence, to buttress their collective self-representation as signal reformers.

To this point, I have emphasized the functions to which the missionaries put the penitential rituals, but what might the faithful have gained from such acts of mortification? Some scholars posit the value of the penitential rituals as potential 'safety valves' for communities riven with social tensions and conflict. In this case, penitence provided a mystical process through which a community could effect unity and maintain social peace.[53] Others, however, present a somewhat different interpretation of how such ceremonies might function. The penitential rituals, particularly the processions in which all members of the community participated, offered community members an appropriate means to cope with the violence endemic to daily life, and 'suppress[ed] the fear of death and the uncertainty of the hereafter.' By participating in ritualized punishments, people could 'avert the punishments of Hell.'[54]

Such diverse theories of the functions that penitential practice played have merit, but they fail to attend adequately to the highly volatile nature of the penitential activities, which both attempted to forge social unity and (paradoxically) provided the precise atmosphere in which such unity might be undermined. In southern Italy, perhaps as much as anywhere in the early modern period, the social fabric was very delicate indeed. Emerging out of the Revolt of Naples (1647–48), maintaining social peace was a grave concern for religious reformers like the Society of Jesus. Although the Spanish military had restored order in the City

---

[52] *S. Francesco di Girolamo*, 111.

[53] Mario Rosa, 'Per la storia della vita religiosa e della Chiesa in Italia tra il '500 e il '600: studi ricenti e questioni di metodo,' *Quaderni Storici* 15 (1970): 673–758, esp. 722–3.

[54] Novi Chavarria, 'L'Attività missionaria dei Gesuiti,' 181.

234   A PARADISE INHABITED BY DEVILS

and Kingdom of Naples, the gross inequalities and high levels of familial and community violence which had fueled the insurrections had not abated. If the penitential missions provided an outlet for social tensions by encouraging gestures of solidarity and the 'carnivalesque' example of social elites humiliating themselves before their 'inferiors,' they also reinforced the very rigid social and gender hierarchy which characterized early modern southern Italy. An examination of the penitential missions, then, in all of their complexity, sheds light on the peculiar dynamics of social relations in the late seventeenth-century *Mezzogiorno*, while also showing how the Jesuits sought to position themselves as arbiters of a very curious form of civility during this period.

Among all of the activities associated with the Jesuits' internal missions, the penitential exercises (along with the reconciliations) were the most highly ritualized. The mortifications practiced during evening sermons produced a spectacular atmosphere for the (ideally) all-male parishioners who would assemble during such events. But such rituals also reveal potential fissures within the supposedly unified community of worshipers. In the penitential rituals, as in all other areas of social existence, religious devotion represented both a site of potential equality and a mirror of the very real inequities which plagued early modern southern Italy.

Although penitence was encouraged among all members of the social body, for elites it took on all the markers of status. For example, confraternities such as the so-called 'Slaves to Our Lady the Virgin,' which practiced special acts of penitence and debasement, were composed almost exclusively of nobles. As Paolucci's narrative suggests, noble members of the confraternity, bound together by chains, would arrive at the church 'preceded by the leader with Crucifix in hand,' and beg 'the people's pardon for their sins, prostrated before the sacred Altar.'[55] In these instances, members of the nobility and leading clergy apparently offered a model for others through their examples of self-debasement and mortification. Paolucci expresses the belief that greater piety will issue from those possessing more civility. In this view, the nobles demonstrated greater zeal in attending to missionary functions, and apparently traveled longer distances to participate in the penitential missions.[56]

In other instances, an apparent paradox emerges in representations of the penitential missions: social status is rewarded. For example, in a mission carried out in Bitonto, near Bari, we learn of the social tensions

---

[55] Paolucci, *Missioni*, 54–5.
[56] Paolucci, *Missioni*, 57. On his perceptions of the greater degree of fervent attention to missions on the part of the nobility, see 80.

that might emerge during the course of a penitential mission. This mission, out of which a small pamphlet was published in 1646,[57] led off in the usual manner for such occasions. The Jesuit missionaries began by modeling 'edifying mortifications,' then initiated a competition among the nobility to determine who would be among the elite 'twelve' who would be permitted to engage in 'special mortifications.' As the pamphlet's author Giovanni Battista di Elia suggests, the selection of an elite group of twelve favored *disciplinati* disturbed the rest of the community who remained locked out of the ritual enactment.[58]

The situation was apparently exacerbated when Di Elia and his companion missionary attempted to segregate the people from the evening's disciplinary exercises. While one led the 'gentlemen' down into some catacombs to participate in the exercises, another assembled the rest of the community above. But Di Elia describes a scene both poignant and fraught with potential chaos, when the crowd, dissatisfied with this segregation, surged toward the entrance to the sacralized catacombs: '[It] was necessary to use great effort to hold the people back from coming down [into the catacombs], so that nobody fell on the ground. And because the gentlemen and Priests wanted to have room, one had to use many stratagems in order to detain the people, who were either staying on the stairs of said Catacomb, or in the same Church up above [. . .].'[59] When the signal was given for the select group of penitents to begin their mortifications in the Catacombs, the crowds just above them would follow suit. Even more marginal than the male commoners were the women, who assembled 'outside in the street by the windows of the Catacomb, beating themselves on the breast, and [they] did not make less noise, nor shed fewer tears than the men.'[60]

Thus, the penitential missions highlighted a profound paradox in early modern Catholicism in the Kingdom of Naples and elsewhere: while Catholicism was theoretically an egalitarian faith, and the missions themselves were seen as civilizing projects aimed at all of the faithful, they might also reinforce existing social relationships, whether socio-economic or gender-based. In the penitential processions, people customarily were divided according to their social status, age, gender and even neighborhood or parish. These were certainly identity markers for early modern people. According to Paolo Segneri, after the missionaries

---

[57] ARSI, *Neap.* 74 (1646), Giovanni Battista Di Elia, *Relatione di una Missioni fatta da due Reverende Padri della Compagnia di Giesù nella Città di Bitonto del Regno di Napoli, nell'Anno 1646*, ff. 163–78.

[58] Ibid., f. 166.

[59] Ibid.

[60] Ibid.

236   A PARADISE INHABITED BY DEVILS

themselves had set a good example of penitential fervor, the people would participate according to their specific status within the community. Here, as in indoor penitential exercises, missionaries sought to balance fervent activity with the perennial concern of maintaining good order and discipline.[61]

Similarly, women were often excluded from many disciplinary exercises because their presence would have been deemed inappropriate and distracting. In the case of a mission from Foggia (1665), for example, women's involvement was curtailed because of the fear that they would pose a threat to good order. In the event, however, this news was not welcomed by the assembled women:

> From the windows, one could hear the cries of the Women, and a great many of them came down from their houses, wanting to follow the procession but noticing this, [and] in order that no disorders occurred that night, the Father stopped them, [but ...] because not everyone had heard him, he was forced, from time to time, to say in a loud voice that women must not follow the procession, but should wait at home until the men returned.[62]

Such exclusion of women was symptomatic of a more generalized process of separating the sexes in post-Tridentine religious ritual. While men could engage in collective penitential violence to deal with their anxieties over sin, or to expiate guilt, women were expected to grieve in a manner appropriate to their gender, and preferably in private. Although women were permitted to don penitential garb in the highly organized processions, which often served as the culminating ritual in the popular mission, they were proscribed from practicing public mortifications. Rather, for women, such traditionally female practices as wailing, beating on their chests with their fists and pulling their hair were deemed appropriate.[63]

Although this kind of gender separation was considered ideal, the Neapolitan sources make it clear that efforts to keep women from practicing mortifications in public were futile. Scipione Paolucci offers several examples of women's fervent participation in such rituals, revealing a begrudging respect for such shows of piety, while also reinforcing conventional concerns over female weakness and suggestibility. In one example, Paolucci describes a gathering of about two thousand *discipli-*

---

[61] Segneri and Fontana, *Pratica delle Missioni*, 12–13; cf. ARSI, *Neap.* 74 (1645–1646), 'Missioni di P. Prella,' ff. 137–152v, esp. 139.

[62] ARSI, *Neap.* 76, 'Relatione ... di Foggia,' (1665), f. 11v.

[63] Novi Chavarria, 'L'attività missionaria dei Gesuiti,' 172. Novi Chavarria notes that women's penitential practices hearken back to the classic image of the southern Italian female's funereal lamentations. On the range of penitential instruments that women used, cf. Paolucci, *Missioni*, 32.

JESUIT MISSIONARY THEATER IN NAPLES   237

nati near Bari. Following social norms, the local notables began the penitential rituals, followed by local clergy. Although women were formally barred from the proceedings, Paolucci notes approvingly their unwillingness to be sent away:

> I cannot report without wonder the holy obstinacy of the women, including noble and primary women, who, excluded from mortifying themselves with the others, would not leave the place where they were beating themselves [. . .] There, in order to not remain hateful eavesdroppers of the others' service, not only with tears alone, and with the cries which accompanied the moans of the penitents, but violently tearing at their hair, they began hitting themselves harshly on the cheeks, and occasionally also on the chest with stones. They demonstrated that in opportunity alone, not in courage, did they cede anything to the men through such a bountiful [display of] mortification.

In this passage, Paolucci seems particularly struck by a small group of about six women who 'hid themselves in the sepulcher of the Mother Church, so that they could be present during the disciplining which took place there.' Such women, Paolucci argues, allowed their desire to participate in the mortification rituals to 'prevail over the native female fear of dead bodies and burial vaults.'[64] Casting Paolucci's bizarre supposition about female fears of the dead aside, this account offers another glimpse at the profoundly ambivalent nature of the penitential missions for the Jesuits in the Kingdom of Naples. Although they hoped to use these missions to promote greater piety, moral reform and cohesiveness in communities that had perhaps recently emerged from tense social conflict, the desire to promote the enthusiastic involvement of the laity sometimes meant breaking social codes, or unleashing the pent up emotions of parishioners whose lives might be deeply troubled.

Promise and danger in the penitential missions

If Jesuit missionary theatricality and the participatory penitential rituals associated with such spectacles served a variety of possible functions in southern Italian society during the seventeenth and early eighteenth centuries, they also engendered growing controversy and criticism. As was true during the medieval period, collective demonstrations of penitential discipline did not always sit well with the Catholic Church. Increasingly, by the turn of the eighteenth century, many worried that the use of spectacle in religious rituals only served to weaken social

---

[64] Paolucci, *Missioni*, 26.

238 A PARADISE INHABITED BY DEVILS

discipline and accommodate to the more 'superstitious' aspects of popular piety.

From the fourteenth century, Pope Clement VI's injunction against penitential processions in the German lands of the Holy Roman Empire had argued that such activities could pose a threat. In his bull, *Inter solicitudines*, Clement maintains that the processions represented 'a type of vain religion of superstitious invention, through which many of the simple people, who are called flagellants, have allowed themselves to betray and drag down and vilify the power of the church and ecclesiastical discipline, abandoning themselves to acts completely foreign to normal life.'[65] By the early eighteenth century, the Jesuits increasingly became accused of accommodating to superstitious tendencies among the faithful. Such an outcome was certainly at odds with the Jesuits' long-standing goal of civilizing their southern Italian charges.

From their earliest interventions in southern Italy, the Jesuits had sought very much to challenge what they considered the more 'superstitious' aspects of popular piety and cultural practice in Naples, yet their missions in many ways accommodated just such practices, at least in the eyes of critics. The Jesuits had attempted to substitute unacceptable, so-called 'pagan' practices with more tolerable ones as a means of binding people to their program of religious education and (in their minds) cultural betterment. This kind of substitution allowed the order to adapt itself to what the sociologist Michael Carroll has referred to as the 'logic' of popular Catholicism, in the hopes that this might effect desired reforms.

Ironically, the seventeenth- and early eighteenth-century missions, with their 'heroic' missionary preachers and highly articulated missionary technique, represented a bittersweet watershed in the history of the Jesuit civilizing mission in the Kingdom of Naples. While substitutions like the 'Forty Hours' represented an apparent repudiation of the profane revelries of Carnival, the Jesuits' assimilation of popular theatrical techniques and adoption of a highly emotional penitential practice in their mature missions left them open to attack as the political and religious climate changed on the eve of the Enlightenment.

From about the middle of the seventeenth century, Jesuit authors hint at growing opposition to the Society of Jesus and its missionary methods. Scipione Paolucci devotes the entirety of Chapter Eleven in his chronicle of Jesuit missions in the Kingdom of Naples to the 'Impediments posed

---

[65] Pope Clement VI, papal bull, *Inter solicitudines* (1349), cited in Magli, *Gli uomini della penitenza*, 82–3. Although the political context of the fourteenth-century Catholic Church and the unofficial nature of the Flagellant Movement created particular concerns that might not have been so significant in the later period, the comparison is still intriguing.

JESUIT MISSIONARY THEATER IN NAPLES 239

by the Devil in order to diminish the fruit of the Missions.' Beyond citing the usual litany of examples of parishioners possessed by the devil and valorizing the Jesuit missionaries' apparent role in combating these demonic incursions, Paolucci also cites the more worldly obstacles that the Jesuits could expect to face from their detractors.

Particularly troublesome, Paolucci suggests, were those critics who appeared to be speaking from a position of piety when, in fact, their accusations betrayed a hostile intent. In such locales, he warns, the Jesuits could anticipate being ill-received, 'even rejected with contempt,' while their nay-sayers 'greeted their arrival very badly.'[66] The penitential missions became an increasingly common target of critics who opposed such missionary techniques on principle as an apparent perversion of Catholic piety and a threat to public order. In order to build support for the penitential missions, Jesuit authors like Paolucci first sought to present a fairly faithful representation of their critics' viewpoint before critiquing it. Anticipating later Jansenist polemic against the supposedly impious nature of Jesuit missionary endeavors, Paolucci writes:

> 'Which new methods,' they replied, 'are these which the Jesuits use? Whatever are they trying to do with these ashes, with these thorns, with those ropes? In order to be truthful, penitence must be of the heart, and in consequence, completely internal; [instead] it is being given over to who knows what kind of useless appearances and extrinsic demonstrations.'[67]

As a consequence of their use of theatricality, Paolucci continues in his imagined opponent's voice, the penitential missions have come to resemble nothing so much as an empty mine whose explosion causes only smoke, since there is nothing of substance to be found within it. From this perspective, the penitential exercises might be alluring to crowds, but they could also do unseen damage, because ' "virtue is like a vice when it is given over to excesses." ' Honing in closer to the Jansenist Blaise Pascal's later claims that the Jesuits encouraged moral laxity among the faithful, Paolucci's faux Jesuit critic suggests that the road between passionate exercises of penitence and sinful behavior is a short one: ' "How many have we seen who pass quickly from those ropes to a most licentious life and from those ashes to most dishonest fires [. . .?]." '[68]

Of course, in these passages Paolucci articulates a rhetorical vision of the effects of Jesuit missionary labors that is diametrically opposed to

---

[66] Paolucci, *Missioni*, 206. For similar concerns beyond the Neapolitan context, compare Segneri and Fontana, *Pratica delle Missioni*, 25.

[67] Paolucci, *Missioni*, 207–208.

[68] Ibid., 208.

240 A PARADISE INHABITED BY DEVILS

the claims that the Society of Jesus made for its own civilizing mission. His primary defense against the claims of Jesuit critics is to cite the ecclesiastical and secular sanction for the kinds of penitential activities in which the Jesuits engaged. For example, Paolucci cites the example of Catholic Reformation heroes like the mid-sixteenth-century Archbishop of Milan, Carlo Borromeo, to justify the legitimacy of penitential exercises, stressing the increased fervor which the missions obtained in the face of adversity. But in an uncanny way, Paolucci anticipates the gist of future criticisms against the Society of Jesus.

Beyond Naples, the most pointed criticisms of the Jesuits' missionary practices came to be inspired by the work of Paolo Segneri. While his innovations in missionary technique and practice in northern and central Italy had proven to be highly influential, often reflecting strategies adopted earlier in the Neapolitan mission field, criticism of the 'Segner-ian' method focused on the ultra-theatrical nature of the penitential missions. Critics like the Modenese Benedictine Mauro Alessandro Laza-relli (1662–1729) seem especially perturbed by the use of 'studied artifice' in the Jesuit missions. Commenting upon a missionary tour in 1712 by Paolo Segneri Jr, the more famous missionary's nephew, Lazarelli contends that while the mission 'brought much good,' its theatricality struck him as symptomatic of the Jesuits' wrong-headed orientation toward 'rustic folk.' He also worried over the apparent excessiveness of the mortifications practiced in the mission.[69] To another local Benedictine, the popular missions produced a 'convulsive state' in the citizenry and took people away from their legitimate employment.[70]

Even those most supportive of the Jesuits' civilizing mission, such as Ludovico Antonio Muratori (1672–1750), a good friend of the younger Segneri and a prolific eighteenth-century author and religious commen-tator, express concern over possible abuses. Betraying cultural biases well-rooted in his milieu, Muratori focuses his criticisms on the poten-tially harmful effects that penitential exercises might produce on those most vulnerable to suggestion, especially common folk and women, who might grow overly agitated by public flagellations.[71]

In response to their critics, supporters of the Segnerian missions, like the elder Segneri's missionary colleague, Pietro Pinamonti, argued that

---

[69] Giuseppe Orlandi, 'L.A. Muratori e le Missioni di P. Segneri Jr.,' *Spicilegium Historicum Congregationis Ssmi Redemptoris* 20 (1972): 158–294. Mauro Alessandro Lazarelli's *Relazione* of the younger Paolo Segneri's 1712 missionary reconnoiters in and around Modena is reprinted on 279–94, see esp. 281–2.

[70] Orlandi, 'L.A. Muratori,' 178.

[71] Muratori's chronicle of Segneri's 1712 missions, reprinted in Orlandi, 'L.A. Mura-tori,' 92–257. For one of the best studies of Muratori within the context of eighteenth-century Italian intellectual life, see Venturi, *Dal Muratori a Beccaria*.

JESUIT MISSIONARY THEATER IN NAPLES 241

those who spoke badly of the penitential missions had obviously never been touched by them. But even among these Jesuit defenders, who echoed Scipione Paolucci's ecclesiastical sanction for such rituals, commentators acknowledged that the penitential processions did hold the potential to unleash disorder. According to Pinamonti, for example: 'Some spoke badly [of Segneri's methods], but these people were not those who had been reduced [by the missions], nor the bishops of those places, who not only did not forbid these night processions, but commended them greatly! *One needs, however, to advise all possible caution in carrying out these processions.*'[72]

At the inside of the Society of Jesus, the efficacy of penitential exercises, a hallmark of the mature civilizing mission in the Kingdom of Naples in particular, began to be questioned more widely. By the end of the seventeenth century, for example, the Jesuits' Venetian Provincial, Vincenzo Imperiali, argued that the popular missions in Modena needed to be stripped of their penitential flavor, so that they could be truly effective. Decrying the use of theatrical methods, Imperiali's 'Rule' evokes a nostalgia for the supposed 'glory days' of early Jesuit missions, when such approaches were not in such evidence, perhaps reflecting an unease and defensiveness with the growing criticisms that the Society was facing at the turn of the eighteenth century.[73]

Regardless of how problematic it may have proven, the Society of Jesus' deployment of theatrical techniques and emphasis on corporeal discipline in its civilizing mission reflects the many paradoxes that lay at the heart of their history in Old Regime southern Italy. In their eagerness to stage their missions, the Jesuits relied upon many of the very methods that they decried when used by their secular competitors. Nevertheless, they developed sharp polemics against theater artists, while actively competing with comedians for the favor and attentions of the public. Nor do the paradoxes end there. The Jesuits self-consciously developed a missionary science that included an elaboration of the technical virtuosity that missionaries should ideally master. Their efforts to justify their 'craft' to potential critics (past or present) also bears striking similarity to the learned comedians' own defense of *their* professional ethics and standards of quality.

Finally, the Society of Jesus' embrace of penitential disciplining as a worthy component of its missionary regime highlights the ambiguous role that the Jesuits came to play in Baroque southern Italy and beyond. Penitence, as we have seen, was meant to encourage greater piety, alongside the potentially pacifying social ends to which it might be put.

---

[72] Pietro Pinamonti, cited in Baldinucci, *Avvertimenti*, ff. 41–2 (emphasis mine).

[73] Orlandi, 'L.A. Muratori,' 167.

242 A PARADISE INHABITED BY DEVILS

Had not the Jesuits claimed their own signal role in fostering and maintaining social peace as one of the hallmarks of their civilizing mission in Naples? And yet, by the eighteenth century, critics believed that the penitential missions might also unleash profound disorder, and critics soon implicated the Jesuits in a swirling tempest of suspicion and hostility that ultimately contributed to the Society's suppression in the latter half of the eighteenth century.

Conclusion

The Jesuits left an instructive legacy in early modern Naples. The southern Italian capital and its hinterlands played a vital and fascinating role in the Jesuits' construction of a collective institutional identity. For the Society of Jesus, Naples was not simply an ideal locus in which to effect a civilizing mission – in close proximity to the organizational center in Rome, yet mythologized as a so-called *Other Indies* – but also proved to be an important training ground for building a new kind of religious order that drew an essential part of its *raison d'être* from its members' self-proclaimed, and widely publicized, heroic missionary labors. But operating in Naples was also fraught with its own risks.

As we have seen, contemporary accounts of Jesuit missions in Naples highlighted the strategies, goals and overall philosophy of the civilizing mission, but they also reveal some of the paradoxes inherent in such work. The published histories of Paolucci (1651), Schinosi (1717) and Santagata (1757), as well as countless missionary relations, correspondences and other sources, reflect the fine line that the Jesuits walked between chronicling the successes that they claimed for their missionary endeavors and educational initiatives, and reinforcing precisely those images of Neapolitan backwardness that they needed to justify their ongoing presence.

In this respect, internal missions in southern Italy shared a great deal conceptually with the missions in the Indies. As Acosta had argued in his *De Procuranda*, disparate societies around the globe had reached different levels of civilization, leaving many of them far from the Jesuits' desired goal of being truly Christianized and civilized. Missionaries had to take such differences into account when devising appropriate strategies to work among diverse cultures. In this way, the Jesuits had learned the significance of accommodation, refined their collective institutional identity so that members of the Society felt a sense of shared purpose and recognized the most efficacious methods to achieve their goals, and instructed newcomers to the company in all aspects of the missionary vocation.

But whereas the role of the missionary was relatively clear in the context of the Indies of America or Asia, where the 'otherness' of indigenous populations (and, for that matter, of the missionaries themselves) stood out in sharp relief, things were far murkier in the Kingdom of Naples. Although the Jesuits contributed in no small part to dissemi-

244 A PARADISE INHABITED BY DEVILS

nating a myth of southern Italian backwardness in the early modern period, they increasingly counted among their members in the *Mezzogiorno* those native to the region. Here then, unlike the case for their work across the globe, the Jesuits were both insiders and outsiders – perched precariously atop a lookout post that both afforded a more intimate view of the society that they hoped to transform and made them vulnerable to criticisms and, ultimately, expulsion.

As I have suggested, while the Society of Jesus had faced a wide range of critics from its earliest history, these voices grew more insistent and their polemics more elaborate between the mid-seventeenth and mid-eighteenth centuries. In Naples, the second half of the seventeenth century witnessed a number of political and cultural shifts that ultimately fueled anti-curialism in general, and, more specifically, created an atmosphere hostile to the Jesuits. While anti-curialism in the eighteenth-century was a complex phenomenon with juridical, political, economic and ideological dimensions, it can be defined broadly as a strong current of opposition to the hegemonic power that the Roman Catholic Church and its constituent institutions held within early modern society. For secular monarchs and their bureaucratic officials, anti-curialism also represented a tool in efforts to legitimize an extension of centralized monarchical authority. Among Enlightenment intellectuals who placed great faith in the willingness of progressive-minded secular rulers to reform society, government and law, the Catholic Church represented backwardness and stagnation.

Which factors contributed to anti-curialism in general, and growing opposition to the Society of Jesus in particular? On the one hand, religious orders became ever more competitive after the dust settled from the mid-seventeenth-century revolts. This was followed fairly closely by a cataclysmic plague in 1656 that devastated the population of urban Naples. In the aftermath of the epidemic, religious orders had apparently bickered over the greater efficacy of their respective patron saints in preventing future crises. Yet these religious organizations also began to face public criticisms for their efforts to collect donations from a beleaguered populace in the wake of the epidemic. As the Neapolitan chronicler and gazetteer known as 'Innocenzo Fuidoro' (1618–92), himself a cleric, claimed: 'the religious have impoverished most of the people in this Kingdom, and more precisely, in our city of Naples, through the donations procured by them for their monasteries during the recent plague [. . . .]'[1] Fuidoro' s comments suggest a broader climate of growing opposition to the Church and its personnel.

---

[1] See Guiseppe Galasso, *Napoli Spagnolo dopo Masaniello. Politica, cultura, società* (Florence: Sansoni, 1982), 1: 41–50; 60. Galasso notes, especially, the squabbles between

CONCLUSION   245

Yet the Church's financial claims in the aftermath of the 1656 plague were only part of the picture of anti-curialism in Naples. A number of other factors contributed to an increasingly troubled climate in which the Jesuits became targets of both lay and ecclesiastical criticisms. Building on a longstanding tradition, lay critics argued against the abuses of ecclesiastical immunity and the proliferation of churches and religious houses. They proffered the notion that religious traditionalists stood against 'modern science', and laid a familiar charge against the apparent immorality of the clergy.[2] In their advocacy of increasing the secular powers of the monarchy as the best means to effect reforms, these critics viewed religious orders like the Jesuits as emblematic of the feudal cast of southern Italy that they wished to transform.

By the mid-eighteenth century, Naples faced a worsening economic climate, which increased the anti-curial atmosphere still further. This was fueled in part by recurrent bad harvests, which led to that familiar and tragic cycle of famine and epidemic, and by price-fixing by a group of grain merchants with whom the reformist government of royal counselor Bernardo Tanucci had to negotiate. In any event, the Church was held, alongside other members of the Neapolitan elites, to be corrupt and unduly powerful.[3] Despite the vast population of metropolitan Naples, the Kingdom of Naples remained overwhelmingly an agricultural economy with relatively few advantages when competing in an increasingly tight international market. As one historian has recently noted: 'The Kingdom's position in the international market subjected it to continuing commercial instability and so discouraged long-term investment, particularly in the areas most vulnerable to market fluctuations. And this in turn hindered the development of a competitiveness that would have strengthened her position in the market.'[4] For several key eighteenth-century reformers, any efforts to civilize southern Italy had to urge not simply moral reform, but contend with its economic marginality by endorsing full modernization.

---

the Jesuits and the Theatines, which had roots in the immediate aftermath of the 1647–48 Revolts when the two reform orders apparently competed to demonstrate greater loyalty to the Spanish Crown; Innocenzo Fuidoro, *Giornali di Napoli dal MDCLX al MDCLXXX*, cited in Galasso, *Napoli Spagnolo*, 1: 60–61.

[2] Galasso, *Napoli Spagnolo*, 2: 419–24; on the changing intellectual climate in eighteenth-century Naples, in particular, cf. Franco Venturi, *Dal Muratori a Beccaria*, Vol. 1 of *Settecento Riformatore* (Turin: Einaudi, 1969; 1998), esp. Chapter Eight, 'La Napoli di Antonio Genovesi,' 523–644.

[3] Franco Venturi, cited in cf. Girolamo Imbruglia, 'Enlightenment in Eighteenth-Century Naples,' *Naples in the Eighteenth Century*, 70–94, esp. 78.

[4] Biagio Salvemini, 'The Arrogance of the Market,' 53.

246   A PARADISE INHABITED BY DEVILS

In the face of these widespread economic hardships, the Jesuits appeared suspiciously successful to many, both because of their healthy patrimony (including land, buildings and the relatively generous allowances to maintain the roughly four hundred members of the Neapolitan Province) and the meticulous management of their business interests. Although other religious orders and the secular clergy had land holdings and had acquired considerable wealth, critics perceived the Jesuits as being overly fixated upon their investments. As one commentator aptly suggests: 'That which characterized the Jesuits [. . .] was not the fact of their patrimony, but the intense care, even passion that they put into making it produce and bear fruit.'[5] This criticism suggests that the Jesuits' very adeptness at accommodating themselves to new conditions fueled opposition to the Society of Jesus. In Naples, as elsewhere, the Jesuits were perceived as having expended prodigious energies in cultivating their financial interests, just as they had in instructing novices in the best means to evangelize and civilize disparate communities. Thus, an institutional strength could also be viewed as a vulnerability in the changing landscape of late seventeenth- and eighteenth-century Naples. While the Jesuits would have objected to such characterizations of their members as greedy, or involved in unseemly financial dealings, countering that in fact their investments were necessary to finance the free education that they provided to young boys across the lands in which they worked, alongside other important charitable works, the perception nonetheless had its impact.

Beyond widespread concern over the Jesuits' apparent economic successes, the emergence of a vibrant and politically engaged lay intellectual community rooted in the newly invigorated University of Naples contributed to the rising chorus of secular criticism of the Society of Jesus. One of the linchpins of this criticism was the contention that the Jesuits had undue power among the nobility and within the viceregal government.[6] Many intellectuals held that the Society of Jesus epitomized the kind of religious traditionalism that could only hold back

---

[5] 'L'Espulsione dei Gesuiti dal Regno di Napoli,' in *La Soppressione della Compagnia di Gesù* (Naples: Istituto Pontano, 1992), 67–83, esp. 76–7. (NB There is no author nor editor credited with this work.) For a broader study of the suppression of the Society of Jesus in Italy, cf. Umberto Padovani, *La Soppressione della Compagnia di Gesù* (Naples: Instituto Editoriale del Mezzogiorno, 1962).

[6] Innocenzo Fuidoro, for example, argued that the Jesuits were more concerned with 'the dominion that they have over the nobility' than with saving souls in their missions. Cited in Galasso, *Napoli Spagnolo* 2: 429 (makes comparison with the Dominicans, noting that if it had been the Jesuits 'fusse stata di Giesuiti, e certo che con la loro politica e destrezza averiano operato assai piu, per il dominio c'hanno con la nobilita, della quale piuttosto si approfittano per il loro proprio commodo').

CONCLUSION   247

economic and social progress. As early as the mid-seventeenth century, anti-Jesuit polemics, like those most famously of the French philosopher and Jansenist Blaise Pascal, gained an audience in Naples.[7] In his *Lettres écrites à un provincial* (1656–57), Pascal lambasted the Jesuits for their supposed moral laxity.

Tensions in Naples culminated at the end of the seventeenth century with an inquisitorial trial against a group of accused 'atheists' that quickly degenerated into a bitter jurisdictional dispute between Church and civil authorities. An anonymous pamphlet, published in 1695 at the tail end of the dispute, attacked the defenders of civil authority and, by extension, the 'new culture' that criticized unfettered ecclesiastical power. The pamphlet was quickly attributed to the Society of Jesus, only adding to the already present (if often contradictory) suspicions that critics held toward an organization perceived as beholden to its elite patrons and hostile to the more 'enlightened' among them.[8]

Within this context, two of the most salient institutional characteristics that helped build the *old* Society of Jesus (that is, the pre-suppression Jesuits) – its methodical and articulated approach to its labors and the organization's emphasis on accommodation and pragmatic flexibility – became implicit targets for reprobation. Ironically, a secularized program for civilizing Naples came to challenge the Jesuits' vision and program for moral reform. This is perhaps one of the unexpected consequences of the Jesuits' early modern civilizing mission in the Kingdom of Naples: that their secular critics took up the mantle of the civilizing project, albeit advocating divergent methods and visions for cultural uplift. This historical contiguousness, along with the highly rationalized institutional character of the Society of Jesus, suggests the order's very modernity, though early modern critics might not have viewed things this way.

By the middle of the eighteenth century, Neapolitan intellectuals like Antonio Genovesi (1712–69) offered a secularized version of a civilizing mission for the Kingdom of Naples more in keeping with the emerging Enlightenment culture. While they shared many of the Jesuits' preconceptions about the backwardness of the Neapolitan poor, these critics' recipes for reform were quite different. For Genovesi, among the most

---

[7] Cf. Galasso, *Napoli Spagnolo*, 2: 395. Pascal (1623–62), the illustrious French natural philosopher, was among the harshest critics of the Jesuits for their supposed moral laxity and encouragement of 'superstition' through their missionary methods. For this anti-Jesuit polemic, see Blaise Pascal, *Lettres écrites à un provincial*, ed. Antoine Adam (Paris: Garnier-Flammarion, 1967).

[8] For a description of this episode and the accusations leveled at the Society of Jesus, cf. Galasso, *Napoli Spagnolo*, 2: 425–73, esp. 443–71.

248 A PARADISE INHABITED BY DEVILS

influential and recognizable figures of the Neapolitan Enlightenment, the clergy represented a drag on the economic, cultural and moral development of the South. Like the Jesuits, Genovesi believed in the power of education to effect individual and cultural transformation. And, interestingly, Genovesi also shared their anxieties over the violence and social decadence into which an unregulated poor might be drawn. But where the Jesuits and other religious reformers looked to the power of conversion, ritual behavior, building and sustaining charitable institutions and lay congregations and inculcation in Catholic orthodoxy as keys to civilizing southern Italian commoners and their more unruly elite counterparts, Genovesi believed that only by creating a 'culture of talents' could Naples escape what he saw as its perennial backwardness and provide moral, cultural and material uplift to its populace.[9]

In his *Elementi del Commercio* (1765), Genovesi articulated a modern vision of taking specific measures to increase prosperity among wider layers of Neapolitan society, 'not only the artisans, but also the peasants and the women.' Doing so, Genovesi believed, 'would make civility more universal' by making a greater number of families engines of economic development, encouraging talent and ingenuity in the mass of the population and improving technical expertise because education and training would be more widespread.[10] Genovesi did not argue for these reforms because he was committed to an egalitarian society, nor because he was in favor of political democratization, but because he saw them as central to southern Italy's economic viability. To this end, Genovesi saw the Catholic Church as a problem, because for him it represented one of the pillars of the feudal society that he hoped to transform.

Criticisms such as those of Enlightenment reformers like Genovesi reflect the profound tension that lay at the heart of the Jesuits' enterprise in Naples. On the one hand, the Society of Jesus was committed to pursuing a multi-faceted civilizing mission among the laity, both elites and commoners. And yet the Jesuits also needed to cultivate and maintain productive relationships with local elites who served as patrons, missionary subjects and, ideally, potential members of the Society. Perhaps for this reason, the Jesuits often targeted the popular classes as the source of both potential disorder and irreligiosity. While

---

[9] While stereotypes of southern Italian backwardness and barbarity remain largely consistent across the early modern period, as I suggested in Chapter One, responses to this 'problem' do shift. For Genovesi's characterization of Neapolitan 'backwardness,' see Venturi, 'La Napoli di Antonio Genovesi,' 575–85; cf. Imbruglia, Enlightenment in Naples, ibid., 74.

[10] Genovesi, *Elementi del Commercio*, cited in Venturi, 'Dal Muratori a Beccaria,' 580–81. My use of the term 'modern' here does not imply a value judgment.

CONCLUSION

missionary accounts include examples of dissolute nobles or wealthy commoners, they derive much of their dramatic power from their representations of the barbarity of the Neapolitan lower orders and of the Jesuits' efforts to tame and reform these communities. Missionary reports interweave examples of 'savagery' with edifying tales of repentance, reconciliation and the restoration of good order and Catholic morality. In these accounts, large-scale popular insurrections such as the Neapolitan revolts of 1585 and (more dramatically) 1647–48, are presented as proof positive that local elites needed Jesuit reformers and peacemakers not merely to educate their sons and aid them in penitential exercises to expiate collective guilt, but also to contain and redirect the rage of the plebe.

Certainly, the Jesuits were not the first nor the only early modern commentators to develop or disseminate the image of Naples as a 'paradise inhabited by devils,' a physically beautiful city and region mired in backwardness and viewed with concern over its potential volatility. Yet their more than 200-year-long project to provide 'stable culture' to the 'rough and licentious' people of Naples could not but help to perpetuate this myth. Whether striving to Christianize prisoners, reform prostitutes or convert Muslim slaves, the Jesuits were self-consciously positioned themselves as central actors in a civilizing project. Yet, it would be simplistic and historically inaccurate to portray them as cunning, amoral power brokers. Indeed, the conditions that provoked the early modern Jesuits' expulsion from the Kingdom of Naples in 1767 – in particular, their paradoxical association with both traditional elites and with the kind of superstitions regularly linked to the popular classes – suggest that, in spite of its institutional prerogatives and sense of collective purpose, the Society of Jesus, like all historical actors, could not completely control its own image-making, nor its destiny.

Bibliography

Manuscripts

Archivum Romanum Societatis Iesu (ARSI)

Fondo Gesuitico (F.G.)

Indipetae 2 Italia mss 733–45 (1580–1647)

Institutes
Vol. 74 (1647–50) Vincenzo Carafa, 'Lettera di Padre Nostro Vicenzo Carafa à tutti li Provinciali della Compagnia in Europa intorno alle Missioni,' *Missiones Populares*, 1647–50, ff. 24–57.

Istruttioni
ms 720A/I/1/1 'Istruttione per quelli che vanno à missione per la Provincia (Romana) fatta nell'anno 1590.'
ms 720A/I/1/6 Cesare Croilo, 'Istruttioni per li Missionanti data à N.P. Dal P. Cesare Croilo, Prefetto delle Missioni Nella Provincia Romana.'
ms 720A/I/1/9 Fabio Fabi, 'Instruttione per li Padri che vanno à fruttificare nella Sabina' (*c.* 1590), unfoliated.
ms 720A/I/1/11 'Avvisi per le Missioni.'
ms 720A/I/1/12 'Instruttioni per li Padri della missione della Campagne di Roma' (*c.* 1620).
ms 720A/I/1/13 'Instruttioni . . .'

Litterae Annuae Historia Provinciae Neapolitanae (Neap.)

Neap., Vols 72–6 (1551–1767), Missionary Relations.
Neap., Vol. 202 (1590), Claudio Acquaviva, 'Lettera di Nostro Padre Claudio Acquaviva quando mando il 2' Giubileo impresato da Nostra Compagnia. Sisto V' et ordina che si mandano alcuni Padri in missione. Dei 2' di Maggio, 1590. Al Padre Antonio Lisio, Provinciale di Napoli,' ff. 31–33v.

Operum Nostrorum (Opp. Nn.)

ms 211 Paolo Segneri, 'Ragionamenti per la Missione' (*c.* 1690).
ms 299 Antonio Baldinucci, 'Avvertimenti a Chi Desidera impiegarsi

252 BIBLIOGRAPHY

nelle Missioni. Cavati dall' Esperienza di Quei che le Hanno fatte per Molti Anni' (*c.* 1710–17), 67ff.

Archivio Segreto Vaticano (ASV)

Congregazione del Concilio, Relationes ad Limina, Neapolitana I and II

mss 560 A/B Cardinal Mattei, 'Discorso sopra le Reforme delle Parocchie della Città di Napoli che al presente si ritrovano, et del modo di erigerne altre nuove da darle al Signore Cardinale Illustrissimo et Reverendissimo Mattei' (12 May 1595), ff. 24–5.

mss 560 A/B Alfonso Gesualdo, Visita Limina Apostolorum, 'Relationi del[lo] stato della Chiesa di Napoli per il 4' et 5' triennio' (1599), ff. 27–36v.

mss 560 A/B Cardinal Carracciolo, Untitled Report of Cardinal Carracciolo to the Congregation of the Council on the state of the Neapolitan Church (1683), ff. 243–253v.

Biblioteca Apostolica Vaticana (BAV)

Chigiani

mss G. VII 210, 'Delle Rivolutioni di Napoli' Vol. 1, 'Succinto Relatione della sollevatione di Napoli occorso nel presente anno 1647 à 7' di Luglio giorno di Domenica sinco alla mort' di Tomm'Aniello,' ff. 63–102.

Ferraioli IV 9186, Ascanio Filomarino, 'Lettere al pontefice Innocenzio X sulla sommossa di Masaniello'.

Printed Sources

Acosta, José de, *De Procuranda Indorum Salute.* 2 vols, ed. Luciano Pereña Vicente. Madrid: CSIC, 1987.

——, *Obras del Padre José de Acosta*, ed. Francisco Mateos. Madrid: Atlas, 1954.

——, 'Tercero Cathecismo y exposicion de la Doctrina Christiana, por Sermones. Para que los curas Y otros ministros prediquen y enseñen a los Yndos y a las demas personas' (1585), *Monumenta Catechetica Hispano-Americana (Siglos XI–XVIII)*, Vol. II, ed. Juan Guillermo Duran. Buenos Aires: Facultad de Teologia de la Uneversidad Catolica Argentina, 1990.

BIBLIOGRAPHY

Andreini, Giovan Battista, *La Ferza. Ragionamento Secondo. Contra L'Accuse Date Alla Commedia*. Paris, 1625.

Araldo, Giovan Francesco, *Napoli, L'Europa e La Compagnia di Gesù Nella 'Cronica' di Giovan Francesco Araldo*, ed. Francesco Divenuto. Naples: Edizioni Scientifiche Napoletane, 1998.

Bacco, Enrico, *Naples. An Early Guide*, ed. and trans. Eileen Gardiner. New York: Italica Press, 1991.

Baldinucci, Antonio, *Lettere inedite del P. Antonio Baldinucci della C . d. G. corredate di note per cura del P. Luigi Rosa*. Prato, 1899.

Barnaba, Fabrizio, 'Letter of 23 April, 1607,' in 'Documenti Sulla Storia Economica e Civile del Regno Cavati dal Carteggio degli Agenti Del Granduca di Toscana in Napoli, Dall'Anno 1582–1648,' *Archivio Storico Italiano* IX, 245–53.

Barone, Antonio, *Della Vita del Padre Pierantonio Spinelli della Compagnia di Giesù*. Naples, 1707.

Bartoli, Daniello, *Della Vita del P. Vincenzo Carafa*, 2 vols, Turin, 1825.

Bartolini, Ludovico, *Relatione delle missioni fatte su le montagne di Modena dalli molto R.R.P.P. Paolo Segneri e Foi. Pietro Pinamonti della Compagnia di Gesù l'anno 1672*. Modena, 1673.

Beltrano, Ottavio, *Descrittione del Regno di Napoli. Diviso in Dodeci Provincie*. Bologna: Forni, 1969.

Bulifon, Antonio, *Giornali di Napoli dal 1547 al 1706*, ed. Nino Cortese. Naples: Società Napoletana di Storia Patria, 1932.

Bursati, Lucretio, *La Vittoria delle Donne*. Venice, 1621.

Capaccio, Giulio Cesare, 'Napoli Descritta ne' Principii del Secolo XVII' (*c.* 1607), ed. B. Capasso, *Archivio Storico per le province napoletane* VII (1882): 68–103; 531–54; 776–804.

———, *Il Forastiero*. Naples, 1634.

Collenuccio, Pandolfo, *Compendio dell'Istoria del regno di Napoli*. Venice, 1591.

Di Elia, Giovanni Battista, *Relatione di una Missione fatta da due Reverendi Padri della Campagnia di Giesù nella Città di Bitonto del Regno di Napoli nell'Anno 1646*. Trani and Bologna, 1647.

Di Girolamo, Francesco (a.k.a. De Geronimo), *San Francesco Di Girolamo e Le Sue Missioni. Dentro e Fuori di Napoli*, ed. Giuseppe Boero. Florence: Raffaelo Ricci, 1882.

Donzelli, Giuseppe, *Partenope liberata. Overo Racconto dell'Heroica Risolutione fatta dal Popolo di Napoli per Sottrarsi con Tutto il Regno dall'insopportabil Giogo delli Spagnuoli*, ed. Antonio Altamura. Naples, 1970.

Fuidoro, Innocenzo, *Successi del Governo el Conte D'Oñatte*, ed. Alfredo Parente. Naples, 1932.

254   BIBLIOGRAPHY

Galante, G.A., *Guida Sacra della Città di Napoli*, ed. Nicola Spinosa. Naples, 1985.

Galanti, Giuseppe M., *Nuova Guida per Napoli e Suoi Contorni*. Naples: Fausto Fiorentino, 1845.

Genovesi, Antonio, *Discorso sopra il vero fine delle lettere e delle scienze*. Naples, 1753.

Giannone, Pietro, *Istoria Civile del Regno di Napoli*. Naples, 1840.

Giraffi, Alessandro, *Le Rivolutioni di Napoli*. Venice, 1647, trans. James Howell as *An Exact History of the Late Revolutions of Naples; And of their Monstrous Successes, not to be Parallel'd by any Antient or Modern History*, 2 vols. London, 1650–52.

Las Casas, Bartolomé de, *Witness. Writings of Bartolomé de Las Casas*, ed. and trans. George Sanderlin. Maryknoll, NY: Orbis Books, 1971.

Loyola, Ignatius, *The Constitutions of the Society of Jesus*, trans. and with an introduction by George E. Ganss. St Louis: The Institute for Jesuit Sources, 1970.

——, 'Instructions for the Undertaking of at Trent (1546), in *Saint Ignatius Loyola, Personal Writings*. London: Penguin, 1996.

——, *Saint Ignatius Loyola: Letters to Women*, ed. Hugo Rahner, trans. Kathleen Pond and S.A.H. Weetman. Edinburgh and London: Nelson, 1960.

——, *The Spiritual Exercises of Saint Ignatius*. ed. and trans. George E. Ganss. St Louis: The Institute for Jesuit Sources, 1992.

Lupis, Antonio, *Compendio di una Missione fatta da due RR. PP. Dell'Ill.ma Compagnia di Gesù nella città di Molfetta della provincia di Bari, nel Regno di Napoli il'anno 1647*. Naples, 1647.

Mainardi, Piovano Arlotto, *Facezie Motti e Burle del Piovano Arlotto*, ed. Chiara Amerighi. Florence: Libreria Editrice Fiorentina, 1980.

Marcaldo, Francesco, 'Cose principali di una Relazione sul Regno di Napoli, fatta al Granduca di Toscana da Francesco Marcaldo, nell'anno 1594,' in 'Documenti Sulla Storia Economica e Civile del Regno Cavati dal Carteggio degli Agenti Del Granduca di Toscana in Napoli, Dall'Anno 1582–1648,' *Archivio Storico Italiano* 9 (1846): 245–353.

Palermo, F., ed. 'Documenti sulla storia economica e civile del regno [di Napoli],' *Archivio Storico Italiano*, IX (1846): 348–53.

——, 'Sette Lettere del Cardinal Filomarino al papa,' *Archivio Storico Italiano*, IX (1846): 379–93.

Paolucci, Scipione, *Missioni de Padri della Compagnia di Giesù nel Regno di Napoli*. Naples, 1651.

Parrino, Domenico Antonio, *Teatro Eroico e Politico dei Governi de' Vicere del Regno di Napoli*. 2 vols. Orig. Publ. Naples, 1692; Naples: Mariano Lombardi, 1875.

BIBLIOGRAPHY

Pascal, Blaise, *Lettres écrites à un provincial*, ed. Antoine Adam. Paris: Garnier-Flammarion, 1967.

Porzio, Camillo, *Relazione del Regno di Napoli al Marchese Di Mondesciar, Vicere di Napoli* (1579), in *La Congiura dei Baroni del Regno di Napoli Contra il Re Ferdinando Primo e Gli Altri Scritti*, ed. Ernesto Pontieri. Naples, 1964.

Ragguaglio della miracolosa protezione di San Francesco Saverio Apostolo delle Indie, verso la città e il Regno di Napoli nel contagio del 1656. Naples, 1660.

Riaco, C.F., *Il giudicio di Napoli. Discorso del passato contaggio rassomigliato al giudicio Universale*. Perugia, 1658.

Rosso, Andrea, 'La rivoluzione di Masaniello visto dal residente veneto a Napoli,' ed. A. Capograssi, *Archivio storico per le province napoletane* 33 (1952): 167–235.

Santagata, Saverio, *Istoria della Compagnia di Giesù appartenente al Regno di Napoli*. 2 vols. Naples, 1756–7.

Sauli, Ottaviano, 'Relazione dei tumulti napoletani del 1647,' ed. L. Correra, *Archivio storico per le province napoletane* XV (1890): 355–87.

Schinosi, Francesco, *Istoria della Compagnia de Giesù appartenente al Regno di Napoli*. 2 vols. Naples, 1706–11.

Segneri, Paolo, *Il Cristiano Istruito nella sua Legge. Ragionamenti Morali di Paolo Segneri della Compagnia di Gesù*. Venice: Giuseppe Bortoli, 1745.

_____, 'L'Arte di Predicar Bene,' *Opere*, Vol. IV. Milan: Società Tipografica de' Classici Italiani, 1845.

_____, *Lettere Inedite del P. Paolo Segneri (D.C.D.G.) Raccolte e Pubblicate per Cura di Giuseppe Boero*. Naples, 1850.

_____ and Fontana, Fulvio, *Pratica delle Missioni del Padre Paolo Segneri della Compagnia de Giesù predicatore Pontificio continuata dal P. Fulvio Fontana della Medesima Religione, per lo spazio d'anni ventiquattro, per una gran parte d'Italia e di la da monti nella Elvezia, Rezia, Valesia e Tirolo, con l'aggiunta delle prediche, discorsi e metodo distinto tenutosi nelle funzioni sacre*. Venice, 1714.

Seward, Desmond, ed., *Naples: A Traveller's Companion*. London: Constable & Co., 1984.

Summonte, Giovanni Antonio, *Historia della Città e Regno di Napoli*. 4 vols. Naples, 1602–43.

Suriano, Michele, 'Diplomatic Report to the Venetian Senate' (1559), in *Pursuit of Power. Venetian Ambassadors' Reports on Turkey, France, and Spain in the Age of Philip II*, ed. and trans. James C. Davis. New York: Harper Torchbooks, 1970.

BIBLIOGRAPHY

'(Il) Tumulto napoletano dell'anno 1585,' *Archivio Storico per le province napoletane*, no pagination.

Tutini, Camillo, *Dell'origine e fondazione de' Seggi di Napoli*. Naples, 1644.

Xavier, Francis, *The Letters and Instructions of Francis Xavier*, trans. M. Joseph Costelloe. St Louis: The Institute of Jesuit Sources, 1992.

Secondary sources

Alden, Dauril, *The Making of an Enterprise: The Society of Jesus in Portugal, its Empire, and Beyond, 1540–1750*. Stanford: Stanford University Press, 1996.

Allegra, Luciano, 'Il Parocco: un mediatore fra alta e bassa cultura,' in *Storia d'Italia. Annali IV: Intelletuali e potere*. Turin: Einaudi, 1981.

Allen, D.F., 'Anti-Jesuit Rioting by Knights of St. John During the Malta Carnival of 1639,' *AHSI* 65 (January–June 1996): 3–30.

Ambrasi, Domenico, *Riformatori e ribelli a Napoli nella seconda metà del Settecento: Ricerche sul giansenismo napoletano*. Naples: Regina, 1979.

Angelini, Franca, *Il Teatro Barocco*. Bari: Laterza, 1975.

Astarita, Tommaso, *The Continuity of Feudal Power. The Caracciolo di Brienza in Spanish Naples*. Cambridge, UK: Cambridge University Press, 1992.

Bangert, William V., 'Some International Aspects of the Activity of the Jesuits in the New World,' *The Americas* 14 (1958): 432–6.

——, *Claude Jay and Alfonso Salmerón. Two Early Jesuits*. Chicago: Loyola University Press, 1985.

——, *A History of the Society of Jesus*, 2nd edn. St Louis: Institute of Jesuit Sources, 1986.

——, *Jerome Nadal, S.J. (1507–1580): Tracking the First Generation of Jesuits*, ed. and completed by Thomas M. McCoog SJ. Chicago: Loyola University Press, 1992.

Barish, Jonas, *The Antitheatrical Prejudice*. Berkeley, CA: University of California Press, 1981.

Bentley, Jerry, *Politics and Culture in Renaissance Naples*. Princeton, NJ: Princeton University Press, 1987.

Bilinkoff, Jodi, 'The Many "Lives" of Pedro de Ribadeneyra,' *Renaissance Quarterly* 52 (1999): 180–95.

Biondi, Albano, 'Aspetti della cultura cattolica post-tridentina. Religione e controllo sociale,' in *Storia d'Italia. Annali IV: Intellettuali e Potere*. Turin: Einaudi, 1981.

BIBLIOGRAPHY 257

Bireley, Robert, 'Two Works by Jean Delumeau,' *The Catholic Historical Review* 77 (1991): 78–88.

Black, Christopher, *Italian Confraternities in the Sixteenth Century.* Cambridge, UK: Cambridge University Press, 1989.

Black-Michaud, Jacob, *Cohesive Force: Feud in the Mediterranean and the Middle East.* Oxford: B. Blackwell, 1975.

Blaisdell, Charmarie J., 'Calvin's and Loyola's Letters to Women: Politics and Spiritual Counsel in the Sixteenth Century,' in *Calviniana: Ideas and Influence of John Calvin*, ed. Robert V. Schnucker. Kirksville, MO: The Sixteenth Century Journal Publishers, 1988, 235–53.

Boccadamo, Giuliana, 'Maria Longo, L'Ospedale degli Incurabili e la sua Insula,' *Campania Sacra* 30 (1999): 37–170.

Bono, Salvatore, 'Schiavi Musulmani in Italia nell'età moderna,' *Erdem* 3, No. 9 (July 1987): 829–38.

Borromeo, A., 'Contributo allo studio dell'Inquisizione e dei suoi rapport con il potere episcopale nell'Italia spagnola del Cinquecento,' *Annuario dell'Istituto Storico italiano per l'età moderna e contemporanea*, 29–30 (1977–78): 219–76.

Bossy, John, *Peace in the Post-Reformation.* Cambridge, UK: Cambridge University Press, 1998.

Braudel, Fernand, *The Mediterranean and the Mediterranean World in the Age of Philip II*, 2 vols. Berkeley and Los Angeles: University of California Press, 1995.

Brizzi, Gian Paolo, *La Formazione della classe dirigente nel Sei-Settecento: I seminaria nobilium nell'Italia centro-settrentionale.* Bologna: Il Mulino, 1976.

———, ed., *La 'Ratio Studiorum.' Modelli Culturali e Pratiche Educative dei Gesuiti in Italia tra Cinque e Seicento.* Rome: Bulzoni, 1981.

Burckhardt, Jacob, *The Civilization of the Renaissance in Italy.* New York: Harper Torchbooks, 1958.

Burgaleta, Claudio, *José de Acosta, S.J. (1540–1600): His Life and Thought.* Chicago: Loyola Press, 1999.

Burke, Peter, *Popular Culture in Early Modern Europe.* New York: Harper and Row, 1978.

———, 'A Question of Acculturation?,' in *Scienze, credenze occulte, livelli di cultura. Convegno internazionale di studi.* Florence: Olschki, 1982.

———, 'The Virgin of the Carmine and the Revolt of Masaniello,' *Past and Present* 99 (May 1983): 3–22.

———, *Historical Anthropology in Early Modern Italy.* Cambridge, UK: Cambridge University Press, 1987.

Calabria, Antonio, *The Cost of Empire: the finances of the Kingdom of Naples in the time of Spanish Rule.* Cambridge, UK: Cambridge University Press, 1991.

Campbell, Thomas, *The Jesuits 1534–1921. A History of the Society of Jesus from its Foundations to the Present Time.* New York: The Encyclopedia Press, 1921.

Camporesi, Piero, 'Cultura popolare e cultura d'elite fra Medioevo ed età moderna,' in *Storia d'Italia. Annali IV: Intellettuali e Potere.* Turin: Einaudi, 1981.

Canosa, Romano and Colonello, Isabella, *Storia del Carcere in Italia. Dalla Fine del Cinquecento all'Unità.* Bari: Sapere2000, 1984.

Carroll, Michael P., *Madonnas that Maim. Popular Catholicism in Italy Since the Fifteenth Century.* Baltimore and London: Johns Hopkins University Press, 1992.

_____, *Veiled Threats: The Logic of Popular Catholicism in Italy.* Baltimore and London: Johns Hopkins University Press, 1996.

Castiglione, Miriam, *I Professionisti dei sogni. Visioni e devozioni popolari nella cultura contadina meridionale.* Naples: Liguori, 1981.

Châtellier, Louis, *The Religion of the Poor: Rural Missions in Europe and the Formation of Modern Catholicism, ca. 1500–ca. 1800,* trans. Brian Pearce. Cambridge, UK: Cambridge University Press, 1997.

Chiabò, Maria and Doglio, Federico, eds, *I Gesuiti e i Primordi del Teatro Barocco in Europa.* Rome: Centro Studi Sul Teatro Medioevale e Rinascimenti, 1995.

Christian, William, *Local Religion in Early Modern Spain.* Princeton, NJ: Princeton University Press, 1981.

Cipolla, Carlo, *Before the Industrial Revolution. European Society and Economy, 1000–1700.* New York: Norton, 1976.

Cocchiara, Giuseppe, *The History of Folklore in Europe,* trans. John N. McDaniel. Philadelphia: Institute for the Study of Human Issues, 1981.

Cochrane, Eric, *Italy 1530–1630,* ed. Julius Kirshner. London: Longman, 1988.

Cohen, Sherrill, *The Evolution of Women's Asylums Since 1500. From Refuges for Ex-Prostitutes to Shelters for Battered Women.* New York and Oxford: Oxford University Press, 1992.

Cohen, Thomas V., 'The Social Origins of the Jesuits, 1540–1600,' 2 vols. PhD diss., Harvard University, 1973.

Coleman, David, 'Moral Formation and Social Control in the Catholic Reformation: The Case of San Juan de Avila,' *The Sixteenth Century Journal* 36, No. 1 (Spring 1995): 17–30.

Conelli, Maria Ann, 'The *Guglie* of Naples: Religious and Political Machinations of the Festival *Macchine,*' *American Academy in Rome Publications* 45 (2000): 153–83.

Cortese, Nino, *Cultura e politica a Napoli dal Cinquecento al Settecento.* Naples: Edizioni Scientifiche Italiane, 1965.

BIBLIOGRAPHY 259

Croce, Benedetto, 'Il "Paradiso Abitato da Diavoli," ' in *Uomini e Cose della Vecchia Italia*. Bari: Laterza, 1927.

——, *History of the Kingdom of Naples*, ed. H. Stuart Hughes, trans. Frances Frenaye. Chicago and London: University of Chicago Press, 1970.

——, *I Teatri di Napoli: dal Rinascimento alla fine del secolo decimottavo*, ed. Giuseppe Galasso. Milan: Adelphi, 1992.

Croix, Alain, *La Bretagne aux 16e et 17e siècle: la vie, la mort, la foi*. Paris: Maloine, 1980.

Cucinotta, Salavatore, *Popolo e clero in Sicilia nella dialetta socioreligiosa fra Cinque-Seicento*. Messina: Edizioni Storiche Siciliane, 1986.

Daniel, E. Randolph, *The Franciscan Concept of Mission in the High Middle Ages*. Lexington, KY: University of Kentucky Press, 1975.

D'Aria, F.M., *Un Restauratore Sociale. Storia Critica della vita di san Francesco de Geronimo da documenti inediti. Saggio sui suoi autografi. Le sue lettere inedite*. Rome: Edizioni Italiane, 1943.

D'Ascoli, Arsenio, *La Predicazioni dei Cappuccini nel Cinquecento Italia*. Loreto: Libreria S. Francesco D'Assisi, 1956.

Davis, Natalie Zemon, 'The Reasons of Misrule,' in *Society and Culture in Early Modern France*. Stanford: Stanford University Press, 1975.

——, *Women on the Margins: Three Seventeenth-Century Lives*. Cambridge, MA: Harvard University Press, 1995.

Davis, Robert, 'Counting European Slaves on the Barbary Coast,' *Past and Present* 172 (2001): 87–124.

De Boer, Wietse, *The Conquest of the Soul: Confession, Discipline and Public Order in Counter-Reformation Milan*. Leiden and Boston: Brill, 2001.

Delumeau, Jean, *Catholicism between Luther and Voltaire: A New View of the Counter-Reformation*, trans. Jeremy Moiser. Philadelphia: Westminster Press, 1977.

——, *Cristianità e Cristianizzazione*, trans. Alberta Rizzi. Casale Monferrato: Marietti, 1983.

——, *Sin and Fear. The Emergence of a Western Guilt Culture, 13th–18th Centuries*, trans. Eric Nicholson. New York: St Martin's Press, 1990.

De Maio, Romeo, *Pittura e Controriforma a Napoli*. Rome-Bari: Laterza, 1983.

——, *Religiosità a Napoli, 1656–1799*. Naples: Edizioni Scientifiche Italiane, 1997.

De Martino, Ernesto, *La terra del rimorso: Contributo a una storia religiosa del Sud*. Milan: Il Saggiatore, 1961.

260 BIBLIOGRAPHY

De Rosa, Gabriele, *Vescovi, popolo e magia nel Sud. Ricerche di storia socio-religiosa dal XVII al XIX secolo.* Naples: Guida, 1971.

——, *Chiesa e Religione popolare nel Mezzogiorno.* Rome-Bari: Laterza, 1978.

——, *La vita religiosa nel seicento nel regno.* Naples: Istituto Suor Orsola Benincasa: Edizioni Scientifiche Italiane, 1989.

——, Tullio, Gregory and Vauchez, Andre, eds, *Storia dell'Italia religiosa II: L'età moderna.* Rome-Bari: Laterza, 1994.

Deslandres, Dominique, 'Exemplo aeque ut verbo: The French Jesuits' Missionary World,' in *The Jesuits. Cultures, Sciences, and the Arts, 1540-1773,* ed. John W. O'Malley SJ, Gauvin Alexander Bailey, Steven J. Harris and T. Frank Kennedy SJ. Toronto: University of Toronto Press, 1999.

De Seta, Cesare, *Storia della Città di Napoli dalle origini al Settecento.* Rome-Bari: Laterza, 1973.

Di Constanzo, Angelo, *Storia del Regno di Napoli.* Cosenza: Brenner, 1984.

Di Giacomo, Salvatore, *La Prostituzione in Napoli Nei Secoli XV, XVI, e XVII Documenti Inediti.* Naples, 1899.

Di Nola, Annalisa, 'De Martino's "Critical Ethnocentrism" in South Italy,' in *Italy's 'Southern Question': Orientalism in One Country,* ed. Jane Schneider. New York: Berg, 1998.

Divenuto, Francesco, ed., *Napoli, L'Europa e la Compagnia di Gesù nella 'Cronica' di Groian Francesco Araldo.* Naples: Edizioni Scientifiche Italiane, 1999.

Elias, Norbert, *Power and Civility,* Vol. 2 of *The Civilizing Process,* trans. Edmund Jephcott. New York: Pantheon, 1982.

Elliott, John H., *The Old World and the New, 1492-1650,* Cambridge, UK: Cambridge University Press, 1970.

——, *Spain and its World, 1500-1700. Selected Essays.* New Haven and London: Yale University Press, 1989.

Errichetti, Michele, 'La Chiesa del Gesù nuovo in Napoli. Note storiche,' *Campania Sacra* 5 (1974): 34-75.

'L'Espusione dei Gesuiti dal Regno di Napoli,' in *La Soppressione della Compagnia di Gesù.* Naples: Istituto Pontano, 1992.

Fabbri, Maurizio, 'Il Teatro tragico ispano-italiano dei gesuiti espulsi,' in *I Borbone di Napoli e I Borbone di Spagna,* Vol. 2, ed. Mario Di Pinto. Naples: Guida, 1985.

Faralli, Carla, 'Le missioni dei Gesuiti in Italia (sec. XVI–XVII): Problemi di una Ricerca in Corso,' *Bolletino della Società di Studi Valdesi* 82, No. 138 (1975): 97–116.

Feldhay, Rivka, 'The Cultural Field of Jesuit Science,' in *The Jesuits.*

BIBLIOGRAPHY   261

Culture, Sciences, and the Arts, ed. John W. O'Malley et al. Toronto: University of Toronto Press, 1999.

Ferrante, Lucia, 'Honor Regained: Women in the Casa del Soccorso di San Paolo in Sixteenth-Century Bologna,' in *Sex and Gender in Historical Perspective*, ed. Edward Muir and Guido Ruggiero. Baltimore and London: Johns Hopkins University Press, 1990.

Ferrone, Siro, *Attore mercanti corsari. La Commedia dell'Arte in Europa tra Cinque e Seicento*. Turin: Einaudi, 1993.

Findlen, Paula, *Possessing Nature: Museums, Collecting and Scientific Culture in Early Modern Italy*. Berkeley and Los Angeles: University of California Press, 1994.

Fumaroli, Marc, *Eroi e oratori. Retorica e drammaturgia secentesche*. Bologna: Il Mulino, 1990.

Galasso, Giuseppe, *L'Altra Europa. Per Un'Antropologia storica del Mezzogiorno d'Italia*. Milan: Mondadori, 1982.

——, *Napoli Spagnolo dopo Masaniello. Politica, cultura, società*, 2 vols. Florence: Sansoni, 1982.

——, 'Trends and Problems in Neapolitan History in the Age of Charles V,' in *Good Government in Spanish Naples*, ed. and trans. Antonio Calabria and John Marino. New York: Peter Lang, 1990.

——, *L'Altra Europa. Per Un'Antropologia storica del Mezzogiorno d'Italia*, new revised edn. Lecce: Argo, 1997.

—— and Valerio, Adriana, *Donne e Religione a Napoli: secoli XVI–XVII*. Milan: Angeli, 2001.

—— and Russo, Carla, eds, *L'Archivio Storico Diocesano di Napoli*. Guida: 1978–79.

—— and Russo, Carla, eds, *Per la storia sociale e religiosa del Mezzogiorno d'Italia*, 2 vols. Naples: Guida, 1982.

Gentilcore, David, *From Bishop to Witch. The System of the Sacred in Early Modern Terra d'Otranto*. Manchester, UK: Manchester University Press, 1992.

——, 'Methods and Approaches in the Social History of the Counter-Reformation in Italy,' *Social History* 17, No. 1 (January 1992): 73–98.

——, ' "Adapt Yourselves to the People's Capabilities": Missionary Strategies, Methods and Impact in the Kingdom of Naples, 1600–1800,' *Journal of Ecclesiastical History* 43, No. 2 (April 1994): 269–96.

Ghirelli, Antonio, *Storia di Napoli*. Milan: Einaudi, 1973.

Gilmore, David, *Aggression and Community: Paradoxes of Andalusian Culture*. New Haven: Yale University Press, 1987.

Ginsburg, Paolo, 'Folklore, magia e religione,' in *Storia d'Italia I: I caratteri originali*. Turin: Einaudi, 1972.

262 BIBLIOGRAPHY

____, *The Cheese and the Worms. The Cosmos of a Sixteenth-Century Miller*, trans. John and Anne Tedeschi. Baltimore and London: Johns Hopkins University Press, 1980.

Gioia, Mario, 'Per una biografia di san Bernardino Realino, S.J. (1530–1616): Analisi delle fonti e cronologia critica,' *AHSI* 39 (1970): 3–101.

Gleason, Elisabeth G., 'On the Nature of Sixteenth-Century Italian Evangelism: Scholarship 1953–1978,' *Sixteenth Century Journal* 9, No. 3 (1978): 3–26.

____, *Gasparo Contarini: Venice, Rome, and Reform*. Berkeley and Los Angeles: University of California Press, 1992.

Gramazio, Maria Iris, 'Gesuiti Italiani Missionari in Oriente nel XVI Secolo,' *AHSI* 66 (July–December 1997): 275–300.

Grandieri, Michelino, 'Della moderazione onesta. Introduzione al teatro dei Gesuiti in Italia,' *Storia dell'Arte* 32 (1978): 59–70.

Grendler, Paul, *Schooling in Renaissance Italy. Literacy and Learning 1300–1600*. Baltimore and London: Johns Hopkins University Press, 1989.

Gruzinski, Serge, 'Délires et visions chez les indiens du Mexique,' *Mélanges de l'École française de Rome* (Moyen Age-temps modernes) 86 (1974): 445–80.

____ and Sallmann, J.M., 'Une Source d'ethno-histoire: les vies des "vénerables" dans l'Italie meridionale et le Mexico baroque,' *Mélanges de l'École française de Rome* 88, No. 2 (1976): 789–822.

____, *La colonisation de l'imaginaire. Sociétés indigèn et occidentalisation dans le Mexique espagnol XVI–XVII siècle*. Paris: 1988.

Guerci, Luciano, *La Sposa obbediente. Donna e matrimonio nella discussione dell'Italia del Settecento*. Turin: Terrenia, 1988.

Guidetti, Armando, *Le Missioni Popolari: I Grandi Gesuiti Italiani: Disegno Storico Biografico delle Missioni Popolare dei Gesuiti d'Italia dalle Origini al Concilio Vaticano II*. Milan: Rusconi, 1988.

____, 'Il Metodo Missionario del P. Segneri,' *Appunti di Spiritualità* 31 (1991): 27–45.

Gutiérrez, Ramon, *When Jesus Came, the Corn Mothers Went Away: Marriage, Sexuality, and Power in New Mexico, 1500–1846*. Stanford: Stanford University Press, 1991.

Harline, Craig, 'Official Religion – Popular Religion in Recent Historiography of the Catholic Reformation,' *Archiv für Reformationsgeschichte* 81 (1990): 239–62.

Harris, Steven J., 'Mapping Jesuit Science: The Role of Travel in the Geography of Knowledge,' in *The Jesuits. Cultures, Sciences, and the Arts*, ed. John W. O'Malley et al. Toronto: University of Toronto Press, 1999, 212–40.

BIBLIOGRAPHY

Hartnoll, Phyllis, ed. *The Oxford Companion to the Theatre*, 3rd edn. London: Oxford University Press, 1967.

Hills, Helen, 'Cities and Virgins: Female aristocratic convents in early modern Naples and Palermo,' *Oxford Art Journal* 22, No. 1 (1999): 29–54.

Hollis, Christopher, *The History of the Jesuits*. London: Weidenfield and Nicolson, 1968.

Hudon, William V., 'Religion and Society in Early Modern Italy – Old Questions, New Insights,' *American Historical Review* 101, No. 3 (June 1996): 783–804.

Iapelli SJ, Filippo, 'Gesuiti e Seicento napoletano,' *Societas* 34 (1985): 23–5.; 73–90; 110–20.

——, 'Gesuiti e Barocco fra Napoli, Sardegna, e Roma,' *Societas* 38 (1989): 112–24.

——, 'Gesuiti a Nola, 1558–1767,' *Societas* 41 (1992): 20–35.

——, 'Missioni di San Francesco De Geronimo in Campania in un Inedito di Di Francesco D'Aria,' *Campania Sacra* 32 (2001): 311–24.

Illibato, Antonio, ed., *Il 'Liber Visitationis' di Francesco Carafa Nella Diocesi di Napoli (1542–1543)*. Rome: Edizioni di Storia e Letteratura, 1983.

Imbruglia, Girolamo, *L'Invenzione del Paraguay. Studio sull'idea di comunità tra Seicento e Settecento*. Naples: Bibliopolis, 1983.

——, 'Dalle storie dei santi alla storia naturale della religione. L'idea moderna di superstizione,' *Rivista Storica Italiana* 101 (1989): 35–84.

——, 'Enlightenment in Eighteenth-Century Naples,' in *Naples in the Eighteenth Century. The Birth and Death of a Nation State*, ed. Girolamo Imbruglia. Cambridge, UK: Cambridge University Press, 2000.

Jed, Stephanie, *Chaste Thinking. The Rape of Lucretia and the Birth of Humanism*. Bloomington, IN: Indiana University Press, 1989.

Jedin, Hubert, et al., *History of the Church, Vol. V: Reformation and Counter Reformation*, trans. Anselm Biggs and Peter W. Becker. New York: The Seabury Press, 1980.

Jordan, Constance, *Renaissance Feminism. Literary Texts and Political Models*. Ithaca: Cornell University Press, 1990.

Kadulska, Irene, 'La Tradition de la Commedia Dell'Arte dans le Théâtre Jésuite du XVIII° Siècle,' in *Le Théâtre dans l'Europe des Lumières*. Wroclaw: University of Wroclaw Press, 1985.

Lacroutre, Jean, *Jesuits: A Multibiography*, trans. Jeremy Leggatt. Washington, DC: Counterpoint, 1995.

Lakshminarasimha, K.A., *Debunking a Myth, or the re-discovery of St. Francis Xavier: The true story of his life and deeds*. Bombay: Dikshitji Maharaj, 1964

264 BIBLIOGRAPHY

Lazar, Lance, 'The First Jesuit Confraternities and Marginalized Groups in Sixteenth-Century Rome,' in *The Politics of Ritual Kinship. Confraternities and Social Order in Early Modern Italy*, ed. Nicholas Terpstra. Cambridge, UK: Cambridge University Press, 2000.

Leone, Nino, *Napoli ai Tempi di Masaniello*. Milan: Biblioteca Universale Rizzoli, 1994.

Le Roy Ladurie, Emmanuel, *Carnival in Romans*, trans. Mary Feeney. New York: George Braziller, 1980.

Lewis SJ, Mark A., ' "Preachers of Sound Doctrine:" The Social Impact of the Jesuit College of Naples, 1552–1600,' PhD diss., University of Toronto, 1995.

——, 'The Development of Jesuit Confraternities in the Kingdom of Naples in the Sixteenth and Seventeenth Centuries,' in *The Politics of Ritual Kinship. Confraternities and Social Order in Early Modern Italy*, ed. Nicholas Terpstra. Cambridge, UK: Cambridge University Press, 2000.

—— and Selwyn, Jennifer D., 'Jesuit Activity in Southern Italy during the Generalate of Everard Mercurian,' in *The Mercurian Project: Forming a Jesuit Culture, 1572–1580*, ed. Thomas M. McCoog SJ. St Louis and Rome: The Jesuit Historical Insitute (forthcoming).

Liebowitz, Ruth P., 'Virgins in the Service of Christ: The Dispute Over an Active Apostolate for Women During the Counter-Reformation,' in *Women of the Spirit: Female Leadership in the Jewish and Christian Traditions*, ed. Rosemary Ruether and Eleanor McLaughlin. New York: Simon and Schuster, 1979.

Lopez, Pasquale, *Riforma Cattolica e vita religiosa e culturale a Napoli: dalle fine del Cinquecento ai primi anni del settecento*. Naples: Istituto Editoriale del Mezzogiorno, 1964.

——, 'Le confraternite laicali in Italia e la Riforma cattolica,' *Rivista di studi salernitani* 2 (1969): 152–238.

——, *Clero, Eresia e magia nella Napoli del Viceregno*. Naples: Adriano Gallina, 1984.

Maccarone, M., et al., eds, *Problemi di Vita Religiosa in Italia nel Cinquecento. Atti del Convegnodi Storia della Chiesa in Italia (Bologna, 2–6 Sett., 1958)*. Padua: Editrice Antenore, 1960.

Magli, Ida, *Gli uomini della penitenza. Lineamenti antropologici del medioevo italiano*. Milan: Garzanti, 1977.

Majorana, Bernadette, 'Un *Gemino Valor*: mestiere e virtù dei comici dell'arte nel primo Seicento,' *Medievo e Rinascimento* 3 (1992): 173–93.

——, 'Lo pseudo-Segneri e il Teatro celeste: due tracce secentesche,' *Teatro e Storia* 9 (1994): 357–88.

Manfredi, Clelia, *Il Cardinale Ascanio Filomarino, Arcivescovo di*

BIBLIOGRAPHY

Napoli nella Rivoluzione di Masaniello. Naples: Istituto della Stampa, 1950.

Manfredi, Rosario, 'Le "Descrittioni" di Napoli (1450–1692). Appunti per una Ricerca Bibliografica,' *Rendiconti della Accademia di Archeologia Lettere e Belle Arti* 63 (1992): 63–108.

Marciani, Corrado, 'Il Commercio degli schiavi alle fiere di Lanciano nel sec. XVI,' *Archivio Storico per le province napoletane* 41 (1961): 269–82.

Marino, John, *Pastoral Economics in the Kingdom of Naples*. Baltimore: Johns Hopkins University Press, 1988.

Marotti, Ferruccio and Romei, Giovanna, eds, *La Commedia dell'Arte e la società barocca. La professione del teatro*. Rome: Bulzoni, 1991.

Marranzini, Alfredo, 'I Gesuiti Bobadilla, Croce, Xavierre e Rodriguez tra I Valdesi di Calabria,' *Rivista Storica Calabrese* 4 (1983): 393–420.

Martin, A. Lynn, *The Jesuit Mind: the Mentality of an Elite in Early Modern France*. Ithaca: Cornell University Press, 1988.

Mayer, Thomas F., *Reginald Pole. Prince and Prophet*. Cambridge, UK: Cambridge University Press, 2000.

—— and Woolf, D.R., eds, *The Rhetorics of Life-Writing in Early Modern Europe. Forms of Biography from Cassandra Fedele to Louis XIV*. Ann Arbor: University of Michigan Press, 1995.

Mazzoleni, Joli, ed., *Aspetti della Riforma Cattolica e Del Concilio di Trento a Napoli. Mostra Documentaria*. Naples: L'Arte Tipografica Napoli, 1966.

McCabe SJ, William H., *An Introduction to Jesuit Theater*, ed. Louis J. Oldani SJ. St Louis: The Institute of Jesuit Historical Sources, 1983.

McGinness, Frederick J., *Right Thinking and Sacred Oratory in Counter-Reformation Rome*. Princeton, NJ: Princeton University Press, 1995.

Meikeljohn, Norman, *La Iglesia y los Lupaqas de Chucuito durante la Colonia*. Cuzco: Instituto de Estudios Aymaras, 1988.

Melossi, Dario and Pavarini, Massimo, *The Prison and the Factory. Origins of the Penitentiary System*, trans. Glynis Cousins. London: The Macmillan Press, 1981.

Mendella, Michelangelo, *Il Moto Napoletano del 1585 e il Delicto Storace*. Naples: Giannini, 1967.

Meseguer Fernández, Juan, 'Contenido misionológico de la *Obediencia* e *Instrucción* de Fray Francisco de los Angeles a los doce apóstoles de México,' *The Americas* 11 (1955): 473–500.

Mezzadri, Luigi, 'Le missioni popolari della congregazione della missione nello stato della Chiesa (1642–1700),' *Rivista di storia della Chiesa in Italia* 33 (1979): 12–44.

266 BIBLIOGRAPHY

Miele, Michele, *La Riforma Domenicana a Napoli nel periodo post-Tridentino*. Rome: S. Sabina, 1963.

——, 'Sisto V e la riforma dei monasteri femminili di Napoli,' *Campania Sacra* 21 (1990): 123–209.

Mitchell, David, *The Jesuits. A History*. London: MacDonald, 1980.

Moe, Nelson, *The View from Vesuvius. Italian Culture and the Southern Question*. Berkeley and Los Angeles: University of California Press, 2002.

Morgan, Ronald J., 'Jesuit confessors, African slaves and the practice of confession in seventeenth-century Cartagena,' in *Penitence in the Age of Reformations*, eds Katharine Jackson Lualdi and Anne T. Thayer. Burlington, VT: Ashgate, 2000, 222–39.

Mormando, Franco, *The Preacher's Demons: Bernardino of Siena and the Social Underworld of Early Renaissance Italy*. Chicago: University of Chicago Press, 1999.

Mozzillo, Atanasio, *Passaggio a Mezzogiorno. Napoli e il Sud nell'immaginario barocco e illuminista europea*. Milan: Leonardo, 1993.

Muir, Edward, *Civic Ritual in Renaissance Venice*. Princeton, NJ: Princeton University Press, 1981.

——, 'The Virgin on the street corner: the place of the sacred in Italian cities,' in *Religion and Culture in the Renaissance and Reformation*, ed. Steven Ozment. Sixteenth Century Essays and Studies, XI. Kirksville, MO: Sixteenth Century Journal Publishers, 1989.

——, *Mad Blood Stirring. Vendetta and Factions in Friuli during the Renaissance*. Baltimore and London: Johns Hopkins University Press, 1993.

Musi, Aurelio, *La Rivolta di Masaniello nella scena politica barocca*. Naples: Guida, 1989.

Nalle, Sara, *God in La Mancha: Religious Reform and the People of Cuenca, 1500–1650*. Baltimore: Johns Hopkins University Press, 1992.

Nardi, Gennaro, 'Nuove Ricerche sulle istituzioni napoletane a favore degli schiavi. La Congregazione degli Schiavi dei PP. Gesuiti,' *Asprenas* 14 (1967): 294–313.

Nicolini, Fausto, *Sulla vita civile, letteraria e religiosa napoletana alla fine del Seicento. Note in margine a un libro del Burnet con nuove notizie e documenti inediti sul 'Quietismo.'* Naples, 1929.

Noel, Charles C., 'Missionary Preachers in Spain: Teaching Social Virtue in the Eighteenth Century,' *American Historical Review* 90, No. 4 (October 1985): 866–92.

Novi Chavarria, Elisa, 'L'Attività missionaria dei Gesuiti nel Mezzogiorno d'Italia tra XVI e XVII Secolo,' in *Per la Storia Sociale e*

BIBLIOGRAPHY 267

Religiosa del Mezzogiorno d'Italia tra XVI e XVII, Vol. I, ed. Giuseppe Galasso and Carla Russo. Naples: Guida, 1982.

———, 'Ideologia e comportamenti familiari nei predicatori italiani tra Cinque e Settecento. Tematiche e modelli,' *Rivista Storica Italiana* 100, No. 3 (December 1988): 679–723.

———, 'Le Missioni dei Gesuiti in Calabria in età moderna,' in *I Gesuiti e la Calabria. Atti del convegno, Reggio Calabria, 27–28 febbraio 1991*, ed. Vincenzo Sibilio. Reggio Calabria: Laruffa, 1992.

———, *Il Governo delle Anime. Azione pastorale, predicazioni e missioni nel Mezzogiorno d'Italia. Secoli XVI–XVIII.* Naples: Editoriale Scientifica, 2001.

Oldani SJ, L.J. and Bredeck SJ, M.J., 'Jesuit Theater in Italy: A Bibliography,' *AHSI* 66, no. 131 (January–June 1997): 185–235.

Olin, John. C., ed., *The Catholic Reformation: Savonarola to Ignatius Loyola. Reform in the Church 1495–1540.* New York: Harper & Row, 1969.

O'Malley SJ, John W., 'To Travel to Any Part of the World: Jerónimo Nadal and the Jesuit Vocation,' *Studies in the Spirituality of Jesuits* 16, No. 2, 1984.

———, ed., *Catholicism in Early Modern History. A Guide to Research.* St Louis: Center for Reformation Research, 1988.

———, 'Was Ignatius Loyola a Church Reformer? How to Look at Early Modern Italy – Old Questions New Insights,' *Catholic Historical Review* 77 (1991): 177–93.

———, *The First Jesuits.* Cambridge, MA: Harvard University Press, 1993.

———, 'The Society of Jesus,' in *Religious Orders of the Catholic Reformation: Essays in Honor of John C. Olin on His Seventy-Fifth Birthday*, ed. Richard L. De Molen. New York: Fordham University Press, 1994.

———, Bailey, Gauvin Alexander, Harris, Steven J. and Kennedy SJ, T. Frank eds, *The Jesuits. Cultures, Sciences, and the Arts, 1540–1773.* Toronto: University of Toronto Press, 1999.

———, *Trent and All That.* Cambridge, MA: Harvard University Press, 1999.

Orlandi, Giuseppe, 'L.A. Muratori e le Missioni di P. Segneri, Jr.,' *Spicilegium Historicum Congregationis Ssmi Redemptoris* 20 (1972): 158–294.

———, 'Missioni Parrocchiali e Drammatica Popolare,' *Spicilegium Historicum Congregationis Ssmi Redemptoris* 22, No. 2 (1974): 313–46.

———, 'S. Alfonso Maria de Liguori e l'ambiente missionario napoletano nel settecento: La Compagnia di Gesù,' *Spicilegium Historicum Congregationis Ssmi Redemptoris* 38 (1990): 5–195.

———, 'La Missione popolare in età moderna,' in *Storia dell'Italia Reli-*

268 BIBLIOGRAPHY

giosa II: L'Età Moderna. ed. Gabriele De Rosa, Tullio Gregory and Andre Vauchez. Rome-Bari: Laterza, 1994.

Osborne, Kenan B., *Reconciliation and Justification. The Sacrament and its Theology*. New York: Paulist Press, 1990.

Padberg, John W., O'Keefe, Martin D. and McCarthy, John L., eds, *For Matters of Greater Moment. The First Thirty General Congregations. A Brief History and a Translation of the Decrees*. St Louis: Institute of Jesuit Sources, 1994.

Pagden, Anthony, *The Fall of Natural Man. The American Indian and the Origins of Comparative Ethnology*. Cambridge, UK: Cambridge University Press, 1982.

Paglia, Vincenzo. *'La Pietà dei Carcerati.' Confraternite e Società a Roma nei Secoli XVI–XVII*. Rome: Edizioni di Storia e Letteratura, 1980.

Pane, Roberto, ed., *Seicento Napoletano. Arte, costume e ambiente*. Milan: Edizioni di comunità, 1984.

Parascandolo, L., *Memorie storiche critiche diplomatiche della chiesa di Napoli*. Naples, 1851.

Parente, Ulderico, 'Alfonso Salmerón a Napoli (1551–1585),' *Campania Sacra* 20 (1989): 14–51.

_____, 'Nicolò Bobadilla e gli esordi della Compagnia di Gesù in Calabria,' in *I Gesuiti e la Calabria*, ed. Vincenzo Sibilio. Reggio Calabria: Laruffa, 1992.

Pate, Dennis Edmond, 'Jerónimo Nadal and the Early Development of the Society of Jesus, 1545–1573,' PhD diss., University of California, Los Angeles, 1980.

Pelizzari, Maria Rosaria, 'Dalle Descrizioni per I Forestieri Alle Guide Turistiche: Cinque Secoli di Napoli in Vetrina,' *Campania Sacra* 32 (2001): 429–57.

Petraccone, Claudia, *Napoli dal '500 al '800: problemi di storia demografica e sociale*. Naples: Guida, 1974.

_____, *Napoli moderna e contemporanea*. Naples: Guida, 1981.

Phelan, John Leddy, *The Millenial Kingdom of the Franciscans in New Spain*, 2nd edn. Berkeley and Los Angeles: University of California Press, 1970.

Picón-Salas, Mariano, *Pedro Claver, el Santo de los Esclavos*. Madrid: Ediciones de la Revista de Occidente, 1969.

Polecritti, Cynthia, *Preaching Peace in Renaissance Italy: San Bernardino of Siena and his Audience*. Washington, DC: Catholic University Press, 2000.

Porter, Jeanne Chenault, ed., *Baroque Naples. A Documentary History*. New York: Italica Press, 2000.

BIBLIOGRAPHY   269

Poska, Allyson. *Regulating the People. The Catholic Reformation in Seventeenth-Century Spain.* Leiden: Brill, 1998.

Prodi, Paolo and Penuti, Carla, eds, *Disciplina dell'anima disciplina del corpo e disciplina della società tra medioevo ed età moderna.* Bologna: Il Mulino, 1988.

Prosperi, Adriano, 'America e Apocalisse. Note sulla "Conquista Spirituale" del Nuovo Mondo,' *Critica Storia* 13, No. 1 (March 1976): 1–61.

———, 'Intellettuali e Chiesa all'inizio dell'età moderna,' *Storia d'Italia. Annali IV: Intellettuali e Potere.* Turin: Einaudi, 1981.

———, ' "Otras Indias": Missionari della Controriforma tra Contadini e Selvaggi,' in *Scienze, Credenze, Occulte e Livelli di Cultura.* Florence: Olschki, 1982.

———, 'Il Missionario,' in *L'Uomo Barocco*, ed. Rosario Villari. Rome-Bari: Laterza, 1991.

———, 'L'Europa Cristiana e il Mondo: Alle Origini dell'Idea di Missione,' *Dimensioni e Problemi della ricerca storica* 2 (1992): 189–220.

———, 'Riforma Cattolica, controriforma, disciplinato sociale,' in *Storia dell'Italia religiosa II: L'età moderna*, ed. Gabriele De Rosa, Tullio Gregory and Andre Vauchez. Rome-Bari: Laterza, 1994.

———, 'La Chiesa Tridentina e il Teatro: Strategie di Controllo del Secondo '500,' in *I Gesuiti e i Primordi del Teatro Barocco*, ed. Maria Chiabò and Federico Doglio. Rome: Centro Studi Sul Teatro Medioevale e Rinascimenti, 1995.

———, *Tribunali della Coscienza. Inquisitori, confessori, missionari.* Turin: Einaudi, 1996.

Pullan, Brian, *Rich and Poor in Renaissance Venice: The Social Institutions of a Catholic State to 1620.* Cambridge, MA: Harvard University Press, 1971.

———, 'Support and Redeem: Charity and Poor Relief in Italian Cities from the Fourteenth to the Seventeenth Century,' *Continuity and Change* 3 (1988): 177–208.

Ranft, Patricia, 'A Key to Counter Reformation Women's Activism: The Confessor-Spiritual Director,' *Journal of Feminist Studies of Religion* 10, No. 2 (Fall 1994): 7–26.

Ricard, Robert, *The Spiritual Conquest of Mexico. An Essay on the Apostolate and the Evangelizing Method of the Mendicant Orders in New Spain, 1523–1572*, trans. Lesley Byrd Simpson. Berkeley and Los Angeles: University of California Press, 1966.

Rienzo, Maria Gabriella, 'Il processo di cristianizzazione e le missioni popolari nel Mezzogiorno. Aspetti istituzionale e socio-religiosi,' in

270 BIBLIOGRAPHY

Per la Storia Sociale e Religiosa del Mezzogiorno d'Italia, Vol. 1, ed. Giuseppe Galasso and Carla Russo. Naples: Guida, 1982.

Rizzi, Armido, ed., 'José de Acosta. *De Procuranda indorum salute. L'evangelizzazione degli Indios: Problemi e metodi,' Futuro dell'Uomo* (Special Issue: America Latina: 1492–1992. Quattro Voci del 1500) 29, No. 2 (1992): 69–88.

Romano, Antonio, *Memorie di Tommaso Aniello d'Amalfi Detto Masaniello. Responsibilità della Chiesa nella Sconfitta Della Rivoluzione Napoletana e Guerra d'Independenza Antispagnola, 1647–48*. Naples: Edizioni del Delfino, 1990.

Romeo, Giovanni, *Aspettando il Boia. Condannati a morte, confortatori e inquisitori nella Napoli della Controriforma*. Florence: Sansoni, 1993.

Romeo, Rosario, *Le Scoperte Americane nella Coscienza Italiana del Cinquecento*. Milan-Naples: R. Ricciardi, 1971.

Roper, Lyndal, *The Holy Household. Women and Morals in Reformation Augsburg*. Oxford: Clarendon, 1989.

Rosa, Mario, 'Per la storia della vita religiosa e della Chiesa in Italia tra il '500 e il '600: studi ricenti e questioni di metodo,' *Quaderni Storici* 15 (1970): 673–758.

——, *Religione e Società nel Mezzogiorno tra Cinque e Seicento*. Bari: Donato, 1976.

——, 'L'Onda che ritorna: Interno ed esterno Sacro nella Napoli del '600,' in *Luoghi Sacri e Spazi della Santità*, ed. Sofia Boesch Gajano and Lucetta Scaraffia. Turin: Rosenberg and Sellier, 1990.

Roscioni, Gian Carlo, *Il Desiderio delle Indie. Storie, sogni e fughe di giovani gesuiti italiani*. Milan: Einaudi, 2001.

Ross, Andrew C., *A Vision Betrayed: The Jesuits in Japan and China, 1542–1742*. Edinburgh: Edinburgh University Press, 1994.

Rurale, Flavio, 'Carlo Borromeo and the Society of Jesus in the 1570s,' in *The Mercurian Project: Forming a Jesuit Culture, 1572–1580*, ed. Thomas M. McCoog, SJ, St Louis and Rome: Jesuit Historical Institute, 2004.

Rusconi, Roberto, 'Predicatori e predicazione,' in *Storia d'Italia. Annali IV: Intellettuali e potere*. Turin: Einaudi, 1981.

——, *Predicazione e Vita Religiosa nella Società Italiana da Carlo Magno alla Controriforma*. Turin: Loescher, 1981.

——, 'Gli ordini maschili dalla Controriforma alle soppressioni settecentesche. Cultura, predicazione, missioni,' in *Clero e società nell'Italia moderna*, ed. Mario Rosa. Rome-Bari: Laterza, 1992.

Russo, Carla, *I Monasteri feminili di clausura a Napoli nel secolo XVII*. Naples: Istituto di storia medioevale e moderna, 1970.

BIBLIOGRAPHY 271

——, *Società, Chiesa e vita religiosa nell'Ancien Regime*. Naples: Guida, 1976.

——, 'La religiosità popolare nell'età moderna. Problemi di prospettive,' *Prospettive Settanta* 1 (1979): 345–79.

——, *Chiesa e comunità nella diocesi di Napoli tra Cinque e Settecento*. Naples: Guida, 1984.

Ryan, Michael T., 'Assimilating New Worlds in the Sixteenth and Seventeenth Centuries,' *Comparative Studies in Society and History* 23 (1981): 519–38.

Ryder, Alan, *The Kingdom of Naples Under Alfonso the Magnanimous. The Making of a Modern State*. Oxford: Clarendon Press, 1976.

Salvemini, Biagio, 'The Arrogance of the Market: The Economy of the Kingdom Between the Mediterranean and Europe,' in *Naples in the Eighteenth Century. The Birth and Death of a Nation State*, ed. Girolamo Imbruglia. Cambridge, UK: Cambridge University Press, 2000.

Scaduto SJ, Mario, 'Tra Inquisitori e riformati,' *Archivum Historicum Societatis Iesu* 15 (1946): 1–76.

——, *Catalogo dei Gesuiti D'Italia, 1540–1565*. Rome: Institutum Historicum Societatis Iesu, 1968.

——, *L'Epoca di Giacamo Laínez, 1556–1565*, 2 vols. Rome: La Civiltà Cattolica, 1974.

——, *L'Opera di Francesco Borgia, 1565–1572*. Rome: La Civiltà Cattolica, 1992.

Scagione, Aldo, *The Liberal Arts and the Jesuit College System*. Amsterdam and Philadelphia: Benjamins, 1986.

Schutte, Anne Jacobson, 'Periodization of Sixteenth-Century Italian Religious History: The Post-Cantimori Paradigm Shift,' *The Journal of Modern History* 61 (1989): 269–84.

Schütte SJ, Josef Franz, *Valignano's Mission Principles for Japan*, trans. John J. Coyne SJ. St Louis: The Institute for Jesuit Sources, 1980.

Selwyn, Jennifer D., ' "Procuring in the Common People these Better Behaviors": The Jesuits' Civilizing Mission in Early Modern Naples, 1550–1620,' *Radical History Review*, 67 (Winter 1997): 4–34.

——, 'Schools of Mortification: Theatricality and the Role of Penitential Practice in the Jesuits' Popular Missions,' in *Penitence in the Age of Reformations*, ed. Katharine Jackson Lualdi and Anne T. Thayer. St Andrews Studies in Reformation History. Burlington, VT and Aldershot, UK: Ashgate, 2000.

——, 'Angels of Peace: The Social Drama of Reconciliation in the Jesuit Missions in Southern Italy,' in *Beyond Florence: The Contours of Medieval and Early Modern Italy*, ed. Paula Findlen, Michelle Fon-

272 BIBLIOGRAPHY

taine and Duane Osheim. Stanford, CA: Stanford University Press, 2003.

Simioni, Attilio, 'Per la Storia del teatro gesuitico in Italia nel secolo XVIII,' *Rassegna critica della letteratura italiana* 12 (1907): 145–62.

Simonut, Noe, *Metodo d'evangelizzazione dei francescani tra musulmani e mongoli nei secoli XIII–XIV*. Milan: Pontificio Istituto Missioni Estere, 1947.

Sodano, Giulio, 'Miracoli e ordini religiosi nel Mezzogiorno d'Italia (XVI–XVIII secolo),' *Archivio Storico per le Province Napoletane* 105 (1987): 293–414.

_____, *Modelli e selezione del santo moderno: periferia napoletana e centro romano*. Naples: Liguori, 2002.

Sommervogel, Carlos, *Bibliothèque de la Compagnie de Jésus*, 11 vols. Brussels: O. Schepens, and Paris: A. Picard, 1890–1932.

Spence, Jonathan D., *The Memory Palace of Matteo Ricci*. New York: Penguin Books, 1984.

Sposato, Pasquale, *Aspetti e figure della riforma cattolica-tridentina in Calabria*. Naples: F. Fiorentino, 1964.

Strazzullo, Franco, *Edilizia e Urbanistica a Napoli dal '500 al '700*. Naples: Arte Tipografica, 1995.

Symonds, John Addington, *The Catholic Reaction*, 2 vols. London, 1886.

Tacchi Venturi SJ, Pietro, *Storia della Compagnia di Gesù in Italia*, 3 vols. Rome: La Civiltà Cattolica, 1930–1950.

Tanturri, Alberto, 'Sinodi a Chieti alla fine del secolo XVI,' *Campania Sacra* 28 (1997): 321–45.

Taviani, Ferdinando and Schino, Mirella, *Il Segreto della Commedia dell'Arte. La Memoria delle compagnie italiane del XVI, XVII, e XVIII secolo*. Florence: Casa Usher, 1982.

Taylor, Larissa, *Soldiers of Christ: Preaching in Late Medieval and Reformation France*. New York and Oxford: Oxford University Press, 1992.

Terpstra, Nicholas, *Lay Confraternities and Civic Religion in Renaissance Bologna*. Cambridge, UK: Cambridge University Press, 1995.

Thompson, E.P., 'The Moral Economy of the English Crowd in the Eighteenth Century,' in *Customs in Common: Studies in Traditional Popular Culture*. New York: New Press, 1991.

Toppi, Francesco Saverio, *Maria Lorenza Longo. Donna della Napoli del '500*. Pompeii: Pontifico Santuario, 1997.

Torre, Angelo, 'Faide, fazioni e partiti, ovvero le ridefinizione della politica nei feudi imperiali della Longhe tra Sei e Settecento,' *Quaderni Storici* 63 (1986): 775–810.

BIBLIOGRAPHY

Tortora, Alfonso, *Congregazioni sacerdotali e strategia missionaria dei gesuiti nel Cinquecento leccese*. Naples: F. Fiorentino, 1988.

Trexler, Richard, *Public Life in Renaissance Florence*. New York: Academic Press, 1980.

——, 'We Think, They Act: Clerical Readings of Missionary Theater,' in *Understanding Popular Culture. Europe from the Middle Ages to the Nineteenth Century*, ed. Steven L. Kaplan. Berlin and New York: Mouton, 1984.

Turtas, Raimondo, 'Missioni popolari in Sardegna tra '500 e '600,' *Rivista di Storia della Chiesa in Italia* 44 (1990): 369–412.

Venturi, Franco, *La Chiesa e la Repubblica dentro i loro limiti*, Vol. 2 of *Settecento Riformatore*. Turin: Einaudi, 1976.

——, *Dal Muratori a Beccaria*, Vol. 1 of *Settecento Riformatore*, 2nd edn. Turin: Einaudi, 1969; 1998.

Villani, Pasquale, 'La Visita Apostolica di Tommaso Orfini nel Regno di Napoli (1566–1568): Documenti per la Storia dell'Applicazione del Concilio di Trento,' *Annuario dell'Istituto Storico Italiano per l'età moderna e contemporanea* 8 (1956): 5–79.

——, Veneruso, Danilo and Bettoni, Margherita, eds, *Nunziature di Napoli (1570–1591)*, 3 vols. Rome: Istituto Storico per l'età moderna e contemporanea, 1962–70.

Villari, Rosario, 'Naples: The Insurrection of 1585,' in *The Late Italian Renaissance*, ed. Eric Cochrane. New York: Harper and Row, 1970.

——, *Elogio della dissimulazione. La lotta politica nel Seicento*. Rome-Bari: Laterza, 1987.

——, *The Revolt of Naples*, trans. James Newell. Cambridge, UK: Polity Press, 1993.

Vismara Chiappa, Paola, 'L'abolizione delle missioni urbane dei gesuiti a Milano (1767),' *Nuova Rivista Storica* 62 (1978): 549–71.

Watts, Pauline Moffitt, 'Prophecy and Discovery: On the Spiritual Origins of Christopher Columbus's "Enterprise of the Indies,"' *American Historical Review* 90, No. 1 (February 1985): 73–102.

——, 'Hieroglyphs of Conversion: Alien Discourses in Diego Valadés's *Rhetorica Christiana, Memorie Domenicane* 22 (1991): 405–33.

——, 'Languages of Gesture in Sixteenth-Century Mexico,' in *Reframing the Renaissance: Visual Culture in Europe and Latin America*, ed. Claire Farago. New Haven: Yale University Press, 1995.

Webb, Diane, 'Penitence and Peace-making in City and Contado: The Bianchi of 1399,' in *Studies in Church History: The Church in Town and Countryside*, ed. Derek Baker. Oxford: Oxford University Press, 1979.

Zagorin, Perez, *Ways of Lying. Dissimulation, Persecution, and Con-*

274 BIBLIOGRAPHY

formity in Early Modern Europe. Cambridge, MA: Harvard University Press, 1990.

Zanlonghi, Giovanna, *Teatri di Formazione. Actio, parola e immagine nella scena gesuitica del Sei-Settecento a Milano*. Milan: Vita e Pensiero, 2002.

Zarri, Gabriella, *Finzione e santità tra medioevo ed età moderna*. Turin: Rosenberg & Sellier, 1991.

———, 'From Prophecy to Discipline 1450–1650,' in *Women and Faith. Catholic Religious Life in Italy from Late Antiquity to the Present*, ed. Lucetta Scaraffia and Gabriella Zarri. Cambridge, MA: Harvard University Press, 1999.

———, *Recinti: donne, clausura e matrimonio nella prima età moderna*. Bologna: Il Mulino, 2000.

Zupanov, Ines G., *Disputed Mission: Jesuit Experiments and brahmanical knowledge in seventeenth-century India*. Oxford: Oxford University Press, 1999.

Index

Abruzzi, 42, 62, 228
Accommodation, 18, 51, 65, 78, 91–2, 94, 110, 118, 120, 126–7, 243, 247
Acosta, José de, 17, 18, 63, 84, 96, 103, 105, 108, 117, 119, 121–37, 140, 141, 243
Acquaviva, Claudio, 62–3, 75, 92, 99, 100, 110, 117, 140, 142, 149
Africa, 89, 90, 120
Africans, 73, 89, 114, 117
Alcalá, 121, 122, 169
Alexander the Great, 79
Alexander VI (Pope), 79
Alfonso V (King of Naples), 24
Almagro, Diego de, 121
Amerindians, 63, 84, 89, 91, 117, 118, 119, 122, 125, 126, 130, 132, 133, 135, 229
Angevin Kingdom, 23–4
Aniello, Tommaso (*see also* Masaniello), 196
Aquinas, Thomas, 89
Araldo, Giovan Francesco, 13, 14, 55–9, 67, 74, 83, 86
Augustine (of Hippo), 222
Aversa, 113, 115, 116, 117, 137, 183, 184, 185

Baldinucci, Antonio, 146, 164, 166, 190, 191
Bandini, Francesco, 24
Bari, 46, 151, 152, 222, 234, 237
Barone, Antonio, 71, 74, 91
Basilicata, 46, 129
Bitonto, 151, 152, 159, 174, 234
Bobadilla, Nicolás, 42, 57, 106
Boccaccio, Giovanni, 23–4
Borja (Borgia), Francisco, 61, 122
Borja (Borgia), Gaspar (Cardinal), (*see also* Viceroys of Naples), 183
Borja (Borgia), Rodrigo (Pope Alexander VI), 79
Brazil, 1, 120, 128, 129

Brindisi, 46, 47, 48
Bursati, Lucretio, 175

Calabria, 42, 46, 70, 96, 129
Capaccio, Giulio Cesare, 26–7, 35, 41, 129, 175–6
Capua, 113, 168, 202
Capua, Annibale di (Archibishop), 51
Capuchins, 72, 170
Caracciolo, Innico, 52
Carafa, Alfonso, 45
Carafa, Francesco (Archbishop), 45
Carafa, Gian Pietro (Pope Paul IV), 69
Carafa, Vincenzo, 62, 142
Carnival 93, 216, 217, 218, 234
Castelli, Pierantonio, 104
catasti, catasto (*see also* tax records), 36
Cava, 154
Charles V, Holy Roman Emperor, 30, 56, 132
China, 1, 99–101, 107, 133
Cicala, Antonio, 102
circular letters, 108, 141, 145
Citarelli, Stefano, 87
civilizing mission (*see also* civilizing project), 1, 2, 3, 6, 7, 17, 18, 19, 38, 52, 56, 62, 70, 73, 76, 78, 84, 88, 92, 93, 95, 97, 98, 110, 112, 117, 118, 120, 121, 125, 132, 133, 137, 140, 141, 149, 155, 167, 180, 185, 190, 200, 205, 208, 230, 240, 241, 242, 243, 247, 248
civilizing project (*see also* civilizing mission) 19, 87, 235, 247, 249
Claver, Pedro, 115
Clement VI (Pope), 238
Cocollo, Giuseppe, 104, 136
Collective identity, 1, 7, 18, 56, 103, 137, 139, 180
Colleges, 14, 18, 38, 57, 58, 59, 70, 120, 121, 143, 144, 145, 151, 187, 211, 214, 217

276 INDEX

commedia dell'arte, 19, 215, 219, 220, 223
Confraternities, 67, 74, 76, 81, 83, 191, 234
Congregation of the Epiphany, 90, 92
Conversano, 47
Conversion, 3, 13, 17, 42, 62, 69, 76, 81, 89, 90, 91, 92, 107, 108, 113, 117, 119, 120, 128, 132, 133, 134, 135, 173, 174, 188, 192, 193, 207, 208, 213, 215, 228, 229, 231, 233, 248
Council of Trent, 44, 46, 50, 61, 161, 162, 187
Criminality, 22, 41, 42, 44, 53, 221
Croce, Benedetto, 8, 9, 22, 25
Croilo, Cesare, 146, 150, 157, 167
Cusola, Antonio, 129

D'Argenzio, Agostino, 87
D'Orta, Carlo, 112, 113, 114, 137, 183
Da Ponte, Bernardo, 153, 156, 162
Daniello, Bernardino, 25
De Geronimo (a.k.a. Di Girolamo), Francesco, 190, 192, 203, 204, 209, 212, 225, 230
Di Cordova e Di Aguilar, Consalvo Ferdinando, (*see also* Viceroys of Naples), 80
Di Elia, Giovanni Battista, 151, 174
Di Ribera, (Don) Parafan, (*see also* Viceroys of Naples), 41
Díaz, Bernal, 98
Dissimulation, 163
Dominicans, 18, 63, 70, 119
Duke of Ossuna, 74, 75

Economic conditions, 40, 73
Elites, 29, 30, 35, 37, 38, 39, 40, 52, 60, 67, 75, 78, 131, 141, 188, 191, 200, 234, 245, 248, 249
Epidemics, 32, 34, 186, 244, 245

Fabi, Fabio, 143, 146, 153, 162, 167
Famine, 32, 33, 34, 201, 245
Ferdinand (King of Aragon), 30, 80, 98
Ferrante, 24
Filomarino, Ascanio (Archbishop), 195, 196, 197, 198, 200

Florida, 122, 129
Fontana, Fulvio, 147, 161, 162, 215
Franciscans, 23, 63, 70, 119, 140, 186, 227
Franco, Veronica, 79

Galasso, Giuseppe, 10, 12, 29, 49, 50
Genoino, Giulio, 196, 199
Gesualdo, Alfonso, 51, 86
Giraffi, Alessandro, 195
Goa, 103, 106, 120
Gonzaga, Margherita (Duchess of Mantua), 59
Gramsci, Antonio, 9

Howell, James, 195

Incas, 121, 128
India, 1, 17, 99, 106, 107, 108, 113, 116, 120, 122, 133, 172
Indies Down Here, 3, 95, 104, 137
Indonesia, 107
Innocent X (Pope), 197

Japan, 99, 107

Laínez, Diego, 58, 162
Las Casas, Bartolomé de, 91, 125, 132
Lecce, 2, 11, 45, 77, 78, 163, 193
Longo, Maria, 69
Longobardo, Niccolò, 102, 103
López de Gómara, Francisco, 98
Loyola, Ignatius, 52, 55, 56, 57, 63, 64, 72, 82, 106, 108, 169
Luther, Martin, 187

Mainardi, Arlotto, 26
Malleus Maleficarum, 170
Marcaldo, Francesco, 29
Marian cults, 50
Masaniello (*see also* Aniello, Tommaso), 196, 197, 199
Massella, Luigi, 61
Mastrilli, Carlo, 74, 77, 88, 188
Mastrilli, Nicolò, 100
Mendoza, Cristobal, 60
Mercurian, Everard, 95, 126
Mexicas/Aztecs, 128
Mexico, 17, 119, 120, 121, 229

INDEX

missionary identity, 7, 15, 16, 98, 104, 105, 117, 118, 136, 137, 185, 224

missionary relations, 13, 48, 115, 129, 134, 141, 145, 146, 150, 151, 153, 155, 159, 167, 173, 174, 209, 218, 219, 224, 243

missionary science, 13, 118, 140, 146, 147, 155, 224, 241

Muslim slaves, 52, 56, 62, 73, 78, 88, 89, 90, 91, 92, 93, 107, 213, 249

Myth of Naples, 2–3, 16, 21, 27, 244, 249

Nadal, Jerónimo, 122

Navarra, Pietro Paolo, 99

Navarro, Miguel, 95, 104, 137

Neapolitan Province, 99, 101, 105, 129, 139, 143, 144, 145, 146, 167, 173, 246

nobles, 16, 29, 31, 35, 36, 37, 38, 39, 40, 59, 199, 201, 234, 248

nobility, 21, 22, 24, 25, 27, 30, 35, 37, 38, 39, 40, 44, 75, 183, 194, 197, 198, 199, 200, 201, 207, 234, 235, 246

Nola, 111, 218

nomadism, 128

nuns, 48, 82, 83, 170, 189, 190, 203

O'Malley, John, 5, 12, 16

Ochino, Bernardino, 62

Oratory of Divine Love, 69

Orfini, Tommaso, 16, 45, 46, 47, 48, 188

Orsini, Giovanni, 44

Ostuni, 47

Ottaviano, Bernardo, 77

Oviedo, Andrea, 57, 68

Palma, Francesco, 110

Palmio, Benedetto, 84

Paolucci, Scipione, 7, 13, 135, 145, 147, 150, 152, 159, 163, 173, 174, 175, 189, 190, 201, 214, 228, 229, 231, 234, 236, 237, 238, 239, 240, 241, 243, 251

'paradise inhabited by devils', 1, 3, 21, 22, 25, 249

Parrino, Domenico, 38

Pascal, Blaise, 239, 247

Paul IV (Pope), 69

Pavone, Francesco, 101, 103

penitential exercises, 19, 208, 211, 227, 228, 229, 230, 233, 234, 236, 239, 240, 249

Peru, 1, 3, 17, 104, 117, 120, 121, 122, 123, 126

Petrarch, Francesco, 23

Philip II (King of Spain), 122

Pignatelli, Ettore (Duke of Monte Leone), 57

Pinamonti, Pietro, 240–41

Pius V (Pope), 45

Pizarro, Francisco, 121

plague(s), 34, 35, 50, 51, 52, 109, 201, 244, 245

Polanco, Juan de, 58, 59, 60, 82, 103, 105, 117

Polignano, 46, 47

Ponce De Leon, Rodrigo (Duke of Arcos), (see also Viceroys of Naples), 195, 198

population, 2, 31, 32, 33, 35, 36, 37, 40, 44, 51, 56, 79, 82, 84, 89, 107, 176, 245

Porzio, Camillo, 22, 23, 27, 28, 42

Possevino, Antonio, 59

Prisoners, 62, 69, 73, 78, 84, 85, 86, 88, 93, 187, 196, 199, 249

Prisons, 64, 84–6, 93, 187

Prosperi, Adriano, 3, 4, 63, 97, 120, 248

Prostitutes, 47, 62, 69, 78–84, 166, 205, 207

Prostitution, 22, 53, 56, 78–84, 166, 205, 207

Razzi, Serafino, 180

Realino, Bernardino, 213

Rebellion(s), 34, 39, 44, 76, 84, 176

Revolt of 1585, 34, 73, 78

Revolt of Masaniello (see also Revolt of Naples), 31, 52, 194

Revolt of Naples (see also Revolt of Masaniello), 13, 114, 188, 194, 196, 197, 201, 208

Ricci, Bartolomeo, 102

Rodríguez, Cristóbal, 42

Roman Province, 143, 146, 149, 150, 151, 158

Romano, D. Francesco, 130

278 INDEX

Rome, 2, 6, 7, 11, 45, 52, 60, 61, 62, 70, 79, 82, 86, 87, 93, 101, 107, 109, 118, 120, 131, 145, 149, 153, 155, 170, 171, 177, 197, 207, 230, 240, 243
Ruggieri, Michele, 99, 101
Ruvo, 47

Sabina, 153
saints' cults, 50, 51
Salamanca, 121, 122
Salerno, 163
Salmerón, Alfonso, 56, 59, 60, 61, 162
San (Saint) Gennaro, 50
San Bernardino di Siena, 186, 188
Sandoval, Alonso de, 111
Schinosi, Francesco, 7, 13, 14, 68, 74, 75, 83, 147, 176, 188, 213, 216, 243
Segneri, Paolo, 142, 147, 150, 154, 155, 156, 157, 158, 159, 160, 161, 165, 172, 177, 178, 179, 180, 190, 191, 192, 205, 212, 215, 219, 221, 222, 223, 224, 229, 230, 235, 241
Segneri, Paolo, Jr., 240
Sepúlveda, Juan Gínes de, 132
Sforza, Francesco, 25
Slavery, 89, 195
Slaves, 52, 56, 62, 73, 78, 84, 88–93, 107, 114, 115, 117, 125, 132, 179, 213, 234, 249
Social groupings, 35–6
Spectacle, 18, 216, 218–20, 237
Spinelli, Pierantonio, 17, 62, 68, 70–72, 83, 86, 87, 89, 91–4, 101, 104, 113, 118, 189, 190
St Francis of Assisi, 170
St Jerome, 170
Summonte, Giovanni Antonio, 34
Suriano, Michele, 43

Taranto, 193
tax records (see also catasti), 36
taxes, 31, 32, 43, 44, 80

taxation, 43, 195, 199
Téllez-Girón, Pedro, (see also Viceroys of Naples), 74, 271
Terra di Bari, 46, 47
teschio (death skull), 213, 228
Theatine Order, 69
Theatricality, 19, 151, 206, 212, 214, 216, 217, 227–33, 237, 239, 240
Thiene, Gaetano, 69
Toledo, Francisco de, 121
Toledo, Pedro de (see also Viceroys of Naples), 31–3, 38, 39, 41, 57
Training Manuals, 145, 146, 147
Tupinamba, 128
Tutini, Camillo, 40

Valignano, Alessandro, 96, 107
Vernazza, Ettore, 69
Viceroys of Naples
    Borja (Borgia), Gaspar (Cardinal), 183
    Di Cordova e Di Aguilar, Consalvo Ferdinando, 80
    Di Ribera, (Don) Parafan, 41
    Ponce De Leon, Rodrigo (Duke of Arcos), 195, 198
    Téllez-Girón, Pedro, 74, 271
    Toledo, Pedro de, 31–3, 38, 39, 41, 57
Vignapiano, Vito, 102
Vignes, Hieronimo, 57
Visconti, Filippo Maria, 25
Vitelleschi, Muzio, 62, 111, 113, 142

Women, 36, 69, 73, 78, 79, 80, 81, 82, 83, 84, 90, 129, 130, 134, 135, 157, 158, 166, 168–73, 175–80, 189, 206, 215, 221, 225, 226, 230, 231, 235, 236, 237, 240, 248

Xavier, Francis, 17–18, 75, 96–8, 103, 105–10, 112, 115–18, 120, 136, 137, 141–6, 152, 170–73, 179

Lightning Source UK Ltd.
Milton Keynes UK
UKOW06n0328101017
310715UK00007B/245/P